International Library of Ethics, Law, and the New Medicine

Volume 75

Series editors

Founded by

The book series International Library of Ethics, Law and the New Medicine comprises volumes with an international and interdisciplinary focus. The aim of the Series is to publish books on foundational issues in (bio) ethics, law, international health care and medicine. The 28 volumes that have already appeared in this series address aspects of aging, mental health, AIDS, preventive medicine, bioethics and many other current topics. This Series was conceived against the background of increasing globalization and interdependency of the world's cultures and governments, with mutual influencing occurring throughout the world in all fields, most surely in health care and its delivery. By means of this Series we aim to contribute and cooperate to meet the challenge of our time: how to aim human technology to good human ends, how to deal with changed values in the areas of religion, society, culture and the self-definition of human persons, and how to formulate a new way of thinking, a new ethic. We welcome book proposals representing the broad interest of the interdisciplinary and international focus of the series. We especially welcome proposals that address aspects of 'new medicine', meaning advances in research and clinical health care, with an emphasis on those interventions and alterations that force us to re-examine foundational issues.

More information about this series at http://www.springer.com/series/6224

Egon Jonsson • Sterling Clarren • Ian Binnie
Editors

Ethical and Legal Perspectives in Fetal Alcohol Spectrum Disorders (FASD)

Foundational Issues

Springer

Editors
Egon Jonsson
Faculty of Medicine, Department of Psychiatry
University of Alberta
Edmonton, AB, Canada

Sterling Clarren
Faculty of Medicine
University of British Columbia
Vancouver, Canada

Ian Binnie
The Supreme Court of Canada
Ottawa, ON, Canada

ISSN 1567-8008 ISSN 2351-955X (electronic)
International Library of Ethics, Law, and the New Medicine
ISBN 978-3-319-71754-8 ISBN 978-3-319-71755-5 (eBook)
https://doi.org/10.1007/978-3-319-71755-5

Library of Congress Control Number: 2018932340

Printed on acid-free paper

This Springer imprint is published by Springer Nature
The registered company is Springer International Publishing AG
The registered company address is: Gewerbestrasse 11, 6330 Cham, Switzerland

Foreword

Fetal alcohol spectrum disorder (FASD) includes both mental and physical disabilities prevalent during the lifespan.

All FASD's are caused by embryo/fetus exposure to alcohol during the time of pregnancy. A developing child, who prenatally has been exposed to alcohol, may experience some, several, or even all of the following consequences in different grades of severity: growth retardation, malformations of the face, other organ malformations, ongoing medical problems as heart defects, cleft palate, kidney failure, hearing loss, gastroenteritis, pneumonia, bronchitis, sleeplessness, and bone and joint problems, as well as neurological disorders, and cognitive deficiencies such as problems with memory, learning, attention, and social communication. Most sections of this book deal with the cognitive issues of FASD in the perspective of their ethical and legal implications in the criminal justice system.

FASD is a spectrum of disorders and a spectrum of levels of disability, which can then be improved or made more severe through environmental, social, and other factors mentioned below. As described in Part 1, Chap. 3, on the origins of FASD, heavy drinking early on during pregnancy may cause brain damage in the offspring even before a woman usually is aware of being pregnant.

FASD is also related to a higher risk of secondary disabilities later in life, such as dropping out of school, family and placement breakdown, becoming unemployed, homelessness, abuse of alcohol and drugs, and being involved with the criminal justice system. The burden for individuals living with FASD, their parents/caregivers, and the society including health, social, educational, and legal services is huge as is described in Part 1, Chap. 4. The cost of FASD related to police, court, and correctional services is significantly higher than that for healthcare, educational, and social services. Without appropriate support, it may be devastating for the individual, the family, and other caregivers. With strong and orderly support, many of these secondary problems may not appear or can be dealt with satisfactorily. However, a person who may not fully understand the difference between what is right and wrong or cannot conceptualize legal proceedings and language needs to be supported not only by family/caregivers but also by frontline police, judges, prosecutors, other lawyers in courts, probation officers, and from staff in correctional services, through a better understanding of and appropriate dealing with people living with FASD. The implications of the current inequality related to people with FASD in different stages of the criminal justice system are laid out in Part 1, Chap. 2 as well as in all Chapters of Part 4, and in Part 5, Chap. 1.

The contributions to this book reflect the situation mainly in North America. Mental incompetence has been recognized in the USA and in Canada as an appropriate defense in some criminal cases. Similarly, brain-based disabilities may help to qualify an individual for assistance in education and social services. In recent decades, it has become appreciated in medicine and psychology that serious incompetence defined by a very low score on an IQ test or by psychosis excludes many persons who should by all accounts be considered incompetent in all or in some arenas of daily life. The legal, educational, social, and health service systems have not been averse to considering the possibility of incompetence or disability in individual cases with more subtle presentations, but clear standards for expanding the definitions have not yet been consistently applied. This problem of appreciating subtle to moderate cognitive disabilities leading to extreme problems in adaptive and behavioral situations is especially true of individuals with fetal alcohol spectrum disorders (FASDs).

The idea for this book began when the editors organized and participated in a consensus development conference on legal issues related to FASD. The appendix describes the content and outcome of that consensus development conference, and includes a number of recommendations useful for policy makers and all professions of the criminal justice system as well as for law students. Some of the questions raised in the conference but hardly fully answered included:

- To what extent was it necessary to prove that a person who had broken the law had some form of brain damage if it did not rise to the extreme levels of insanity, cognitive impairment, or physical dysfunction currently accepted as "disability"?
- What should the courts accept as evidence that the crime was linked to the brain dysfunction and hence not committed in the usual context of knowing right from wrong?
- If these concepts were accepted, how would they/should they amend punishment?

Before such important questions can be fully answered, it is critical that all groups responsible for the answers fully understand all sides of the situation. The testimonies from the experts at the consensus development conference confirmed that the brain damage associated with FASD and the sophistication necessary to fully evaluate individual patients are a complicated issue and, also, that the barriers that might exist in translating these findings into the social, educational, and legal systems are not fully understood. As well, the effective routes to change within complex and multifaceted systems are unclear. It was also obvious from the presentations that there are gaps between the understanding of the condition among medical and legal experts. Now, several years later, these questions still remain largely open and need to be further addressed, as is done in this volume.

The answers to the many questions within the boundaries of ethical, legal, and social issues in FASD are of course relevant to many other disabilities which manifest themselves to similar forms of brain damage from any cause. Still, the FASD population, which represents an estimated 1–2% of the general population in the USA and Canada and much higher prevalence figures in many other countries, could be used as the spearhead to engage in this important problem.

Throughout most of the world, alcohol is largely a legal substance that is widely enjoyed. But it has also been widely abused for thousands of years. Part 1, Chap. 1 of this book, focuses on the history of FASD and justice and how issues surrounding alcohol have challenged public policy and the legal system. As Warren and Chezem states in that chapter: "But the interplay between pregnancy, alcohol and the law has only come to the forefront in recent years following the recognition of the existence of the fetal alcohol syndrome (FAS) and fetal alcohol spectrum disorders (FASD) less than a half century ago."

When used during pregnancy, alcohol becomes a potent chemical agent known to cause a variety of lifelong disabilities especially within the brain. No amount of alcohol can be confirmed to be safe for the unborn child at any stage during pregnancy, although most individuals diagnosed with an FASD were exposed to substantial amounts of alcohol especially in the early weeks after conception. Alcohol easily penetrates the placenta and enters the developing conceptus and may cause a range of developmental defects in the brain, based on volume of exposures, timing within gestation interactions with other potential teratogens, and issues in maternal health. These brain anomalies may be obvious, resulting in abnormally small head size, obvious malformations on clinical images of the brain (CT or MRI as described in Part 2, Chap. 2), and/or general performance in the intellectually impaired categories, but more often the structural brain changes are very subtle if detectable at all with current imaging techniques and only found through wide-ranging test of brain performance. These more subtle brain changes may still result in global performance deficits that are subsumed in categories that are recognized as intellectual disabilities. But most of the time, these changes do not cause a person to have a generalized IQ score that falls in the lowest 2 or 3 percentiles. Rather, there are specific problems in learning, memory, problem solving, etc. These are still significant issues that may have lifetime implications for normal functioning in society (normal adaptation). How should society assist these individuals? Sometimes, these cerebral deficits lead to poor judgment that results in illegal acts both minor and serious. How the courts should respond to this is indeed a great challenge. The basic principles of sentencing, which assume that offenders are capable of making choices, understanding the consequences of their actions, and learning from their mistakes so as not to repeat them, are also challenged by FASD. This is discussed in several sections of this book, in particular in Part 3, Chaps. 8, 9, 10, and 11, and in Part 5, Chap. 16. As Binnie et al. have stated elsewhere (1):

- "Issues associated with the cognitive and behavioural deficits of individuals affected by FASD surface frequently in criminal proceedings. However, people with FASD may not have been diagnosed for their problems and rarely exhibit any visible signs of the disorder. This may put them in a disadvantaged position in the justice system. When these individuals face criminal charges, they often do not fully appreciate the nature and consequences of their actions, nor can they fully understand and attend to the legal proceedings and potential outcomes of their cases. Problems with memory, organizing, and contextualizing may make it difficult for them to remember or to relate important facts that would assist counsel in making a proper defense.
- They tend to be suggestible and to have a desire to please others, and therefore to agree with leading questions and, potentially, false confessions. They often misunderstand basic legal terminology and procedures, such as the difference between 'guilty' and 'not guilty' or the fact that a false confession cannot be retracted – as a result, individuals with FASD are at increased risk of wrongful convictions. Their cognitive impairments also reduce their reliability as witnesses and complainants. When they are the victims of crime, their victimizers are therefore less likely to be convicted.
- General deterrence, meaning that the punishment given to one person for breaking the law will operate to deter other persons, presupposes the ability to process and translate information as well as to remember it. Similarly, rehabilitation, as it is conventionally understood, is largely a cognitive process premised on the ability of those other persons to understand, to learn, to remember, and to make choices. None of these assumptions fits well with what is known about FASD. Offenders with FASD are held to a standard that they cannot attain, given their impairments."

The need to identify and to address FASD more effectively within the context of the law is increasingly acknowledged in many judicial and legislative branches in North America as well as by caretakers and families of individuals who have FASD. Many plans and strategies on FASD stress the importance of awareness and the synthesizing of findings from research. It is our hope that this book will contribute to the knowledge exchange needed for change. Many complex legal issues associated with FASD need to be resolved in order to ensure that FASD-affected individuals receive fair and equitable treatment in the criminal justice system. This requires that the legal system, including the police services, prosecutors, defense counsels, judges, and staff in correctional services, be better served with information about the nature of FASD and its potential cognitive and behavioral dysfunctions. Above all, we hope that this book will contribute to initiatives that specifically support people with FASD to avoid coming into conflict with the law in the first place and assist them to qualify for necessary services that will keep them from running afoul of the law and hope that measures for prevention of FASD will be strengthened.

Edmonton, Canada — Egon Jonsson
Kelowna, Canada — Sterling Clarren
Ottawa, Canada — Ian Binnie

Reference

Binnie I., M. Trussler, and E. Jonsson. 2013. Legal Issues of FASD. Fetal alcohol spectrum disorder. In *Proceedings from a consensus development conference*. ISBN 978-1-897443-36-1. www.ihe.ca.

Contents

Editor and Contributors

Editors

Egon Jonsson graduated from the Stockholm School of Economics and trained as a research associate at Harvard School of Public Health. He was a co-founder and long-term CEO of the Swedish Council on Technology Assessment in Health Care, leader of the WHO Health Evidence Network, and co-editor of the *International Journal of Technology Assessment in Health Care*. He is an elected member of the US National Academy of Sciences/Medicine since 1992. Until recently, he was the CEO of the Institute of Health Economics in Edmonton, Canada. Dr. Jonsson is now a professor at the University of Alberta, Department of Psychiatry. He has published frequently on the economic, social, legal, and policy implications of FASD.

Sterling Clarren is the recently retired CEO and scientific director of Canada FASD Research Network; professor of pediatrics at the University of British Columbia, Faculty of Medicine, Canada; and Robert A. Aldrich Professor of pediatrics at the University of Washington, School of Medicine, USA. Dr. Clarren was instrumental in many advancing knowledge of FASD in etiology, diagnostics, interventions, and prevention since 1976.

Ian Binnie Hon. Ian Binnie CC QC is a former justice of the Supreme Court of Canada.

Contributors

Tricia Aiken received her doctorate degree in clinical psychology in 2003. Dr. Aiken has worked full-time for the State of Minnesota as a forensic psychologist since 2006. In addition, Dr. Aiken owns and operates Minneapolis Forensic Psychological Services (www.mplsforensicpsych.com), where she conducts evaluations and offers professional trainings. Dr. Aiken was certified by the American Board of Professional Psychology in the field of forensics in 2009.

Christian Beaulieu is a professor of biomedical engineering, an Alberta Innovates Health Solutions Scientist, and the scientific director of the Peter S. Allen MR Research Centre at the University of Alberta in Edmonton, Canada. His research focuses on the development of novel MRI methods for better visualization and quantification of brain structure, with applications to neurological disorders.

Jerrod Brown is the treatment director for Pathways Counseling Center, Inc. Pathways provides programs and services benefitting individuals impacted by mental illness and addictions. Jerrod is also the founder and CEO of the American Institute for the Advancement of Forensic Studies (AIAFS) and the editor in chief of *Forensic Scholars Today* (*FST*) and *The Journal of Special Populations* (*JSP*). Jerrod is also currently pursuing his doctorate degree in psychology.

Teresa Brown has several years' experience working with adolescents in residential treatment and within youth corrections. In 2005, Teresa began working with the FASD Youth Justice Program coordinating assessments for youth and providing ongoing FASD education to community resources and corrections staff. Teresa previously managed the FASD Youth Justice Program that involved working directly with youth and their families to identify supportive services. She currently is the acting assistant superintendent at the Manitoba Youth Centre.

Andrew Burke is the manager of the Forensic Assessment and Community Services program in Edmonton, Alberta, an outpatient clinic which offers assessment and treatment for forensic adult patients living in Central and Northern Alberta. He has worked in the field of forensics since 1998. He received his master's degree in counseling psychology from the University of Calgary and is currently completing his PhD at the University of Alberta. His research to date has focused on treatment outcomes among forensic patients, evaluation of risk assessment instruments, and the impact of the therapeutic alliance on work with forensic patients. Recently, he has begun research on the effectiveness of telemental health (video conferencing) technology with forensic patients.

Linda L. Chezem began her judicial career as a trial court judge followed by serving for 22 years as a judge on the Indiana Court of Appeals. She is also a professor emerita at the College of Agriculture, Purdue University, and an adjunct professor at the Indiana University School of Medicine. Her current service includes chairing the Indiana Juvenile Justice State Advisory Group and as a member of the Indiana Criminal Justice Institute Board of Trustees.

Albert E. Chudley is a professor emeritus in the Departments of Pediatrics and Biochemistry and Medical Genetics, University of Manitoba. His interests are in the recognition, delineation, and prevention of birth defects, including FASD. He has authored numerous scientific publications on a variety of topics related to medical genetics and birth defects. He is a recipient of several awards including the Founders Award from the Canadian College of Medical Geneticists.

Nikki Freeman is a licensed professional clinical counselor and a certified facilitator of the FASCETS Neurobehavioral Model. She has clinical experience in many settings: school-based mental health, in-home therapy, therapeutic foster care, behavioral health coaching, and case management. She specializes in using the neurobehavioral approach with people who have FASD and their caregivers at Hardy & Stephens Counseling Associates in Elk River, MN. Nikki has a master's degree in counseling psychology and a graduate certificate in child and adolescent mental health from Bethel University in St. Paul, MN.

Stephen Greenspan is professor emeritus of educational psychology at the University of Connecticut and now resides in Colorado, USA. His writings and testimony on social vulnerabilities of people with intellectual disabilities involved in criminal justice proceedings won recognition from the American Association on Intellectual and Developmental Disabilities, which awarded him its Gunnar and Rosemary Dybwad Award for Humanitarianism.

Mary Kate Harvie was appointed to the Provincial Court of Manitoba in 2000 and previously served as associate chief judge. Judge Harvie initiated a process for youth in the criminal justice system to be assessed for FASD. The FASD Youth Justice Program was awarded the Manitoba Service for Excellence Award – "partnership" category – in June 2008. Judge Harvie has presented at national and international conferences on FASD and has served on a number of community and educational boards.

Jeffrey Haun is employed as a forensic examiner at Minnesota State Operated Forensic Services (SOFS), where he conducts a variety of forensic evaluations with juveniles and adults. He is on the clinical faculty of the SOFS Postdoctoral Fellowship in Forensic Psychology and the University of Minnesota Forensic Psychiatry Fellowship programs. He also provides consultation and peer-review services at PsyBar, LLC, and is an adjunct instructor in the Forensic Mental Health program at Concordia University, St. Paul. He is certified in forensic psychology by the American Board of Professional Psychology.

Sarah Herrick has worked with sexual abusers ranging in age from 10 to elderly since 1991, in residential, community mental health, and secured settings. Currently, she is working with civilly committed sexual abusers and is an adjunct professor with Concordia University's (St. Paul, MN) forensic mental health online graduate program.

Fia Jampolsky worked for the Yukon Legal Services Society for over a decade representing clients in family, criminal, and child protection matters. Ms. Jampolsky represented residential school survivors in their sexual and physical abuse claims under the Indian Residential Schools Settlement Agreement Independent Assessment Process. She is presently counsel with the Aboriginal Law Group for the Yukon Government. Ms. Jampolsky received her master's in law from Osgoode Hall Law School in 2015.

Patricia Jones has served as a guest lecturer, an associate editor for several peer-reviewed journals, a forensic mental health specialist, and a counselor. Over the last 4 years, she has worked exclusively in a community forensic mental health setting, providing research, grant writing, and clinical services. Her clinical focus includes complex forensic assessment, test construction, and research design. Her professional publications include the mental health correlates of juvenile fire setting behaviors and discussions of coping with mental illness presented by inmate populations.

Avril J. Keller is a professor of psychology at the University of Calgary.

Cathy Lane Goodfellow has practiced law in Alberta since 1984, spending most of that time as a defense lawyer and advocate for youth in criminal court. During the decades of representing youth, she developed a real and practical knowledge of the impact FASD has on all stages of the criminal justice process. Cathy has lectured to both community and professional groups about this issue, most recently at the Legal Aid of Western Australia's Summer Series Criminal Law Day in February 2016. Cathy achieved her master's degree in law in 1995 and was appointed Queen's Counsel in 2010. She volunteers in her community and is currently a board member of the Calgary Fetal Alcohol Network.

Sally Longstaffe is a professor of pediatrics in the Department of Pediatrics, University of Manitoba. Dr. Longstaffe is a developmental pediatrician who has held positions as section head of developmental pediatrics and as medical director of the MB FASD Centre and Network. She has had a longstanding commitment and participation in healthcare initiatives and research for children and youth who are marginalized and experience special challenges including those with FASD.

Trevor Markesteyn is the chief correctional psychologist for the Community Safety Division and has been with Manitoba Justice for more than 20 years. He developed a Provincial Program Strategy, helped implement new youth justice legislation, and subsequently worked on developing and implementing a new case management and risk assessment system for Manitoba. Dr. Markesteyn holds a PhD in psychology from the University of Manitoba and an undergraduate degree in criminology.

Kaitlyn McLachlan is an assistant professor in the Department of Psychiatry and Behavioural Neurosciences at McMaster University and a clinical psychologist in the Forensic Psychiatry program at St. Joseph's Healthcare Hamilton. Dr. McLachlan is a clinician and researcher with a program focused on understanding the experiences, abilities, and needs of individuals with fetal alcohol spectrum disorder and neurocognitive disabilities who become involved in the criminal justice system.

Kathi Osmonson Minnesota Deputy State Fire Marshal, coordinates the Minnesota State Youth Fire Intervention Team (YFIT). YFIT partners with law enforcement, mental health, justice, and social agencies to sustain a network of professionals who collaborate to provide intervention. Osmonson started her firefighting career in 1987 specializing in fire prevention, investigation, and youth fire setting intervention. She publishes and reviews articles and presents for national and international audiences. She is currently pursuing her master's degree in forensic mental health.

Arlin Pachet is a board-certified clinical neuropsychologist and an assistant clinical professor in the Department of Clinical Psychology at the University of Calgary. Also a practicing registered psychologist, Dr. Pachet continues to complete a wide range of assessments with youth, adults, and seniors experiencing cognitive and neurobehavioral issues. Dr. Pachet provides training workshops regarding the assessment of decisional capacity, and he has published and completed many presentations in the areas of test construction, capacity assessment, and neuropsychological evaluation.

Hal Pickett is a clinical psychologist and clinical director of Headway Emotional Health Services in Minneapolis, Minnesota. He has been practicing in the field of child and adolescent psychology for 20 years and specializing in forensic assessment of youth for the past 9 years predominantly with adolescent sex offenders. His major clinical interest is how trauma affects delinquent behavior.

Jacqueline Pei is an associate professor in the Department of Educational Psychology and assistant clinical professor in the Department of Pediatrics at the University of Alberta in Edmonton, Canada. Also a practicing registered psychologist, Dr. Pei began her career as a criminologist and has continued in this vein, studying youth at risk and interventions for those with FASD. Dr. Pei currently leads the Intervention Network Action Team for the Canada FASD Research Network.

Carmen Rasmussen is an associate professor in the Department of Pediatrics at the University of Alberta and a research affiliate at the Glenrose Rehabilitation Hospital. She is also a Canadian Institutes of Health Research (CIHR) New Investigator. Her research is focused on understanding neurobehavioral difficulties among children with FASD.

Jonathan Rudin graduated from Osgoode Hall Law School. In 1990, he was hired to establish Aboriginal Legal Services of Toronto and has been with this organization ever since. He has appeared before all levels of court, including the Supreme Court of Canada. Mr. Rudin is the chair of the FASD Justice Committee. The committee created a website on FASD and the justice system: www.fasdjustice.ca. Mr. Rudin also teaches on a part-time basis in the Law and Society program at York University.

Deepa Singal is in the Department of Community Health Sciences, University of Manitoba. Her research interests are utilizing administrative data to investigate child and maternal health. Her doctoral dissertation is the first to investigate the characteristics, health, and service utilization of women who give birth to children with FASD at a population level. Deepa has received funding from provincial and national granting agencies and was awarded the Research Manitoba Dissertation Award, demonstrating research excellence in a doctoral thesis.

Kathleen K. Sulik is a professor emeritus of cell biology and physiology at the University of North Carolina, Chapel Hill, NC, USA. Dr. Sulik spent her academic career conducting basic research on birth defects, with an emphasis on understanding the genesis of abnormalities resulting from early prenatal alcohol exposure. She is a past president of the US Teratology Society and FASD Study Group and has received awards for her contributions to the FASD field by these organizations as well as by the US National Institute on Alcohol Abuse and Alcoholism.

Nguyen Xuan Thanh is an adjunct professor with the School of Public Health, University of Alberta, and a health economist with the Institute of Health Economics in Edmonton, Canada, specializing in health economics, evaluation in public health, biostatistics, and epidemiology. He received training as a medical doctor at Hanoi Medical University in Vietnam and holds both a master's and PhD in public health from the Umea International School of Public Health in Sweden. Thanh has a wide range of experience working with economic evaluations of health services, interventions, programs, and policies, including cost, cost-effectiveness, cost-benefit, and social return on investment analyses. He has published several articles on epidemiology and economics of FASD and causes of alcohol consumption.

Sarah Treit is a research associate in the Department of Biomedical Engineering at the University of Alberta in Edmonton, Canada. Her work focuses on structural MRI of brain development in children and adolescents with fetal alcohol spectrum disorders, specifically aiming to identify how deviations in cognitive development link up with deviations in brain structure.

Aaron J. Trnka is a Minnesota Board-approved supervisor clinical director and the CEO of Lighthouse Psychological Services, Inc., Fridley, MN, USA. Aaron has been practicing psychotherapy for over 10 years. He specializes in treating special needs adults who have issues of sexuality. Aaron has a focus on trauma and is Eye Movement Desensitization and Reprocessing (EMDR) certified.

Kenneth R. Warren is a former deputy director and acting director of the National Institute on Alcohol Abuse and Alcoholism (NIAAA), a part of the National Institutes of Health in the USA. He currently serves as a senior advisor to NIAAA. He has been active in research and administration related to FASD for 40 years and continues to chair the US government's Interagency Coordinating Committee on FASD.

Anthony P. Wartnik was a trial judge for 34 years, presiding judge of juvenile court, family law court chief judge, dean emeritus of the Washington Judicial College, Judicial College Board of Trustees chair, and the Washington Supreme Court's Judicial Conference Education Committee chair. Judge Wartnik is a nationally and internationally recognized speaker, author, and trainer on issues involving FASD and the law and teaches postgraduate courses on forensic mental health and special needs populations at Concordia University, St. Paul, MN.

Erin Watts has been working with dually diagnosed people and their families for over 10 years, primarily those with schizophrenia and neurodevelopmental disorders. After working for the Department of Human Services providing clinical services to people who are civilly committed as mentally ill and dangerous, Ms.

Watts now brings her expertise to the Institute on Community Integration at the University of Minnesota. Her primary focus is building capacity of community providers by providing training and technical assistance to teams implementing evidence-based practices and person-centered planning while simultaneously developing sustainable systems change through organization-wide action planning.

George Woods is the president of the International Academy of Law and Mental Health. He is a forensic and neuropsychiatrist consultant in courts of law, mental illness, and crime. Dr. Woods teaches at the University of California, Berkeley Law, and Morehouse School of Medicine, Atlanta.

Margaret R. Wimberley was a field operations manager for news, sports, and entertainment for ABC TV, New York. Shows included World News Tonight, Monday Night Football, Nightline, World Series Baseball, the Academy Awards, Good Morning America, and the Tour de France. Subsequent to a career change, she turned her focus to forensic study and has a strong research interest in topics related to the criminal justice and forensic mental health aspects of fetal alcohol spectrum disorder (FASD).

Patricia A. Zapf is a professor in the Department of Psychology at John Jay College of Criminal Justice and was appointed fellow of the American Psychological Association in 2006 for outstanding contributions to the field of law and psychology for her work in competency evaluation. She has published 10 books and manuals and over 100 articles, chapters, and reports on forensic psychology. Her research involves the assessment and conceptualization of various types of competencies and the utility of various methods of competency.

Part I
Overview

Chapter 1
FASD and Justice: An Historical Perspective

Kenneth R. Warren and Linda L. Chezem

> *Those who don't know history are doomed to repeat it.*
> – Edmund Burke
>
> *Those who cannot remember the past are condemned to repeat it.*
> – Santayana (in The Life of Reason, 1905)

Abstract Alcohol has been widely used in societies for thousands of years so it is not surprising that issues surrounding alcohol have challenged public policy and the legal system for many years. But the interplay between pregnancy, alcohol and the law has only come to the forefront in recent years following the recognition of the existence of the fetal alcohol syndrome (FAS) and fetal alcohol spectrum disorders (FASD) less than a half century ago. In the context of prevention, some communities have enacted ordinances requiring the placing of warning signs informing the public of the risks of drinking in pregnancy at locations associated with alcohol use. A more formidable issue stems from the observation that FASD individuals are over-represented in all court systems as defendants and victims.

The review of criminal cases involving an FASD have been few to date, but even that experience illuminates the challenges that lie ahead in addressing the impact of FASD associated intellectual impairments for achieving appropriate justice. There is a need for statutes directly addressing FASD issues within the society and a model is put forth to aid communities in achieving fair and just outcomes.

Keywords Fetal Alcohol Syndrome (FAS) · Fetal Alcohol Spectrum Disorders (FASD) · Evidence · Expert Experts · History · Caselaw · Statutes

K. R. Warren (✉)
National Institute on Alcohol Abuse and Alcoholism (NIAAA), Bethesda, MD, USA
e-mail: kwarren@willco.niaaa.nih.gov

L. L. Chezem
Professor Emerita, College of Agriculture, Purdue University, West Lafayette, IN, USA

E. Jonsson et al. (eds.), *Ethical and Legal Perspectives in Fetal Alcohol Spectrum Disorders (FASD)*, International Library of Ethics, Law, and the New Medicine 75,
https://doi.org/10.1007/978-3-319-71755-5_1

1.1 Introduction

Alcohol has had a significant impact on many aspects of human history. Issues surrounding its use and consequences have often been addressed through policy and law. This review will describe one unique aspect of alcohol and the law: those policies, laws and court history that surround pregnancy and fetal outcome.

Laws and judicial practices involving alcohol overall, not just with respect to pregnancy, are often not evaluated for their effectiveness. At the extreme, some laws and practices have actually resulted in increasing the problem they were enacted to prevent. One case in point known to most Americans is the Eighteen Amendment to the U.S. Constitution, which brought prohibition into existence in the years 1920 to 1933. While some aspects of prohibition legislation achieved a positive outcome (i.e., a decrease in liver cirrhosis deaths), there was an accompanying increase in violence and disrespect for the law that was counter-productive. This led to the repeal of prohibition through the passage of the Twenty-first Amendment to the Constitution 14 years later.

As discussed in other reviews (Warner and Rosett 1975; Warren and Hewitt 2009; Warren 2015) societal reaction to prohibition impacted contemporary views on the use and safety of alcohol during pregnancy and may have delayed modern recognition of alcohol as a teratogenic agent. However, after that recognition, various legislative actions have been put in place in some U.S. states and Canadian provinces that are meant to reduce the occurrence of birth defects caused by alcohol and advance public health. These actions range from requiring the posting of warnings in bars, restaurants, and rest rooms about alcohol use in pregnancy (Kaskutas and Graves 1994), to laws criminalizing alcohol use by pregnant women (Guttmacher Institute 2017). In the U.S. and in France, for example, legislation currently requires the posting of a warning with respect to use in pregnancy on all beverage containers (Warren 2015). In the case of statutes that criminalize drinking in pregnancy, the number of criminal prosecutions that have taken place has been limited and primarily have focused on drug rather than alcohol use. This may change in years to come despite the overwhelming viewpoint of the medical establishment which emphasizes that drinking in pregnancy should remain a medical rather than legal issue.

Today, a generally accepted view is that individuals with fetal alcohol syndrome (FAS) or the broader category of fetal alcohol spectrum disorders (FASD) are over-represented in ~~all~~ the courts of the judicial system (Streissguth et al. 1996, 1997a, b; Fast et al. 1999; Popova et al. 2011; National Council of Juvenile and Family Court Judges 2015). Characteristic deficits in cognition and executive function make those with FASD more likely to be involved in crime, or, as is often the case, more likely to be the person who is left behind to be arrested after others have committed a crime and fled (Fast et al. 1999). These same neuro-cognitive deficits also make those with FASD more likely to be a victim of crime. Because they live in families with heavy alcohol use and alcohol use disorders they are more likely to appear in family, divorce and adoption court. Regardless of the court system, the cognitive deficits resulting from prenatal alcohol exposure can seriously complicate the situation for affected individuals in their roles as defendant or witness.

1.2 Brief History of Alcohol, Pregnancy, and the Law

In eighteenth century England, a natural experiment involving alcohol, infant and child death rates, and the legislative ~~al~~ system occurred. That period of time has been referred to as both the "gin epidemic" and the "gin craze". The backdrop of events that led to the beginning of the gin epidemic included the ascension of William III (from the Netherlands) to the throne of England in 1689, resulting in increased political conflict between England and France. Legislation was passed in England resulting in decreased importation of French wine (brandy) and a marked increase in local gin distillation (George 1965; Coffey 1966).

The gin epidemic has been typically considered to have occurred from 1690 through 1751 (George 1965; Coffey 1966) although recent analysis suggests that it did not end until later in the 1750s or 1760s (Warner et al. 2001). The London College of Physcians petitioned the House of Commons on 17 January 1725 stating that they had "*observed, for some years past, the fatal effects of the frequent use of several sorts of distilled Spirituous Liquors... and too often the cause of weak, feeble, distempered children, who must be instead of an advantage and strength, a charge to their Country.*"

Parliament did take action passing three Gin Laws in 1929, 1736 and 1751 specifically related to the gin craze, but the impetus for their action related to economics and military strength rather than public health; with increasing death rates and decreasing infant survival, there was less manpower available for the workforce and the military (Warner et al. 2001; George 1965; Coffey 1966).

These Gin Laws provide interesting lessons in how legislation may or may not achieve the desired individual and societal changes in behavior. While the first two of these gin acts are generally regarded as not achieving the desired end of reduction of excessive gin consumption, the 1751 law was considered to have been successful in its purpose, bringing an end to the gin epidemic, a view that was expressed by M. Dorothy George (George 1965) in her 1925 book, *London Life in the Eighteenth Century*. But this conclusion was recently challenged in an analysis undertaken by Jessica Warner and her colleagues (Warner et al. 2001). Through a quantitative time series analysis examining annual per capita consumption of spirits and beer, excise tax records, real wages, and other legislative and economic variables, Warner and colleagues found that the 1751 gin act, similar to prior laws, resulted in only a short term reductions in consumption which was followed by a rebound of drinking and even higher gin consumption. It was put forth that the end of the epidemic was the result of social and cultural changes in views toward excessive gin consumption and the realization of the harm this excessive imbibing was causing (George 1965). This argument is supported, in part, by the fact that only the city of London experienced the gin epidemic though the same tax policies that had led to the London gin craze existed throughout England. The cultural and social norms outside of London prevented the epidemic, and similar attitudes toward gin finally took hold in London with the recognition among the populace of the problems gin has caused (George 1965; Warner et al. 2001).

The ineffectiveness of the three socially motivated gin acts raises real questions as to whether statutes addressing taxation, price, production and outlets can truly change consumption behavior. The Warner and colleagues' analyses revealed that the harsher the restrictions, the more the public negatively reacted by refusing to pay fees and by harassing magistrates and tax collectors to the point that neither group would enforce the laws (Warner et al. 2001). The most restrictive of the gin laws – the 1736 law brought about the greatest increase in gin consumption as a protest to the intent of the law. The 1736 law was not only repealed, but fees paid by those few merchants who had complied with the law were actually returned.

The Warner and colleagues' analysis strongly suggests that it was not legislation but rather education (even if self-acquired) that brought the gin epidemic to its demise. Contributing to the diminution of the appeal of gin were scholarly works produced at that time including those by three important social commentators: Henry Fielding, Corbyn Morris, and the artist William Hogarth (Fielding 1751; Morris 1751; Hogarth 1751).

1.3 Legal System, Laws, and Cases

The legal systems within the United States and Canada are primarily derived on the principles of English Common Law, and the laws that relate to alcohol as well as alcohol and pregnancy derive from that same English Common law context, with accretions to the law that may or may not make clear logical sense. Because the common law is court written law, as opposed to statutes or codes, it requires a greater recognition of the judicial role than is required for law set by codes. A code jurisdiction is one that does not recognize law created by courts (common law). This is not to ignore the importance of courts in code jurisdictions but merely notes a greater reliance on statutes. Regardless of common law or codes, the constant hope is that the laws function as an expression of policy resulting from the application of good science. When alcohol is involved, that hope has not often been achieved.

1.3.1 FASD Issues Impact Every Court

The ubiquity of FASD spreads the impact of this disorder across the full justice system and the cases on any single docket (from adoption, family, probate, civil to criminal) may involve individuals with an FASD in some aspect of the case from litigant to witness to defendant. However, gaining reliable data on the number of cases at the trial court level that involve an individual with an FASD is not an easy task. Such data is often not recorded unless a case moves to the appellate level, and cases do not enter the appellate system unless a claim is made of an error in the trial court action. Consequently, there is no simple formula to derive the number of cases involving FASD from appellate court records.

Though their numbers are fewer, cases at the appellate court level are important for their precedential value in the common law system. The opinions provide legal precedent that can be of the same weight and import as statutory law for the trial courts located in the jurisdiction of that appellate court. If an appellate court opinion affirms a trial court's action in accepting the impairments caused by prenatal alcohol exposure into consideration in deciding a case, other trial courts may do the same. The appellate court thereby sets a precedent for all cases coming after that until or unless a statute is passed that, in effect, overrules precedent as the law of that jurisdiction.

1.3.2 How Do FASD Issues Fare in the Court System?

In addressing the law and FASD one might do well to ask three questions:

1. What research-based evidence is reliable and relevant to the population that might be used to inform law and justice?
2. What should the law say?
3. What does the law say?

These three questions can be addressed in turn:

What research-based evidence is reliable and relevant to the population that might be used to inform law and justice?

The admission of evidence from lay and expert witnesses alike is governed by precedent, court rules of evidence, and statutes. There are barriers that must be passed before any type of evidence is permitted into the court. The evidence to be presented must be established as relevant to the case and reliable. Facts pertaining to an individual's FASD deficits, whether as a defendant or witness, must be accepted by the court if they are to have an impact on the court decision.

We see the reluctance of courts to consider medical findings related to neurocognitive defects in an overview provided by U.S. District Judge Jed S. Rakoff who presented at the annual 2015 meeting of the Society for Neuroscience (Davis 2015). Rakoff is a founding member of the MacArthur Foundation Research Network on Law and Neuroscience. He explained that judges are still cautious about allowing neuroscientific evidence in court. "The attitude of judges toward neuroscience is one of ambivalence and skepticism," Rakoff said. "You ask them about the hippocampus, they say it's something at the zoo." Rakoff noted that judges have reason for caution. In the not too distant past, the courts and the law allowed science to be used that was inhumane and harmful—and has been discarded. An example he described was eugenics. State laws allowed the forced sterilization of women, and the U.S. Supreme Court upheld the practice in 1927 (Davis 2015).

Returning to the question of FASD in the court, until recently there has been a paucity of probative research about deficits caused by prenatal alcohol to answer justice system questions about reliability and relevance to the case at hand. Fortunately, court knowledge about FASD is increasing, and expert witness testimony on FASD issues will likely be increasingly admissible with time.

What should the law say?

Many advocates propose that the law should mandate the consideration of an FASD diagnosis and appropriately address the individual's deficits within each case. They propose requiring expert assessment of the individual's deficits, to be done regardless of socio-economic or legal status. An even more comprehensive statute would require judges to assure that information derived from the assessment is applied in the action of the court.

What does the law say?

The answer today would most often be "not enough". A large void of direct references to FASD exists in both statutes and appellate opinions. But courts have recognized lack of mental capacity as precluding a guilty finding. In a case where the individual with FASD is the defendant, and the question is mental capacity, the same criteria should apply to FASD as with a mental illness, even though there is no statutory basis for finding "not guilty by reason of an FASD". In determining guilt or innocence of an offence, a court could find:

(a) The defendant's impairments were such that the individual did not meet the McNaughton rule[1] requirement to have the capacity to understand the nature and quality of his acts or that the acts were wrong.
(b) The defendant's impairments were such that the individual misunderstood the circumstances of the setting of the crime.
(c) The defendant cannot assist as needed in his or her own defense because of a disability.

In determining the sentence or penalty, the courts are not prohibited from taking into account the effects of FASD on defendants' ability to obey conditions of probation or parole.

The court can require the screening and assessment of defendants for FASD as a part of the psycho-social investigation before a sentencing order is made to determine what might be reasonable terms to impose as a sentence.

---

[1] In the mid 1850s, the "McNaughton rule" created a presumption of sanity, unless the defense proved "at the time of committing the act, the accused was laboring under such a defect of reason, from disease of the mind, as not to know the nature and quality of the act he was doing or, if he did know it, that he did not know what he was doing was wrong." The rule remains the standard to determine whether a person shall be held criminally responsible for acts in many states and a variant in other states. The Canadian criminal code is also based on the McNaughton rule.

Even though U.S. and Canadian trial courts do have the authority to take FASD into account based on their common law tradition, the existing evidence indicates that this is rarely what happens; it would appear that the FASD status is largely ignored in most cases to date. Appellate court actions could also come into play in FASD cases but this does not happen often enough. A court's refusal to make a finding based on being unable to assist in one's defense or an impairment severe enough to meet the McNaughton requirements are not frequently grounds for a reversal upon appeal in the appellate system. Indeed, few cases reach the appellate system absent some egregious error. The data on rates of reversal at the appellate level (combined civil and criminal) runs less than 20% in most United States jurisdictions. The two explanations for the trial court's failure to consider FASD factors seem obvious. They are: (1) the attorneys are not presenting the evidence needed about the effects of FASD on the litigants' or defendant's behavior; and (2) the judges do not recognize the importance of the effects of FASD.

As noted below, there is a dearth of FASD precedent in the case law in Canada and US. There is, however substantial acknowledgement of the suspicion of the seriousness of FASD in the criminal justice system of both countries. More empirical evidence is needed about the outcomes for those with FASD in the justice system across the dockets.

Research to date clearly suggests that individuals with FASD have a high level of repeated justice system involvement (Streissguth et al. 1996, 1997a, b, 2004) whether the involvement is civil or criminal, whether as a witness, a victim or an offender. With respect to the adult population in the justice system, it is important to note that these numbers may be deceptively low, consequent to the difficulty of diagnosing FASD in adults. Yet, whether derived from anecdotal observations or structured research, FASD seems to be a greater burden in the justice system populations than has been documented by analysis to date. The difficulties of conducting research on any subject in the justice system added to the difficulties of obtaining an FASD diagnosis for an adult, speaks to the need for new study approaches on FASD and law. This holds true as well for the juvenile court population. Without better designed studies of the justice system populations and the inclusion of other dockets such as family, divorce, bankruptcy courts and small claims, the full burden of FASD will not be recognized by the justice system policy and decision makers.

In addition, a great deal more work is needed in the design of effective dispositional orders from the courts for cases involving persons with FASD. And, last, but not the least, research is needed to determine the most effective ways of disseminating knowledge about FASD to the courts in order to get the judges to use the evidence based programming.

1.4 Cases

The common law heritage of Canada and the United States provide the two countries with a shared jurisprudential approach to problems presented in court (Streissguth et al. 2004). Even so, the case law of each country differs. A review of the case law for each country is instructive and should be undertaken in more detail than is provided here.

A foundational Canadian precedent in the Supreme Court of Canada is Winnipeg Child and Family Services (Northwest Area) v. G. (D.F.), [1997] 3 SCR 925, 1997 CanLII 336 (SCC). In this case the focus was on glue sniffing rather than alcohol but sets a precedent that would be applicable to alcohol as well. The court held that "The law of Canada does not recognize the unborn child as a legal person possessing rights." The court's decision has been applied to efforts to stop (or rather not stop) the consumption of alcohol by pregnant women.

There is a range of case law in Canada that is captured through the website "FASD and the Justice System" located at http://fasdjustice.ca/main/about.html. The site was developed by The Justice Committee of FASD ONE (FASD Ontario Network of Expertise) with funding from the Public Health Agency of Canada and the Department of Justice Canada, Youth Justice Policy. The FASD ONE site was created for justice system professionals and others seeking legal information about FASD who want to understand more about FASD. The information about FASD that is provided on the site includes case law, legal resources, and strategies. The resources are intended to assist professionals to better represent or serve persons with FASD who enter the justice system as accused, victims, or witnesses. The Canadian legal record contains many more cases than the United States.

In the United States, few civil or criminal cases actually address the issues that might be presented by the presence of an FASD. This is disappointing because many cases at trial and appellate levels may have an individual as party or witness who has an FASD. Thus precedential guidance is rarely available either as a mandate or an illumination of the problems FASD presents to the justice system. Trial court decisions are often not published in records of court actions known as "reporters" and are only published in the lay media if the editor finds them of news or other commercial value. While those cases reaching the appellate system will be reported and accessible, few FASD involved cases reach the appellate level. The rarity of the appellate opinions is further exacerbated by the narrowness of their applicability. The appellate courts are bound by the record transmitted to them and the issues preserved for appeal by the parties. An appellate court will only decide those issues raised specifically upon appeal. It is rare to see a court on its own rule on an issue that has not been briefed, unless the issue constitutes a fundamental error in the trial.

The case of Ferguson v. Charleston (99–936) 532 U.S. 67 (2001) is often cited for its prenatal care ruling, specifically, that a pregnant women cannot be compelled into treatment by threats of criminal prosecution. But in actuality, the case is far narrower in its precedential value than often described by commentators. This is because the hospital which served as the litigant was government owned and therefore, deemed to be a state actor. The hospital staff had collected the urine of pregnant women without the informed consent of the women and used the results to threaten those who tested positive for alcohol and drugs with criminal law violations. Though the case relates to the issue of using threat of prosecution as a means of preventing prenatal drinking, it does not fully resolve the legal status of such an approach given the unique circumstances of this case.

In another FASD case, Holmes v. Louisiana (08–1358)130 S.Ct. 70 (2009), Brandy Aileen Holmes, was a 29-year-old woman with FAS on death row who had been convicted of a 2003 murder in Louisiana. Despite the amicus brief filed detailing her disability from FASD, the petition for writ of certiorari (that is, a request for review) to the Supreme Court of Louisiana was denied by the United States Supreme Court.[2]

In the case Trevino v. Thaler, 133 S. Ct. 1911, 185 L. Ed. 2d 1044 (2013), a claim of ineffective assistance of trial counsel alleges that the attorney should have included fetal alcohol syndrome (FAS) as a mitigating circumstance. The Supreme Court of the United States opinion did not address the implications of FAS, or the merits of the claim, and remanded the case back to the lower court. On remand, the district court order declined to consider Trevino's proposed new evidence showing that he suffers from FAS or an FASD. The court found that the claim was unsupported by any showing of evidence that the petitioner's mother abused alcohol. The court further noted that there was no showing that the evidence was not reasonably available at the time of petitioner's 1997 capital murder trial (Trevino v. Stephens, Civil No. SA-01-CA-306-XR, United States District Court For The Western District Of Texas, San Antonio Division, 2015 U.S. Dist. LEXIS 75400, June 11, 2015).

In one death sentence state case, while considering the defendant's FASD status, the Court of Criminal Appeals of Texas in Soliz v. Texas wrote (432 S.W.3d 895; 2014 Tex. Crim. App. LEXIS 874, US Supreme Court certiorari denied by Soliz v. Texas, 2015 U.S. LEXIS 696 (U.S., Jan. 20, 2015): "There was sufficient evidence to support his death sentence because a rational trier of fact could have found that there was a probability that he would commit criminal acts of violence constituting a continuing threat to society; the jurors weighed his evidence of brain damage and partial fetal-alcohol syndrome along with other relevant evidence and made a normative judgment that the evidence did not warrant a life sentence."

Thus, as it pertains to criminal cases in the U.S. a number of conclusions may be drawn: First, the courts are not giving persuasive weight to the evidence of FASD as a mitigating circumstance. Next, the requirement for evidence of maternal alcohol use in one of these cases (beyond the medical FASD diagnosis) adds another barrier, for it would have seemed that in place of testimony related to the defendant's mother use of alcohol, the dysmorphological and neurocognitive assessment should have sufficiently defined the defendant's FASD mental and functional impairment. Lastly, if the evidence of FASD is not admitted at trial, it appears that the chances of reversal on appeal, alleging inadequate counsel or other errors, are quite small. Therefore, it is not surprising that the admission of evidence about FASD in civil or other cases varies greatly across both Canadian and American jurisdictions.

---

[2]The entire opinion consisted of this paragraph: "Motion of National Organization on Fetal Alcohol Syndrome for leave to file a brief as amicus curiae granted. Motion of Constitution Project for leave to file a brief as amicus curiae granted. Motion of Louisiana Association of Criminal Lawyers for leave to file a brief as amicus curiae granted. Motion of National Center on Domestic and Sexual Violence, et al. for leave to file a brief as amici curiae granted. Petition for writ of certiorari to the Supreme Court of Louisiana denied."

1.5 Statutes

To be most effective, policies for the prevention or mitigation of FASD should be grounded in explicit statutory provisions. One of the reasons argued for a statute is to promote equal access to justice informed by science. A second reason is that the judges are more clearly bound to consider the effects of FASD in the cases if the requirements are "hard wired" into statute.

We can analyze and organize FASD policy by using levels of state action as a way of classifying the importance attached by the government to the action. In the diagram in Fig. 1.1, the nature of the government's role and actions expected from lower priority to higher priority would reflect the level of importance of the policy. The successful use of Bloom's taxonomy (Overbaugh and Schultz 1956) in pedagogy[3] provides a possible model for the creation of a taxonomy of law and regulations to signal the priority and importance of the actions or programs to deal with FASD. Such taxonomy would provide common structure to advance legislative and regulatory provisions regarding FASD in importance and to analyze the effectiveness of the level of priority. In other words, a hierarchy matching the level of importance of the law to level of government action could be designed. Such a design would help make it clear that the tasks that are most important are performed by government as essential government functions. The tasks mandated by the statutes would be in the next lower priority.

Fig. 1.1 Hierarchy of Response

[3] Bloom's Taxonomy was created under the supervision of Dr. Benjamin Bloom as an organization approach to promote higher forms of thinking, such as analyzing and evaluating concepts, processes, procedures, and principles, rather than just memorization of facts.

Table 1.1 Legislative needs related to FASD

1.	The state's efforts to prevent the use of alcohol by women who are pregnant
2.	The treatment options for women who have an alcohol use disorder
3.	The neonatal and childhood care for a child exposed to alcohol in utero
4.	The social services and educational agencies preparation to offer appropriate services for a child or adult who has a FASD
5.	The criminal justice and juvenile justice implementation of screening efforts to better identify the disabilities resulting from FASD
6.	The justice system, civil and criminal, development of approaches and provision of services that might be appropriate to the needs of the person with FASD who is in court
7.	Service coordination as the statutes are brought to alignment with other statues for population with disabilities
8.	The development of a research agenda will be developed to guide research in ways that will better inform law and policy

An example is that the state itself carries out critical functions such as fire service protection but the next lower level of services such as smoke detectors are mandated by building codes and the building owner must install the detectors or face fines. A third and even lower level of fire prevention might be undertaken to forbid individuals from building a campfire in unapproved areas in the woods. One can see the fire engines as the most critical response to preventing injury and damage from fires. The government assists by inspections and education in the lessor order actions. Merely forbidding an activity is even less emphatic. That same hierarchy also might assist in the analysis of the importance given to the law. Then, if in such a hierarchical table, the highest level of the of law is the performance of acts by the state, it would follow that a statute mandating a court to provide screening and assessment for FASD denotes that the screening and assessment for FASD are an essential function of the court.

Other statutes and regulations can outline the importance of the government in providing essential services for FASD. The required performance does not have to be by a state agency. If the state or province requires the acts by other entities, then it might be justified in considering that performance or required performance as the indicator of a higher priority for the policy addressed by that statute. In considering whether the government "requires", "facilitates" or "permits" the acts, an indicator of the level of the government's awareness and commitment is found. Does the jurisdiction "ignore" or "forbid" the actions by policy? In Table 1.1 one can chart a statute or regulation according to the action verb in the language of the provision. Each level indicates a priority, and the highest priority is at the top of the chart where the government performs the task itself.

A more sophisticated approach would compare the policy to the action actually taken recognizing that the policy implementation could be impacted by the amount of community resources available. In other words, while the statute might define a specific priority level, the actual implementation may differ. An example of where "theoretical intent" differs from "implementation" can be found in the laws setting a minimum drinking age. The aim of the law is to prevent individuals under age 21 (in the U.S.) from consuming alcohol. When law enforcement officers do not act to prevent the use of alcohol in the under 21 population they are not acting at the highest level of "perform" but lowering the status of the efforts against underage drinking to the fifth level of status, to wit: "ignore".

In an attempt to sort out which FASD laws are in place, we have sought to better understand how and where the law and the science match up. A process that examines and classifies the statutes of the individual states that specifically address FASD should be developed to elucidate the impact of the statutes in a logical fashion. The process might also include statutes that do not specifically identify alcohol to determine if they could have an impact on FASD-related behaviors. In this context, it is important to note that legislative provisions that refer to drugs or substance abuse may confound the review and discussion unless the statutory definition specifically included alcohol. Substance abuse, as a term, is meaningless in the law as well as in the understanding of the general population. Traditionally, the law names alcohol and defines it, when the law or policy is intended to regulate use or possession of alcohol.

The word "drugs" can often mean illegal drugs to non-medical people, as well as to the law trained person. In the law, "drugs" also may include the scheduled drugs that may be legally prescribed. Because criminal law must define each element of the crime, state statutes have to define what drugs are addressed within the meaning of substance abuse for each specific law. Without statutory definition, substance abuse could include caffeine, food, chocolate, etc. In contrast, alcohol is more clearly defined in the law and holds a common, widely understood meaning.

But the issue of legal drugs versus illegal drugs in pregnancy goes even further. Mary Ellen Rimsza, chairwoman of Arizona's Child Fatality Review Board, provided an interesting perspective on this subject, as reported: "She fears a slippery slope when states begin prosecuting women for drug abuse during pregnancy – first, prosecutions for illegal drugs such as cocaine and methamphetamine, then for legal substances such as alcohol and tobacco, then for potentially risky behavior such as not taking prenatal vitamins and not eating properly" (Scharnberg 2003).

The discussion of how to improve our response to the needs of pregnant women who drink alcohol is often sidetracked by a number of issues such as debates over the status of the fetus as a human, social and economic discrimination, respect for women and their right to their bodies, and all of the religious and emotional fervor that accompanies strong beliefs. Putting all of the emotion and passionate views aside, this rather daunting task of analysis requires a framework to organize the statutes and science across the widely varying statutory schemes. The challenge is to relate the statutes to the peer reviewed research and to assign appropriate categories and maintain consistency with the other statutes of the state. The assumption is that a coherent and consistent set of statutes and polices would improve all of the goals in Table 1.1.

While the statutes are the foundation of a government's policy and articulate its general policies, it is in the regulations of administrative agencies where the policy meets human life on the streets. The regulations of health and child protection agencies are more intrusive on a day to day basis than are the prosecution of criminal laws when dealing with pregnancy and family life. For families under the supervision of the Child Protection Services, it may at times seem like the case worker has moved in with them as they visit and send others to visit the home on a frequent basis.

A comprehensive review of the regulatory provisions as well as the relevant case law in the states is beyond the scope of this article. The aim here is to describe a generalized picture of the legal status of FASD in Canada and US, and suggest future directions. This is a first attempt to lay out an approach that should be comprehensive and coherent, and contain a clear set of statutes to deal with the issues around FASD.

It is important for any legislation to explicitly articulate its purpose, the rationale for the policy, and the goals that are to be accomplished by the legislation. It is especially timely to consider how states or provinces can best design their statutes pertaining to FASD, as there is a growing body of new science which can inform legislation. The next part of this discussion lays out a potential model statute for FASD to enact a substantial response to the needs of the state to deal with effects of FASD. A suggested preamble is set out below as a simple and direct explanation.

1.6 Authorizing and Justification Language Preamble

The Province or State of (insert name) has substantial social, legal, financial and ethical interests in protecting children from the harm that results from the use of alcohol by their mothers during pregnancy, for the sake of the child and of the family. The financial costs of fetal alcohol spectrum disorders (FASD) can be enormous to the state in providing medical and other care to those children damaged by the alcohol use of their parents. Alcohol is a teratogen, and arguably presents the highest risk because it is legal, widely consumed, and frequently consumed at doses that can result in harm, even death, to the fetus. Alcohol affects the fetus through transplacental transfer. Alcohol can produce a range of defects in the fetus that are irreparable either in childhood or adulthood. Such effects may include serious neurobehavioral deficits. No safe level of use of alcohol during pregnancy is known.

Of all of the concerns that properly demand the attention of a society, the protection of the health and capabilities of its young should be among the most pressing. Hence, this discussion of the urgency and sadness of the need to address the law around prenatal alcohol exposure is warranted. Law, medicine, social work, justice systems, and research – all need a clear focus on how we should deal with FASD.

It is recognized that the preferable, most effective, and most ethical means of preventing birth defects and health problems due to alcohol use during pregnancy requires informed leadership. The significant cross-disciplinary, community, and multi-level efforts that are needed must be supported by the state (province). To that end, this statute sets out necessary goals, requirements, and responsibilities. Further, as needed, this statute identifies the state (province) and local agencies with the corresponding responsibilities and assigns the responsibilities to the appropriate entity.

Table 1.2 Legislative needs related to FASD

Prevention	Marriage license requirements
	Education
	State Department of Education
	Secondary schools
	Course work in health classes
	Other curriculum materials
	Pregnant women
	By treating physicians
	Broad education – public
	Alcohol serving establishment signs
	Alcohol container labels
	Professional Schools with special focus for those who work with women or children as teachers and pediatricians, as well as, the justice system
	Department of Children and Family Services
Mitigation of the effects of FASD	Reporting to authorities
	Adoptions and records
	Reporting of mother for intervention or prosecution
	Community Health Services
	Children in need services
	Juvenile system requirements
	Criminal justice system requirements

Further, this statute creates the state (province)-wide *"Commission to Prevent and Mitigate FASD"* to provide oversight and coordination. The statute shall address the following index items.

Specific issues that should be addressed within the statute across the dimensions of prevention, education and mitigation are outlined in Table 1.2.

It is undeniable that the most controversial statutory provisions related to FASD are those that provide criminal punishment for drinking alcohol during pregnancy. The Canadian Supreme Court delivered a well-reasoned opinion about the state's role in Winnipeg Child and Family Services (Northwest Area) v. G. (D.F.), [1997] 3 SCR 925, 1997 CanLII 336 (SCC) at 927. The court explained, "To extend the law of tort to permit an order for the detention and treatment of a pregnant woman for the purpose of preventing harm to the unborn child would require major changes, involving moral choices and conflicts between fundamental interests and rights. [This] would affect women, who might find themselves incarcerated and treated against their will for conduct alleged to harm the fetus. The proposed changes to the law have complex ramifications impossible for a court to fully assess, giving rise to danger that the proposed order might impede the goal of healthy infants more than it would promote it."

No research provides persuasive evidence that coercion through prosecution will prevent FASD. As many judges have learned by experience, punishment does not constitute effective prevention.

Table 1.3 Goals of enacted statues

Category of activity	Target audience	Level of learning (after Bloom's taxonomy)
Inform	General population	Lower
Prevent	Parents, medical and social service providers	Higher and targeted to audiences
Create resources	Parents and community, justice	High
Treat and remediate	Social services, medical, justice	High and intense
Punish	Justice	High
Research	Body politic	High, sophisticated science

The chart in Table 1.3 is a schematic illustration of an approach to thinking about how to enact the desired statutory provisions. An effective scheme will deliver the statutory support for a specific audience with the aim of education, not regulation, for a healthy pregnancy.

1.6.1 Specific Programs and Possibilities to Provide FAIR (Fetal Alcohol Interventions and Responses) in Justice

As part of the efforts to assure equal access to Justice, the criminal justice system is attempting to incorporate scientifically based knowledge about human health and behavior in programs such as "Reentry" and "Justice Reinvestment." Prenatal alcohol exposure is a pressing condition that the justice system must confront. The research on FASD is advancing, although much work remains. When dealing with FASD, it is penny wise and pound foolish to underfund research, intervention, and treatment of alcohol misuse. Observations to date would indicate that persons with FASD are the single most over represented, under-recognized, and underserved group in the justice system (Fast et al. 1999).

The questions presented by the justice reform efforts are:

1. How might we develop and evaluate programs that are in collaboration with the justice system to divert persons with an FASD from the justice system?
2. Who will inform the justice system of the science about FASD?
3. What quality assurance measures can be developed and applied to assure equal access to justice for those persons with an FASD?

A Lexis-Nexis search shows that 395 appellate cases in the U.S. are listed as mentioning fetal alcohol. This includes federal district courts, US Courts of Appeals, and unpublished appellate opinions from the state courts. The Canadian courts have over 1000 appealed cases including a case before the Supreme Court of Canada, Winnipeg Child and Family Services (Northwest Area) v. G. (D.F.), [1997] 3 SCR 925, 1997 CanLII 336 (SCC). Canada reports more judicial attention to the considerations of justice systems approaches to FASD than does the United States. Yet, in both countries, the results are not adequate in terms of prevention of FASD, as well as provision of equal access to justice for those persons who are affected by FASD. In both countries much work remains to adequately inform law and policy and the justice system with science-based evidence. Most importantly, work needs to be done so that efforts to prevent FASD do not create more ineffective laws and regulations. The aim is to educate effectively, with law and policy support. Our mantra is to educate, not regulate and provide more education for the public about the causes and effects of FASD.

1.7 Some Final Comments on Law, Policy, and Ethics

One of the aims of this chapter is to consider how a community might provide a more just, more effective and ethical response to prevent and remediate the deficits caused by prenatal exposure to alcohol, using law and policy approaches. The relationship of law and ethics in issues surrounding prenatal alcohol exposure is fraught with more challenges than in other areas of alcohol and justice interaction. In the law, a response may be legal but not ethical; but in order for an action to be ethical, it must be permitted by the law.

Law and policy, both past and current, also shape the ethical issues that determine how a community might best address the needs of persons living with fetal alcohol spectrum disorders, (FASD) and the programs which help prevent future alcohol exposed pregnancies. The establishment of good policy and law is dependent on sound data, but the potential for data flaws within the justice system can be greater than that derived from other systems such as health care or science. Justice data often lacks accuracy and completeness and the collected data elements often vary across sites and systems. Even when data elements carry the same label, the meanings may differ. Unless data dictionaries are established for each system and agency and are compared it could be a critical mistake to assume that two fields with the same label contain the same data. The many cultural influences on alcohol use can blur useful conclusions about what the data might mean for law and policy purposes.

Historically, there has been a lack of effort to obtain good data on alcohol and the law. This seems remarkable in light of the fact that from the very first written civil codes and religious writings, the use and misuse of alcohol has been front and center in the language of laws and regulations. Alcohol use has an influence on many human activities, and law and policy efforts remain inadequately informed by science. Often the aim of law and regulation on alcohol has not been to improve society or ensure justice but rather to raise revenue for governments through taxation.

For law trained professionals, there is an assumption that if the law forbids or requires a certain action, then disregarding such law is an unethical action. When it comes to the law and policy for the pregnant woman and her child of the pregnancy, the complexity of rights versus harms make the validity of that assumption less assured. This lack of clarity makes ethical responses more difficult for legal professionals who are subject to disciplinary action, including loss of professional licenses, if they are found to violate statutory or Constitutional rights or fail to act in ways their professional ethics require. For example, balancing client confidentiality with the protection of a baby or the life of a fetus is a tough decision for a lawyer. Lawyers are ethically bound to maintain client confidentiality. The attorney-client privilege is sacrosanct. An examination of the law and policy around the mother's consumption of alcohol, as well as the law and policy aimed to protect the child before and after birth from prenatal alcohol exposure may inform ethical decisions. Going beyond the fact that what may be ethical for a medical professional may be unethical in a province or state for a lawyer, the question also presents as to whether an action can be ethical for one law professional and the same response unethical for a different lawyer based on the law of the different jurisdictions in which they practice.

The conflicting legal and ethical issues between the professions of medicine and law also come into play. An example might be determining the ethical decision of the treating obstetrician with patients in two clinics, each in a different state or province or for a lawyer who represents the two pregnant women. One clinic or client is in a jurisdiction that has a law making it a criminal offense for a pregnant woman to consume alcohol and the second is devoid of such provision. For the physician, the ethical decision is centered on his or her judgment as to what is best for the patient. For the lawyer, it is an unethical decision to advise a client to violate the law. The lawyer's ethical requirement is to advise the client she cannot consume alcohol regardless of whether there is detoxification treatment available to the client or what might be in her client's best medical interest. The dilemma becomes even more complex in a state where the lawyer is held to a statutory duty to report child endangerment and disciplinary actions have been taken against lawyers for not reporting the child endangerment. At what point is the mother's prenatal alcohol use an endangerment to the child and how does that mesh with the law? The duty to report has trumped client confidentiality in some cases.

Another question is whether an examination of the laws across multiple jurisdictions is likely to illuminate the use or the non-use of science to inform the law. One would expect, at least from a logical approach that many U.S. states and Canadian provinces would have relatively similar provision in their laws and court decisions. After all, Canada and the Unites States share a common law heritage, not to mention the unifying effect of science about prenatal exposure to alcohol which does not change according to political subdivisions. Nonetheless, attempts to catalog the laws reveal the haphazard content of laws from different jurisdictions and variations and swings in law over time. A part of this complexity is that in some jurisdictions courts rely exclusively on statutes (so called "code" law jurisdictions), as compared to "common" law jurisdiction where the courts make law as well as interpret it. To expand on this distinction, code law jurisdictions restrict the actions of the court to those that have been set in legislation (be it local, state or federal) while common law jurisdictions (based on the original English common law) have more flexibility to interpret the law and rely heavily on precedents set in previous court decisions.

One important goal is to examine statutes, regulations and case law, to identify provisions that are more effective than others in dealing with prenatal alcohol exposure (PAE) issues. Proof of effectiveness of a law will promote the enactment of more effective laws to advance the justice system response for persons who have been affected by an FASD.

In summary, this chapter set out to provide a brief review of the history of legal response to prenatal alcohol exposure and then review the current status of legislation in two countries that share the legal tradition of English common law derived from their prior English colonial histories. Finally, a structural analysis was suggested and some current trends in the justice system were identified that may support the advancement of system reform in dealing with persons affected by prenatal alcohol exposure.

References

Coffey, T. 1966. Beer street – Gin lane – Some views of 18th century drinking. *Quarterly Journal of Studies on Alcohol* 27: 669–692.

Davis, K. 2015. Federal judge says neuroscience is not ready for the courtroom – yet. *American Bar Association Journal* [Internet]. 2015 Oct 15. Available from: http://www.abajournal.com/mobile/article/federal_judge_says_neuroscience_is_not_ready_for_the_courtroom_yet/

Fast, D.K., J. Conry, and C.A. Loock. 1999. Identifying fetal alcohol syndrome among youth in the criminal justice system developmental and behavioral. *Pediatrics* 20: 370–372.

Fielding, H. 1751. *An enquiry into the causes of the late increase of robbers...with some proposals for remedying this growing evil.* London: A. Millar.

George, M.D. 1965. *London life in the eighteen century*. 2nd ed. New York: Harper Torchbooks.

Guttmacher Institute. Updated 2017. *Substance use during pregnancy*. https://www.guttmacher.org/state-policy/explore/substance-use-during-pregnancy

Kaskutas LA, Graves K 1994. Relationship between cumulative exposure to health messages and awareness and behavior-related drinking during pregnancy American Journal of Health Promotion 9: 115–124.

Morris, C. 1751. *Observation on the past growth and present state of the city of London*. London.

National Council of Juvenile and Family Court Judges. 2015. *Fetal alcohol spectrum disorders: Implications for juvenile and family court judges*. http://www.ncjfcj.org

Overbaugh, R.C., and L. Schultz. 1956. *Blooms Taxonomy*. Old Dominion University [Internet], Retrieved from http://ww2.odu.edu/educ/roverbau/Bloom/blooms_taxonomy.htm. Last viewed 20 Nov 2015.

Popova, S., S. Lange, D. Bekmuradov, A. Mihic, and J. Rehm. 2011. Fetal alcohol spectrum disorder prevalence estimates in correctional systems: A systematic literature review. *Canadian Journal of Public Health* 102: 336–340.

Scharnberg, K. 2003. Report on comments of Mary Ellen Rimsza. *Chicago Tribune*. 23 Nov 2003.

Streissguth, A.P., H.M. Barr, J. Kogan, and F.L. Bookstein. 1996. *Final report: Understanding the occurrence of secondary disabilities in clients with fetal alcohol syndrome (FAS) and fetal alcohol effects (FAE)*. Seattle: University of Washington Publication Services.

———. 1997a. Primary and secondary disabilities in fetal alcohol syndrome. In *The challenge of fetal alcohol syndrome: Overcoming secondary disabilities*, ed. A.P. Streissguth, J. Kanter, et al., 25–39. Seattle: University of Washington Press.

Streissguth, A.P., and J. Kanter, et al., eds. 1997b. *The challenge of fetal alcohol syndrome: Overcoming secondary disabilities*. Seattle: University of Washington Press.

Streissguth, A., F. Bookstein, H. Barr, P. Sampson, K. O'Malley, and J. Kogan. 2004. Risk factors for adverse life outcomes in fetal alcohol syndrome and fetal alcohol effects. *Journal of Developmental and Behavioral Pediatrics* 25 (4): 228–238.

Warner, R.H., and H.L. Rosett. 1975. The effects of drinking on offspring an historical survey of the American and British literature. *Journal of Studies on Alcohol* 36: 1395–1420.

Warner, J., M. Her, G. Gmel, and J. Rehm. 2001. Can legislation prevent debauchery? Mother gin and public health in 18th century England. *American Journal of Public Health* 91 (3): 375–384.

Warren, K.R. 2015. A review of the history of attitudes toward drinking in pregnancy. *Alcoholism, Clinical and Experimental Research* 39: 1110–1117. https://doi.org/10.1111/acer.125757.

Warren, K.R., and B.G. Hewitt. 2009. Fetal alcohol spectrum disorders: When science, medicine, public policy and law collide. *Developmental Disabilities Research Reviews* 15: 170–175.

Chapter 2
FASD and the Denial of Equality

Ian Binnie

2.1 Introduction

One of the most important guarantees in the *Canadian Chart of Rights and Freedoms* is the entitlement of "every person" to the equal protection and benefit of the law. At a formal level, the courts have been active in addressing issues of discrimination where it can be established that differential treatment is based on one of the prohibited grounds of race, national origin, ethnicity, skin colour, religion, sex, age or mental or physical disabilities.

There is no doubt that individuals who suffer from Fetal Alcohol Syndrome Disorder ("FASD") often exhibit functional disabilities that, in an ideal world, would be accommodated in the legal system, or at least treated as a *mitigating* rather than an *aggravating* factor. However, at a practical level, when decisions have to be made in a hurry by a judge or public trustee or other official, often based on incomplete diagnosis and fragmentary information, the guarantee of equal protection and benefit of the law may often be illusory.[1]

The problem was made manifest in a case in the British Columbia Court of Appeal, *R. vs Harris,* 2002 BCCA 152, in which the appellate court rapped the knuckles of a trial judge for giving a lighter sentence than might otherwise be imposed for convictions of breaking and entering and breach of probation. The sentencing judge inferred from various observations and bits of information in the pre-sentence report that the accused (now convicted) "probably" suffered from FASD, and on that account was handed a conditional sentence of only 9 months with 3 years' probation. The important point about a conditional sentence is that it is served in the community under strict conditions. It may amount to house arrest, but the offender is

[1] See the very helpful discussion of many of these issues in Roach and Bailey (2009) at p. 1.

I. Binnie (✉)
The Supreme Court of Canada, Ottawa, ON, Canada
e-mail: ibinnie@litigate.com

E. Jonsson et al. (eds.), *Ethical and Legal Perspectives in Fetal Alcohol Spectrum Disorders (FASD)*, International Library of Ethics, Law, and the New Medicine 75,
https://doi.org/10.1007/978-3-319-71755-5_2

not incarcerated in a jail or penitentiary. It is important, where practical, to keep FASD sufferers out of potentially violent settings. In effect, the trial judge had taken what is called "judicial notice" of the signs of FASD, that is to say he inferred the existence of FASD without expert evidence to establish the diagnosis.

The Court of Appeal concluded that the trial judge could not properly take "judicial notice" of the likely presence of FASD. Judicial notice is generally reserved for matters that are beyond controversy. The appellate judges said that "it is wrong in principle for a sentence to be based on a conclusion about the mental capacity of an individual offender derived from assumptions and general knowledge." At the same time, the Court of Appeal was candid enough to recognize "that it is practically impossible for an adult to be assessed for FASD/FAE/ARND in the Province" because in most cases the funds are simply unavailable. An assessment may take more time than the legal system is able to give it, and the cost of $3000 to $4000 for a full assessment is more money than the state is willing to spend. The result is that FASD is a much under diagnosed disability, and the people suffering from this disability pay the price.

2.2 The Dilemma Posed by FASD

Here then is the dilemma: the courts appreciate that FASD can express itself in functional disabilities that challenge some of the fundamental assumptions of our legal system, namely that an individual is presumed to be able to foresee the probable consequences of his or her conduct, and by going ahead anyway is presumed to have intended to bring about the consequences of that conduct,. If caught and punished in the criminal courts (or bounced from foster home to foster home), he or she is likely incapable of personal reassessment and reform. Yet the courts are by and large unable to give effect to the reduced capacity of the FASD victim to live up to these expectations. The law is applied equally to people of greatly unequal capacity to comply with its demands.

Apart from distortions of the victim's facial morphology in serious cases, such as unusually small eyes and a narrow space between the nose and the upper lip, and a diminished vertical cleft in the upper lip, the FASD individual may look quite normal, and is therefore expected by the community to act normally. But in serious cases of FASD such an expectation may be completely unrealistic and because of his or her inability to live up to "normal" expectations, the FASD sufferer may be denied the equal protection and benefit of the legal system.

2.3 Functional Disabilities

In September 2013, Consensus Development Conference on "Legal Issues of FASD" organized by the Institute of Health Economics in Alberta (see appendix at the end of the book), the view amongst the experts appeared to be that both the legal system and various support programs in the community should focus on addressing functional disabilities rather than diagnosis because it is at the *functional* level that discrimination occurs. A girl suffering from FASD may get into trouble in a foster home because (to take one possibility) she is violent, not because the *cause* of her violent behaviour is FASD.

That is not at all to say that a positive diagnosis of FASD is unimportant. Very often an accurate diagnosis, as early as possible in the life of a child, can help in the formation of a management plan to help the child deal in a practical way with functional disabilities and live a useful and rewarding life in the community. However, some years ago, then Chief Justice of Saskatchewan, Ed Bayda, told a legal audience that the single biggest challenge to justice in the Prairie Provinces was FASD. His statement went beyond the criminal law, and included everything from adoption, guardianship, child welfare, correctional services and embraced virtually every aspect of life touched by the law. There continues to be a lack of proportionality between the scale of the FASD challenge and the minimal support systems that exist in the community.

2.4 Where Do the Judges Stand?

The Courts are better at discussing the problem of FASD than in giving practical relief. For example, any effort by the state to intervene against an expectant mother with a history of serious substance abuse to protect the unborn child is fraught with human rights issues. At this point in our judicial history the rights of an addict mother who refuses treatment and insists on carrying her baby to term will be protected even at the likely expense of her unborn child. This was decided by a 7 to 2 majority in the Supreme Court of Canada in *Winnipeg Child and Family Services (Northwest Area) v.* G. *(D.F),* [1997] 3 SCR 925.

In that case, the Child and Family Services authority sought to detain for treatment, against her will, a 22 year old pregnant woman with a history of serious addiction to glue-sniffing. Some of the judgments made stray references to FASD, but for our purposes the distinction between glue-sniffing and alcoholism may not make much difference. Both "life-style choices", as the Supreme Court majority characterized the mother's behaviour, lead potentially to similar sorts of neurodevelopmental disabilities.

FASD is always the result of the mother's alcohol consumption, but it is unpredictable whether disabilities develop at all, and if they do, the severity and type of physical and functional deficits vary from barely discernible to the catastrophic. The *Winnipeg* mother-to-be might well have given birth to a perfectly normal child, or she might not.

In the *Winnipeg* case, the woman had already given birth to three children, two of whom had been born brain damaged as a result of her addiction and had been made permanent wards of the state. She had refused all offers of treatment to deal with her addiction problem [para 73]. She declared her determination to carry the fourth child to term, which she did.

The trial judge issued a detention order confining the expectant mother for treatment, but he was reversed by the Manitoba Court of Appeal, and the mother again prevailed in the Supreme Court of Canada by a majority of 7 to 2 judges. The majority essentially rested their decision on the familiar ground that an unborn child is not a legal person. It possesses no legal rights. "A pregnant woman and her unborn child are one," the majority said, and to make an order protecting the foetus would "radically impinge on the fundamental liberties of the mother, both as to lifestyle choices and how and as to where she chooses to live and be" (emphasis added). The statement, so far as it went, reflects orthodox legal principle, although at the 2013 conference we were told that Norway and Finland do assume the power to confine an expectant mother with a serious addiction problem to protect the unborn child.

There are strong echoes in the majority judgment of the abortion debate, and the 7 judges were determined to stand firm on the fundamental question of principle of when a foetus acquires legal status. If there is to be a change, the majority said, it should be left in the hands of the legislature. Of course, the judges were well aware that following *R.* v. *Morgenthaler* [1988] 1 SCR 30 no government has dared raise in Parliament the wildly controversial issue of the status and rights, if any, of an unborn child.

In the *Manitoba* case, the dissenting judges ventured onto more adventurous legal ground. They were less concerned about the lifestyle choices of the mother than the life prospects of the foetus. Would the result have been different, they asked, "if the state had been trying to restrain a pregnant mother from taking thalidomide to deal with her morning sickness?" [para 123]. In their view, invoking the *parens patriae* jurisdiction, the state need not "stand idly by ... watching the birth of a permanently and seriously handicapped child who has no future other than as a permanent ward of the state" [para 63].

In fact, as mentioned, at least in the case of FASD, there is a huge variation in the potential physical and functional effects. In experiments with genetically modified mice, whose DNA is programmed to produce genetically identical pups, researchers have observed a bewildering range of effects among pups in the same litter as a result of dosing the mother with alcohol. Some of the pups seem normal, others have virtually no forebrain. Experiments with mice may not always be good predictors of effects in humans, but at the 2013 conference we heard of an autopsy of a human foetus aborted from an alcoholic mother where the large fibre bundle that forms the essential connection between the right and the left half of the brain was entirely missing. Other children born in similar circumstances may have no physical or functional disabilities at all.[2] An IQ below 70 is generally regarded as deficient,

[2] There can be enormous variance in the range of resulting *functional* handicaps in human beings, including poor executive decision making, the inability to foresee the consequences of taking certain actions, and to learn from mistakes, poor self-regulation, hyperactivity, suggestibility, a lack of capacity to communicate and to meet the challenges of daily living in an appropriate way.

but many FASD victims score much higher. The unpredictability makes FASD a tough issue for the law to deal with.

At the conference on Fetal Alcohol Syndrome in Edmonton, mentioned above, we were addressed by a young man, apparently well educated, who had been diagnosed with FASD, yet had managed to make a relative success of his life. He spoke for about 20 min without a note about the challenges of living with FASD. We learned later that after his speech he left the conference hotel and became so disoriented he had difficulty finding his way home. Eventually he was spotted by an acquaintance who knew he was a FASD sufferer and helped him to his lodging.

2.5 Likely Candidates for Trouble with the Law

Assuming that the fourth child of the mother in the *Winnipeg* case followed the pattern of two of her earlier children, and, again it is stressed that this would not necessarily be the situation, the child could have been quite normal, but assuming things turned out badly, there is a high probability that the child with FASD would find himself or herself caught up in the grinding complexities of the legal system.

If the history of the earlier of the *Winnipeg* siblings was repeated, the fourth child could well suffer from a range of cognitive and functional deficits such as poor memory, impulsiveness, inability to appreciate adequately the consequences of his or her actions, a lack of capacity to learn from mistakes and a weakness for being easily influenced and manipulated by others. The executive functions of the brain are frequently diminished in persons with FASD. The child would simply be unable "to get his act together" in the way children without such a disability will normally do. Moreover, the functional disabilities often lead to a third level of consequence, namely poor employment prospects, a high level of homelessness, and a general inability to integrate successfully into the community.

The diminished capacity to deal with authority of every description is often mistaken for intransigence. The victim of FASD is as likely to be re-victimized by having his or her functional disabilities treated in the legal system as an *aggravating* factor thereby compounding the misery even in cases where the safety of the community is not at risk.

As mentioned earlier, FASD may create a barrier to justice in many aspects from adoption to guardianship to the evolving doors or foster homes. However, here I will focus my remarks on the criminal law consequences.

2.6 FASD in the Criminal Justice System

At the 2013 conference, our attention was drawn to a striking observation by Judge Barry Stuart of the Yukon Territorial Court as follows:

> In a couple of cases, I have conducted trials where the accused, the victim, and the witnesses all suffer from FAS, and it is very difficult to get an understanding of what happened in the actual case. Your first impression is to think, 'Everybody is lying here. Nobody is telling the truth.' And then you begin to appreciate, 'No, they are trying their best,' but because of the brain damage they have suffered as a result of FAS or FAE, they are doing the best that they possibly can.

In expressing his sympathy for persons suffering from the effects of FASD, Judge Barry Stuart was not underestimating the need to control violent conduct, and the need for punishment where punishment is required, including incarceration to protect the safety of the community. A victim of FASD may well bear a diminished responsibility for his or her conduct, but if the diminished responsibility leads to dangerous conduct, the conduct is no less dangerous because the cause is FASD. The public must be protected.

The media often gives the impression that FASD is concentrated amongst aboriginal communities. However, although aboriginal people are said to have a heightened sensitivity to alcohol, and this may be a factor in the incidence and expression of FASD, the situation is not necessarily tied to ethnicity. The 2013 jury was told that because FASD individuals tend to be easily lead by others, if he or she grows up in a situation of domestic violence or substance abuse (regardless of any connection to First Nationhood or reserves) FASD will tend to express itself in antisocial or violent behaviour. On the other hand, an aboriginal child with FASD who is fortunate enough to be diagnosed and be supported by a management plan that enhances integration into a stable home on or off a reserve there may be few if any marked departures from socially acceptable behaviour.

A striking illustration of a court attempting to come to terms with FASD is *R v Charlie,* 2012 WKTC 5, a decision of the Yukon Territorial Court. The case involved the very serious matter of a home invasion by a drunken youth armed with a club. Charlie likely suffered from FASD. He and two of his friends had been out drinking. They ran out of money and beer. Charlie was aware of the existence of a quite elderly and inoffensive local resident. While the two drunken companions were smart enough to stay outside, Charlie rushed into the home armed with a make-shift club, terrorized the elderly man, took about $30 for beer money and the car keys to the elderly man's vehicle, which he then drove towards Watson Lake. Ultimately he crashed the car and continued on to Watson Lake by other means. Charlie was eventually apprehended by the RCMP.

2.6.1 An Initial Encounter with the Police

The judgment of the Territorial Court does not address all of the factual circumstances surrounding Charlie's detention and arrest. Suppose however for illustrative purposes, that Charlie was seen walking along the street in the town of Watson Lake a few days after the crime, and was stopped for no particular reason by an RCMP officer and told to identify himself. In some jurisdictions this police practice is quite common (though highly controversial) and known as "carding". The Supreme Court of Canada has affirmed that when the police have no cause to detain someone on suspicion of criminal activity, the individual is free to walk away, *R v Mann*, 2004 SCC 52. However, many people (and this must be particularly true of FASD victims) are unlikely to do so. Most people do not pick fights with a policeman. On the other hand, people with normal instincts are unlikely to lean over backwards to get themselves into trouble.

In the case of an FASD sufferer like Charlie there may be no real appreciation that he has a choice in the matter. For such people any order from the constabulary to stand still and answer questions may result in a form of psychological detention. One of the common expressions of FASD is a desire to please. Charlie's natural inclination, if he possessed this characteristic, would be to be as helpful with the policeman as he could, even if he had no very accurate recollection of what had happened. He would be less able than most people to watch out for his own interest. Candour would likely not operate in Charlie's favour, but he would be unable to appreciate that fact. Nor might he foresee the consequences for his future of telling his story to police. In short, even at this early stage of interaction with the law, Charlie would be at a disadvantage in a system designed for people with normal self defence mechanisms.

2.6.2 *Charlie's Illusory Right to Remain Silent*

The next in Charlie's (imagined) trajectory through the criminal law system would be a stop at the RCMP detachment at Watson Lake. The police would have lots of questions for Charlie, based on the information he volunteered in casual conversation on the street, and possible information from the Whitehorse RCMP. Of course, the police would be required to advise Charlie of his right to legal counsel. Charlie may or may not have much of an idea what the "counsel" business was all about, and might not be much enlightened by the stilted language of the standard warning. Suppose however the policeman was helpful and put Charlie in touch with a local lawyer. Charlie might not have much to say to the lawyer. The lawyer would almost inevitably tell Charlie not to say anything.

The police, of course, are accustomed to dealing with suspects who have been advised by their lawyers not to say anything. One of their techniques is to agree entirely with the suspect that he received good advice and was absolutely free to remain silent but then to go on asking questions anyway. Charlie would then be in something of a quandary. His lawyer told him to say nothing but this policeman was proceeding as if he expected Charlie to answer the questions. Charlie has a constitutional right to keep silent, but is he really capable of exercising that right and thereby receiving the equal protection and benefit of the law? Probably not.

Even in the case of a person without disabilities, the Supreme Court of Canada has given great latitude to police questioning. The court seeks a proper balance between the rights of a detained person under investigation and the public interest in the investigation and solution of crime. In the case of *R v Singh,* 2007 SCC 48, the accused, who so far as the record shows was under no disability, kept asking to end the interrogation and be returned to his cell, but the police carried on with putting questions despite his protestations. According to the record, he asserted his right to silence on eighteen (18) occasions before the police, ignoring his insistence on not talking, got him talking and ultimately secured a confession. In the robust atmosphere of a police interrogation room the FASD sufferer may have no real capacity at all to assert effectively a right to silence. The concept of ignoring questions may not be understood. There is likely to be little appreciation on Charlie's part of the risks of putting aside his lawyer's advice to remain silent.

If a quite normal individual like Mr. Singh could have his repeatedly asserted right to silence overridden by police insistence, and yet the police conduct upheld as quite legitimate by the Supreme Court of Canada, would not Charlie with his FASD disability be even less capable of claiming the protection of the right to silence? If the right to silence was unavailing for Mr. Singh, it would likely have been completely illusory for someone in Charlie's position. According to the majority judges, Mr. Singh had the capacity to persist in his silence. Charlie would likely lack such capacity. But it would likely be an "undiagnosed" incapacity rooted in "undiagnosed" FASD. Therein lies another example of the unequal protection of the law.

2.6.3 Charlie Is Mixed Up About the Legal Advice

In the hypothetical situation leading up to Charlie's arrest and eventual trial, suppose for a moment that Charlie didn't have much of a clue about what to ask the lawyer, and did not appreciate the consequences of opening up to the police. He recalled his lawyer's advice not to talk to the police, but had begun to have doubts as to whether he had properly understood the lawyer. Why else would the police keep asking him all these questions?

The experienced police office might tell Charlie that one of the other members of the drunken threesome had now admitted the home invasion in Whitehorse but claimed it was all Charlie's idea and Charlie was in fact the only "home invader". If the police confronted Charlie with this statement, true or false, Charlie might well recognize that this left him in a bad situation.

However, Charlie's inability to think clearly would put him at a pronounced disadvantage. In *R v Sinclair*, 2010 SCC 35, [2010] 2 SCR 310, the Supreme Court of Canada held that the right to consult a lawyer does not generally include a right to re-consult the lawyer during the continuing interrogation. Charlie would be on his own unless there were new developments (such as if the elderly victim of the home invasion had died, and the police were now considering elevating the charge to homicide rather than break and enter) in which case he could again get to talk to a lawyer if he demanded it. The protections of the law for individuals dealing with the police are not of much protection to a FASD sufferer who understands the investigation process even less than a FASD-free person who has his wits about him.

2.6.4 Charlie Meets Mr. Big

Take another hypothetical situation. Suppose the police are not satisfied with Charlie's admissions. Charlie is released but becomes a candidate for a "Mr. Big"[3] undercover police operation. In the Mr. Big scenario, as is apparently by now quite well known through the media except to people like Charlie, undercover police officers pretend to a suspect that they are members of a violent but profitable criminal gang, and hold out the promise of great wealth and advantage to Charlie if he joins their number. In one variation, Charlie is introduced to "Mr. Big" who demands that Charlie make a full confession of his past misconduct in order to show he has a real aptitude for a life of serious crime. In another variation, Mr. Big may say he insists on a confession to gain a "hold" over Charlie to deter Charlie at a later date from trying to quit the gang while in possession of all the (supposed) secrets[4] of the criminal organization.

The "Mr. Big" technique, which has been used with enormous success, has come under much criticism for the psychological pressure it imposes on suspects who are possibly misfits or marginal people eager to join such a group just for a sense of "belonging". They may well be prepared to make a false confession just to gain entry to the magic circle. If ordinary people without disabilities are considered to be unfairly treated in a Mr. Big situation, how much more so is the FASD sufferer whose ability to think straight is severely compromised at the best of times. How can it be said that, at a practical level, the FASD sufferer enjoys the equal protections of the law?

[3] As discussed in *R v Mentuk*, 2001 SCC 76 [2001] 3 SCR 44 at para 4. Following the first trial, the respondent was targeted by the Royal Canadian Mounted Police in an undercover operation codenamed Operation Decisive. The undercover operation followed a pattern commonly employed by Canadian police. The respondent was invited by undercover officers to join a fictitious criminal organization. He was then asked to undertake certain tasks, the claimed importance of which was increased over time. The tasks included counting large sums of money and delivering parcels. The respondent was then told to be honest about his involvement in the murder of Amanda Cook. When he denied involvement, he was told that the "Boss" of the organization was angry with the person who had recruited the respondent as the respondent was a liar. The respondent was again encouraged to discuss the murder honestly. He was told that the criminal organization would arrange for a person dying of cancer to confess to the crime, and therefore would provide assistance to the respondent in suing the government for wrongful imprisonment. As a result of evidence gathered during this undercover operation, the indictment was reinstated on January 28, 1999.

[4] The "Mr. Big" method has been sanctioned by the Supreme Court of Canada on the basis that Mr. Big is an undercover police officer and the suspect has absolutely no reason to think that. Mr. Big is a policeman or otherwise in a "position of authority" to hold out fear or favour within the scope of the prohibited confessions rule.

2.6.5 The Prospect of False Confessions

Charlie would be easily manoeuvered by skilled police questioning into making a full confession to the home invasion. In Charlie's case, the confession might be true but would it be *voluntary*? Some northern judges have been skeptical about the voluntariness of confessions made by victims of FASD even in situations where the police have kept within the bounds of legal propriety. In the 1996 case of *R v Henry,* 1996 YKTJ No. 39, for example, a man suspected of suffering from FASD and described as having "neurological damage such as mental retardation and speech defects" that resulted in an IQ of about 55–65, was said to operate "at a level of a seven-and-a-half year-old child". In that case, the judge threw out the confession on the basis that the accused had not been alerted to his right to counsel, but at the same time noted that in terms of the "confession", the accused related "to authority in a child-like passive manner and would have felt compelled to answer the police" (emphasis added). A compelled confession is not a voluntary confession.

In *Henry* the police behaved themselves. The suspect was relatively unpressured. However, in general, police work is not a game in which prizes are given out for sportsmanlike conduct. The police have a job to do and some of them are very good at doing it. In the case of *R v Oickle,* [2008] 2 SCR 3, para 37, the Supreme Court upheld as voluntary a confession of a Nova Scotia man who had more or less come apart under police questioning.[5] The Court was careful to analyze whether the police had misconducted themselves in any way in bringing about the breakdown of the accused, and determined that they had not. Mr. Oickle was simply a vulnerable sort of character who in the end decided to make a full confession to various acts of arson in Nova Scotia. In doing so, the Supreme Court not only kept in mind fairness to Mr. Oickle, and respect for his civil rights, but the interest of society in solving crime. Exclusion of a confession may result in a wrongful acquittal.

The general practice now is to videotape police interrogations so that the trial court can see for itself that the suspect has not been abused or otherwise denied his or her rights. It is uncertain where this leaves the FASD sufferer. In *R v Henry,* referred to above, the Court held at paragraph 33 that although the police had conducted themselves properly, there was nevertheless "evidence of cognitive ability and lack of appreciation of consequences which raises a reasonable doubt that the statements were voluntary". In other words, as Kent Roach and Angela Bailey point out,[6] while the Court in *Oickle* focused on police misconduct, the Court in *Henry* considered it more important to reflect upon the disabilities of the suspect, and to

---

[5] See *Oickle* at para 8: "The respondent was arrested, warned of his right to counsel, given the secondary police warning, and driven to the police station at 8:15 p.m. En route he was very upset and was crying. He was placed in an interview room equipped with videotaping facilities, which recorded the subsequent interrogation where Corporal Deveau questioned him about the other fires. Around 8:30 p.m. and 9:15 p.m. the responded indicated that he was tired, and wanted to go home to bed. He was informed that he was under arrest, and he could call a lawyer if he wanted, but that he could not go home. Questioning did not cease."

[6] Roach and Bailey (2009) at pp. 18–19.

determine whether in all the circumstances the confession was voluntary and on that basis should be admitted into evidence.

There is some indication even post *Oickle* that some trial judges will continue to take into account symptoms of FASD in the absence of a full multidisciplinary assessment. Possibly they will draw an inappropriate inference from bits and pieces of information gleaned during the *voir dire* on the admissibility of the confession. They will consider FASD as an element capable of undermining the voluntary nature on the statement. In *R v Bohenier,* [2002] MJ No. 313 at para 46 (QB), a case decided after *Oickle* (2000), the Manitoba Court of Queen's Bench excluded a confession given by an accused who appeared to suffer from FASD on the basis that the police conduct "while perhaps not oppressive in terms of an individual with a normal development state, did become oppressive" because the police were somewhat aware of the accused's mental condition. But of course the police will often not be aware of (or indeed not very interested in exploring) the mental condition of a suspect. Their focus is to solve the crime. Yet it is an unequal contest. Safeguards against the stresses and strains of a criminal investigation which are designed to give reasonable protection to the normal person, are often not adequate to give an equivalent level of protection to a person suffering FASD. On this view of the matter, the FASD sufferer is thereby denied the equal protection and benefit of the law.

2.6.6 Sentencing of a FASD Offender

If the criminal justice system is to deal effectively with FASD victims, diversions and alternative measures are essential tools, but across the country rehabilitation or other programs are grossly underfunded. The northern judges in Nunavut, the Northwest Territories and the Yukon, regard such programs to be unrealistic to the point of fantasy given the chronic lack of resources in their regions. The *Criminal Code* can provide as many options as Parliament wishes, but if the funds are not available then the options are not there in any practical sense.

In the 2013 conference, the jury heard from a number of experienced judges, including a judge of the Provincial Court of Alberta, who sat on our jury and spoke of the challenges facing the sentencing judge in the fast-moving, high volume situation of a big city provincial criminal court. As a practical matter FASD is often not reflected in sentencing because there will be no formal diagnosis before the Court and the sentencing judge is not supposed to act on a hunch.

The fundamental principle of sentencing is found in section 781.1 of the *Criminal Code,* namely that a fit sentence must be "proportionate to the gravity of the offence and the degree of responsibility of the offender". These twin objectives, of course, may pull in opposite directions. Charlie's home invasion wielding a dangerous piece of timber was a very grave offence, and called for a severe sentence. But assuming, as did the sentencing judge, that Charlie had a lesser degree of blameworthiness because FASD resulted in a reduced degree of responsibility for his actions, the companion principle would pull the judge in the opposite direction, namely to treat FASD as a *mitigating* factor notwithstanding the gravity of the offence.

The great objectives of sentencing are denunciation, rehabilitation and deterrence. In terms of rehabilitation, however, to the extent that FASD has resulted in permanent and irreparable brain damage, there may be little scope for rehabilitation other than to seek a situation where the FASD individual can be integrated into the community under a program which at least reduces the prospect of reoffending.

One of the favoured sentencing techniques in this regard used to be the conditional sentence which permits the judge to sentence the offender to serve a sentence "in the community". In many cases, as mentioned, this means in effect confinement to home (if there is a home) under strict conditions. At least the offender is kept out of the prison environment where he or she is likely to get into trouble. However, if the underlying cause of sociopathic behaviour is brain damage, and the offender has already experienced a life of instability and violence, "rehabilitation" may be an unlikely outcome. In any event, recent changes in the law have sharply curtailed the discretion of sentencing judges to make use of conditional sentences.

Deterrence is also a question mark. A common characteristic of FASD is an inability to learn from experience. The FASD offender is a prime candidate to reoffend. At the same time, if the idea is not individual deterrence but to send the FASD offender to prison as a deterrent to others, the courts bear the condemnation of the Provincial Court judge in *R v Abou,* [BC Provincial Court 1995] who said, "it is simply obscene to suggest that a court can properly warn other potential offenders by inflicting a form of punishment upon a handicapped person."

From the judge's perspective, the choices are difficult. In Charlie's case, where the sentence was effectively mitigated by 50% by reason of Charlie's supposed FASD condition, what about the senior citizen who was terrorized by Charlie's home invasion and what is the victim or his family or indeed the broader community to think of a system that lets Charlie walk free in half the time than would be served by other offenders? The impact on the victim of the home invasion is no different.

One of the purposes of sentencing is denunciation of the crime. In *R v Harper*, 2009 YKTC 18 (YTC), a 36 year old man was found guilty of sexually touching a 3 year-old girl with his penis. He similarly was given a reduced sentence on account of a supposed FASD condition. Does this accord with the community's sense of justice? Is the outcome fair to the 3 year-old victim?

At the 2013 conference, Professor Allan Manson of Queens University proposed that the *Criminal Code* sentencing provisions be amended to permit the sentencing judge to have regard "to the offender's diminished capacity to comply with the law due to an intellectual deficiency or neurodevelopmental condition or disorder". His point was that the *Criminal Code* ought not to fashion a separate system for FASD because there are other disorders, including those resulting from traumatic brain damage, that result in a diminished capacity to comply with the law.

Moreover, Professor Manson's approach conforms to the view prevalent at the 2013 conference that the law is more properly focused on functional deficiencies not the issue of diagnosis. (Note that Professor Manson's proposal would exclude such self-inflicted and temporary conditions as drunkenness.) At present, there would appear to be little appetite in Parliament for such a reform.

2.7 Conclusion

It seems apparent from the foregoing, that in dealing with the FASD individual, society has not adequately integrated medical science and the exigencies of the law.

Legal theory takes into account the individual circumstances of the offence and the offender up to a point but "the point" often falls short of what is required to justly accommodate the FASD sufferer. As a result, a person who suffers from FASD may operate at a morally unacceptable disadvantage in the legal system, particularly in the criminal courts.

To some extent, of course, it is always difficult for a judge to assess on short notice and with limited information whether the alleged "diminished responsibility" is in fact true, or simply a tactic by an accused or his or her counsel to achieve a more lenient result. The high incidence of FASD in the criminal courts however is an established fact.

The primary objective should be to keep the FASD sufferer altogether out of the criminal law system by creating situations in the community to accommodate the disability and permit as normal a life as possible. However, governments seem not prepared to make available sufficient resources for this to happen.

The FASD sufferer cannot be blamed for his or her condition. The diminished capacity of the individual suffering FASD to comply with normal expectations is rarely either properly diagnosed or accommodated. That reduced blameworthiness should be better reflected in our legal system. Otherwise progress towards the goal of the equal protection and benefit of the law promised by the *Canadian Charter of Rights and Freedoms* will, in this respect, continue to go unfulfilled.

Reference

Roach, K., and A. Bailey. 2009. The relevance of fetal alcohol spectrum disorder in Canadian criminal law from investigation to sentencing. *University of British Columbia Law Review* 42 (1): 1–68. Available from: http://ubclawreview.ca/issues/42-1/kent-roach-andrea-bailey-the-relevance-of-fetal-alcohol-spectrum-disorder-in-canadian-criminal-law-from-investigation-to-sentencing/.

Chapter 3
Prenatal Alcohol Exposure and Abnormal Brain Development – Findings from Basic Research

Kathleen K. Sulik

Abstract The focus of this chapter is on description of normal and alcohol-induced abnormal embryogenesis of the brain and face. Emphasis is placed on early mammalian developmental stages and the vulnerability of early embryos to birth defects caused by maternal alcohol use. Regarding normal development, the prenatal stages described are present from the 3rd through the 6th weeks of human gestation (i.e., mid 5th through 8th weeks after the beginning of the last normal menstrual period [LNMP]; a time that is prior to pregnancy recognition by many women). This presentation of basic embryology concepts is designed to provide a foundation for the appreciation of alcohol-induced teratogenesis. The alcohol-induced abnormalities described result from accurately timed acute prenatal exposures in mice that were subsequent to maternal alcohol administration at times that correspond to the mid-3rd to early 4th week post-fertilization (mid-5th to early 6th week post-LNMP) in humans. The animal model-based research findings show that the characteristic facial features of Fetal Alcohol Syndrome result from insult as early as the mid-3rd week of human development; that later exposures affecting development in the 4th week yield a different pattern of facial defects; and that at both of these exposure periods embryos are vulnerable to induction of structural brain abnormalities. Demonstration of the vulnerability to alcohol-induced birth defects of embryos at developmental stages that are present at a time prior to typical human pregnancy recognition has major implications for Fetal Alcohol Spectrum Disorder prevention approaches and is important for legal and ethical considerations involving both mothers and their affected offspring.

Keywords Animal model · Fetal alcohol spectrum disorder · Embryology · Malformation · Teratology

K. K. Sulik (✉)
Department of Cell Biology and Physiology and Bowles Center for Alcohol Studies, University of North Carolina, Chapel Hill, NC, USA
e-mail: mouse@med.unc.edu

E. Jonsson et al. (eds.), *Ethical and Legal Perspectives in Fetal Alcohol Spectrum Disorders (FASD)*, International Library of Ethics, Law, and the New Medicine 75,
https://doi.org/10.1007/978-3-319-71755-5_3

3.1 Introduction

The objective of this chapter is to provide a foundation for understanding how maternal alcohol use can affect the brain, with emphasis on the damage incurred at the early stages of in utero development that occur prior to typical pregnancy recognition. Demonstration of the vulnerability of embryos to alcohol-induced birth defects at these early developmental stages has major implications for Fetal Alcohol Syndrome (FAS) and Fetal Alcohol Spectrum Disorder (FASD) prevention approaches and is important for legal and ethical considerations involving both mothers and their affected offspring. Regarding prevention, as opposed to messages simply stating that pregnant women should not drink alcohol (a message that may not get the necessary attention of women prior to the time that they realize they are, indeed, pregnant), it is critical to communicate that maternal alcohol use should be reduced or curtailed if there is even a chance of pregnancy. Regarding legal and ethical considerations, actions and attitudes associated with the liability of birth mothers and of individuals with alcohol-induced birth defects, should be influenced by an appreciation for the biological basis of the damage caused by this pervasive toxin.

The basic research described is based on the mouse-model system employed in the author's laboratory. Indeed, rodents (both mice and rats) have been very commonly used for research on FAS and FASD, as have other species including those that we consider both lower (fish and chicks) and higher (subhuman primates) forms. Animal models allow identification of critical exposure periods, definition of dose-response relationships, and correlation of structural and functional changes. In model systems, alcohol-affected areas including the brain and other organ systems such as the kidney and the heart can be examined in great detail and at varying stages of the life cycle. Importantly, the results obtained from the use of animal models can verify and potentially expand the FASD diagnostic criteria.

From animal model systems, it has been learned that virtually every stage of prenatal development is vulnerable to alcohol-induced damage, but different types of damage/birth defects result from alcohol exposure at different points in time. In the 1st trimester, alcohol can cause structural abnormalities. Commonly, these changes can be observed grossly. The structural damage may be accompanied by functional changes. Additionally, in the 1st trimester, alcohol can cause functional damage without obvious structural changes. In the 2nd and 3rd trimesters, most of the defects caused by alcohol are functional. That is, an obvious structural change cannot be identified, at least not with most of the imaging techniques that are typically used.

It is known that the most severe alcohol-induced birth defects are a result of very heavy prenatal exposures, especially binge exposures, and that peak maternal blood-alcohol levels are a strong determinant of the severity of the insult. However, variability from individual to individual with respect to genetic background, as well as in exposure to other predisposing or protective environmental factors makes it difficult, if not impossible, to define a universally safe maternal dose of alcohol. This difficulty is compounded by the fact that it is impossible to know what someone's potential may have been in the absence of maternal alcohol use.

While animal model-based research has provided clear evidence that early stages of embryogenesis are vulnerable to permanent alcohol-induced damage, many, if not most individuals remain ignorant of normal human developmental events and their timing and, consequently, can not appreciate how and when alcohol can cause birth defects. In this chapter, the prenatal stages briefly described are present from the 3rd through the 6th weeks of human gestation (i.e., from the 5th through 8th weeks following the beginning of the last normal menstrual period [LNMP]). During these early weeks, women commonly remain unaware of pregnancy. For additional detail, reference to standard embryology textbooks or to the following website are recommended: https://embryology.med.unsw.edu.au/embryology/index.php/Main_Page.

3.2 Normal Embryogenesis

As evidenced in the human developmental timeline shown in Fig. 3.1, much of human embryogenesis occurs before pregnancy is typically recognized. The normal menstrual cycle is typically 28 days long, and if fertilization is going to occur, it happens at the middle of that time period. Thus, on the 1st day of the 1st missed menstrual period, the embryo is typically 14 days old. At this time, the embryo consists of only 2 layers of cells and it has implanted in the uterine wall. With implantation-associated bleeding commonly being mistaken for a light period instead of as a sign of the 1st missed period, the problem of inadvertent alcohol exposure due to failure of pregnancy recognition is compounded. From studies of animal models we have learned that developmental stages that are present in humans as early as the middle of the 3rd week after fertilization are very vulnerable to the teratogenic effects of alcohol. This chapter concentrates on the teratogenic results of alcohol exposure at this time through the beginning of the 4th week after fertilization (i.e., mid 5th week through the beginning of the 6th week post-LNMP).

Figure 3.2 shows a histological section, as well as a graphic illustration of the human embryo as it appears in the early to mid-3rd week after fertilization (beginning to mid 5th week post-LNMP). The embryo is suspended between 2 fluid-filled cavities (an amniotic and a yolk sac cavity), all of which is surrounded by an additional fluid-filled space termed the chorionic cavity. During its 3rd week, the bilayered embryo (ectoderm and endoderm) begins to form a 3rd cell layer (mesoderm), and is in the shape of a thin disc that is only 0.5 to 1 mm in diameter. Even at this early point in time the head (cranial) end, with its prochordal plate, and the tail (caudal) end, with its primitive streak, are distinguishable and genes that are programming how the brain, as well as other tissues, will develop are being expressed.

Embryonic growth is extremely rapid; a factor that contributes to the vulnerability of the embryo to insult by a number of different teratogens, including alcohol. By the

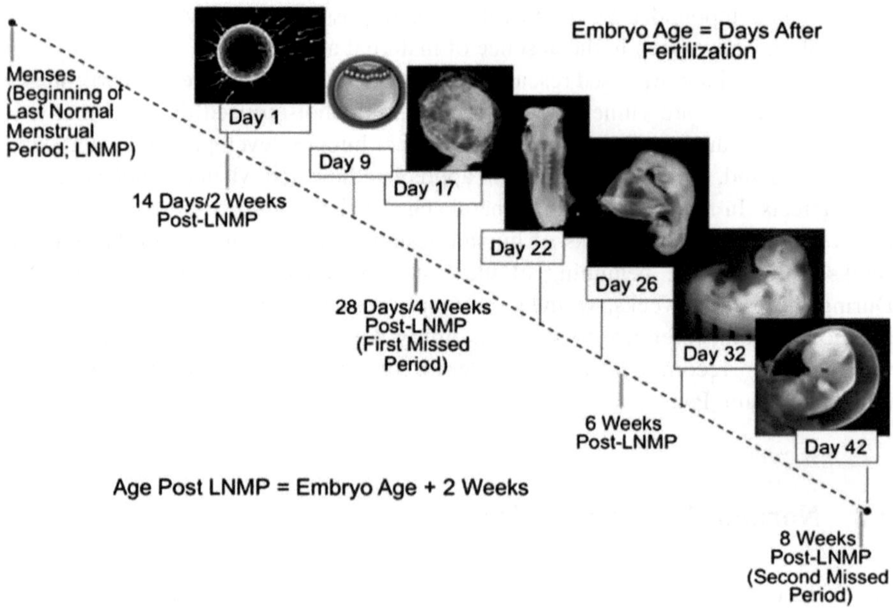

Fig. 3.1 A human developmental timeline illustrating the first 6 weeks of embryonic development. Fertilization typically occurs 2 weeks after the beginning of the last normal menstrual period (LNMP). By the end of the 6th week of development (i.e., by 8 weeks post-LNMP), the human brain, eyes, face and limbs can be readily identified. With much of embryogenesis occurring prior to the time that pregnancy is typically recognized, unintended alcohol exposure is common

beginning of the 4th week after fertilization (beginning of the 6th week post-LNMP), when the heart begins to beat, the human embryo is approximately 3 mm long, having tripled in length over the course of only 4–5 days. During this time, the form of the developing brain and spinal cord changes as the cell population termed the neural plate begins to be reconfigured to form a tube. Neural tube closure begins near the junction of the brain and spinal cord and progresses both cranially (toward the head) and caudally until closure is complete in the middle of the 4th week. Figure 3.3 shows both a light micrograph (a) and a scanning electron micrograph (b) of a human embryo that is 23 days old, with arrows indicating the direction of neural tube closure. As shown in (b; dashed line), at this age the junction between the tissue that covers the developing face and that which will form the brain is readily demarcated.

Focusing on the developing head, Fig. 3.4 further illustrates the progression of cranial neural tube closure (arrows) and accompanying facial development. Notable is that the developing eyes (open arrows) are extensions of the brain, a fact that helps to explain the typically concurrent induction of brain and eye defects following alcohol exposure at early stages of embryogenesis. The approximate boundary between the facial tissues that surround the developing cerebral hemispheres and those tissues that are associated with more caudal brain structures is indicated by a dashed line in the older 2 embryos (b, c).

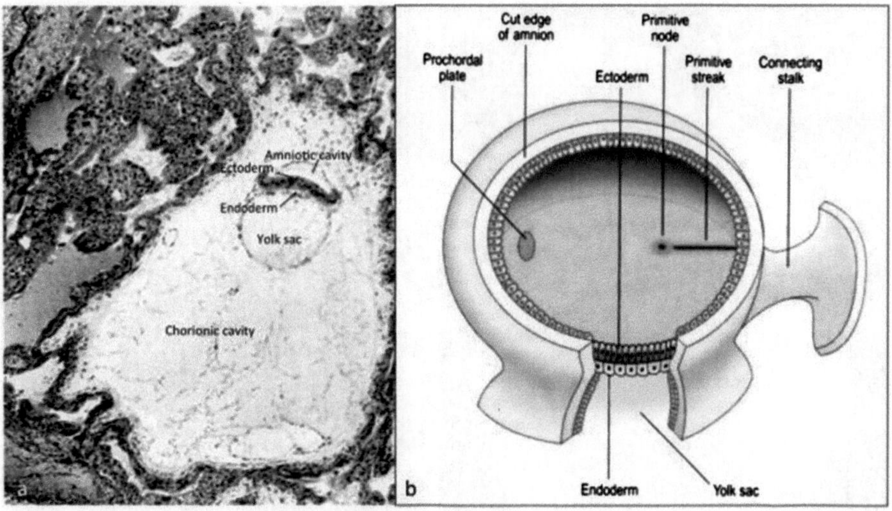

Fig. 3.2 A histological section (**a**) and a graphic illustration (**b**) of a human embryo in the early to mid-3rd week of development. Notable is that the embryo, proper, is a bilayered disc of cells (ectoderm and endoderm) located between the amniotic and yolk sac cavities. The head end of the embryo is marked by the presence of a prochordal plate and the tail end of the embryo contains the primitive streak. Histological section from Heuser et al. (1945). Graphic illustration from Mitchell and Sharma (2005)

Figure 3.5 shows a human embryo that is in its 5th week of development. By this time, evident on the cerebrum-associated portion of the developing face are the developing nostrils. These are best seen in the scanning electron micrograph (b) and are widely spaced, with placement just in front of the developing eyes. In the light microscopic image (a), subdivisions of the brain can be readily appreciated; the cerebrum and cerebellum being labeled.

In the 6th week, the nostrils become more evident and more closely approximated (Fig. 3.6). The facial tissue in between them will form the tip of the nose as well as the philtrum (the region of the central groove of the upper lip) (b). A cut through the midline of the embryo illustrates the interior surface of the neural tube/brain; the developing cerebrum and cerebellum being labeled. The embryo that is cut in this way and shown in (c) is a mouse; the form of the concurrently developing brain and face being virtually the same as that of a human at this time in development. Indeed, the similarity between human and mouse embryogenesis is one of the factors that allows extrapolation of research findings from mouse models to humans.

By the end of the embryonic period, i.e., by the end of the 8th week after fertilization in humans (end of the10th week post-LNMP), the developing face has a distinctly human appearance. The majority of readily identifiable structural birth defects (virtually all of which are associated with functional changes) are induced during the embryonic period. The fetal period (i.e., the remaining 30 weeks of the

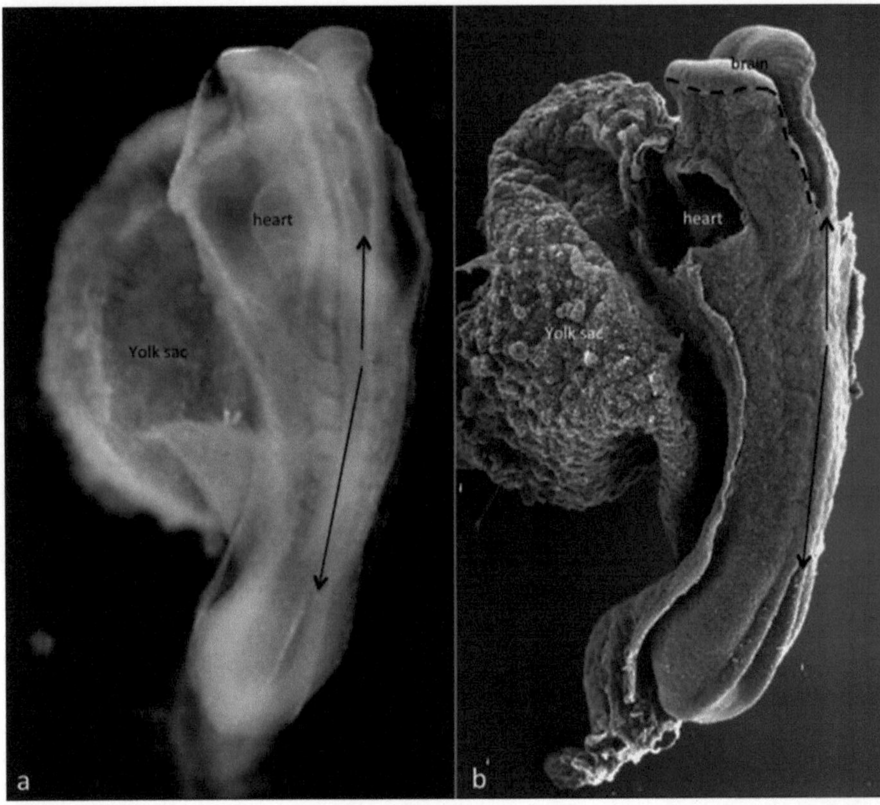

Fig. 3.3 A light micrograph (**a**) and a scanning electron micrograph (**b**) of a 23 day old human embryo. Arrows indicate direction of neural tube closure with the arrowheads at the location of the most recent union. At the head end, the junction between the yet unclosed brain and the tissue that will cover the developing face and neck is indicated by a dashed line

normal 38 week gestational period) remains vulnerable to teratogenesis, though the defects are primarily functional and occur in the absence of readily observable structural changes.

3.3 Alcohol-Induced Birth Defects

For more than 30 years it has been known that exposure of a mouse embryo to alcohol on just 1 day of its development (gestational day [GD] 7) can cause all of the facial features that are considered classic for/or characteristic of full-blown fetal alcohol syndrome (FAS) (Sulik et al. 1981). This time in gestation corresponds to the mid-3rd week of human development. Figure 3.7 shows a mouse fetus (b) whose mother was given alcohol at this time in her pregnancy. As compared to a normal

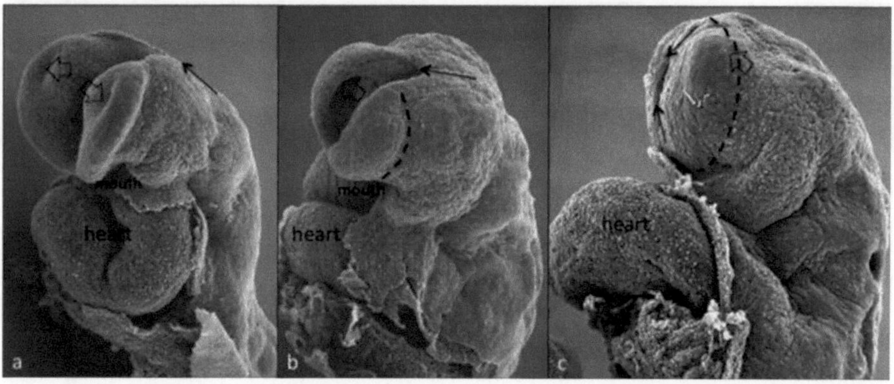

Fig. 3.4 Scanning electron micrographs illustrating closure of the human anterior neural tube, as occurs during the 4th week of human development. Embryos in (**a**), (**b**), and (**c**) are progressively more advanced in age. Arrows indicate the site and direction of cranial neural tube closure; arrowheads indicate position of the developing eyes

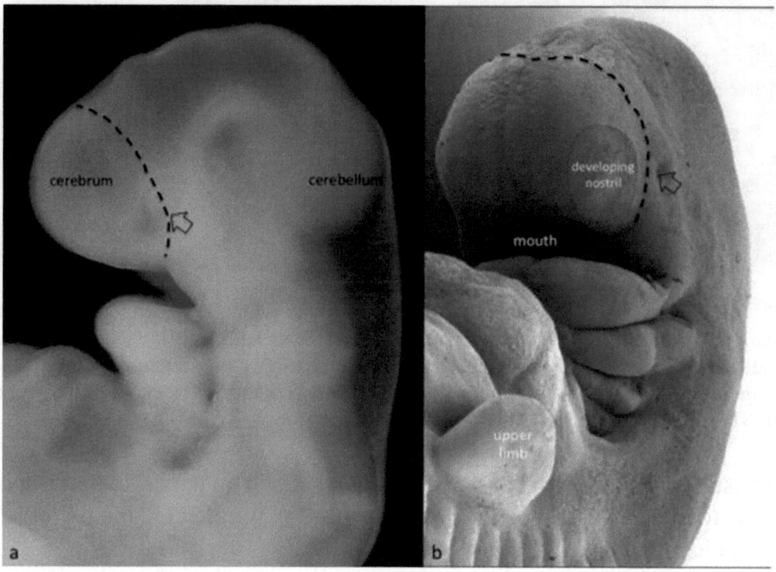

Fig. 3.5 A light micrograph (**a**) and a scanning electron micrograph (**b**) of a human embryo in its 5th week of development. The dashed line indicates the boundary between the cerebrum and more caudal aspects of the brain. The dotted line surrounds the developing (left) nostril. Open arrow indicates the eye

mouse (c), it has short palpebral fissures, indicating that the eyes are too small; a small nose with the nostrils too close together; and a very abnormal looking philtral region of the upper lip. The upper lip change is the result of failure of the philtral tissues to form, or reduction in their size, and subsequent over-convergence of more

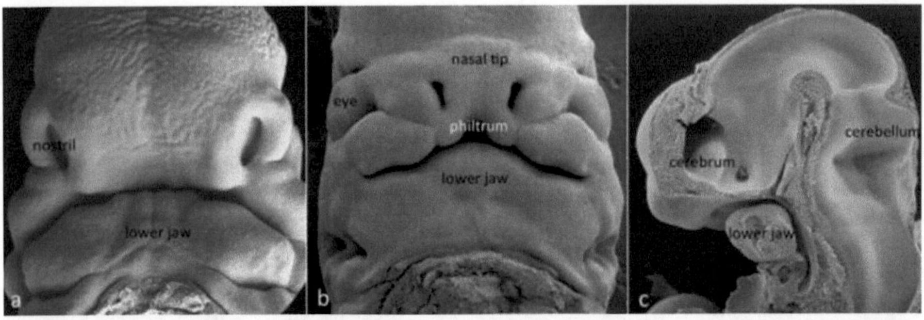

Fig. 3.6 Scanning electron micrographs of human embryos early (**a**) and late (**b**) in the 6th week post-fertilization and of a comparably staged, mid-sagittaly cut mouse embryo. At this time in development, the nostrils become more closely approximated and the tissues that will form the nasal tip and philtrum of the lip become evident. The brain is essentially a hollow tube, the walls of which include the developing cerebrum and cerebellum. (**c**) from Hinrichsen (1985)

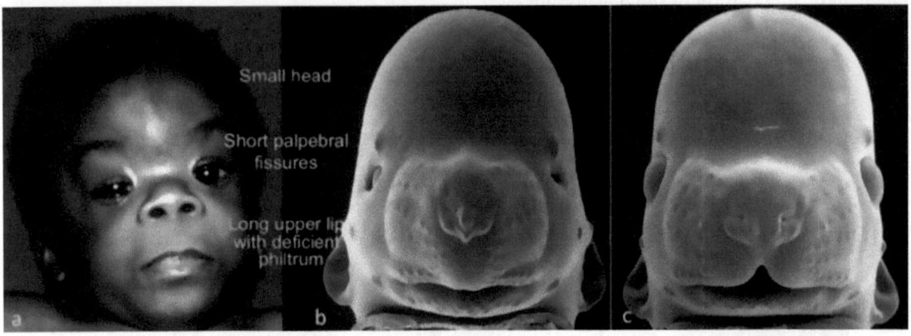

Fig. 3.7 A child with Fetal Alcohol Syndrome (FAS; **a**), an alcohol-affected fetal mouse (**b**), and a comparably-staged normal fetal mouse (**c**) are shown. The characteristic facial features of FAS were induced in the mouse by maternal alcohol treatment only on gestational day 7, when the mouse embryo is at a stage corresponding to that in humans in the 3rd week. Modified from Sulik et al. (1981)

lateral tissues; a combination of changes that results in an upper lip that is too long from nose to mouth. Also apparent is that the head of the affected mouse fetus is too narrow, indicating that the brain is abnormal.

Following early prenatal alcohol exposure in mice, the affected animals show varying degrees of abnormality. This can be readily seen in images acquired using magnetic resonance microscopy to visualize the brains and faces of fetal mice whose dams had been alcohol-treated on their 7th day of pregnancy (Fig. 3.8). As the severity of effect increases, there is typically increasingly greater loss of facial midline structures (esp. nasal tip and philtral components), resulting in abnormally close approximation of the nostrils. As expected, considering that the teratogenic alcohol exposure occurred at an early embryonic stage, when the development of

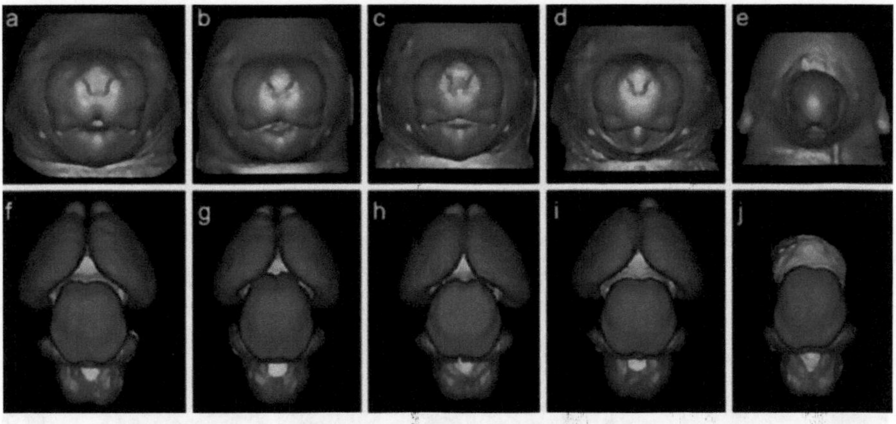

Fig. 3.8 3-D reconstructions of magnetic resonance images of fetal mice allow ready comparison of normal (**a** and **f**) and alcohol-induced abnormal (**b–e**; **g–j**) face and brain morphology. Notable is that, as compared to normal (**a**), the nostrils become increasingly more closely approximated in the alcohol-exposed fetuses, with the most severely affected fetus (**e**) having so much midline tissue deficiency that no nostrils are present. Accompanying this midline facial deficiency is abnormal approximation and reduced size of the cerebral hemispheres (red) and olfactory bulbs (pink), to the point of virtual absence of these structures in the most severely affected fetus. As evident in all of the affected animals, the gestational day 7 alcohol exposure selectively damages the cerebrum, while more caudal parts of the brain, including the midbrain (fuschia), cerebellum (teal), and remaining hindbrain (dark green) remain relatively normal in appearance. Light green = diencephalon; light blue-green = roof of the fourth ventricle. Modified from O'Leary-Moore et al. (2011)

the face and brain are interdependent, with increasing severity the cerebral hemispheres (red), like the nostrils, become abnormally closely approximated and are diminished in size. This can be seen in the reconstructed, pseudo-colored brain images in Fig. 3.8. In the most severely affected animal shown (e, j) the cerebrum in virtually absent while the more caudal brain structures appear relatively intact. While in some mildly affected individuals the brain can appear grossly normal following GD 7 insult, histological defects have been observed (Godin et al. 2010).

Further work has shown that the defects that alcohol can cause in mouse embryos can persist post-natally (O'Leary-Moore et al. 2011b). This is documented in Fig. 3.9 in mouse brain images created using a technology called diffusion tensor imaging. The colored images are of normal (a) and alcohol-exposed (c, e) adolescent mouse brains. In the abnormal brains the corpus callosum (pseudo-colored red and indicated by an arrow), which is the fiber tract that connects the two cerebral hemispheres, is deficient. These defects appear comparable to those in individuals with FAS (d, f).

Animal studies have also shown that alcohol can cause differing kinds of brain and facial defects depending on the time during development that the embryo is exposed. Exemplary is work showing that using a treatment paradigm comparable to that for the mouse GD 7 alcohol exposures, but with maternal alcohol administration limited to one day later and corresponding to early in the human 4th

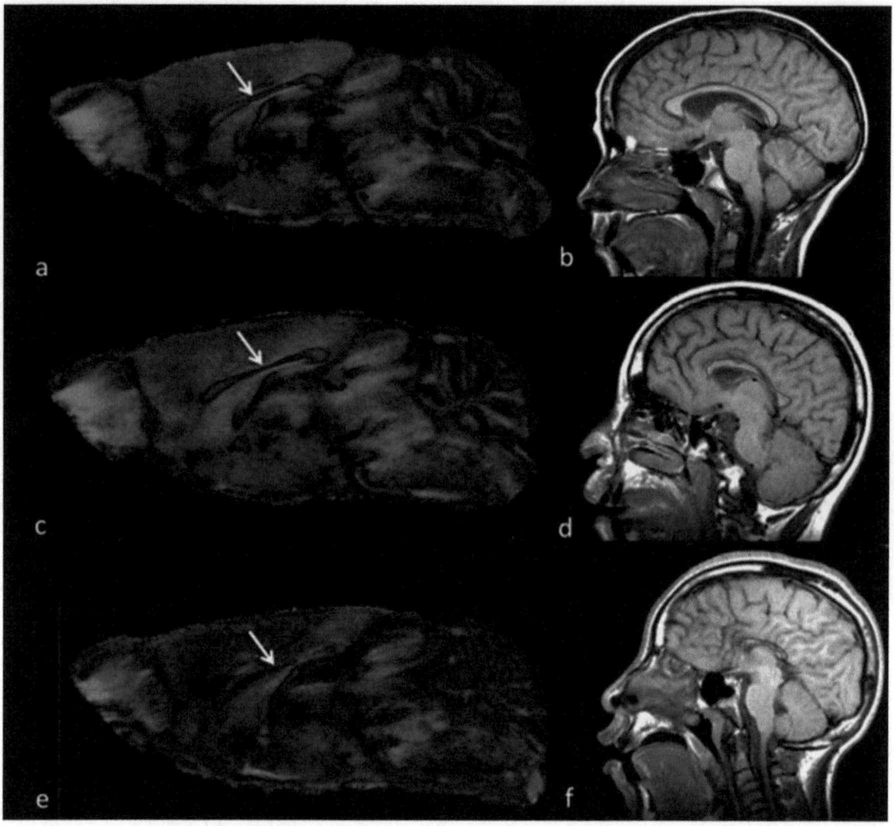

Fig. 3.9 Pseudo-colored midline sections of adolescent mouse brains created using diffusion tensor imaging illustrate fiber tract changes resulting from gestational day 7 alcohol exposure. Corpus callosum (colored red in **a**, **c**, **e** and surrounded by a red line in the human magnetic resonance images, **b**, **d**, **f**) deficiencies are comparable and vary in degrees of severity in mice and in individuals with FAS. Modified from O'Leary-Moore et al. (2011b); human images courtesy of S. Mattson

week post-fertilization, affected individuals have a different constellation of facial and brain abnormalities; defects that may not be clinically recognized as typical for FAS or as part of FASD (Sulik et al. 1986; Sulik 2005; Parnell et al. 2009; Lipinski et al. 2012).

In addition to the insights that utilization of new imaging technologies provides, application of new knowledge in the fields of developmental biology and genetics and their associated research technologies have advanced our understanding of susceptibility and resistance to alcohol-induced teratogenesis. For example, recognizing the importance of a particular developmental gene signaling pathway, i.e., the sonic hedgehog (Shh) pathway, for normal face and brain embryogenesis, studies employing mice having (man-made) modifications in genes in this pathway have been conducted (Kietzman et al. 2014). Animals in which developmental signaling through Shh pathway genes is reduced have been found to be much more vulnerable to the effects of alcohol than their normal littermates. The implications of these genetic findings for human FASD relate to the difficulty/impossibility of defining a universally non-teratogenic alcohol dosage.

While the focus of this chapter has been on developmental stages present early in the 1st human trimester and on damage that alcohol causes to the developing brain at this time, it is important to recognize that at virtually every stage of its prenatal development the brain is vulnerable to alcohol-induced defects. Importantly, knowledge that the brain is vulnerable to alcohol insult prior to the time of typical pregnancy recognition has major implications for FASD prevention approaches, as well as for ethical and legal considerations. Everyone needs to be made aware of the fact that for women of child bearing age, alcohol consumption and unprotected sex don't mix. Clearly, a key approach for dissemination of this universal message will be the education of our youth.

Acknowledgments Research in the author's laboratory has been funded by the US National Institute on Alcohol Abuse and Alcoholism and conducted as part of the Collaborative Initiative on Fetal Alcohol Spectrum Disorders (CIFASD). Information about the CIFASD can be found at www.cifasd.org. Any opinions, findings, and conclusions or recommendations expressed in this material are those of the author(s) and do not necessarily reflect the views of the National Institutes of Health.

References

Godin, E.A., S.K. O'Leary-Moore, A.A. Khan, S.E. Parnell, J.J. Ament, D.B. Dehart, B.W. Johnson, A.G. Johnson, M.A. Styner, and K.K. Sulik. 2010. Magnetic resonance microscopy defines ethanol-induced brain abnormalities in prenatal mice: Effects of acute insult on gestational day 7. *Alcohol Clinical and Experimental Research* 34 (1): 98–111. https://doi.org/10.1111/j.1530-0277.2009.01071.x.

Heuser, C.H., J. Rock, and A.T. Hertig. 1945. Two human embryos showing early stages of the definitive yolk-sac. Carnegie Institution. *Contributions to Embryology* 81: 85–99.

Hinrichsen, K. 1985. The early development of morphology and patterns of the face in the human embryo. *Advances in Anatomy, Embryology and Cell Biology* 98: 1–79.

Kietzman, H.W., J.L. Everson, K.K. Sulik, and R.J. Lipinski. 2014. The teratogenic effects of prenatal ethanol exposure are exacerbated by Sonic hedgehog or Gli2 haploinsufficiency in the mouse. *PLos One* 9 (2): e89448. https://doi.org/10.1371/journal.pone.0089448.

Lipinski, R.J., P. Hammond, S.K. O'Leary-Moore, J.J. Ament, S.J. Pecevich, Y. Jiang, F. Budin, S.E. Parnell, E.A. Godin, J.L. Everson, D.B. Dehart, H.R. Holloway, M.A. Styner, G.A. Johnson, and K.K. Sulik. 2012. Ethanol-induced face-brain dysmorphology patterns are correlative and exposure-stage dependent. *PLoS One* 7 (8): e43067. https://doi.org/10.1371/journal.pone.0043067.

Mitchell, B., and R. Sharma. 2005. *Embryology: An illustrated colour text*. London: Elsevier.

O'Leary-Moore, S.K., S.E. Parnell, R.J. Lipinski, and K.K. Sulik. 2011a. Magnetic resonance-based imaging in animal models of fetal alcohol spectrum disorder. *Neuropsychology Review* 21 (2): 167–185. https://doi.org/10.1007/s11065-011-9164-z.

O'Leary-Moore, S.K., S.E. Parnell, E.A. Godin, and K.K. Sulik. 2011b. Focus on: Magnetic resonance-based studies of fetal alcohol spectrum disorders in animal models. *Alcohol Research and Health* 34: 99–105.

Parnell, S.E., S.K. O'Leary-Moore, E.A. Godin, D.B. Dehart, B.W. Johnson, G.A. Johnson, M.A. Styner, and K.K. Sulik. 2009. Magnetic resonance microscopy defines ethanol-induced brain abnormalities in prenatal mice: Effects of acute insult on gestational day 8. *Alcohol Clinical and Experimental Research* 33: 1001–1011. https://doi.org/10.1111/j.1530-0277.2009.00921.x.

Sulik, K.K. 2005. Genesis of alcohol-induced craniofacial dysmorphism. *Experimental Biology and Medicine (Maywood)* 230 (6): 366–375.

Sulik, K.K., M.C. Johnston, and M.A. Webb. 1981. Fetal alcohol syndrome: Embryogenesis in a mouse model. *Science* 214 (4523): 936–938.

Sulik, K.K., M.C. Johnston, P.A. Daft, W.E. Russell, and D.B. Dehart. 1986. Fetal alcohol syndrome and DiGeorge anomaly: Critical ethanol exposure periods for craniofacial malformations as illustrated in an animal model. *American Journal of Medical Genetics Supplement* 2: 97–112.

Chapter 4
Total Cost of FASD Including the Economics of FASD Associated with Crimes

Nguyen Xuan Thanh and Egon Jonsson

Abstract This chapter reports a systematic review of studies of the economics of fetal alcohol spectrum disorder (FASD) with a focus on costs that are associated with crimes. It shows that the total cost of FASD for Canadian society is $9.4 billion per year (2015 price level), of which crimes account for the largest share (42% or $3.9 billion), followed by health care (21%), indirect costs (19%), social services (9%), and special education (9%). Of the costs of FASD associated with crimes ($3.9 billion), Criminal Justice System (CJS) accounts for the largest share (54% or $2.1 billion), followed by victims of crime (41%), and third-party (5%). Of the cost for CJS ($2.1 billion), police services accounts for the largest share (57%), followed by correctional services (23%) and court services (20%).

Keywords FASD · Cost · Crime · Canada

4.1 Introduction

In 2010, we published a review of available studies from the international literature on the cost of fetal alcohol spectrum disorder (FASD). In that review, the annual cost per person with FASD was estimated at CA$ 25,000, the lifetime cost per person with FASD at CA$ 1.8 million (2009 price level), and the annual cost of FASD in Canada was estimated at CA$ 6.2 billion and in Alberta at CA$ 520 million. Cost of health services accounted for 30%, followed by educational services 24%, social services 19%, correctional services 14%, and other cost 13% (Thanh et al. 2010). At that time there was no study available on other cost of FASD-related legal services, such as cost of police, courts, and of victims of crime.

N. X. Thanh
Institute of Health Economics, Edmonton, AB, Canada

E. Jonsson (✉)
Faculty of Medicine, Department of Psychiatry, University of Alberta, Edmonton, AB, Canada
e-mail: egon@ualberta.ca

E. Jonsson et al. (eds.), *Ethical and Legal Perspectives in Fetal Alcohol Spectrum Disorders (FASD)*, International Library of Ethics, Law, and the New Medicine 75,
https://doi.org/10.1007/978-3-319-71755-5_4

Five years have elapsed since the review mentioned above was published. During that time there seems to be a broadened and increased interest in FASD, which is reflected in the escalation of the number of publications (manuscripts, books and reports) and different events (local, national and international conferences, workshops, showcases, and webinars) on the subject. In 2013, the first consensus development conference on Legal Issues of FASD (Institute of Health Economics 2013)[1] was held back to back with an international conference on prevention of FASD (Jonsson et al. 2015), which may have contributed to a greater world-wide interest in FASD and its legal and other implications. The consensus development conference on Legal Issues of FASD was attended by about 400 people and the prevention conference was attended by more than 700 people from 35 countries around the globe, including senior government officials, scholars and policymakers, indigenous people, lawyers, clinicians, social workers, and other front-line service providers, parents and family members to people with FASD. That conference produced an International Charter on Prevention of FASD which was published in *The Lancet Global Health* (Jonsson et al. 2014). Some of the scientific studies published during the last 5 years deal with the economics of FASD and a few includes costs of FASD related to the Criminal Justice System (CJS).

In this chapter, we report results of a systematic review of studies on the economics of FASD that have been published from 2010 until the end of 2015 with a focus on costs of FASD associated with crimes. One of the many devastating consequences of FASD is that the disorder frequently lead to secondary disabilities, such as school drop-out, unemployment, homelessness, alcohol/drug abuse, and criminal behaviour, which eventually involves interaction with the police, courts and at the end often incarceration for coming in conflict with the law. It has been reported that of adolescents and adults with FASD, 60% come in trouble with the law and 35% are incarcerated for a crime at least once in their lifetime (Streissguth et al. 2004). It has also been reported that youths with FASD are 19 times more likely to be incarcerated than those without FASD (Lang et al. 2012).

The main findings from the current updated study are that the total cost of FASD for Canadian society is $9.4 billion per year (range $7.0 billion–$13.0 billion), of which crimes account for 42% (range: 28–55%), health care for 21% (range: 16–29%), social services for 9% (7–11%), special education for 9% (range: 6–12%), and indirect costs for 19% (range: 17–21%). The prevalence of FASD in the legal system is about 10% (range 5–18%). The total costs of FASD associated with crimes in Canada are $3.9 billion per year (range: $1.9 billion–$7.0 billion) with $2.1 billion or 54% for CJS, $1.6 billion or 41% for victims, and $0.2 billion or 5% for third-party. Of the cost for CJS ($2.1 billion), police services account for 57% or $1.2 billion, court services for 20% or $422.4 million, and correctional services for 23% or $485.7 million.

[1] Also published in Appendix of Chap. 17 in this book.

4.2 Methods

We performed a systematic review of the literature on the economics of FASD associated with crimes. The following databases were searched (Medline, Embase, PsycINFO, and Google) using numerous subject headings and keyword terms for the concepts of FASD, crime, and economics. We limited the search to year 2010 onward and to English language. Reference lists of included studies were also searched in order to identify further studies. After scanning titles and abstracts, we selected studies examining economics of FASD and crime for review and data extraction.

4.3 Results

In total 15 new studies were included, including 8 about cost of FASD in health care, 1 about cost of social services, 2 about productivity losses, 2 about economic evaluations, and 2 about crime related costs. One study was from the US and all others were from Canada. The Canadian studies were all performed by two research teams: the Center for Addictions and Mental Health (www.camh.ca) in Toronto (10 studies) and the Institute of Health Economics (www.ihe.ca) in Edmonton (4 studies).

4.3.1 Summary of Included Studies

4.3.1.1 Health Care Related Costs

Amendah et al. (2011) analyzed the expenditure data of Medicaid in the United States and found that the mean medical expenditures per year per child with fetal alcohol syndrome (FAS) were $16,782, which is nine times higher than that per child without FAS ($1859 in 2005). Intellectual disability (ID) was more common among children with FAS than among those without FAS (12% vs. 0.5%). The mean expenditures per child with FAS and ID were 2.8 times higher than those per child with FAS but without ID.

Thanh et al. (2014a, b) included all patients recorded in the Alberta Health administrative databases of inpatients, outpatients, and practitioner claims from 2003 to 2012 to study incidence, prevalence, and health services utilization (HSU) of people with FASD in Alberta, Canada. People with FASD, and their HSU costs, were calculated from available data on fetal alcohol syndrome (FAS) (ICD-9 code 760.71 and ICD-10 codes Q86.0 and P04.3) and estimates of the prevalence of FASD in individuals diagnosed with 21 FASD-related conditions for which there are ICD codes, such as learning disability, oppositional defiant disorder, mental retardation, nervous system defects, etc. The authors systematically reviewed cohort and case-control studies and performed a meta-analysis to estimate fractions of FASD-related diagnoses that can be attributed to alcohol. Of the 21 FASD-related conditions, 12 contained a statistically significant fraction of cases attributable to alcohol, and these were included in the analyses. The authors estimated the incidence, prevalence, and HSU cost for each FASD-related condition and then weighted it based on the number of cases. Incidence of FASD was defined as the number of new cases per 1000 births. Prevalence of FASD was defined as the number of alive cases per 1000 population. The HSU costs included costs for physician, outpatient, and inpatient services estimated from the Alberta Health administrative databases, and then the authors inflated them by 30% for the cost of medications (as the drug utilization is unavailable in mentioned databases, the figure of 30% was based on published studies of cost of drugs in FASD). The costs per person-year were estimated by multiplying the average number of hospitalizations, outpatient visits, and physician visits per person-year by the average cost for these services. The annual HSU cost of FASD for Alberta was estimated by multiplying the annual HSU cost per person with FASD with the number of people who were living with FASD in Alberta in 2012. The lifetime HSU cost per person with FASD was estimated for several lifespans ranging from 10 years to 70 years. Results showed that incidence of FAS was 2.2–6.8 per 1000 births, and of FASD was 14.2–43.8 per 1000 births, depending on the length of follow-up (1–9 years). There were about 46,000 people living with FASD in Alberta in 2012, including 6000 FAS cases and 40,000 FASD-related cases. Prevalence of FAS was 1.5 per 1000 population, and of FASD was 11.7 (range 8.2–15.1) per 1000 population. The annual cost of HSU for people with FASD in Alberta was $259 million (2014 Canadian dollars), of which FAS accounted for 26%. The annual HSU cost per person with FAS and FASD were $6200 and $5600, respectively. The incremental annual HSU cost per person with FAS is $4100 and with FASD is $3400 as compared to the general population. The lifetime (70 years) HSU cost per person with FAS was $506,000 and with FASD was $245,000. Males had higher HSU costs than females and HSU costs of FAS and FASD varied greatly by age group.

Popova et al. (2012) used the ICD-10 code of FAS (Q86.0) to estimate health care utilization, associated cost, and mortality of people with FAS in the official Canadian databases (Canadian Institute of Health Information for health data and Statistics Canada for mortality data). The study showed surprising results that the total direct health care cost of acute care, psychiatric care, day surgery, and emergency department services associated with FAS in Canada in fiscal year 2008–2009 was as low as $6.7 million. Compared to 2002–2003, the burden and cost of acute care hospitalizations due to FAS in 2008–2009 was increasing 1.6 times. Mortality data from 2000 to 2008 showed there were totally six deaths documented as being attributable to FAS, including one male and five females. Authors concluded that the official data on the utilization of health care services by individuals diagnosed with FAS are likely to be underreported. The mortality data due to FAS may be underreported, and are likely invalid.

In another study by Popova et al. (2013a) estimated the annual cost for multidisciplinary teams to diagnose FASD in Canada. Authors estimated 2 types of cost: the cost per person diagnosed with FASD and the annual cost for all FASD diagnoses in Canada. The diagnostic cost per person was based on the number of hours (based on expert opinion) required by each specialist involved in the diagnostic process and the average rate per hour for each respective specialist (based on hourly costs across Canada). The annual cost of FASD diagnoses for the country based on the number of FASD cases diagnosed per year in Canada (based on the existing clinical capacity of all FASD multidisciplinary clinics in Canada) and the per person cost of FASD diagnosis were estimated in their study. Results showed that the cost per FASD diagnosis was from \$3110 to \$4570. The total cost of FASD diagnostic services in Canada ranged from \$3.6 to \$5.2 million (lower estimate), up to \$5.0–\$7.3 million (upper estimate) per year. The authors concluded that the estimated cost of FASD diagnostic services in this study is most likely underestimated as it was based on the most conservative approach.

Stade et al. (2010) performed an incremental cost analysis to estimate the cost of conducting an FASD assessment via Telemedicine Program in comparison with a clinic in Toronto. The authors found that an average cost savings of \$1280 per patient was demonstrated for the Telemedicine program. Caregivers and youths participated in the Telemedicine also demonstrated a higher level of satisfaction compared to those participated in the Toronto clinic. The authors concluded that diagnosis of clients via Telemedicine was cost-effective and demonstrated a higher level of satisfaction by clients than the Toronto clinic. The findings support increasing diagnostic capacity by the use of Telemedicine in other Northern Communities.

Popova et al. (2013b) performed a modeling study to estimate the utilization of specialized addiction treatment services (SATS) and the associated cost, as a part of the total cost of health care associated with FASD in Canada. Authors used Ontario's data and then extrapolated those data to the total Canadian population. The estimate based on assumptions that 37% (range: 21.6–54.5%) of individuals with FASD abuse or are addicted to alcohol and/or drugs and that their utilization rate of SATS is the same as that for people with a lifetime mental disorder (1.4%). Results showed that the cost of SATS for clients with FASD in Canada in 2010–2011was relatively small, ranging from \$1.65 million to \$3.59 million, based on 5526 outpatient visits and 9529 resident days. The sensitivity analysis showed the cost of SATS varied between \$0.98 million and \$5.34 million.

Another modeling study by Popova et al. (2014b) estimated the cost of 1:1 speech-language interventions among children and youth with FASD for Canada in 2011. The number of children and youth with FASD and speech-language disorder(s) (SLD), the distribution of the level of severity, and the number of hours needed to treat were estimated using data from the available literature. 1:1 speech-language interventions were computed using the average cost per hour for speech-language pathologists. The authors estimated that 37,928 children and youth with FASD had SLD in Canada in 2011 and that the annual cost of 1:1 speech-language interventions among children and youth with FASD was from \$72.5 million to \$144.1 million Canadian dollars.

4.3.1.2 Social Services Related Costs

Popova et al. (2014a) used the data on prevalence of children in care by province/territory (obtained from the Canadian Child Welfare Research Portal) and the estimated proportion of FASD cases among children in care (based on available epidemiological studies) to estimate the number of children (0–18 years) in care with FASD and to determine the associated cost by age group, gender, and province/territory in Canada in 2011. Results showed that the estimated number of children in care with FASD ranged from 2225 to 7620, with an annual cost of care ranging from $57.9 to $198.3 million. The highest overall cost ($29.5–$101.1 million) was for age group 11–15 year-olds. The authors concluded that the study findings demonstrate the substantial economic burden that FASD places on the child welfare system, and that attention towards the needs of this population and prevention efforts to reduce FASD incidence in Canada, and other countries are urgently needed.

4.3.1.3 Productivity Losses Related Costs

Easton et al. (2014, 2015) used a demographic approach with a counterfactual scenario in which nobody in Canada is born with FASD to estimate the productivity losses due to morbidity and premature mortality of individuals with FASD in Canada in 2011. Population estimates were calculated using data on the population of Canada by provinces, the labor force, unemployment rate, and the average weekly wage, all of which were obtained from Statistics Canada. To estimate the number of FASD cases in Canada in 2011, the prevalence of FASD, obtained from the available epidemiological literature, was applied to the general population. The level of impairment that would affect the ability of individuals with FASD to participate in the workforce or reduce their productivity were based on data obtained from the current epidemiological literature and experts' opinions. The number of FASD-related deaths was estimated based on data from Statistics Canada and pooled prevalence estimates of the major disease conditions associated with FASD were obtained from a meta-analysis. The estimates of FASD-related mortality rates were used as a basis for the length of working life span estimation. The authors estimated that about 0.03% of the Canadian workforce experiences a loss of productivity because of FASD-attributable morbidity in the order of $418 million–$1.08 billion. Regarding mortality, the authors estimated that in total 327 individuals with FASD aged 20–69 died in Canada in 2011 resulting in 2877 years of potential employment lost, which translated to a loss of $88 million–$126 million.

4.3.1.4 Economic Evaluation

Thanh et al. (2013) used a decision analytic modeling technique to performed a cost-benefit analysis of potential impacts of the Alberta's 12 FASD Service Networks on secondary disabilities, including crime, homelessness, mental health problems, and school disruption (for children) or unemployment (for adults). From 2008/9 to 2010/11, the 12 Service Networks served 804 children and 471 adults (totalling 1275 people) for FASD diagnostic and supportive services. If there was no such service networks in place, the secondary disabilities of FASD among these people would cost $22.85 million (including 8.62 million for adults and $14.24 million for children) per year. Given that the cost of service networks was $6.12 million per year, the break-even effectiveness was estimated at 28% (range: 25–32%). This means that the economic and social burden associated with secondary disabilities will "pay-off" if the effectiveness of the Networks in reducing secondary disabilities is only 28%.

Thanh et al. (2014c) performed an economic evaluation of the Parent-Child Assistance Program (P-CAP), a three-year home visitation/harm reduction intervention to prevent alcohol exposed births, thereby births with fetal alcohol spectrum disorder, among high-risk women, in Alberta, Canada using a modeling technique. Authors used the discounted incremental lifetime cost per case with FASD of approximately $800,000 (2013 Canadian dollars) and the discounted P-CAP cost per women over the 3 year period of approximately $20,000 for their calculation. The results showed that 56 live births with FASD would be delivered by women who consumed alcohol during pregnancy and who participated in the Alberta P-CAP program. If the P-CAP program did not exist, that number would have been 87. Therefore, the number of FASD cases prevented by the P-CAP program was estimated at 31 (range 20–43). The incremental cost per prevented FASD case was $97,000 (range $72,000–$153,000) and the net monetary benefit of the P-CAP program was $22 million (range $13 million–$31 million). The authors concluded that P-CAP is cost-effective and produces a significant net monetary benefit for Alberta. The sensitivity analyses point at the increased use of contraceptives, (which is central in the P-CAP program) has a significant impact on the outcomes. This finding speaks for placing a high priority not only on reducing alcohol use during pregnancy but also on providing effective measures for family planning and pregnancy protection when a P-CAP program is launched.

4.3.1.5 Cost of FASD Associated with Crimes

Popova et al. (2015a) estimated the direct cost for youths (12–17 years old) and adults (18 + years old) with FASD to the Canadian correctional system in 2011/2012. The prevalence of FASD in the Canadian correctional system, obtained from the current epidemiological literature, was applied to the average number of youths and adults in the correctional system in 2011/2012. The average daily cost for corrections was then applied to the estimated number of youths and adults with FASD in custody. Results showed that the cost of corrections among youths with FASD in Canada in 2011/2012 was calculated to be approximately $17.5 million (2013 Canadian dollars) ($13.6 million for males and $3.8 million for females). Among adults with FASD, it was estimated at $356.2 million ($140 million for provincial and territorial custody and $216.2 million for federal custody). It should be noted that this study includes cost of correctional services only and does not include CJS cost.

Thanh and Jonsson (2015) reviewed literature to estimate the costs of Fetal Alcohol Spectrum Disorder (FASD) in the Canadian Criminal Justice System (CJS) by applying the percentage of people with FASD in CJS to the government expenditures for CJS and to the estimates of crime costs for victims and third-party. The results showed that the costs of FASD associated with the CJS were estimated at $3.9 billion a year, with $1.2 billion for police, $0.4 billion for court, $0.5 billion for correctional services, $1.6 billion for victims, and $0.2 billion for third-party.

4.3.1.6 Total Costs of FASD for Associated Sectors in Society

In the same study on costs of FASD associated with the CJS, Thanh and Jonsson (2015) updated the total costs of FASD in Canada to be $9.7 billion a year, of which CJS accounts for 40%, healthcare 21%, education 17%, social services 13%, and others 9%.

Popova et al. (2015b) performed a cost-of-illness study examining the impact of FASD on the material welfare of the Canadian society in 2013 (combined all the studies by CAMH described above). The authors included the direct costs of health care, law enforcement, children and youth in care, special education, supportive housing, long-term care, prevention and research, as well as the indirect costs of productivity losses of individuals with FASD due to their increased morbidity and premature mortality. This study maintains that the total cost of FASD was approximately $1.8 billion (range: $1.3 billion–$2.3 billion). Of this, the cost of productivity losses accounted for that largest share (41%), followed by the cost of corrections (29%), and the cost of health care (10%).

4.3.2 Costs of FASD Associated with Crimes

As mentioned above, there were 2 studies about costs of FASD associated with crimes. Popova et al. (2015a) estimated costs of FASD in the correctional system only while Thanh and Jonsson (2015) assessed costs of FASD in the entire CJS, which includes not only correctional services but also police and court services as well as costs for victims of crimes. Both studies reviewed the literature to estimate the prevalence of FASD in the legal system and then applied it to either the number of people in custody multiplied by cost per day per person in custody (Popova et al. 2015a) or the expenditures for CJS and costs for victims of crimes (Thanh and Jonsson 2015).

Table 4.1 Prevalence of FASD in legal system reported in 2 studies

Study	Mean	Range (%)	Note
Popova et al. (2015a)	16.6% for youths	10.9–23.3	No meta-analysis
	9.9% for adults		
Thanh and Jonsson (2015)	10.1% for both adults and youths	5–17.9	Meta-analysis

4.3.2.1 Prevalence of FASD in Legal System

Popova et al. (2015a) reviewed 4 studies reporting different prevalence of FASD in the legal system and the authors used a range of the lowest to the highest prevalence for analysis. Thanh and Jonsson (2015) performed a meta-analysis of those studies to estimate a pool prevalence for both youth and adult (Table 4.1). Of the reviewed four studies, three investigated the prevalence in youth, and one in adults.

Fast et al. (1999) assessed 287 youths aged 12–18 who were remanded to the Inpatient Assessment Unit of Youth Forensic Psychiatric Services in Burnaby, British Columbia between 1 July 1995 and 30 June 1996 for fetal alcohol syndrome (FAS) and fetal alcohol effects (FAE). The sample represented approximately 2.5% of youth in custody in British Columbia and Yukon at the time of study. The authors found 3 FAS cases and 64 FAE cases, totaling 67 FASD cases. The prevalence of FASD among youth offenders was therefore estimated at 23.3% (67 out of 287).

Murphy et al. (2005) surveyed 137 youths aged 14–19 in custody in British Columbia in 2004. Of the sample, 90% were male, 47% were Aboriginal, 82% had a history of involvement with the youth justice system, and only 18% were in custody for the first time. As 16 of the youth surveyed (12 Aboriginals and 4 non-Aboriginals) were assessed by a health care professional as having FAS or FAE, this study suggested a prevalence of FASD among youths in custody at 11.7%. The prevalence specific to Aboriginals and non-Aboriginals was 18.8% and 5.5%, respectively.

Rojas and Gretton (2007) examined the background, offence characteristics, and criminal outcomes of youths who had committed sexually offences. The sample included 102 Aboriginal and 257 non-Aboriginal youths aged 12–18 who had been ordered by the courts or by their probation officers to attend the Youth Sexual Offence Treatment Program in British Columbia between 1985 and 2004. The presence or absence of FASD was based on formal diagnosis or suspicion from a physician that the adolescent suffered from FAS or FAE. Information about the presence or absence of FASD was available for 67 Aboriginals and 163 non-Aboriginals. The authors found that the prevalence of FASD was 26.9% among Aboriginals, and 4.3% among non-Aboriginals. Although it was not reported by the authors, based on these figures, the prevalence of FASD for both groups can be estimated at 10.9%.

MacPherson and Chudley (2007) investigated the prevalence of FASD among adult offenders aged 19–30 in Stony Mountain Institution, Manitoba between April 2005 and September 2006. Of 91 participants, 66% were Aboriginal. The authors found 1 partial FAS, 8 alcohol-related neuro-developmental disorder (ARND), and 16 FASD-suspicions (that is, not enough information to confirm or rule out a

Table 4.2 Meta-analysis on the prevalence of FASD in legal system

Study	Sample	FASD cases	FASD rate (%)	95% confidence interval	
				Low (%)	High (%)
Youth					
Fast et al. (1999)	287	67	23.3	18.5	28.2
Murphy et al. (2005)	137	16	11.7	6.3	17.1
Rojas and Gretton (2007)	230	25	10.9	6.8	14.9
Pooled			**14.8**	**12.2**	**17.5**
Adult					
MacPherson and Chudley (2007)	91	9	**9.9**	**4.6**	**17.9**
Weighted average for both adult and youth			**10.1**	**5.0**	**17.9**

Source: Thanh and Jonsson (2015)

diagnosis). Excluding the suspected cases, the prevalence of FASD among adult offenders was estimated at 9.9%.

Using a fixed effect model, the pooled prevalence of FASD among youth in the CJS was estimated at 14.8% (range: 12.2–17.5%) (Table 4.2). Based on a weight of 95% adults and 5% youths in custody on any given day,[2] the weighted average prevalence of FASD in the CJS (regardless of being youth or adult) was estimated at 10.1% (range: 5.0–17.9%) (Table 4.2).

With the total number of youths and adults in custody in Canada in 2011/2012 were 1676 and 39,087, respectively, Popova et al. (2015a) estimated that the number of youths with FASD in custody ranged from 183 to 374, with a mean of 278 (16.6%) and there were 3870 adults (9.9%) with FASD in custody on any given day using the prevalence of FASD among youth in custody was from 10.9% to 23.3% and among adults in custody was 9.9%.

4.3.2.2 Costs of FASD in the Criminal Justice System

Costs of FASD in the CJS include 3 components: police, court, and correctional services. There are 2 studies estimating CJS costs. However, Popova et al. (2015a) included correctional services only. Thanh and Jonsson (2015) included all the 3 components.

By multiplying the number of people with FASD in custody with the cost to imprison an inmate which was estimated at $172 per day ($62,930 per year) for provincial and territorial custody and at $360 per day ($131,382 per year) for federal custody in Canada., Popova et al. (2015a) estimated the cost of corrections among youths with FASD in Canada in 2011/2012 at $17.5 million, of which males accounted for 78% ($13.6 million) and females for 22% ($3.8 million). Among

[2] See: Statistics Canada. Adult and youth correctional services: Key indicators, 2008/2009 (correction). Available at: http://www.statcan.gc.ca/daily-quotidien/091208/dq091208a-eng.htm (Accessed March 3, 2016).

adults with FASD it was $356.2 million, of which provincial and territorial custody accounted for 39% ($140 million) and federal custody for 61% ($216.2 million). Males affected by FASD accounted for 89% ($317 million with $124.6 million in provincial and territorial custody and $192.4 million in federal custody), while females affected by FASD accounted for 11% ($39.2 million with $15.4 million in provincial and territorial custody and $23.8 million in federal custody). Ontario accounted for the highest proportion of the total cost of provincial and territorial corrections, while the Yukon accounted for the lowest proportion. For both youths and adults, the cost of FASD for correctional services was estimated at $373.7 million, of which males accounted for 88% ($330.7 million) and females for 12% ($43 million); provincial and territorial custody accounted for 42% ($157.5 million), and federal custody for 58% ($216.2 million).

Story and Yalkin (2013) performed an expenditure analysis of the CJS in Canada, which included estimates of expenditures of criminal justice for the federal government, provinces, and territories from 2002 to 2012. It included policing, court (judges, prosecutors, legal aid, and youth justice), and corrections (including parole) expenditures. Using data from public accounts, Statistics Canada, and information received through direct request, the authors estimated that in the fiscal year 2011–2012, the federal, provincial, and territorial governments spent $20.9 billion (in 2014 CA$) on criminal justice. This was equal to 1.1% of nominal GDP (that is, a GDP figure that has not been adjusted for inflation), making the CJS expenditures comparable to the budget of National Defence, half the size of the budget of Human Resources and Skill Development, and more than double the budget of Aboriginal Affairs and Northern Development Canada. Of the CJS expenditures, policing accounted for 57% ($11.9 billion), court for 20% ($4.2 billion), and corrections for 23% ($4.8 billion).

Applying the prevalence of FASD in the CJS (10.1%; range: 5.0–17.9%) to the CJS expenditures above, Thanh and Jonsson (2015) estimated the costs of the CJS that can be attributed to FASD at $2.1 billion (range: $1.0 billion–$3.7 billion) (Table 4.3, sub-total 1). Of this, costs of FASD were $1.2 billion for police (57%), $422.4 million for court (20%), and $485.7 million for correctional services (23%).

4.3.2.3 Costs of FASD for Victims of Criminal Acts

The CJS constitutes only one side of the costs related to crimes, with the other side being the victims of criminal incidents. Using data from the Police Administration Survey, the Adult Criminal Court Survey, the Integrated Correctional Services Survey, the Canadian Institute of Health Information, the 2004 General Social Survey, and various governmental publications, Zhang (2008) estimated that criminal cost for victims was about $15.8 billion in 2008. Applying the prevalence of FASD in the CJS to this cost, Thanh and Jonsson (2015) estimated that $1.6 billion (range: $0.8 billion–$2.8 billion) can be attributed to FASD (Table 4.3, sub-total 2). Of this, health care accounted for 10% ($160 million), productivity losses for 47% ($748 million), and stolen/damaged property for 43% ($683 million).

Table 4.3 Costs of FASD associated with crimes in Canada, 2012 (million CA$, 2014 price level)

Cost category	Total costs	FASD costs		
		Mean	Low	High
Criminal justice system				
Police	$11,918.1	$1203.7	$595.9	$2133.3
Court	$4181.8	$422.4	$209.1	$748.5
Corrections	$4809.1	$485.7	$240.5	$860.8
Sub-total (1)	$20,909.0	$2111.8	$1045.5	$3742.7
Victim				
Health care	$1587.3	$160.3	$79.4	$284.1
Productivity losses	$7407.4	$748.1	$370.4	$1325.9
Stolen/damaged property	$6757.3	$682.5	$337.9	$1209.6
Sub-total (2)	$15,752.0	$1591.0	$787.6	$2819.6
Third party				
Funeral and burial expenses	$4.4	$0.4	$0.2	$0.8
Other people harmed/threatened during the incidents	$112.2	$11.3	$5.6	$20.1
Lost production/services of other people	$1159.4	$117.1	$58.0	$207.5
Victim services and compensation programs	$496.1	$50.1	$24.8	$88.8
Shelters for victims	$279.4	$28.2	$14.0	$50.0
Other expenditures related to crime	$261.8	$26.4	$13.1	$46.9
Sub-total (3)	$2313.3	$233.6	$115.7	$414.1
Total (1) + (2) + (3)		**$3936.4**	**$1948.7**	**$6976.4**

Source: Thanh and Jonsson (2015)

4.3.2.4 Costs of FASD for Third Party

Besides victims, others also suffer from crime. For example, family members may have to take time off from their daily activities to accompany/take care of victims who are wounded by criminal acts. Also, governments provide various victim services and compensation programs to help victims. All these costs are reflected in the costs to the third-party, which were estimated at $2.3 billion in 2008 (Table 4.3, sub-total 3). Of this cost, $234 million (range: $116 million–$414 million) can be attributed to FASD (Thanh and Jonsson 2015).

4.3.2.5 Total Cost of FASD Associated with Crimes

Adding together the cost for CJS, the cost for victims, and the cost for third party (sub-totals 1, 2, and 3 in Table 4.3), the total costs of FASD associated with crimes in Canada were estimated at $3.9 billion per year (range: $1.9 billion–$7.0 billion) with $2.1 billion or 54% for CJS (police, court, and correctional services), $1.6 billion or 41% for victims, and $0.2 billion or 5% for third-party (Thanh and Jonsson 2015).

4.3.2.6 Updated Total Cost of FASD for Canadian Society

There are only 2 studies estimating the total cost of FASD for society and both are for Canada (Table 4.4).

Thanh and Jonsson (2015) estimated the total cost of FASD to be $9.8 billion per year (range: $7.8 billion–$12.9 billion), of which health care accounts for 21%, crime/CJS for 40%, social services for 13%, special education for 16%, and other/indirect costs for 9%.

Table 4.4 Updated total cost of FASD by cost component (million 2015 CA$)

	Average		Low		High	
Study/cost component	$	%	$	%	$	%
Thanh and Jonsson (2015)						
Health care	$2020	21	$2020	26	$2020	16
Criminal justice/crimes	$3939	40	$1919	25	$7070	55
Social services	$1313	13	$1313	17	$1313	10
Special education	$1616	16	$1616	21	$1616	13
Other/indirect	$909	9	$909	12	$909	7
Total	$9797	100	$7777	100	$12,928	100
Popova et al. (2015b)						
Health care	$181	10	$131	10	$231	10
Correctional services	$386	21	$386	30	$386	16
Social services	$302	17	$171	13	$433	18
Special education	$55	3	$55	4	$55	2
Indirect	$899	49	$543	42	$1256	53
Total	$1823	100	$1286	100	$2361	100
Average of the 2 studies						
Health care	$1100	19	$1076	24	$1125	15
Criminal justice/crimes	$2162	37	$1152	25	$3728	49
Social services	$807	14	$742	16	$873	11
Special education	$836	14	$836	18	$836	11
Indirect	$904	16	$726	16	$1082	14
Total	$5810	100	$4531	100	$7644	100
Combined results of the 2 studies[a]						
Health care	$2020	21	$2020	29	$2020	16
Criminal justice/crimes	$3939	42	$1919	28	$7070	55
Social services	$807	9	$742	11	$873	7
Special education	$836	9	$836	12	$836	6
Indirect	$1808	19	$1452	21	$2165	17
Total	$9410	100	$6968	100	$12,963	100

[a]Health care cost is from Thanh and Jonsson as the hospital cost in Popova et al. is for FAS only; Criminal justice cost is from Thanh and Jonsson as the one in Popova et al. is for correctional services only; Social and special education services cost is average between the 2 studies; Indirect cost is a sum of the 2 studies as Popova et al. included productivity losses of FASD people and Thanh and Jonsson included productivity losses of FASD care givers

Popova et al. (2015b) estimated the total cost of FASD at $1.8 billion per year (range: $1.3 billion–$2.4 billion), of which health care services accounted for 10%, crime/CJS 21%, social services 17%, special education 3% and indirect cost 49%.

If averaging the 2 studies, the total cost of FASD would be $5.8 billion (range $4.5 billion–$7.6 billion), of which health care accounts for 19%, crime/CJS for 37%, social services for 14%, special education for 14%, and indirect costs for 16%.

However, the average is misleading since there are important differences between the two studies in terms of included/excluded cost components. For example, in Popova et al. (2015b), hospital cost is for FAS only. Moreover the authors concluded that these costs were "underreported" and "invalid". The cost for crime/CJS in the Popova study is for correctional services only, not including cost of police or court services, nor cost for victims of criminal acts. In Thanh and Jonsson (2015), the indirect cost is for productivity losses of care givers, while it is for productivity losses of people with FASD in Popova et al. (2015b).

Nevertheless, we combined the results of these two studies by taking the cost for health care and the cost for crime/CJS from the more complete study by Thanh and Jonsson, adding the indirect costs estimated in both studies, and using the average cost for social services and the cost for special education from both studies. The combined total cost of FASD was then estimated at $9.4 billion (range $7.0 billion–$13.0 billion), of which health care accounts for 21% (range: 16%–29%), crime/CJS for 42% (range: 28–55%), social services for 9% (7–11%), special education for 9% (range: 6–12%), and indirect cost for 19% (range: 17–21%).

4.4 Discussion

There are four main findings of this study. First, the prevalence of people with FASD in the Canadian CJS is 10% (range: 5–18%). Second, the total cost of FASD associated with crimes in Canada per year is $3.9 billion (range: $1.9 billion–$7.0 billion) with $2.1 billion or 54% for the CJS, $1.6 billion or 41% for victims, and $0.2 billion or 5% for third-party. Third, of the cost for CJS ($2.1 billion), police services account for 57% or $1.2 billion, court services for 20% or $422.4 million, and correctional services for 23% or $485.7 million. Fourth, the total cost of FASD for Canadian society per year is $9.4 billion (range $7.0 billion–$13.0 billion), of which health care accounts for 21% (range: 16%–29%), crimes for 42% (range: 28–55%), social services for 9% (7–11%), special education for 9% (range: 6–12%), and indirect for 19% (range: 17–21%).

Of note, all studies on the prevalence of FASD in the CJS are from British Columbia, so that the prevalence may not be representative for the rest of Canada. Screening for FASD among prisoners across the country is therefore needed to have better picture of FASD in the legal system. FASD screening tools (such as the Asante Centre's FASD Screening and Referral Tool for Youth Probation Officers) can be used to trigger a formal diagnosis in the legal system. There is also a need for increasing capacity of multidisciplinary diagnostic teams to provide timely diagnosis in the legal system (Institute of Health Economics 2013).

To minimize the economic burden of FASD for the legal system, several types/stages of prevention can be considered. The prime aim is of course to prevent FASD from happening in the first place. Second to assist people with FASD from coming in conflict with the law. The third is to minimize its consequences.

To prevent FASD from happening is to prevent women from drinking alcohol during pregnancy. There is a number of measures used in different jurisdictions regarding alcohol awareness and harm reduction in the general population and in women of childbearing age in particular. These include alcohol warning labels, ban the sale and service of alcohol to pregnant women, criminalization of alcohol and drug use by pregnant women, interventions targeted at pregnant women with addictions, and subsidization of contraception (Institute of Health Economics 2013). Prevention programs should focus on those areas in which positive effects have been demonstrated. In particular, it may be worthwhile to examine interventions such as parent-child assistance program (PCAP) which helps reduce the likelihood of subsequent children with FASD after a child is found to suffer from FASD (Thanh et al. 2014b). Another potentially promising measure for prevention might be to make use of technology – a cell phone with a breathalyser and a platform with many other functions, to provide feedback to the pregnant woman for her to demonstrate her sobriety for loved ones and for social services.[3]

Every measure has advantages and disadvantages. For example, alcohol and pregnancy warning labels have been found to be effective but lose their impact over time. Also, the labels are least effective with binge or heavy drinkers. Measures to ban selling or serving alcohol to pregnant women have been perceived as discriminatory based on gender. Criminalization of alcohol and drug use by pregnant women have been initiated in the US. Pregnant women have been charged with offences ranging from delivering drugs to a minor, to child neglect and chemical endangerment, which have resulted in arrest and incarceration in some states. Apart from any constitutional issues, medical and public health groups are concerned that these measures deter women from seeking prenatal care, accessing addiction treatment, or speaking openly about their substance use with health care providers. Interventions targeting at pregnant women with addictions, including forced addiction treatment for pregnant women and requirements by health professionals to report prenatal drug and alcohol use to child protection services, along with compulsory screening at birth, raise concerns that they may lead to or encourage under-reporting and may disproportionately impact marginalized women. Since 20 years ago, the country of Norway have had an addendum to its Social Services Act which states that a pregnant drug or alcohol user should be detained (in a hospital) throughout the pregnancy without her consent if the abuse is of such a nature that it is highly probable that the child will be born with defects and if voluntary assistance is insufficient.

[3] See: Alberta Innovates Health Solutions. Preventing the Preventable: New study uses technology to tackle Fetal Alcohol Spectrum Disorder. Available at http://www.aihealthsolutions.ca/news-and-events/media-centre/preventing-the-preventable/ (Accessed August 24, 2016).

This stand is viewed comparable to legislation on mental health, child protection and communicable diseases in many countries, about coercive measures, when a person is in serious danger to herself or others (Nordlie 2016). There is no longer much discussion in Norway about this coercion measure and the fears raised at its introduction about women's rights, going underground, seeking abortions, etc.

The cost to keep a prisoner in federal prison is estimated at $131,382 per year (Popova et al. 2015a), which is much higher than the cost to provide FASD services in community. A cross-sectoral program in Alberta serving people with FASD in community costs below $5000 per person per year or $1.63 per capita (Institute of Health Economics 2013). Note that correctional services account for only 23% of the CJS cost, other components of CJS cost are police (57%) and court services (20%) as shown in this study. Therefore, keeping those with FASD out of prisons/CJS would be cost-saving. Given the fact that people with FASD are more likely involved in the legal system than those without FASD and that people with FASD often get into conflict with the law when they are not involved in a structured program, supports from family members and social service workers creating a therapeutic environment for people with FASD to live in are of importance.

As shown in several other chapters of this book the characteristics of people with FASD make them disadvantaged at all points of a criminal justice process (the initial contact with police, the bail stage, the trial stage, the sentencing stage, and the post-sentencing stage). They may not fully appreciate the criminal nature and consequences of their actions. They may not fully understand the legal proceedings and potential outcomes of their cases. Additionally, those with FASD in custody are particularly vulnerable to exploitation and manipulation by other inmates. If known by correctional officials, they can be housed on a secure range and received a behaviour-based effective correctional program. However, there is still a gap in diagnosis and provision of treatment for FASD in prisons. The current standardized intake screening tools used in the federal corrections context do not explicitly address FASD. Therefore, it is recommended that there should be a broader access to multidisciplinary diagnostic services for individuals suspected of FASD in the correctional system and that a specialized training for correctional staff should be implemented to ensure that staff appreciate the response styles of inmates with FASD (Institute of Health Economics 2013).

4.5 Conclusion

The prevalence of FASD in the legal system was estimated at 10% (range 5–18%). The total costs of FASD associated with crimes in Canada were estimated at $3.9 billion per year (range: $1.9 billion–$7.0 billion) with $2.1 billion or 54% for CJS (police, court, and correctional services), $1.6 billion or 41% for victims, and $0.2 billion or 5% for third-party. Of the cost for CJS ($2.1 billion), police services accounted for 57% or $1.2 billion, court services for 20% or $422.4 million, and correctional services for 23% or $485.7 million. The total cost of FASD for Canadian society was estimated at $9.4 billion per year (range $7.0 billion–$13.0 billion), of which health care accounted for 21% (range: 16–29%), crimes for 42% (range: 28–55%), social services for 9% (7–11%), special education for 9% (range: 6–12%), and indirect for 19% (range: 17–21%).

References

Alberta Innovates Health Solutions (AIHS). *Preventing the preventable: New study uses technology to tackle fetal alcohol spectrum disorder*. Available at: http://www.aihealthsolutions.ca/news-and-events/media-centre/preventing-the-preventable/. Accessed 24 Aug 2016.

Amendah, D.D., S.D. Grosse, and J. Bertrand. 2011. Medical expenditures of children in the United States with fetal alcohol syndrome. *Neurotoxicology and Teratology* 33 (2): 322–324.

Easton, B., L. Burd, A. Sarnocinska-Hart, J. Rehm, and S. Popova. 2014. Productivity losses because of morbidity attributable to fetal alcohol spectrum disorder in Canada: A demographic approach. *Journal of Studies on Alcohol and Drugs* 75 (6): 1011–1017.

———. 2015. The cost of lost productivity due to fetal alcohol spectrum disorder-related premature mortality. *Journal of Population Therapeutics and Clinical Pharmacology* 22 (1): e3–e8.

Fast, D.K., J. Conry, and C.A. Loock. 1999. Identifying fetal alcohol syndrome among youth in the criminal justice system. *Journal of Developmental and Behavioral Pediatrics* 20 (5): 370–372.

Institute of Health Economics. 2013. *Consensus statement on legal issues of FASD*. Institute of Health Economics Consensus Statement, Volume 5 – September 18–20, 2013. Edmonton: Institute of Health Economics. Available at: www.ihe.ca. Accessed 9 Mar 2016.

Jonsson, E., A. Salmon, and K.R. Warren. 2014. The international charter on prevention of fetal alcohol spectrum disorder. *The Lancet Global Health* 2 (3): e135–e137.

Jonsson, E., A. Salmon, S. Clarren, and J. Moffatt, eds. 2015. *Preventing Harm from Alcohol Use during Pregnancy: The Case of Fetal Alcohol Spectrum Disorder (FASD). Plenary Presentations from The first international conference on prevention of FASD*. Edmonton: Institute of Health Economics. Available at: www.ihe.ca. Accessed 22 Aug 2016.

Lang, S., J. Rehm, D. Bekmurakov, A. Mihic, and S. Popova. 2012. Risk of incarceration for individuals with fetal alcohol exposure. *American Journal of Epidemiology* 176 (1): 80–82.

MacPherson, P., and A.E. Chudley. 2007. *Fetal alcohol spectrum disorder (FASD): Screening and estimating incidence in an adult correctional population*. Presented at the 2nd international conference on Fetal Alcohol Spectrum Disorder: Research, Policy, and Practice around the World, Victoria, BC, March 7–10, 2007. Available at: events.onlinebroadcasting.com/fas/090707/ppts/correctional.ppt. Accessed 3 Mar 2016.

Murphy, A., M. Chittenden, and The McGeary Centre Society. 2005. *Time out II: A profile of BC youth in custody*. Vancouver: The McCreary Centre Society. Available at: http://www.mcs.bc.ca/pdf/time_out_2.pdf. Accessed 3 Mar 2016.

Nordlie, E. 2016. Experience in involuntary hospitalization of drug and alcohol addicted mothers during their pregnanbcies at Borgestadklinikken, Norway. In *Fetal alcohol spectrum disorders in adults; ethical and legal perspectives*, ed. M. Nelson and M. Trussler, 49–64. Cham: Springer.

Popova, S., S. Lange, L. Burd, and J. Rehm. 2012. Health care burden and cost associated with fetal alcohol syndrome: Based on official Canadian data. *PLoS ONE* 7 (8): e43024.

Popova, S., S. Lange, L. Burd, A.E. Chudley, S.K. Clarren, et al. 2013a. Cost of fetal alcohol spectrum disorder diagnosis in Canada. *PLoS ONE* 8 (4): e60434.

Popova, S., S. Lange, L. Burd, K. Urbanoski, and J. Rehm. 2013b. Cost of specialized addiction treatment of clients with fetal alcohol spectrum disorder in Canada. *BMC Public Health* 13: 570.

Popova, S., S. Lange, L. Burd, and J. Rehm. 2014a. Canadian children and youth in care: The cost of fetal alcohol spectrum disorder. *Child & Youth Care Forum* 43: 83–96.

Popova, S., S. Lange, L. Burd, K. Shield, and J. Rehm. 2014b. Cost of speech-language interventions for children and youth with foetal alcohol spectrum disorder in Canada. *International Journal of Speech-Language Pathology* 16 (6): 571–581.

Popova, S., S. Lange, L. Burd, and J. Rehm. 2015a. Cost attributable to fetal alcohol spectrum disorder in the Canadian correctional system. *International Journal of Law and Psychiatry* 41: 76–81.

———. 2015b. The economic burden of fetal alcohol spectrum disorder in Canada in 2013. *Alcohol and Alcoholism* 51: 367–375.

Rojas, E.Y., and H.M. Gretton. 2007. Background, offence characteristics, and criminal outcomes of aboriginal youth who sexually offend: A closer look at aboriginal youth intervention needs. *Sexual Abuse: A Journal of Research and Treatment* 19 (3): 257–283.

Stade, B., S. Camera, M. Sgro, C. Bishop, D. Bennett, M. Parkes, et al. 2010. Fetal alcohol spectrum disorder diagnostic telemedicine program: Measurement of cost and client satisfaction. *Journal of Population Therapeutics and Clinical Pharmacology* 17 (2): e284–e301.

Statistics Canada. *Adult and youth correctional services: Key indicators, 2008/2009* (correction). Available at: http://www.statcan.gc.ca/daily-quotidien/091208/dq091208a-eng.htm. Accessed 3 Mar 2016.

Story, R., and T.R. Yalkin. 2013. *Expenditure analysis of criminal justice in Canada*. Office of the Parliamentary Budget Officer, Ottawa, Canada, March 20, 2013. Available at: http://www.pbo-dpb.gc.ca/files/files/Crime_Cost_EN.pdf. Accessed 3 Mar 2016.

Streissguth, A.P., F.L. Bookstein, H.M. Barr, P.D. Sampson, D. O'Mally, and J.K. Young. 2004. Risk factors for adverse life outcomes in fetal alcohol syndrome and fetal alcohol effects. *Journal of Developmental and Behaviour Pediatrics* 25: 228–238.

———. 2015. The costs of fetal alcohol spectrum disorder (FASD) in the Canadian criminal justice system. *Journal of Population Therapeutics and Clinical Pharmacology* 22 (1): e125–e131.

Thanh, N.X., E. Jonsson, L. Dennett, and P. Jacobs. 2010. Costs of FASD. In *Fetal alcohol spectrum disorder: Management and policy perspectives of FASD*, ed. P.R. Edward, S. Clarren, J. Weinberg, and E. Jonsson. Weinheim: Wiley-Blackwell.

Thanh, N.X., J. Moffatt, P. Jacobs, A. Chuck, and E. Jonsson. 2013. potential impacts of the alberta fetal alcohol spectrum disorder service networks on secondary disabilities: A cost-benefit analysis. *Journal of Population Therapeutics and Clinical Pharmacology* 20 (2): e193–e200.

Thanh, N.X., E. Jonsson, A. Salmon, and M. Sebastienski. 2014a. Incidence and prevalence of fetal alcohol spectrum disorder by sex and age group in Alberta, Canada. *Journal of Population Therapeutics and Clinical Pharmacology* 21 (3): e395–e404.

Thanh, N.X., and E. Jonsson. 2014b. Costs of health services utilization of people with fetal alcohol spectrum disorder by sex and age group in Alberta, Canada. *Journal of Population Therapeutics and Clinical Pharmacology* 21 (3): e421–e430.

Thanh, N.X., E. Jonsson, J. Moffatt, L. Dennett, A. Chuck, and S. Birchard. 2014c. An economic evaluation of the parent–child assistance program for preventing fetal alcohol spectrum disorder in Alberta, Canada. *Administration and Policy in Mental Health and Mental Health Services Research* 42 (1): 10–18

Zhang, T. 2008. *Costs of crime in Canada, 2008*. Department of Justice Canada. Available at: http://www.justice.gc.ca/eng/rp-pr/csj-sjc/crime/rr10_5/rr10_5.pdf. Accessed 3 Mar 2016.

Part II
Definition and Identification of FASD

Chapter 5
Understanding the Methods for Diagnosing FASD

Sterling Clarren

Abstract The process of diagnosis for a fetal alcohol spectrum disorder (FASD) and the terminology used within the spectrum may be confusing to those not close to the subject. First the term, FASD, itself has not been used as an actual diagnostic term but rather as a blanket term for a number of more specific conditions caused by alcohol exposure in pregnancy. Second, the reasons or purposes for pursuing this diagnosis vary. The diagnosis might be sought to establish that alcohol was the teratogenic (an agent that can disturb the development of the embryo or fetus causing developmental malformations) cause of the problem. More often, however, the diagnosis is sought to determine if the patient has an elusive form of brain damage that has lead to his/her behavioural and adaptive problems. If that is so, it makes the diagnosis important for intervention and perhaps to understanding a defendant's criminal intentions in a court. The diagnosis can be made for either reason, but does not necessarily need to be made for both. In some cases proving, as best as possible, that alcohol was the principal cause of the individual's problems is the issue, but at other times identifying that brain damage has contributed to behavioural problems, no matter the cause or causes, is the true point of the exercise. This brief chapter is presented in the hope that it can help legal and other non-medical professionals to understand the tasks involved in reaching a diagnosis of FASD.

Keywords Dysmorphology · Medical model for diagnosis · Defuse brain damage · Multidisciplinary team evaluation

S. Clarren (✉)
Faculty of Medicine, University of British Columbia, Vancouver, Canada
e-mail: clarrens@u.washington.edu

E. Jonsson et al. (eds.), *Ethical and Legal Perspectives in Fetal Alcohol Spectrum Disorders (FASD)*, International Library of Ethics, Law, and the New Medicine 75,
https://doi.org/10.1007/978-3-319-71755-5_5

The process of diagnosis for a fetal alcohol spectrum disorder (FASD) and the terminology used within the spectrum may be confusing to those not close to the subject. First the term, FASD, itself has not been used as an actual diagnostic term but rather as a blanket term for a number of more specific conditions caused by alcohol exposure in pregnancy. Second, the reasons or purposes for pursuing this diagnosis vary. The diagnosis might be sought to establish that alcohol was the teratogenic (an agent that can disturb the development of the embryo or fetus causing developmental malformations) cause of the problem. More often, however, the diagnosis is sought to determine if the patient has an elusive form of brain damage that has lead to his/her behavioural and adaptive problems. If that is so, it makes the diagnosis important for intervention and perhaps to understanding a defendant's criminal intentions in a court. The diagnosis can be made for either reason, but does not necessarily need to be made for both. In some cases proving, as best as possible, that alcohol was the principal cause of the individual's problems is the issue, but at other times identifying that brain damage has contributed to behavioural problems, no matter the cause or causes, is the true point of the exercise. This brief chapter is presented in the hope that it can help legal and other non-medical professionals to understand the tasks involved in reaching a diagnosis of FASD.

There are two conceptual frame works that need to be understood, at least basically, in order to place an FASD diagnosis in context: "syndromology" and the "medical model."

Syndromology or dysmorphology is the study of codifying recognizable patterns of human malformation. There are after all, a finite number of ways that any organ in the body can be malformed in development. The terms "major" and "minor" are applied to specific malformations only to express the extent of medical problems that might be associated. Minor malformations are features that occur in only a small percentage of the population and have little or no impact on function. Major malformations generally require medical assessment and interventions. While virtually all malformations have more than one cause, it was appreciated in the early part of the twentieth century that clusters of malformations might be related to a specific etiology – either genetic or environmental in origin. These birth defect syndromes were generally first discerned clinically and then studied for etiology and specificity. Fetal alcohol syndrome is an example. David W. Smith and colleagues recognized a group of less than a dozen children who all had a similar facial appearance, growth delays and cognitive difficulties and all had been heavily exposed to alcohol in pregnancy (Jones et al. 1973). They did not identify an exact description of this same condition in the literature (although there were a couple of earlier articles that had appeared in regional French journals) (Lemoine et al. 1968). It was reasonably certain to that team that the children had the same as yet unrecognized syndrome, but it was a bold leap to declare alcohol the cause and not just a coincident finding after seeing just a hand full of cases. Calling the condition "fetal alcohol syndrome" (FAS) brought the condition to public attention, and stimulated basic research for decades to develop animal models and to "prove" that ethyl alcohol and not cofactors or other factors could produce the cluster of anomalies in the human disorder. Research was successful in clearly establishing alcohol as a teratogen. But somehow, in all the energy that went into proving the reality of the etiology, the permanent and profound problems that individuals with diffuse difficulties faced in brain processing and performance got lost for a while.

Alcohol is not the only cause of the types of brain damage found in children with FAS neither is any one of the specific facial features nor the growth deficiency nor the occasional other organ malformations that occur. It is in the combination of these findings that the person comes to have the "diagnostic phenotype." Slowly it came to be recognized that the patients described in the early literature on FAS had very severe examples of the syndrome and that only these more severe forms could be easily diagnosed by a geneticist or dysmorphologist alone. This was because a physician alone rarely can discerned the crucial findings of brain damage unless there was a very small head (microcephalous) or abnormal neurologic findings. Understanding the brain issues generally required the assistance of teams of developmentalists (Astley and Clarren 1997; Cook et al. 2015).

Western medicine approaches medical evaluation through a system generally called "the medical model" that links the patient's symptoms or complaints to an investigative process that leads first to the specific cause (etiology) and then to a specific treatment or intervention. The physician first takes a history and does a physical examination which lead to a list of possible causes for the patient's complaints or concerns. This is called the "differential diagnosis." The information gleaned from the patient, coupled then with appropriate diagnostic tests, should lead to the selection of one entry on the differential diagnosis as the final diagnosis. That in turn, ideally, leads to a specific and effective treatment. For example, a patient complains of weight gain, fatigue, and hair loss among other things. The medical examination detects among other things, a mass in the anterior center of the neck and a change in deep tendon reflexes. The physician considers many possibilities, but believes that a low amount of thyroid hormone is most likely and laboratory tests confirm poor thyroid function. The specific treatment, oral thyroid supplements, is prescribed. The symptoms disappear. In this approach, the patient was not treated symptomatically for each complaint; a diet, an exercise program, sleep therapy, new shampoo – but rather, the underlying pathophysiology was sought for a more holistic, fundamental solution to the problems. If the thyroid functions had been normal, the doctor would have moved down the list on the differential diagnosis to seek another explanation. When the medical model works, it is elegant. Unfortunately we have not developed a complete pathway for all medical conditions and many conditions can mimic each other. The diagnosis of a fetal alcohol spectrum disorder (FASD) does not always fit the medical model easily and alternative explanations for some of the symptoms are often present. Nevertheless, in this author's view, the legal questions related to FASD must start with understanding the strengths and weaknesses in the FASD diagnostic process that embrace the medical model approach to developmental disabilities.

The symptoms that begin the investigation for an FASD may come from three very different directions at different times in life with different expectations for the diagnosis. A young patient, aged newborn to 4 or 5 years, might be brought to medical attention because his/her mother had used large quantities of alcohol in pregnancy. The issues of concern are the mother's abilities to parent or her risk to bear another affected child. Other patients in this age group might be seen because of unusual facial features or medical conditions like heart or renal disease, or growth problems. The request is for medical help with the specific organ problem or a syndrome diagnosis for genetic counseling proposes. In older children and adult patients, anywhere from 6 to 60 years, things are different and the most likely presenting complaint is, what I have come to summarize in teaching as, "mysterious maladaptation." The patient has not been successful is leading an age appropriate independent life. The specific complaints vary but would include: hyperactivity, poor social judgment, failure to follow directions (even when it is reasonably clear that the person can recite the direction and can say when it is to be used), difficulty with planning, odd patterns of memory, difficulty with transitions from activity to activity and so on. The patterns are not the same patient to patient rather the numbers deficits is comparable. It is the myriad of difficulties large and small that sum to a common final pathway of poor adaptation to daily life. This diagnosis of brain damage by etiology (i.e. fetal alcohol) is different than most developmental conditions where the disorder is defined by a specific cluster of functional problems that are found, such as, dyslexia, nonverbal learning disorder or attention deficit and hyperactivity disorder. Even terms like cerebral palsy or autism are themselves defined by specific functional difficulties and not etiology.

A small percentage of patients who were exposed to alcohol have subtle but observable minor anomalies of the face. These include small palpebral fissures, a thin upper lip and a smooth philtral ridge (Clarren and Smith 1978). Other facials anomalies may be present as well but they are not the features that make the face look like "the face". When these three specific features are present they strongly suggest that alcohol will have been used in the pregnancy and that diffuse brain abnormalities will be detected when sought (Astley and Clarren 2001). Those individuals with these facial stigmata and with conclusive evidence of brain damage will receive a diagnosis of fetal alcohol syndrome (FAS). However the bulk of patients (perhaps 90%) with the same levels of brain damage from alcohol will have no conclusive facial changes and yet they can have the same severities and diversities of brain abnormalities as those with FAS. This is the group that now comprises the rest of the fetal alcohol spectrum disorder (FASD).

There are many entries on a differential diagnosis as for why a person might have poor global adaptive abilities. Explanations might include environmental depravations like abuse or neglect, poor education, significant sleep pattern disturbances or chronic health problems to name a few. There might be psychiatric conditions like chronic depression or psychosis. There could be intellectual handicap. There could be another birth defect syndrome altogether. Finally, there could be complex problems with brain processing that does not bring the intelligence quotient (IQ) down into the intellectually handicapped range, but none-the-less prevents the individual from performing appropriately. A person with FASD may have any and all of these reasons for their cognitive problems! The medical model does lend itself to sorting out the etiology of the maladaptation. This is important in predicting the outcome of the condition. IF the reasons for the adaptive difficulties are actually due to the external environment and learning, then an improved learning environment could lead to a reversal of all of the problems. IF the reasons are due to psychiatric conditions of mood (i.e. depression or anxiety) or mental tone (attention deficit) then a combination of pharmaceuticals and other psychiatric therapies may again lead to a reversal of problems. IF the problems stem from specific learning deficits, educational interventions might improve the circumstances. On the other hand, if the primary cause for the maladaptation is due to performance impaired by diffuse abnormal structure in the brain, then it is likely that while some improvements might be possible with intervention full or nearly full restoration to age appropriate function is not likely.

The tools that lead from the symptoms through to this differential diagnosis are found in a standard medical exam with attention to minor facial anomalies and the neurologic exam and then a complex evaluation of the brain that needs be done by the interdisciplinary team usually consisting of psychologists, speech pathologists, and occupational therapists. Ideally the diagnosis of diffuse brain damage would rest with imaging that would discern the structural problems. Unfortunately, animal studies in numerous species show that the structural damage from embryonic and fetal exposure to alcohol is most commonly microscopic and microcellular and, as such, is not seen on typical currently used clinical brain imaging like CT scans or MRI's. The damage is often found with imaging that is currently only investigatory like functional MRI or PET scans. As a result, the diagnostic team most often uses a broad battery of psychometric tests as proof of global brain dysfunction. These test serve the double function of demonstrating brain dysfunction and itemizing the patterns of strengths and deficit for intervention purposes. These tests are usually given in domains that include:

Domain category	Subdomains of functional assessment
Attention deficit/hyperactivity	Inattention, hyperactivity/impulsivity
Adaptive behaviour	Adaptive behaviour
Executive function/abstract reasoning	Inhibition, flexibility, working memory, planning/problem solving
Communication	Receptive, expressive, narrative, social communication, verbal problem solving
Academic achievement	Reading, writing, math
Memory	Overall, auditory, visual
Cognition	Overall, verbal, non-verbal

Beyond positive results in the tested categories above, the history, physical findings and laboratory tests should exclude other medical and psychiatric causes. With the positive findings coupled with the absence of evidence of alternative causes and a positive history of exposure to alcohol in pregnancy it is likely that the diagnosis is an FASD. Furthermore, the pattern of dysfunction can help to understand the specific reasons for the patient's difficulties and suggest specific interventions, managements or treatments that might improve function.

The positive results of the FASD evaluation place the patients in the following diagnostic categories. It is important to stress that the diagnostic terms that are used all suggest the *level of certainty* that the patients' brain problems relate to alcohol exposure rather than to degree of disability. This is another way that this scheme varies from many others in medicine.

Fetal Alcohol Syndrome (FAS) When the full facial phenotype is seen it is almost always the case that the brain will be found impaired and there a history of alcohol exposure was present BUT the term FAS is not applied until the brain dysfunction can be established not just assumed. Neither growth problems or other anomalies major or minor are needed for the FAS diagnosis, but these things are founds in a minority these patients. Alcohol is the assumed primary etiology of the malformations. FAS is the only FASD diagnosis that can be made without a confirmed history of alcohol exposure because the phenotype is sufficiently distinct that nothing else seems at all likely to have caused the condition.

Partial Fetal Alcohol Syndrome (pFAS) This term is used when a person has been established as exposed to alcohol in pregnancy and has most but not all of the facial features and possibly other anomalies as well. The range of distribution of brain dysfunctions and the variable severity of those deficits is the same as in FAS. Alcohol is somewhat less likely to be the primary etiology in pFAS as other syndrome can over lap (phenocopies) in appearance and these need to be carefully excluded.

Alcohol Related Neurodevelopmental Disorder (ARND) This term is used when a person has been established to have been exposed to alcohol in pregnancy and has one or none of the facial features but the same range of severity and distribution of brain dysfunctions. In the absence of other diagnoses that more likely explain the etiology, this term is applied. But the caution is clear in the term that alcohol exposure was only "related" to the adverse outcomes, but cannot be proven at this time to have been truly etiologic. This term has been favoured in the Canadian Guidelines for FASD diagnosis.

Static Encephalopathy: Alcohol Exposed (SE:AE) This term has been used to describe the same population as ARND but written in a way to emphasize that alcohol can not be generally proven to be the single etiology without the unique facial features. This term has been favoured in the Washington Guide to FASD Diagnosis, the 4 Digit code.

Neurobehavioral Disorder Associated with Prenatal Alcohol Exposure This term will be used in the DMS V in place of pFAS, ARND and SE:AE.

Prenatal Alcohol Exposed (PAE) A term that has been used in research and can be used clinically when a person has been placed "at risk" for an FASD through substantial alcohol exposure in pregnancy but is too young for testing of complex brain function, has not yet had testing, or has had border line abnormal testing and is to be recalled at a later date for more extensive evaluation.

Clinical experience in the United States and Canada would suggest that when 3 or more domains of brain function fall below the performance of 2 or 3% of the population, individuals experience profound difficulties with their day-to-day function regardless of the specific domains that are so impacted. The parts of the brain that are more normally functioning simply cannot compensate for those levels of dysfunction.

This testing process is of limited availability at this time within clinics that are specifically established for this purpose. In Canada less than 2000 diagnostic appointments are available each year in clinics specifically organized for this purpose. These appointments are only available in some provinces and often only available to children. Clearly more infrastructure is needed, but this will take time and individuals may not be able to wait.

This should not mean that the client involved in a legal matter couldn't have such evaluations conducted by appropriate professionals called together to serve as an ad hoc team for that person in a timely fashion.

At the end of the evaluation the two questions discussed initially will be addressed. Does this individual have structural or psychometric evidence of brain damage that explains to a greater extent the troubling maladaptive behaviours? And can a specific cause, like ethanol be posited as the etiology? The answer to the first question is based on positive information culled from the evaluations. The answer to the second is based on both positive and negative information. Ethanol exposure in pregnancy was definitely present or very likely AND no other explanation/etiology was identified that would by itself have caused the problems. Clearly the findings of brain damage and not the fact of ethanol exposure before birth should be the important fact before the court in a legal question of competence or capacity. The physical stigmata of the fetal alcohol syndrome and/or the history of significant alcohol exposure in pregnancy should trigger an evaluation for this elusive form of brain damage in the criminal courts. But it should be the conscientious findings of brain processing difficulties that the courts should understand in reaching their conclusions.

References

Astley, S.J., and S.K. Clarren. 1997. *Diagnostic guide for fetal alcohol syndrome and related conditions; the 4-digit diagnostic code*. Seattle: University of Washington Press.

———. 2001. Measuring the facial phenotype of individuals with prenatal alcohol exposure: Correlation with brain dysfunction. *Alcohol and Alcoholism* 36: 147–159.

Clarren, S.K., and D.W. Smith. 1978. The Fetal alcohol syndrome: A review of the world literature. *The New England Journal of Medicine* 198: 1063–1067.

Cook, J.L., C.R. Green, C.M. Lilley, S.M. Anderson, et al. 2015. Fetal alcohol spectrum disorder: A guideline for diagnosis across the lifespan. *Canadian Medical Association Journal* 188: 191–197. https://doi.org/10.1503/cmaj.141593.

Jones, K.L., D.W. Smith, C.N. Ulleland, and A.P. Streissguth. 1973. Patterns of malformation in offspring of chronic alcoholic mothers. *Lancet* 1: 1267–1271.

Lemoine, P., H. Harousseau, J.-P. Borteyru, et al. 1968. Les enfants de parents alcooliques: Anomalies observees. A propos de 127 cas [Children of alcoholic parents: Abnormalities observed in 127 cases]. *Ouest Medical* 21: 476–482.

Chapter 6
Imaging Brain Structure in FASD

Sarah Treit and Christian Beaulieu

Abstract Although FASD is characterized by physical, behavioral and cognitive deficits that provide compelling evidence of brain damage, routine clinical brain imaging (e.g. magnetic resonance imaging; MRI) often yields non-significant findings that add little insight into the diagnostic process. Nonetheless, research studies using advanced methods have identified numerous abnormalities of brain structure when comparing groups of individuals with FASD to groups of typically developing individuals, including brain volume reductions and abnormalities of cortical thickness and white matter microstructure. In addition, several studies have identified group-level associations between abnormal brain structure and cognitive performance, degree of prenatal alcohol exposure, or other key clinical metrics. This chapter summarizes some of these key findings, highlighting how MRI has advanced our understanding of FASD while also discussing its current limitations as a biomarker of prenatal alcohol exposure.

Keywords MRI · Brain structure · Brain development · Volume · Cortical thickness · Microstructure · Cognition

Preamble

The courts and the criminal justice system in Canada and the United States recognize that defendants need to have adequate degrees of competence and capacity to understand and participate effectively in their own defense. Moreover, their degree of moral and mental culpability must be considered in determining criminal responsibility and sentencing. This book, as a whole, argues that individuals who have been exposed to alcohol in utero may have brain damage that has the potential to impact their competence and capacity. Since the degree of brain damage observed in individuals with prenatal alcohol exposure varies widely from person to person, the simplest way to begin arguing that a person's capacity or culpability has been

S. Treit (✉) · C. Beaulieu
Department of Biomedical Engineering, Neuroscience and Mental Health Institute, University of Alberta, Edmonton, AB, Canada
e-mail: treit@ualberta.ca

E. Jonsson et al. (eds.), *Ethical and Legal Perspectives in Fetal Alcohol Spectrum Disorders (FASD)*, International Library of Ethics, Law, and the New Medicine 75,
https://doi.org/10.1007/978-3-319-71755-5_6

impacted by FASD-related brain damage is to find physical evidence, as is the goal of brain imaging (e.g. MRI). In some cases, imaging reveals lesions that provide objective, observable evidence of abnormal brain structure. However, as this chapter explains, visible "neuroanatomical lesions" associated with prenatal alcohol exposure are rare, and the majority of affected individuals have abnormalities that cannot be resolved with current imaging methods.

Nonetheless, the absence of evidence is not evidence of absence. In many of these cases, neuropsychometric testing confirms that current imaging methods underestimate the degree of brain damage suffered by these individuals. This chapter aims to improve understanding of the strengths and weakness of using brain imaging to identify brain abnormalities following fetal alcohol exposure.

The Editors

6.1 Introduction

One of the fundamental goals of magnetic resonance imaging (MRI) research is to establish 'imaging biomarkers'—distinct and consistent sets of findings that would indicate with a high degree of certainty that an individual has (or doesn't have) a given neurological/psychiatric disorder or disease. In the context of fetal alcohol spectrum disorders (FASD), an imaging biomarker would aid in early screening and diagnosis of the disorder, and may also provide an objective means of predicting and tracking remediation success in affected individuals. In the context of the criminal justice system, an imaging biomarker for FASD could help to confirm if an offender has the disorder, or may help guide sentencing and remediation to reduce recidivism. However, as discussed throughout this book, FASD represents a complex spectrum of cognitive and behavioural symptoms, and likewise, neurological impairments and imaging findings vary greatly between individuals, impeding the establishment of a consistent imaging biomarker for prenatal alcohol exposure.

Nonetheless, MRI has greatly advanced our understanding of brain damage in FASD by uncovering differences in brain structure and development in groups of affected individuals compared to healthy, typically developing individuals. To provide some background, this chapter starts with a brief introduction to the effects of alcohol on the brain and the contributions that autopsy and qualitative imaging studies have made to our understanding of FASD. Key examples from over 20 years of neuroimaging research are provided to summarize the major findings of quantitative structural MRI of the brain in FASD; however, this should not be considered a comprehensive review of the extensive literature on this topic. Importantly, the limitations of this body of work are discussed, as well as the future directions needed for MRI to be used diagnostically for "imaging" FASD.

6.2 Alcohol and the Developing Brain: Autopsy and Qualitative Brain Imaging

When consumed by a pregnant woman, alcohol directly crosses the placental barrier, enters the fetal bloodstream, and impairs brain development by inducing cell death, reducing oxygen availability, and altering the course of dividing and migrating brain cells, among other mechanisms (for review, see Goodlett et al. 2005). The wide spectrum of behavioural and cognitive outcomes observed in an individual who was prenatally exposed to alcohol depends on characteristics of alcohol exposure itself, such as timing (when during pregnancy), frequency (how often) and quantity (how much), but is also mediated by a host of other prenatal factors including maternal nutrition, stress, and genetics (Guerri et al. 2009). Indeed, animal models have demonstrated different degrees of brain damage (i.e. varying susceptibility) among different genetic strains of mice, even with exposure to identical amounts and patterns of alcohol in utero (Chen et al. 2011), suggesting a key role of environment. In humans, this variability challenges efforts to identify a specific set of alcohol-related brain abnormalities, despite growing evidence of alcohol's potent teratogenic effect.

The effects of prenatal alcohol exposure on human brain structure were first described in autopsy studies, such as the famous example shown in Fig. 6.1 which compares a 6 week old who had fetal alcohol syndrome (FAS) with a previously healthy 6 week old (Clarren et al. 1978). It does not take an expert to conclude that

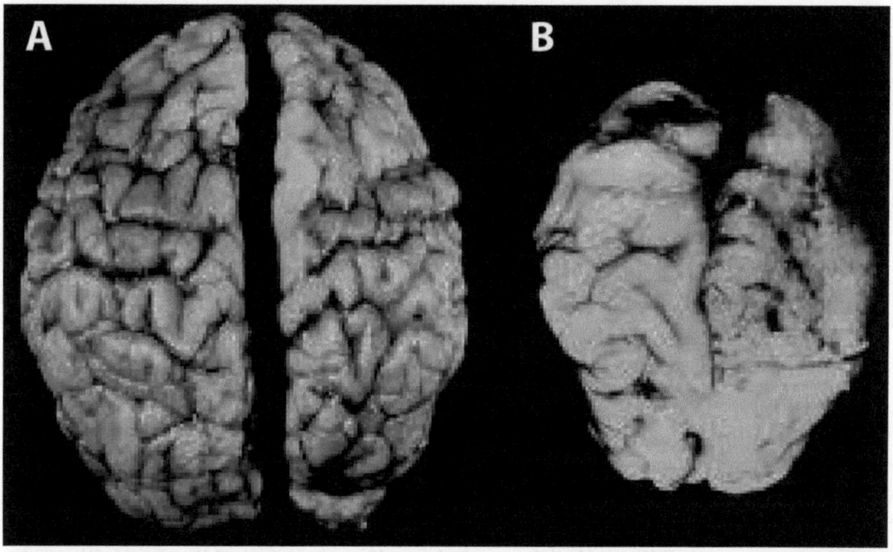

Fig. 6.1 An autopsy study showing the brains of (**a**) a 6 week old previously 'healthy' baby and (**b**) a 6 week old baby that had FAS. The brain of the child with FAS is clearly much smaller, and dissection revealed numerous structural anomalies including a missing corpus callosum and excess fluid. Although this provides a striking example, brain abnormalities associated with FASD are rarely this extreme (Image courtesy of Sterling Clarren)

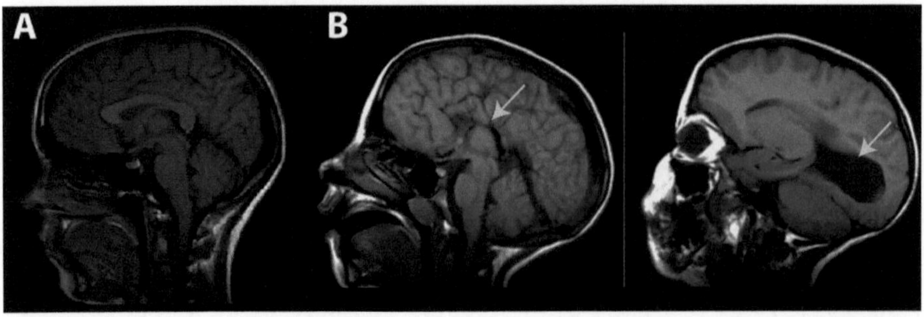

Fig. 6.2 MRI scans showing (**a**) one slice of a healthy brain and (**b**) two slices of the brain of a 9 year old girl with FAS. The girl with FAS is completely missing a corpus callosum and had markedly excess fluid in her brain, resulting from improper division of the two halves of the brain in utero. Although there are several MRI case studies that document severe abnormalities (particularly of the corpus callosum), most children with FASD have brains that are deemed 'normal' on regular MRI (Adapted from Riley et al. (1995), reprinted with permission from John Wiley and Sons)

the alcohol exposed brain is severely damaged; autopsy revealed severe microencephaly (small brain), multiple clusters of brain tissue in abnormal locations (i.e. grey matter clusters in white matter), excess fluid in the brain, and absence of the corpus callosum (the largest white matter tract in the brain that connects the two hemispheres) (Fig. 6.1a). Although these types of studies provide a wealth of detailed macroscopic (visible) and microscopic (cellular) information about the teratogenic effects of alcohol, they also represent only the most severely affected individuals who die in infancy or childhood and do not generalize well to the rest of the much larger population of individuals with FASD.

Insights into the potential effects of prenatal alcohol exposure on the living brain were then afforded by clinical MRI case studies (e.g. Swayze et al. 1997; Riikonen et al. 1999; Reinhardt et al. 2010) such as the example shown in Fig. 6.2 of a 9 year old female with FAS who is entirely missing her corpus callosum and has holoprosencephaly, a birth defect in which the forebrain fails to properly divide into the two hemispheres (Riley et al. 1995). However, even severe abnormalities such as a missing corpus callosum are not specific to prenatal alcohol exposure and can be associated with other conditions such as genetic disorders and prenatal infections (Chouchane et al. 1999), limiting their use diagnostically. Furthermore, although these examples are striking, visible abnormalities are *not* the norm in FASD. Rather, clinical imaging typically yields insignificant or non-specific findings, and is therefore not typically used in the diagnostic process. Figure 6.3 illustrates this point with an example of two fifteen year old boys (a healthy control and a participant with FASD), both of whom have grossly normal-appearing brains, but who are functioning at very different levels, e.g. with a 49-point gap in IQ scores. Given the severity of cognitive and behavioural deficits observed in these individuals, we can assume that conventional brain imaging (that only identifies gross anomalies and lesions) must be underestimating the degree of brain damage in alcohol exposed individuals, highlighting the need for advanced, and importantly, quantitative methods that can identify brain anomalies that are invisible to the naked eye.

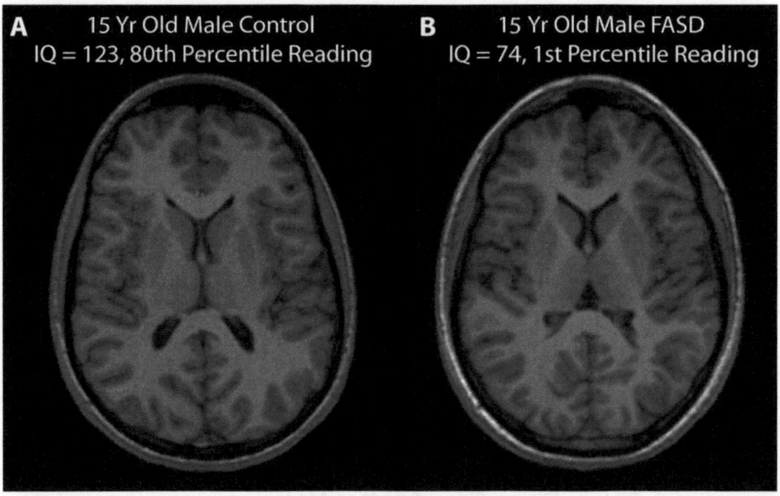

Fig. 6.3 Case example that demonstrates the lack of obvious differences in brain structure between (**a**) a healthy child and (**b**) a child with FASD, both male and of the same age. Both children have normal-appearing brains with no visible lesions or anomalies, yet the child with FASD is functioning at a much lower level

6.3 Advanced Quantitative Structural Brain Imaging

Advanced structural imaging typically relies on quantitative measurements (e.g. calculating the size of a structure) that are compared statistically between groups of subjects, rather than qualitative examination of images from a single individual to look for 'lesions' or gross visible abnormalities. These types of "number generating" methods are particularly valuable in disorders such as FASD where visible abnormalities are not present. For the sake of brevity, this chapter focuses on quantitative *structural* MRI variables that measure 'static' properties of the brain and excludes *functional* MRI (which measures 'brain activation' associated with performing a specific task in the MRI), though a great deal of research in this area also shows impairments in FASD (for review, see Coles and Li 2011).

6.4 Group-Level Differences in Brain Structure Are Widespread

Given that microcephaly (small head) is a hallmark feature used in diagnosis of FASD, it is not surprising that the vast majority of studies show that brain volumes that are ~10% smaller in FASD than healthy control groups (e.g. Astley et al. 2009). This finding holds in studies where the majority of participants do not have facial dysmorphology or growth delays (e.g. Lebel et al. 2008a), suggesting that alcohol has a disproportionate effect on the nervous system. In addition to global reductions

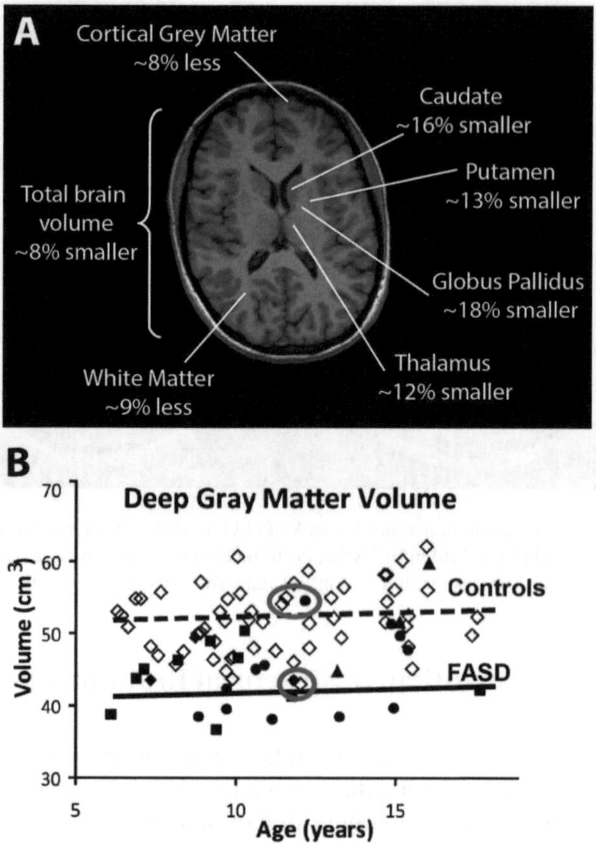

Fig. 6.4 (**a**) Examples of structures that were significantly smaller in participants with FASD than Controls in Nardelli et al. 2011. Panel (**b**) shows deep grey matter volume in controls (open diamonds) and FASD subjects (black filled circles, triangles and squares) at different ages. Despite the distinct group difference (the mean of the control group, dotted line is higher than the mean of the FASD group, solid line), substantial overlap between the two groups precludes differentiation of diagnostic groups at a single subject level. The red circles include examples of FASD and control subjects that can't be differentiated based on absolute deep grey matter volume, even at the mean values for each group (Adapted from Nardelli et al. (2011), reprinted with permission from John Wiley and Sons)

of total brain volume, reductions of white and grey matter, cerebellar, and subcortical volumes are also commonly reported in children, and persist in adult samples (for review, see Lebel et al. 2011; Nunez et al. 2011; Fig. 6.4). Some studies report disproportionate reductions (that remain significant after controlling for total brain volume) in certain regions, including the frontal lobes and caudate nucleus (Archibald et al. 2001; Cortese et al. 2006; Astley et al. 2009; Nardelli et al. 2011); areas that are associated with learning and executive functions commonly impaired in FASD (Rasmussen 2005). Beyond size, studies have also revealed that alcohol exposed individuals have greater variability in the shape and/or relative location of various structures in the brain including the corpus callosum, frontal lobes and cerebellum (Bookstein et al. 2001; Sowell et al. 2001; Sowell et al. 2002; O'Hare et al. 2005), suggesting that global aspects of the structural organization of the brain are impaired in individuals with prenatal alcohol exposure.

In addition to global measures, abnormalities are also observed with finer scale measurements aimed at probing the outer grey matter cortex of the brain. This outer layer of grey matter contains the neuronal cell bodies responsible for sending neural 'electrical' impulses needed for brain function, and is folded into ridges (gyri) and grooves (sulci) to increase surface area, giving the brain its wrinkled appearance. Studies of cortical thickness (which measures the thickness of the cortex along ~80,000 points on the brain's surface) in humans with FASD have yielded conflicting results (Sowell et al. 2008b; Fernandez-Jaen et al. 2011; Yang et al. 2011; Zhou et al. 2011; Rajaprakash et al. 2014), while surface area cortical folding complexity appear to be reduced and the space between cortical folds appears to be increased in participants who were prenatally exposed to alcohol (De Guio et al. 2014; Rajaprakash et al. 2014), suggesting disorganization of this important neuronal layer.

White matter forms connections both within and between the hemispheres of the brain, and is essential for integration of information and higher-order processing. Diffusion tensor imaging (DTI) is an MRI method that enables the reconstruction of various individual white matter tracts, providing quantitative metrics thought to reflect properties of white matter microstructure such as myelination and axonal integrity. DTI studies of FASD suggest that white matter abnormalities in FASD are widespread (e.g. Fig. 6.5), affecting connections between and within the two hemispheres of the brain, between the brain and spinal cord, and across all lobes of the brain (Ma et al. 2005; Lebel et al. 2008a; Sowell et al. 2008a; Fryer et al. 2009; Li et al. 2009; Wozniak et al. 2009; Spottiswoode et al. 2011; Treit et al. 2017). However, findings have not been consistent between studies, suggesting that the relative damage to each tract depends on factors such as timing of exposure and postnatal developmental factors.

6.5 Individuals with FASD Undergo Altered Trajectories of Brain Development During Childhood and Adolescence

The brain undergoes remarkable change across the lifespan, marked by both developmental and degenerative changes that vary regionally throughout the brain. Although total brain volume reaches 95% of its maximum by about age 6 years of age, white matter volume increases and grey matter volume decreases well into adulthood (Giedd et al. 1999). These changes are primarily driven by the myelination of axons and pruning of over-produced connections between neurons, aimed at refining neural networks and maximizing the speed and efficiency of neural impulses.

White matter microstructure undergoes the greatest maturational change early in childhood, continuing at slower rates and then leveling off during adolescence and

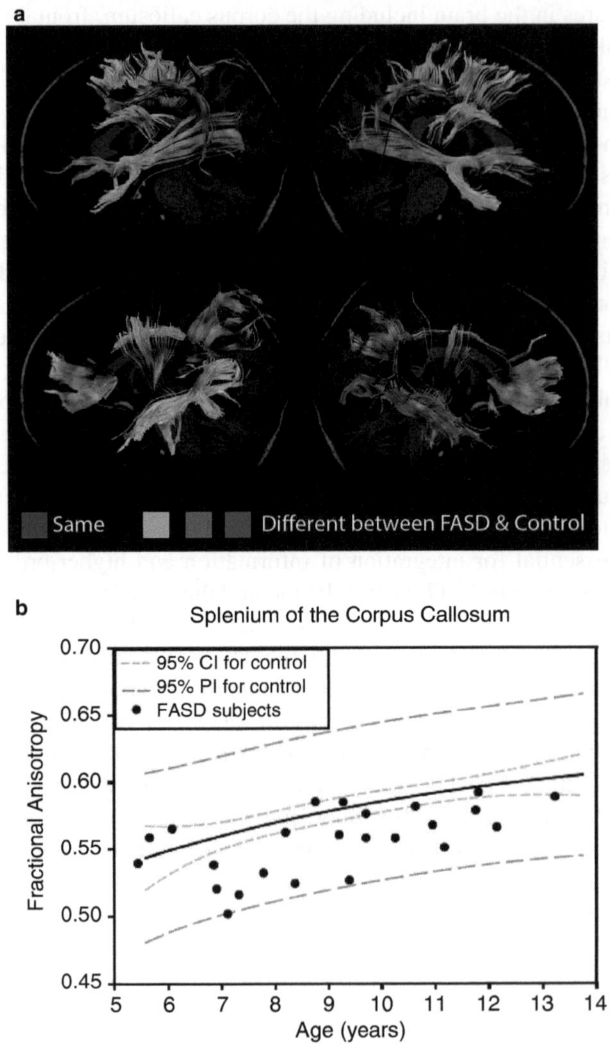

Fig. 6.5 (**a**) White matter tracts shown in red, blue and yellow differed on at least one diffusion tensor MRI metric in children with FASD (ages 5–13 years) compared to healthy controls. This finding provides an example of the widespread differences in white matter integrity found in participants with FASD, including several tracts that are affected on both sides of the brain. (**b**) However, the raw data points of FASD subject DTI metrics (black dots) for one tract (the splenium of the corpus callosum), plotted against the control mean (solid line) have values that fall under the control mean, but within the 95% prediction interval (the values between which 95% of healthy subjects would fall). Given the overlap with control values, this illustrates that these metrics can't alone be used to differentiate individual subjects with FASD (Adapted from Lebel et al. (2008a), reprinted with permission from John Wiley and Sons)

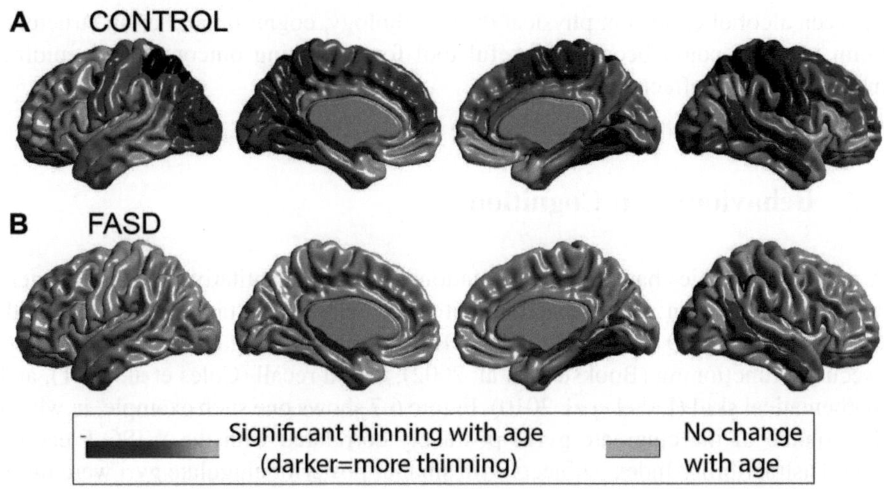

Fig. 6.6 Longitudinal cortical thinning maps in (**a**) controls and (**b**) FASD scanned twice several years apart during childhood and adolescence. Cortical thickness was found to decrease with age in controls across almost the entire cortical mantle (**a**), in keeping with previous literature. Conversely, the FASD group underwent cortical thinning in only few scattered regions (**b**) with most areas showing no change (grey). These findings suggest that cortex development follows an altered trajectory with age during childhood in FASD (Adapted from Treit et al. (2014), reprinted with permission from John Wiley and Sons)

adulthood (Lebel et al. 2008b; Lebel and Beaulieu 2011). Interestingly, longitudinal imaging has shown that white matter parameters changed *more* over several years between brain DTI scans in children and adolescents with FASD than in age-matched controls, which may suggest a form of 'catching up' to compensate for delayed development earlier in childhood (Treit et al. 2013).

Longitudinal studies measuring cortical grey matter have shown less developmental change in both volume (Lebel et al. 2012) and cortical thickness (Treit et al. 2014; Fig. 6.6) in children and adolesents with prenatal alcohol exposure relative to healthy controls, which may reflect reduced pruning of excess cortical connections than is typically expected during the adolescent period.

Collectively, longitudinal imaging of FASD suggests that prenatal alcohol exposure affect downstream developmental mechanisms years beyond when the injury was initiated in utero. However, translation of this to clinical imaging may be impractical as it requires tracking subtle changes over several years.

6.6 Links Between Brain Structure and Clinical Variables

Identifying structural brain damage in subjects with FASD is an important step towards better understanding the effects of prenatal alcohol exposure on the brain, but it is also essential to establish how these findings relate to the variability in clinical presentation observed in FASD. With a better understanding of the relationship between alcohol exposure, physical dysmorphology, cognition and brain structure, brain imaging could become a useful tool for predicting outcomes and guiding interventions for affected individuals.

6.7 Behaviour and Cognition

A number of studies have found correlations between quantitative MRI parameters and performance on standardized cognitive or behavioural tasks in subjects with FASD, including IQ (Roussotte et al. 2011), verbal learning (Sowell et al. 2001), executive functioning (Bookstein et al. 2002), verbal recall (Coles et al. 2011), and mathematical skill (Lebel et al. 2010). Figure 6.7 shows one such example, in which the volume of the cingulate gyrus positively correlated with the WISC Freedom from Distractibility Index; subjects with smaller posterior cingulate gyri were more distractible (Bjorkquist et al. 2010). Although this is a significant correlation, this relationships is not strong enough to make predictions at a single subject level (i.e. measuring the size of an individual person's cingulate gyrus would not reliably reveal their level of distractibility). In addition, many studies have found no significant correlations between brain structure and cognitive performance (e.g. Autti-Ramo et al. 2002; Nardelli et al. 2011), again highlighting the complex relationship between brain structure and function/behaviour.

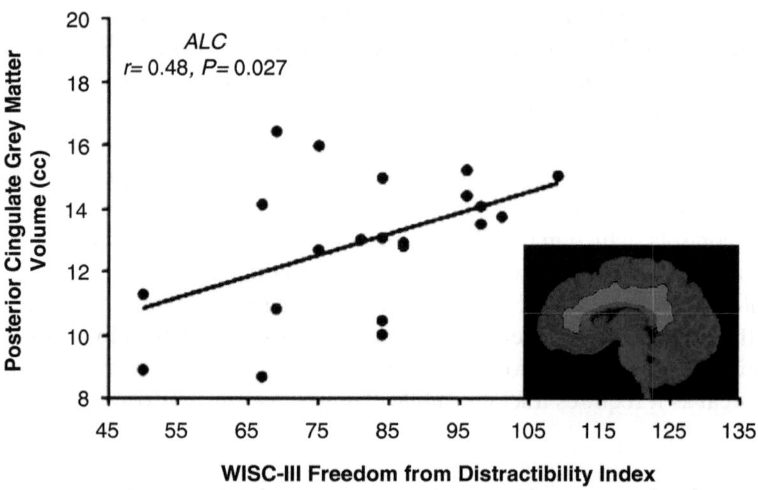

Fig. 6.7 An example of a brain-behaviour correlation demonstrated with MRI, showing a positive correlation between cingulate gyrus volume (shown in orange in the inset picture) and performance on the Freedom from Distractibility Index in children with FASD. As a group, those who had smaller posterior cingulate gyrus volumes were also more distractible. Note, however, the significant scatter in these data (Adapted from Bjorkquist et al. (2010), reprinted with permission from Elsevier)

6.8 Facial Dysmorphology

Animal models have determined that alcohol-related abnormalities in facial structure results from alcohol exposure in the 3rd and 4th weeks of pregnancy in humans, during which precursor cells migrate and divide to form the midline facial features as well as the forebrain (Sulik 2005). The timeline and overlapping lineage of the development of the face and brain has led to interest in associating facial dysmorphology with brain structure in prenatal alcohol-exposed participants. In a study of 65 subjects, Astley et al. (2009) found that brain volume was progressively reduced in participants with FASD who had facial abnormalities, relative to participants with FASD but without facial abnormalities, and finally controls. Other studies have shown more specific relationships, such as correlations between deep grey matter structure (Roussotte et al. 2011) or cortical volumes (Yang et al. 2011) with lipometer score (upper lip and philtrum) and palpebral fissure length (width of the eye opening). Moreover, Lebel et al. (2012) found that children who underwent the least cortical volume development with age also had the highest lipometer scores (Lebel et al. 2012), suggesting that links between the face and brain development may be relevant beyond the initial in utero period. Correlations between facial dysmorphology and brain structure are therefore of scientific interest, as they provide clues about development. However, facial dysmorphology is only evident in ~10% of individuals with FASD (May et al. 2009), limiting the clinical utility of these relationships.

6.9 Alcohol Exposure Patterns

There is significant scientific and public interest in associating the degree of structural and functional abnormalities in the brain with the amount of alcohol exposure in utero. However, like all outcomes in FASD, this relationship is not straightforward, despite animal model evidence of robust teratogenic effects (e.g. cell death) in the brain even from a single binge exposure to alcohol (Farber et al. 2010; Idrus and Napper 2012). Nonetheless, some correlations have been established in human imaging studies. For example, Astley et al. (2009) found that greater frequency of exposures (average number of drinking days per week) correlated with smaller hippocampal and mid-sagittal volume, and shorter corpus callosum length. Likewise, this same study found that greater maximal number of drinks per occasion correlated with smaller frontal lobe, caudate and hippocampus volume among adolescents with FASD. Dose-dependent reductions of grey matter volume of the cingulate gyrus, bilateral middle frontal gyri, middle temporal gyrus and caudate have also been shown in adults who were prenatally exposed to low-moderate amounts of alcohol (Eckstrand et al. 2012). In addition, a longitudinal study found that less cortical development with age during adolescence correlated with a greater number of drinks per week during pregnancy (Lebel et al. 2012).

The brain is vulnerable to damage from alcohol exposure throughout all stages and trimesters of pregnancy, though animal models have still demonstrated varying types of cellular damage from exposure at different developmental stages (West and Goodlett 1990). These relationships remain less clear in humans; however, a few studies have demonstrated time dependencies, e.g. greater relative reductions of frontal lobe volume from alcohol exposure in all 3 trimesters relative to 1st and 2nd, or 1st trimester only (Astley et al. 2009), though it is worth noting that this finding may also be confounded by total cumulative exposure.

Although informative, inconsistencies in these findings have challenged efforts to find a consistent set of brain abnormalities associated with a given amount and timing of alcohol exposure in utero. It is often very difficult to obtain accurate and detailed accounts of alcohol exposure history, particularly given that many FASD participants live in foster or adoptive families and are diagnosed and recruited into research studies many years after birth. Prospective research studies in humans (which recruit women during pregnancy) are a key step toward collecting detailed and accurate exposure histories, as well as other valuable information about socio-economic factors and environmental variables that may impact later developmental outcomes (Jacobson and Jacobson 1996).

6.10 Limitations of Imaging in FASD

MRI studies of FASD have significant limitations that must be considered before drawing conclusions from this body of work, although it is important to keep in mind that each study discussed has additional study-specific limitations.

The first major limitation of MRI research is that outcome parameters are indirect measures of tissue properties, and numerous cellular processes may contribute to each metric, making it challenging to determine the biological mechanism driving a given finding. Even advanced MRI methods provide relatively gross measures of brain structure: 1 mm^3 (a typical MRI resolution) of human frontal cortex contains roughly 20,000 brain cells and roughly one hundred thousand-fold more connections between these brain cells (Huttenlocher, 1979). As such, even for robust effects such as cell death, there is a fairly high minimum threshold to exceed before a change is observable on MRI (even with quantitative methods).

A second limitation is that there are many different ways to acquire and analyze the same type of MRI scan, so results partially depend on the type of MRI scanner used (field strength, vendor), software packages, statistical thresholds, and even the researcher performing the analysis. All of these factors greatly complicate comparisons between studies and limit their widespread clinical utility.

A third limitation is that MRI studies in humans are also almost exclusively observational (rather than experimental), meaning that extraneous variables such as education and nutrition cannot be fully controlled for. Adverse life experiences (such as child abuse and neglect and multiple home placements) are common in individuals with FASD (Streissguth et al. 2004). Some of these may compound defi-

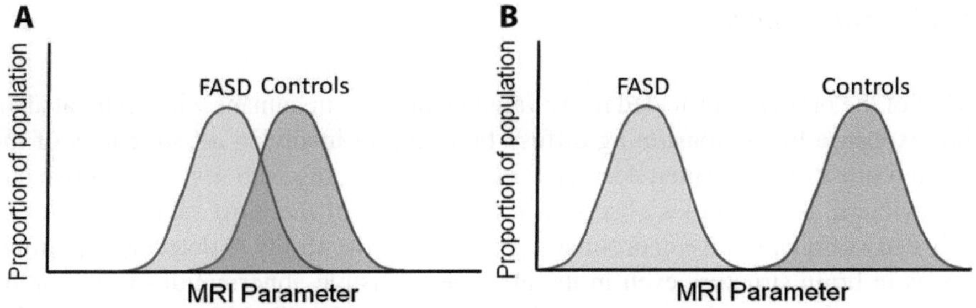

Fig. 6.8 (**a**) It is possible to detect a "statistical" group difference between FASD and Controls for many MRI parameters despite substantial overlap between these curves; however, this overlap precludes diagnostic certainty of a given MRI parameter within an individual. (**b**) In an ideal scenario, the value of a given parameter would be characteristic of, and specific to, the entire population of a given group (FASD versus Control with no overlap of the MRI parameter value) and could then be used to differentiate single subjects with a high degree of certainty. Unfortunately, this latter case is rarely found in quantitative MRI studies of the brain in FASD

cits from alcohol exposure and may even alter brain development through independent mechanisms (McCrory et al. 2010). Where possible, these details are documented for each subject and then controlled for statistically; however, in many cases accurate data from pregnancy and early childhood is difficult to collect in alcohol-exposed subjects, many of whom are not raised by their biological parents. Thus, linking prenatal alcohol-exposure directly with abnormal development during childhood is extremely challenging in humans. Even when brain structure is found to relate to cognition, which increases our confidence that a given finding has functional relevance, it is essential to keep in mind that correlation does not equal causation. In the example provided in Fig. 6.7, one cannot determine if reduced volume of the cingulate gyrus is the cause of attention problems in these individuals, if attention problems led to abnormal development of the cingulate gyrus, or if a 3rd extraneous variable influences both attention and cingulate gyrus volume coincidentally. Thus, correlations between performance and brain structure are intriguing, but often lead to the 'chicken or egg' conundrum.

A fourth and important limitation of this work is that many MRI findings discussed here are not specific to FASD. When taken together with clinical measures and known exposure, it can be reasonably concluded that certain abnormalities (e.g. missing corpus callosum) most likely stem from alcohol exposure, but other genetic and environmental conditions may lead to this same brain structure abnormality.

Lastly, at this point MRI is not a stand-alone indicator of prenatal alcohol exposure, even in extreme cases. As evident in Fig. 6.4, even when advanced imaging identifies group level differences, substantial overlap between FASD and control participants precludes the use of these measures to identify FASD in any given individual. Combining measures (e.g. brain volume + cortical thickness + white matter integrity) may help lead to a more specific indicator linked to prenatal alcohol exposure and thus enable these parameters to be clinically useful at a single-subject level (Fig. 6.8).

6.11 Summary

MRI of the brain has provided many valuable insights in humans with prenatal alcohol exposure by demonstrating diffuse brain injury involving all structures of the brain (cortex, white matter, deep grey matter), in keeping with severe cognitive and behavioural abnormalities observed in FASD. One of the most salient features of this body of quantitative neuroimaging research is the ability to detect group differences in brain structure even in the absence of visible abnormalities in the brain. Given that these metrics are not used in diagnosis of FASD, MRI research has also provided objective, independent evidence associating prenatal alcohol exposure with brain damage in humans. Moreover, longitudinal work (scanning the same individuals as they age) has demonstrated abnormal brain development that continues many years beyond the initial in utero insult, which may underlie worsening behavioural deficits during the key developmental periods of childhood and adolescence. Future work should strive to apply these imaging methods to capture changes in the brain before and after behavioural remediation programs for FASD. Novel imaging methods that measure other aspects of brain structure, metabolism and function also hold promise for detecting and understanding alterations in the brain of those with FASD.

Acknowledgments Salary support was provided by Alberta-Innovates Health Solutions (AIHS; ST & CB) and the Women's and Children's Health Research Institute (WCHRI; ST). CIHR, CLLRNet, WCHRI, and NeuroDevNet provided research funding for our past MRI studies of FASD. We also thank Drs Sterling Clarren, Edward Riley, Catherine Lebel and Susanna Fryer for permission to adapt some of their figures.

References

Archibald, S.L., C. Fennema-Notestine, A. Gamst, E.P. Riley, S.N. Mattson, and T.L. Jernigan. 2001. Brain dysmorphology in individuals with severe prenatal alcohol exposure. *Developmental Medicine and Child Neurology* 43: 148–154.

Astley, S.J., E.H. Aylward, H.C. Olson, K. Kerns, A. Brooks, T.E. Coggins, J. Davies, S. Dorn, B. Gendler, T. Jirikowic, P. Kraegel, K. Maravilla, and T. Richards. 2009. Magnetic resonance imaging outcomes from a comprehensive magnetic resonance study of children with fetal alcohol spectrum disorders. *Alcoholism* 33: 1671–1689.

Autti-Ramo, I., T. Autti, M. Korkman, S. Kettunen, O. Salonen, and L. Valanne. 2002. MRI findings in children with school problems who had been exposed prenatally to alcohol. *Developmental Medicine and Child Neurology* 44: 98–106.

Bjorkquist, O.A., S.L. Fryer, A.L. Reiss, S.N. Mattson, and E.P. Riley. 2010. Cingulate gyrus morphology in children and adolescents with fetal alcohol spectrum disorders. *Psychiatry Research-Neuroimaging* 181: 101–107.

Bookstein, F.L., P.D. Sampson, A.P. Streissguth, and P.D. Connor. 2001. Geometric morphometrics of corpus callosum and subcortical structures in the fetal-alcohol-affected brain. *Teratology* 64: 4–32.

Bookstein, F.L., A.P. Streissguth, P.D. Sampson, P.D. Connor, and H.M. Barr. 2002. Corpus callosum shape and neuropsychological deficits in adult males with heavy fetal alcohol exposure. *NeuroImage* 15: 233–251.

Chen, Y.Y., N.C. Ozturk, L.J. Ni, C. Goodlett, and F.C. Zhou. 2011. Strain differences in developmental vulnerability to alcohol exposure via embryo culture in mice. *Alcoholism* 35: 1293–1304.

Chouchane, M., V. Benouachkou-Debuche, M. Giroud, C. Durand, and J.B. Gouyon. 1999. Agenesis of the corpus callosum: Etiology, clinical features, diagnostic methods and prognosis. *Archives de Pédiatrie* 6: 1306–1311.

Clarren, S.K., E.C. Alvord, S.M. Sumi, A.P. Streissguth, and D.W. Smith. 1978. Brain malformations related to prenatal exposure to ethanol. *Journal of Pediatrics* 92: 64–67.

Coles, C.D., and Z. Li. 2011. Functional neuroimaging in the examination of effects of prenatal alcohol exposure. *Neuropsychology Review* 21: 119–132.

Coles, C.D., F.C. Goldstein, M.E. Lynch, X. Chen, J.A. Kable, K.C. Johnson, and X. Hu. 2011. Memory and brain volume in adults prenatally exposed to alcohol. *Brain and Cognition* 75: 67–77.

Cortese, B.M., G.J. Moore, B.A. Bailey, S.W. Jacobson, V. Delaney-Black, and J.H. Hannigan. 2006. Magnetic resonance and spectroscopic imaging in prenatal alcohol-exposed children: Preliminary findings in the caudate nucleus. *Neurotoxicology and Teratology* 28: 597–606.

De Guio, F., J.-F. Mangin, D. Riviere, M. Perrot, C.D. Molteno, S.W. Jacobson, E.M. Meintjes, and J.L. Jacobson. 2014. A study of cortical morphology in children with fetal alcohol spectrum disorders. *Human Brain Mapping* 35: 2285–2296.

Eckstrand, K.L., Z.H. Ding, N.C. Dodge, R.L. Cowan, J.L. Jacobson, S.W. Jacobson, and M.J. Avison. 2012. Persistent dose-dependent changes in brain structure in young adults with low-to-moderate alcohol exposure in utero. *Alcoholism: Clinical and Experimental Research* 36: 1892–1902.

Farber, N.B., C.E. Creeley, and J.W. Olney. 2010. Alcohol-induced neuroapoptosis in the fetal macaque brain. *Neurobiology of Disease* 40: 200–206.

Fernandez-Jaen, A., D.M. Fernandez-Mayoralas, D. Quinones Tapia, B. Calleja-Perez, J.M. Garcia-Segura, S.L. Arribas, and N. Munoz Jareno. 2011. Cortical thickness in fetal alcohol syndrome and attention deficit disorder. *Pediatric Neurology* 45: 387–391.

Fryer, S.L., B.C. Schweinsburg, O.A. Bjorkquist, L.R. Frank, S.N. Mattson, A.D. Spadoni, and E.P. Riley. 2009. Characterization of white matter microstructure in fetal alcohol spectrum disorders. *Alcoholism* 33: 514–521.

Giedd, J.N., J. Blumenthal, N.O. Jeffries, F.X. Castellanos, H. Liu, A. Zijdenbos, T. Paus, A.C. Evans, and J.L. Rapoport. 1999. Brain development during childhood and adolescence: A longitudinal MRI study. *Nature Neuroscience* 2: 861–863.

Goodlett, C.R., K.H. Horn, and F.C. Zhou. 2005. Alcohol teratogenesis: Mechanisms of damage and strategies for intervention. *Experimental Biology and Medicine* 230: 394–406.

Guerri, C., A. Bazinet, and E.P. Riley. 2009. Foetal alcohol spectrum disorders and alterations in brain and behaviour. *Alcohol and Alcoholism* 44: 108–114.

Huttenlocher, P.R. 1979. Synaptic density in human frontal-cortex – Developmental-changes and effects of aging. *Brain Research* 163: 195–205.

Idrus, N.M., and R.M. Napper. 2012. Acute and long-term Purkinje cell loss following a single ethanol binge during the early third trimester equivalent in the rat. *Alcoholism, Clinical and Experimental Research* 36: 1365–1373.

Jacobson, J.L., and S.W. Jacobson. 1996. Prospective, longitudinal assessment of developmental neurotoxicity. *Environmental Health Perspectives* 104 (Suppl 2): 275–283.

Lebel, C., and C. Beaulieu. 2011. Longitudinal development of human brain wiring continues from childhood into adulthood. *Journal of Neuroscience* 31: 10937–10947.

Lebel, C., C. Rasmussen, K. Wyper, L. Walker, G. Andrew, J. Yager, and C. Beaulieu. 2008a. Brain diffusion abnormalities in children with fetal alcohol spectrum disorder. *Alcoholism: Clinical and Experimental Research* 32: 1732–1740.

Lebel, C., L. Walker, A. Leemans, L. Phillips, and C. Beaulieu. 2008b. Microstructural maturation of the human brain from childhood to adulthood. *NeuroImage* 40: 1044–1055.
Lebel, C., C. Rasmussen, K. Wyper, G. Andrew, and C. Beaulieu. 2010. Brain microstructure is related to math ability in children with fetal alcohol spectrum disorder. *Alcoholism* 34: 354–363.
Lebel, C., F. Roussotte, and E.R. Sowell. 2011. Imaging the impact of prenatal alcohol exposure on the structure of the developing human brain. *Neuropsychology Review* 21: 102–118.
Lebel, C., S.N. Mattson, E.P. Riley, K.L. Jones, C.M. Adnams, P.A. May, S.Y. Bookheimer, M.J. O'Connor, K.L. Narr, E. Kan, Z. Abaryan, and E.R. Sowell. 2012. A longitudinal study of the long-term consequences of drinking during pregnancy: Heavy in utero alcohol exposure disrupts the normal processes of brain development. *Journal of Neuroscience* 32: 15243–15251.
Li, L.C., C.D. Coles, M.E. Lynch, and Hu XP. 2009. Voxelwise and skeleton-based region of interest analysis of fetal alcohol syndrome and fetal alcohol spectrum disorders in young adults. *Human Brain Mapping* 30: 3265–3274.
Ma, X.Y., C.D. Coles, M.E. Lynch, S.M. LaConte, O. Zurkiya, D.L. Wang, and Hu XP. 2005. Evaluation of corpus callosum anisotropy in young adults with fetal alcohol syndrome according to diffusion tensor imaging. *Alcoholism* 29: 1214–1222.
May, P.A., J.P. Gossage, W.O. Kalberg, L.K. Robinson, D. Buckley, M. Manning, and H.E. Hoyme. 2009. Prevalence and epidemiologic characteristics of FASD from various research methods with an emphasis on recent in-school studies. *Developmental Disabilities Research Reviews* 15: 176–192.
McCrory, E., S.A. De Brito, and E. Viding. 2010. Research review: The neurobiology and genetics of maltreatment and adversity. *Journal of Child Psychology and Psychiatry* 51: 1079–1095.
Nardelli, A., C. Lebel, C. Rasmussen, G. Andrew, and C. Beaulieu. 2011. Extensive deep gray matter volume reductions in children and adolescents with fetal alcohol spectrum disorders. *Alcoholism: Clinical and Experimental Research* 35: 1404–1417.
Nunez, S.C., F. Roussotte, and E.R. Sowell. 2011. Focus on: Structural and functional brain abnormalities in fetal alcohol spectrum disorders. *Alcohol Research & Health* 34: 121–131.
O'Hare, E.D., E. Kan, J. Yoshii, S.N. Mattson, E.P. Riley, P.M. Thompson, A.W. Toga, and E.R. Sowell. 2005. Mapping cerebellar vermal morphology and cognitive correlates in prenatal alcohol exposure. *Neuroreport* 16: 1285–1290.
Rajaprakash, M., M.M. Chakravarty, J.P. Lerch, and J. Rovet. 2014. Cortical morphology in children with alcohol-related neurodevelopmental disorder. *Brain and Behavior* 4: 41–50.
Rasmussen, C. 2005. Executive functioning and working memory in fetal alcohol spectrum disorder. *Alcoholism* 29: 1359–1367.
Reinhardt, K., A. Mohr, J. Gartner, H.L. Spohr, and K. Brockmann. 2010. Polymicrogyria in fetal alcohol syndrome. *Birth Defects Research Part A: Clinical and Molecular Teratology* 88: 128–131.
Riikonen, R., I. Salonen, K. Partanen, and S. Verho. 1999. Brain perfusion SPECT and MRI in foetal alcohol syndrome. *Developmental Medicine and Child Neurology* 41: 652–659.
Riley, E.P., S.N. Mattson, E.R. Sowell, T.L. Jernigan, D.F. Sobel, and K.L. Jones. 1995. Abnormalities of the corpus-callosum in children prenatally exposed to alcohol. *Alcoholism: Clinical and Experimental Research* 19: 1198–1202.
Roussotte, F.F., K.K. Sulik, S.N. Mattson, E.P. Riley, K.L. Jones, C.M. Adnams, P.A. May, M.J. O'Connor, K.L. Narr, and E.R. Sowell. 2011. Regional brain volume reductions relate to facial dysmorphology and neurocognitive function in fetal alcohol spectrum disorders. *Human Brain Mapping* 33: 920–937.
Sowell, E.R., S.N. Mattson, P.M. Thompson, T.L. Jernigan, E.P. Riley, and A.W. Toga. 2001. Mapping callosal morphology and cognitive correlates – Effects of heavy prenatal alcohol exposure. *Neurology* 57: 235–244.
Sowell, E.R., P.M. Thompson, S.N. Mattson, K.D. Tessner, T.L. Jernigan, E.P. Riley, and A.W. Toga. 2002. Regional brain shape abnormalities persist into adolescence after heavy prenatal alcohol exposure. *Cerebral Cortex* 12: 856–865.

Sowell, E.R., A. Johnson, E. Kan, Lu LH, J.D. Van Horn, A.W. Toga, M.J. O'Connor, and S.Y. Bookheimer. 2008a. Mapping white matter integrity and neurobehavioral correlates in children with fetal alcohol spectrum disorders. *Journal of Neuroscience* 28: 1313–1319.

Sowell, E.R., S.N. Mattson, E. Kan, P.M. Thompson, E.P. Riley, and A.W. Toga. 2008b. Abnormal cortical thickness and brain-behavior correlation patterns in individuals with heavy prenatal alcohol exposure. *Cerebral Cortex* 18: 136–144.

Spottiswoode, B.S., E.M. Meintjes, A.W. Anderson, C.D. Molteno, M.E. Stanton, N.C. Dodge, J.C. Gore, B.S. Peterson, J.L. Jacobson, and S.W. Jacobson. 2011. Diffusion tensor imaging of the cerebellum and eyeblink conditioning in fetal alcohol spectrum disorder. *Alcoholism* 35: 2174–2183.

Streissguth, A.P., F.L. Bookstein, H.M. Barr, P.D. Sampson, K. O'Malley, and J.K. Young. 2004. Risk factors for adverse life outcomes in fetal alcohol syndrome and fetal alcohol effects. *Journal of Developmental and Behavioral Pediatrics* 25: 228–238.

Sulik, K.K. 2005. Genesis of alcohol-induced craniofacial dysmorphism. *Experimental Biology and Medicine* 230: 366–375.

Swayze, V.W., V.P. Johnson, J.W. Hanson, J. Piven, Y. Sato, J.N. Giedd, D. Mosnik, and N.C. Andreasen. 1997. Magnetic resonance imaging of brain anomalies in fetal alcohol syndrome. *Pediatrics* 99: 232–240.

Treit, S., C. Lebel, L. Baugh, C. Rasmussen, G. Andrew, and C. Beaulieu. 2013. Longitudinal MRI reveals altered trajectory of brain development during childhood and adolescence in fetal alcohol spectrum disorders. *Journal of Neuroscience* 33: 10098–10109.

Treit, S., D.M. Zhou, C. Lebel, C. Rasmussen, G. Andrew, and C. Beaulieu. 2014. Longitudinal MRI reveals impaired cortical thinning in children and adolescents prenatally exposed to alcohol. *Human Brain Mapping* 35: 4892–4903.

Treit, S., Z. Chen, D. Zhou, L. Baugh, C. Rasmussen, G. Andrew, J. Pei, and C. Beaulieu. 2017. Sexual dimorphism of volume reduction but not cognitive deficit in fetal alcohol spectrum disorders: A combined diffusion tensor imaging, cortical thickness and brain volume study. *NeuroImage: Clinical* 15: 284–297.

West, J.R., and C.R. Goodlett. 1990. Teratogenic effects of alcohol on brain-development. *Annals of Medicine* 22: 319–325.

Wozniak, J.R., R.L. Muetzel, B.A. Mueller, C.L. McGee, M.A. Freerks, E.E. Ward, M.L. Nelson, P.N. Chang, and K.O. Lim. 2009. Microstructural corpus callosum anomalies in children with prenatal alcohol exposure: An extension of previous diffusion tensor imaging findings. *Alcoholism* 33: 1825–1835.

Yang, Y., F. Roussotte, E. Kan, K.K. Sulik, S.N. Mattson, E.P. Riley, K.L. Jones, C.M. Adnams, P.A. May, M.J. O'Connor, K.L. Narr, and E.R. Sowell. 2011. Abnormal cortical thickness alterations in fetal alcohol spectrum disorders and their relationships with facial dysmorphology. *Cerebral Cortex* 22: 1170–1179.

Zhou, D., C. Lebel, C. Lepage, C. Rasmussen, A. Evans, K. Wyper, J. Pei, G. Andrew, A. Massey, D. Massey, and C. Beaulieu. 2011. Developmental cortical thinning in fetal alcohol spectrum disorders. *NeuroImage* 58: 16–25.

Chapter 7
Screening and Assessment of FASD in a Youth Justice System: Comparing Different Methodologies

Deepa Singal, Teresa Brown, Sally Longstaffe, Mary Kate Harvie, Trevor Markesteyn, and Albert E. Chudley

Abstract The high association between youth with fetal alcohol spectrum disorder (FASD) and encounters with the law justifies the need for effective means to identify FASD youth in the justice system. This chapter will review the extent of the issue and present a comparison between two screening approaches used at the Manitoba Youth Centre to identify youth at risk for FASD. The chapter will outline information about the history, development and outcomes of youth diagnosed with FASD through the Manitoba Youth Justice FASD Program. Youth who receive an FASD diagnosis can receive additional supports for treatment and management of their disorder. Ultimately, this will increase the well-being of young offenders afflicted with FASD by increasing the fairness and appropriateness of sentences, and tailoring the rehabilitation and treatment.

Keywords Fetal alcohol spectrum disorder · Justice system · Screening tool · Justice program · Prenatal alcohol · Exposure

---

D. Singal
Department of Community Health Sciences, University of Manitoba, Winnipeg, MB, Canada

T. Brown
Former FASD Youth Justice Program, A/Assistant Superintendent of Programs of the Manitoba Youth Corrections, Winnipeg, MB, Canada

S. Longstaffe · A. E. Chudley (✉)
Department of Pediatrics, University of Manitoba, Winnipeg, MB, Canada
e-mail: abchudley@gmail.com

M. K. Harvie
Judge of the Provincial Court of Manitoba, Winnipeg, MB, Canada

T. Markesteyn
Corrections Division, Department of Justice, Manitoba, Winnipeg, MB, Canada

E. Jonsson et al. (eds.), *Ethical and Legal Perspectives in Fetal Alcohol Spectrum Disorders (FASD)*, International Library of Ethics, Law, and the New Medicine 75,
https://doi.org/10.1007/978-3-319-71755-5_7

7.1 Background and Introduction

Fetal Alcohol Spectrum Disorder (FAS) is a term that encompasses various diagnoses associated with prenatal alcohol exposure including: fetal alcohol syndrome (FAS), partial fetal alcohol syndrome (pFAS), alcohol related neurodevelopmental disorder (ARND), and alcohol related birth defects (ARBD) (Chudley et al. 2005). Recently, a revision of the Canadian diagnostic guidelines for FASD recommended the use of the terms Fetal alcohol Spectrum Disorder with sentinel facial features or Fetal Alcohol Spectrum Disorder without sentinenl facial features as acceptable terms for diagnosis (Cook et al. 2016). People with FASD often experience secondary disabilities such as behavior and social difficulties, social ineptness, substance use disorders, school and employment difficulties, poor judgment, trouble understanding consequences of behaviors and lack comprehension of social norms and rules (Streissguth et al. 2004). These factors place people with FASD at increased risk for involvement with the criminal justice system (Streissguth et al. 1997, 2004; Fast and Conry 2004, 2009; Fast et al. 1999; Loeber and Farrington 2000; Zara and Farrington 2010; Conry et al. 1997, 2009).

7.2 FASD Prevalence in the Criminal Justice System

Studies have shown that a substantial proportion of adults and children and adolescents diagnosed with Fetal Alcohol Spectrum Disorder (FASD) are involved with the justice system across Canada and the United States (Fast and Conry 2009; Fast et al. 1999; Conry et al. 1997; Burd et al. 2004; Popova et al. 2011a). A Canadian study conducted in British Columbia and the Yukon in the mid-90s of youth remanded to a forensic psychiatric inpatient assessment unit calculated approximately 23% of cases were diagnosed with FAS, pFAS or ARND (Fast et al. 1999). Another Canadian study surveyed correctional facilities across the country and reported over that there could be over 1300 people with FASD in the Canadian Justice System (Burd et al. 2003). These authors conducted a similar study in the United States and estimated a combined prevalence of FASD and ARND to be over 28,000 inmates (Burd et al. 2004). Another Canadian survey reported approximately 12% of youth (14–18 years of age) in juvenile detention centers in British Columbia had FAS/FAE (Murphy et al. 2005). A study conducted among adult male offenders reported 10% prevalence of FASD in a medium-security penitentiary in Manitoba, Canada (MacPherson et al. 2011). Additionally another Canadian study conducted in a youth sexual offence treatment program in British Columbia reported approximately 11% of youths attending this program were diagnosed or suspected to have FASD (Rojas and Gretton 2007).

These studies used varying methodologies in ascertaining cases of FASD and were conducted in different populations. To date there is no national prevalence rate of FASD among offenders in Canada or the United States. A systematic review of the prevalence of FASD in correctional studies estimated that the number of youth offenders with FASD in the Canadian Justice System on any given day in 2008/2009 ranged from 207 to 423 cases, and the estimated number of adult offenders with FASD in the Canadian Justice system on any given day in 2008/2009 was over 3600 cases (Popova et al. 2011b). These studies demonstrate that there is a high rate of both adult and youth offenders either diagnosed with FASD or who may be un-diagnosed.

The goal of the youth justice system is to rehabilitate, prevent or reduce criminal offences in the future, thus, the Youth Criminal Justice Act stipulates special considerations should be made for young offenders with special needs, including FASD. There is a need for an action-oriented response to deal with the identification, sentencing, management, and rehabilitation of adults and youth with FASD in the criminal justice system.

7.3 The Manitoba FASD Youth Justice Program

The youth justice system is governed by the Youth Criminal Justice Act S.C. 2002, c.1 (YCJA). Section 3 of the YCJA identifies specific principles, which are intended to promote public protection, including rehabilitation, "fair and proportionate accountability", and measures, which are "meaningful for the individual young person given his or her needs and level of development." Section 38 of the YCJA identifies the specific principles to be applied when sentencing a youth, emphasizing the need for sanctions that have "meaningful consequences".

The YCJA includes unique provisions which enable the Court to order an assessment by a qualified person if the Court has reasonable grounds to believe that "the young person may be suffering from a physical or mental illness or disorder, a psychological disorder, an emotional disturbance, a learning disability or a mental disability. As such, the Court can make special considerations for young offenders with special needs, including FASD. There is a need for an action-oriented response to deal with the identification, sentencing, management, and rehabilitation of adults and youth with FASD in the criminal justice system.

To address the complicated needs of young offenders with FASD the Manitoba Youth Justice Program was implemented in Manitoba Youth Corrections (MYC) in 2004. This program screens, diagnoses and aids in the rehabilitation of young offenders with FASD. The primary goals of this program are to: (1) To assess youth involved with the Justice System who may have FASD; (2) To provide recommendations to the Court for appropriate dispositions consistent with sentencing principles of the Youth Criminal Justice Act (YCJA); (3) To build capacity within families and the community while enhancing government and non-government FASD supports and services; (4) To implement multidisciplinary interventions and reintegration plans with supports for youth affected by FASD and their families (Harvie et al. 2011).

The program accepts youth between 12–18 years residing in Winnipeg or The Pas with confirmation of significant prenatal alcohol exposure, no previous diagno-

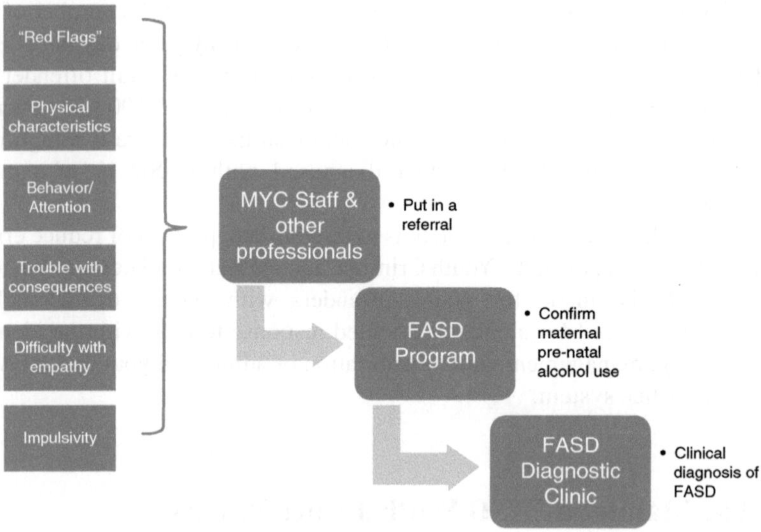

Fig. 7.1 Manitoba Youth Corrections FASD referral process

sis of FASD, and who are in conflict with the law. This program seeks to identify youth with possible FASD who may not have been identified previously through education or health systems, and thus whose criminal behavior is being misconstrued due to a lack of a medical diagnosis and appropriate supports or interventions. Youth are provided access to an FASD assessment.

Currently youth at risk for FASD are identified by multiple professionals who have dealt with the youth including; members of the court, probation and corrections officials, teachers, family members or healthcare professionals. Youth with a confirmation of pre-natal alcohol exposure are then referred to by program staff for a full FASD diagnostic assessment by clinicians specializing in the diagnosis of FASD (see Fig. 7.1 for referral process). A final report completed by physicians and the diagnostic team contains thorough details about the youth's background, the mother's prenatal history, and the youths developmental and medical history including education history, mental health and illness diagnosis, a sensory profile and the results of a psychological, physical and dysmorphology examination. This ensures that the judge who sentences the youth will have relevant information for a proportionate and fair sentence that represents a "meaningful consequence" for the youth, as well as a rehabilitation plan that takes into account the needs identified in the assessment process. All participants in the youth justice system have expressed that there are significant benefits of having access to an FASD assessment for this population. While assessments are obtained as part of the Court process, they are written as a medical report and do not reference the charges, thus allowing the youth to use the assessment in other contexts.

From the beginning of the program in 2004 to June 2017 the program has received 1048 referrals, of which 332 assessments have been completed. The diagnostic assessment involves a thorough review of the medical, social, family, educational and criminal justice histories by trained staff coordinators in the FASD Program. Caregivers and professional support staff are interviewed. Testing using various standardized assessment tools for social adaptive abilities, executive functioning, behavioural rating, cognitive assessments are administered. The adolescent is seen by a physician and a medical geneticist that involves in depth review of health and mental health issues and a physical examination is done with attention to neurological function and dysmorphology, supplemented by FASD facial photographic analysis.[1] A total of 237 youth have been diagnosed with FASD.

7.4 Screening for FASD in Youth Justice System

The purpose of screening is to identify individuals who are likely to have FASD so that a diagnostic assessment can follow. An effective screening tool is generally easily and quickly administered, user friendly, and cost-effective (Goh et al. 2008). Successful screening tools will identify greater number of individuals than the true number of individuals who are affected by the condition. Effective screening tools demonstrate a high sensitivity and specificity. Sensitivity is the ability of a tool to correctly identify persons with the condition within a population who screen positive (Goh et al. 2008). Specificity is the ability to correctly identify persons without the condition within a population who screen negative (Goh et al. 2008). A higher sensitivity and specificity indicates greater accuracy of a test or tool. A reference standard, which is an "alternative method to determine the condition among individuals with a positive test" is required. This standard is not available for FASD at this moment, other than a full diagnostic assessment (Goh et al. 2008).

Currently there are no validated screening tools for identifying FASD in young offenders in Canada (Goh et al. 2008). These youth may fall through the gaps when being ushered through a fragmented legal and health system as there is no systematic approach to screening youth at risk for FASD and referring them for a full diagnostic assessment.

7.5 Screening for FASD in the Manitoba Youth Justice System

The Manitoba FASD Youth Justice Program currently uses a behavior-based approach called the *"Red Flag Method"*. The youth is referred to the FASD Program if the youth exhibits the following "red flags": repeated failure to comply, lack of empathy, trouble in school/drop-out, difficulties with intuitions, compliance and peer interactions, inability to connect actions with consequences, does not seem

---

[1] See: FAS Diagnostic & Prevention Network [Internet], FAS Facial Photographic Analysis Software, https://depts.washington.edu/fasdpn/htmls/face-software.htm

affected by past punishments, followers, rather than leaders in crime, crimes involving risky behavior for little gain and gang involvement.

Although this approach has been successful in referring a large number of youth who may have FASD, it is not a systematic approach with consistent criteria in referring youth for an FASD assessment; therefore youth may be missed using this method. Furthermore, probation officers may not have consistent training regarding identifying youth with FASD and with the Red Flag Method, as there are no mandatory training sessions for new or existing probation officers. All youth and adult institutional staff (not include probation officers) receive a mandatory one-day FASD training during their basic training. The youth institutional staff receive an additional 3 days of FASD training. If a probation officer was previously in a role as another staff member, they may have received this training, but we cannot be sure how many probation officers have this background. Plans are currently being made to train probation officers in FASD in 2014.

7.6 Asante Centre for Fetal Alcohol Syndrome Probation Officer Screening and Referral Tool

The Canadian Association of Paediatric Health Centers (CAPHC), funded by the Public Health Agency of Canada (PHAC), facilitated an initiative to develop a National Screening Tool Kit for people who may be affected by FASD (Goh et al. 2008). The Asante Centre for Fetal Alcohol Syndrome Probation Officer Screening and Referral Tool (hereby referred to the *Asante Screening Tool*) was identified by the FASD Screening Tool Steering Committee involved in this project to be a fast and easily administered tool to facilitate diagnosis of FASD in the youth justice system (Goh et al. 2008). This tool is a pre-coded questionnaire that collects information on social and neurodevelopmental history of the youth as well as the probation officer's knowledge of the youth and FASD (see Appendix 1).

This tool screens youth for referral based on environmental factors and personal and neurobehavioral factors. Referrals are made based on the combination of either one social/environmental factor plus two personal factors or no environmental/social factors but at least three personal factors. This tool was designed to help increase capacity and develop the confidence of probation officers across Canada to identify youth requiring a full FASD assessment.

The Steering Committee for the Development of FASD Screening Tools reviewed the Asante Tool and recommended that the validity of the tool needed to be established prior to wider implementation as there are no other studies outside of the Asante Centre that has validated this tool in the youth justice population (Goh et al. 2008).

7.7 The Manitoba Youth Justice FASD Screen Tool Evaluation Project

In 2008 Manitoba Corrections undertook a review of specific mental health screening tools in use in correctional facilities throughout North America. The Asante Tool was identified as an easily administered, accessible and cost-effective tool, however Manitoba Corrections decided to defer to the steering committee of the FASD National Screening Tool Development Project for direction with implementation. The Manitoba Youth Justice FASD Screening Tool Evaluation Project was initiated in 2011 to assess the validity and applicability of the Asante tool in accurately identifying young offenders at risk for FASD in Manitoba. The goals of this project included: (1) To critically evaluate the applicability of the Asante Centre Screening Tool in the Manitoba Youth Justice System; (2) To evaluate the sensitivity and specificity of the Asante Screening Tool; (3) To generate practical recommendations regarding the possible implementation of the Asante Tool in Manitoba, including highlighting possible barriers to implementation and staff perceptions. This project consists of two studies:

- *Part 1*: A retrospective chart review was conducted to assess the sensitivity and specificity of the Asante Centre FASD Screening and Referral Tool in identifying youth at risk for FASD who are admitted to Manitoba Youth Corrections against the Red Flag Method.
- *Part 2*: A prospective study was conducted to prospectively assess the validity and applicability of the Asante Tool compared to the Red Flag Method, as well as probation officers opinions on the effectiveness and ease of the Asante Tool. The following sections will describe the specific research questions of the retrospective and prospective study, the methodologies used, results and conclusions arising from each study. We will also highlight challenges in conducting this research, limitations and strengths of our study, and will conclude with a discussion of policy implications.

It is our hope that other jurisdictions looking to apply the Asante Tool, or another screening tool in the youth justice population can use lessons learned and the methodology developed for these studies.

7.8 A Community Participatory Research Approach and Knowledge Translation

Our research took a community-based participatory research approach. This approach to research involves key stakeholders including community members, organizational representatives, policy makers, health care professionals and researchers in all aspects of the research process. All partners equitably contribute to the identification of the research problem, choice of methodology and execution of the research study, as well as the interpretation of results and determining how these results should be used to elicit change within a community. This approach ensures the translation of research into locally relevant policies or action by including participants affected by the issue under investigation and policy makers who can influence change.

This approach is particularly useful when assessing the applicability and implementation of a new screening tool. Implementation of tools can be challenging without the support and buy-in of key stakeholders and front line personnel that will eventually apply the tool in their community. There can be resistance to change existing standards and approaches, misunderstandings of intentions and objectives, and a lack of understanding from researchers about practical issues of applicability and a lack of regard of true community needs.

This research project was conceptualized from the need for a more systematic approach to screening youth with potential FASD that was identified by policy makers and physicians associated with the FASD Manitoba Youth Justice Program. However, program staff highlighted concerns regarding the applicability of the Asante Tool in Manitoba Youth Justice, the amount of information needed to fill out the tool and the willingness of probation officers to adapt to this tool. The staff also felt that the current Red Flag Method was effective in generating referrals to the program. Therefore, an epidemiologist was brought on the team to design a study comparing both methods and to make recommendations for the screening process of young offenders with possible FASD in the Manitoba Youth Justice system. This researcher ensured the objective evaluation of both methods of screening and prioritized the needs of the Manitoba Youth Justice Program staff and physicians.

Our project team involved physicians specializing in FASD diagnostic assessments, judges in the youth justice system, the Executive Director of Community and Youth Corrections, the chief correctional psychologist, the program manager of the FASD Youth Justice Program and a PhD Candidate in the Department of Community Health Sciences at the University of Manitoba specializing in health services research.

Physicians and the researcher worked closely with members of the Justice System staff (the community) to identify their needs, and learn from their hands-on experiences. Justice staff recognized the benefit of the research and potential results, and embraced new concepts such as validity and reliability and systematic screening. Incorporating principles of community participatory research increased the quantity and quality of data collected in this project. With support from the program manager of the FASD Program, probation officers were more motivated to ensure completion of screening tools, were able to perceive the benefits of the research project, and took ownership of their participation in the research process. Furthermore, taking a community participatory approach also helped to make findings from this project locally relevant, which is particularly important if implementation of the Asante tool is recommended.

An objective of the study team was knowledge translation of these study results to the academic and the youth justice community. Study methodology and preliminary study results have already been shared with the Public Health Agency of Canada thorough a detailed report highlighting the results of the retrospective chart review, and to health care professionals and youth justice staff through Webinars arranged by the Canadian Association of Pediatric Health Centers, as well as two national conference presentations. Final study results will be shared with study participants through a one-page summary. A final formal report will be written for the Canadian Public Health Agency of Canada upon completion of data analysis. Manuscripts for submission to peer-reviewed medical journals will also be prepared. This thorough knowledge translation plan strengthens the uptake of study recommendations and shares the challenges and limitations of conducting this real world research with other jurisdictions investigating screening for FASD in other youth justice systems.

7.8.1 Part 1: A Retrospective Chart Review Comparing the Asante Screening Tool with the Red Flag Method – Sensitivity and Specificity

We conducted a retrospective review of charts to assess the applicability, sensitivity and specificity of the Asante Centre FASD Screening and Referral Tool in identifying youth at risk for FASD who are admitted to Manitoba Youth Corrections (MYC) against the Red Flag Method.

7.8.1.1 Specific Research Questions

- Is there adequate information in charts from the Manitoba Youth Corrections (MYC) data to administer the Asante Centre screening tool in a useful way?
- What proportion of youth who met inclusion criteria screened positive for being at risk for FASD by the Asante Centre tool, screened negative by the tool, and had missing information?
- How sensitive is the Asante Centre FASD Screening Tool in identifying youth referred to the MYC FASD program?
- How specific is the Asante Centre FASD Screening tool in identifying youth referred to the MYC FASD program?

7.8.1.2 Study Design and Sample

This study was a retrospective chart review of a sample of charts of young offenders admitted to Manitoba Youth Corrections between 2006 and 2009. Only charts of young offenders that have a probation officer and a pre-sentence report (a report written by probation officers summarizing the educational, behavioral, family and legal history of the youth) were included. This ensured that only charts with comprehensive information were reviewed. Researchers and stakeholders decided that this criteria would be applied due to the nature of information required to fill out the

Asante Tool, for example, if charts of youth who were admitted for one day were used and did not have contact with a probation officer, there would not be enough information to use the tool effectively and would bias the results of this evaluation by showing the tool was not valid in identifying youth at risk for FASD.

7.8.1.3 Data Collection and Analysis

A PhD candidate along with the research team conducted data collection and analysis. First a pilot test was conducted to determine if there was enough information in youth files to administer the Asante Tool in meaningful way. Information was abstracted from Manitoba Youth Corrections Program Files, including the Corrections Offender Management Database, the Medical Files, and the Probation files for a random sample of 30 charts that met inclusion criteria. Analysis demonstrated that no additional relevant information was available from the medical files and the probation files versus the presentence report from the Corrections Offender Management Database, therefore data abstraction was restricted to the pre-sentence report for the remainder of the charts.

Data was abstracted using a standardized data collection form that corresponded with questions from the Asante Tool (see Appendix 1). An electronic database was created using excel on a secure, password protected laptop computer. The study was conducted at the Manitoba Youth Corrections Centre, which is a secure environment where the charts are held. Access was restricted only to study personnel and all data was password protected.

Youth with a combination of either one social/environmental factor plus two personal factors or no environmental/social factors but at least three personal factors were considered at being risk for FASD and were recommended for further assessment (as indicated by the Asante Tool). Youth who screened positive using the Asante Centre Screening Tool were compared to a master list from the FASD Youth Justice Program to determine which of these youth were actually referred to the FASD Youth Justice Program for a full FASD diagnostic assessment. The proportion of youth who were screened positive for being at risk for FASD using the Asante tool and were not referred to the program was also determined. True positive cases and false negative case were determined through this verification process.

Statistical analyses were conducted using SPSS Version 18.0 (SPSS Inc., Chicago, IL, United States). A contingency table was used to calculate the sensitivity and specificity of the Asante Tool compared to the Red Flag Method. Sensitivity of the tool was determined using the following calculation: Sensitivity = # of true positives / # of true positives + # of false positives. Specificity of the tool was determined using the following calculation: Specificity = # of true negatives / # of true negatives + # of false negatives.

7.8.1.4 Ethics and Privacy

This study was a retrospective chart review and did not involve contacting young offenders or the offender's family. This study was approved from the University of Manitoba's Human Research Ethics Board and the Manitoba Youth Corrections and Court approval. Privacy of youth records and probation officers was protected and emphasized throughout the research process.

7.8.1.5 Results of Retrospective Chart Review

After reviewing a random sample of 30 charts meeting study inclusion criteria, researchers concluded that there was enough information in charts of young offenders containing pre-sentence reports to administer the Asante Screening Tool to proceed with the study.

Out of 378 charts of youth ages 12–18 who were admitted to the MYC between 2006–2009 who had a probation officer, 55 charts did not have a pre-sentence report and were excluded from the study. Out of the remaining 323 charts, 70 (21.7%) youth screened positive using the Asante Centre Screening Tool (see Table 7.1), and 34 (9.5%) screened negative. A high proportion of charts did not have enough information to definitively answer certain questions on the Asante Tool, for instance if youth had a sibling with FASD (215 charts). Because this information was not explicitly stated in the charts we cannot be certain about the truth regarding these items. A youth may have a sibling with FASD even if it is not recorded in the chart. Notes were kept on these particular items to assess the availability of information in the youth charts at MYC to screen for potential FASD. These items were recorded as "no" on the Asante Tool, as it was assumed for the purpose of this research if the item was not recorded the child did not have this particular characteristic. Charts with missing information and negative screens where used as the total number of charts that screened negative using the Asante Tool (n = 253).

7.8.1.6 Predictive Value of the Asante Centre Screening Tool

The predictive values of the Asante Centre Tool as compared to the Red Flag Method are shown in Table 7.1. Eleven per cent (36) of youth were classified by the Asante Tool as being at high risk for FASD and had been previously referred to the FASD program using the Red Flag Method (true positives) and 60% (193) youth were not referred by the Asante Tool or previously by the Red Flag method (true negatives). Ten percent of youth screened positive on the Asante tool but had not been previously referred by the Red Flag Method (false positives) and 19% (60) youth screened negative on the Asante tool but were referred to the FASD program using the Red Flag Method (false negatives). The sensitivity of the Asante tool compared to current referrals made to the MYC center was 34%.The specificity of the Asante Centre Tool compared to current referral's made to the MYC was 84%.

Table 7.1 Number of young offenders at MYC at risk for FASD as indicated by the Asante Tool compared to the Red Flag Method

	Referred to the FASD program by Red Flag Method	Not referred to the FASD program by the Red Flag Method	Total
At risk of FASD (Asante tool)	36 (true positive)	34 (false positive)	70
Not at risk for FASD (Asante tool)	60 (false negative)	193 (true negative)	253
Total	96	227	323

7.8.1.7 Discussion and Limitations

The aim of this study was to assess the applicability and evaluate the sensitivity and specificty of the Asante Tool in screening for young offenders with possible FASD repremanded to the Manitoba Youth Centre. The Asante Tool had a low senstivity of 34% and a specificity of 84% as compared to the Red Flag method. This means that the Asante Tool may be missing a proportion of adolescent offenders who were referred to the FASD program by the Red Flag method. While the senstivity of the Asante Tool is low compared to the the Red Flag method it is important to consider that *the Red Flag method is not a gold standard in screening for youth offenders with possible FASD.*

Youth could be referred incorrectly by the Red Flag Method, or could be missed by the Red Flag Method. Probation officers may not have consistent knowedlge regarding the Red Flag method, some may have have a lack of tiraning and awareness of FASD, and not be using the Red Flag method effectively or at all. Probation officers may not have the knowedlge to accuartely assess beahvour symptoms exhibted by youth using the Red Flag method, or they might not have spent enough time with a youth to witness red flags, There may also have been a lack of obvious behaviour symptoms exhibted by the youth to use the Red Flag method effectively. Therefore, adefinitive conlcusion cannot be made stating youth who are being screened postive by the Asante Centre tool are not at high risk for FASD because they have not been previously referred to the FASD program by MYC staff, as there is no "gold standard" for referral.

The Asante Centre Screening Tool has reasonable specificity when compared to the Red Flag Method, indicating that is it is more comparable to the Red Flag Method's ability to rule out youth who are not at risk for FASD. However we are not certain that the Red Flag Method is ruling out "true negative" cases because we do not know how many of these youth actuallyreceived a diagnosis of FASD by either the Red Flag Method or the Asante Tool Method.

A high proportion of charts did not contain specific information required to accurately fill out the Asante Tool. For example it is not consistently documented in the charts if youth have siblings with FASD or early devlopment difficulty. Maternal alcohol history is frequently not available in charts. This missing information could be attributed to the fact that staff and probation officers at MYC may not be asking questions to screen youth for further FASD assessments, or this informationhas been asked but wasnot documented in the chart. This is a key limitation in this chart review.

The information that is needed to fill out the Asante Tool may be known by probation officers of youth assigned to their case load but not recorded in their charts. The ability of the probation officers to fill out the Asante Tool with their knowledge of the behaviour and neurodevelopmental charactertiscs of the youth would be more accurately assessed by prospectivley filling out the Asante Tool on youth on their exsiting caseloads. It is important to note that a higher porportion of youth may be have been referred for further FASD assessment using the Red Flag method after 2009 due to an increased awarness of FASD throughout Manitoba Corrections, the development of the Youth FASD Program, and the 3 day FASD training being delivered to staff since 2009. This trend may not be picked up in this review.

7.8.1.8 Conclusions and Recommendations

The goal of this study was to assess if the Asante Centre Screening Tool is applicable and valid in identifying youth at risk for FASD who are admitted to Manitoba Youth Justice. This study established the following primary findings:

1. The Red Flag method and the Asante Screen refer different youth to be at risk for FASD when assessing information available in youth charts. There is not a high rate of overlap of youth who screen positive by both tools. The Asante Tool may miss youth who screen positive by the Red Flag method and Red Flag method may miss youth who screen positive by the Asante Tool.
2. The Asante Centre tool is more comparable to the Red Flag Method when screening out youth who are not at risk for possible FASD, i.e., the Asante Centre Tool is more specific than sensitive when comparing it to the Red Flag Method.
3. There was a high proportion of missing information in existing youth charts that prohibited a definitive conclusion on certain items in the Asante Centre Tool.

These findings have the following implications:

1. The Asante tool should only be used on youth offenders by probation officers who have a relationship with the youth, or have a reasonable amount of information about the youth's family history, cognitive and social behavior. If probation officers apply this tool to youth who are detained for one day and do not have a history with the Justice System they would not have the information needed for a referral to be made to the FASD Program.
2. Due to the high porportion of missing information available in charts pertaining to the Asante Tool, probation staff may be missing youth that could require further FASD assessment. A prospective analysis should be done to see if probation officers have this knowledge of youth and if this information was simply not documented in the charts.
3. A prospective analysis should be done with probation officers filling out the Asante Tool to determine if they would screen a higher proportion of youth at

risk for FASD as compared to using the Red Flag Method using their knowledge of youth on their existing caseload.

4. Due to the fact that the Red Flag Method is not a gold standard in referring young offenders with possible FASD, a prospective study should be conducted that compares the Asante Screening Tool with a full diagnostic assessment to calculate more accurate sensitivity and specificity results before recommending that this tool be implemented at the MYC.
5. The high proportion of missing information in charts to definitively fill out items on the Asante Tool indicate training sessions may be necessary for probation officers to learn how to correctly fill out the Asante Screening Tool as they may not be asking the specific questions required to effectively apply the tool to the MYJC setting. Discussions with staff are necessary for implications this tool may have on current workloads and scarce time and resources.

This retrospective chart review study laid important groundwork highlighting possible areas of difficulty in implementing the tool, i.e., missing information and the difficulty in obtaining it. It also created a strong impetus for a prospective study that compares the current method to the Asante Centre Tool to calculate more valid sensitivity and specificity statistics and to reach a definitive conclusion whether or not the tool should be implemented with Youth Corrections.

7.8.2 *Part 2: The Prospective Study*

Based upon the recommendations of the retrospective chart review, a prospective study to compare youth who screened positive on the Asante Centre Screening Tool and Red Flag method with youth who received full diagnostic assessments was conducted. The objective of this study was to assess which method of referral lends itself to more referrals to the FASD Youth Justice Program from probation officers, and if these referrals are accurate at identifying youth at high risk for having FASD by comparing them to youth who received full diagnostic assessments. This study included a survey component that provides feedback regarding the ease and effectiveness the Asante tool compared to the current red flag system from probation officers. The results from the surveys will be used to identify challenges and possible barriers to implementation of the Asante Tool in the Manitoba Youth Justice System as well as to generate recommendations for successful implementation.

7.8.2.1 Specific Research Questions

- How many youth screened positive using the current red flag methodology at MYC during the study period?
- How many youth who were screened positive using the current red flag methodology at MYC received a full FASD diagnostic assessment and a diagnosis of FASD?

- How many youth screened positive using the Asante Centre Screening Tool at MYC during the study period?
- How many youth who screened positive using the Asante Centre Screening Tool at MYC received a full FASD diagnostic assessment and a diagnosis of FASD?
- What are probation officers opinions on the ease and usefulness of the Asante Centre Screening Tool in identifying youth with potential FASD?

7.8.2.2 Study Participants and Data Collection

Youth Probation officers were recruited throughout all four Manitoba Youth Correction sites in Winnipeg during a study information and training session held for each site. Probation officers who agreed to participate were randomly split into two groups: Asante Tool users and the Red Flag, "business as usual" group. Probation officers in the Asante Tool group received brief training sessions in using the Asante Centre Tool to identify youth with potential FASD. Probation officers assigned to the Red Flag group were re-familiarized with the Red Flag Method. Information from youth assigned to probation officers participating in the study was used to fill out the Asante Tool, therefore these youth were also considered study participants.

Probation officers screened all youth who were assigned to their caseload during the data collection period (September 2012 to February 2013) using the Red Flag or Asante Tool. This consisted of youth who may have been on the caseload before the study period and new youth assigned to the probation officers during the study period. Only youth with presentence reports were screened to ensure adequate information was available to fill out the Asante Tool or to assess behaviors as indicated by the Red Flag Method. At the end of the study period a brief survey was distributed to probation officers in each group assessing the ease, user-friendliness, and effectiveness of either the Red Flag Method (see Appendix 2) or the Asante Tool (see Appendix 3).

7.8.2.3 Survey Tools

Two separate structured surveys were designed to provide feedback about the Asante Tool and the current Red Flag Method using Likert scale responses (strongly disagree, disagree, neutral, agree, strongly agree). Questions for the Red Flag group pertained to the perception of probation officer's familiarity of the red flag method and confidence in using it to refer youth with possible FASD, if they would like more training for screening youth with potential FASD, if the Red Flag method is effective, and if they would prefer to use a standardized tool to help referring youth with possible FASD (see Appendix 2). Questions for the Asante Tool group pertained to the ease of the tool, if probation officers had enough information to answer the questions on the tool, if it could be filled out in less than 20 min, if the tool is an effective way to screen youth for possible FASD, and if they would prefer to use the tool compared to the current red flag method (see Appendix 2). Surveys were constructed by the study team and with feedback from MYC FASD Program staff to ensure the information collected would achieve study objectives and generate applicable and useful feedback. Surveys were kept short and questions were kept specific and direct to increase response rates.

7.8.2.4 Data Analysis

Youth included in the study that screened negative on the Asante Tool will be compared to a master list form the FASD Youth Justice Program to determine if these youth were previously referred to the FASD Youth Justice Program for a full FASD diagnostic assessment by the Red Flag Method, or if they received a diagnosis. Investigators will follow youth who screened positive on the Asante Tool and were referred to the FASD Youth Justice Program to either rule out or confirm pre-natal alcohol exposure and follow-up with an assessment. Information on whether or not these youth receive a diagnosis will be collected. True positive cases and false negative case will be determined through this verification process.

Summary statistics were used to describe the results of the surveys. Statistical analyses were conducted using SPSS Version 12, 20 (SPSS Inc., Chicago, IL, United States). Data are summarized in an electronic database on a password-protected computer. A contingency table will be used to calculate the sensitivity and specificity of the Asante Tool compared to the actual rate of diagnosis of youth screened positive and negative. This will also be calculated for youth referred by the Red Flag Method.

7.8.2.5 Ethics and Consent

The University of Manitoba's Human Research Ethics Board, Provincial Courts and the Manitoba Youth Corrections approved this study. Consent was obtained from all participating probation officers and verbal consent was obtained from all youth whose information was utilized to fill out the Asante Tool. No additional information from youth or families was requested for the purposes of this study.

7.8.2.6 Preliminary Results

We obtained consent for 21 Probation Officers across all four Youth Justice sites in Winnipeg. There were approximately 25 probation officers employed at these four sites during this time. Ten probation officers were randomly assigned to the Red Flag group and 11 were randomly assigned to the Asante Tool Group. Two probation officers dropped out of each group (n = 4 drop outs) due to maternity leave, retirement, and lack of time to fulfill study requirements. A total of 17 probation officers completed the study, among them 8 were in the Red Flag Group and 9 were in the Asante Tool group.

During the study period information from the charts of 59 youth was used in the study. Consent was obtained for all of these youth. Among the 59 youth, 35 of these youth screened positive for possible FASD. Among these 35 youth, 7 were referred to the MYC FASD program from probation officers using the Red Flag Method and 27 referrals were made from probation officers using the Asante Tool. Among these 27 referrals, 13 were new referrals to the program. These youth did not have previous referrals using the Red Flag Method to the FASD Program. Among the 27 referrals using the Asante Tool, 14 had been referred to the FASD Program previously using the Red Flag method. None of these youth had been referred to the Red Flag Method by the same probation officer participating in the study. These youth had either been referred by another probation officer (n = 2), a corrections staff (n = 8), or someone else such as teacher or foster parent (n = 3).Among the 22 youth who screened negative using the Asante Tool, 4 were previously made using the Red Flag Method, other corrections staff referred 3 of these youth and someone other than probation officers and justice staff referred the last youth.

7.8.2.7 Predictive Value of the Asante Centre Screening Tool

Sensitivity and specificity analysis will be conducted for both the Red Flag Method and the Asante Tool Method by comparing youth screened positive for possible FASD using these screens to those that actually received a full diagnostic assessment and diagnosis by the FASD Youth Justice Program. This analysis has not been completed, as data collection of the results of full assessments and possible diagnoses is ongoing. Among the 27 youth who screened positive using the Asante Tool screen, 7 received a diagnosis of FASD, 3 did not, 5 youth did not have confirmation of prenatal alcohol exposure, 9 youth are still waiting assessments and 3 youth turned 18 and were no longer eligible for the program. Among the seven youth who were referred by the Red Flag Method, one youth turned 18 and was no longer eligible for the program, another moved out of province, one did not receive a diagnosis and four are still waiting assessment.

7.8.2.8 Survey Feedback

The majority of probation officers who used the Red Flag Method agreed that they were familiar with this method, that they were confident in using this method to refer youth with possible FASD for further assessment and that they have referred youth with potential FASD for further assessment in the past using this method (see Fig. 7.2). Half the group strongly disagreed that they would like more training for screening youth with potential FASD and the other half agreed that they would like more training. The majority of probation officers were neutral as to the effectiveness of the Red Flag methods effectiveness in screening youth with potential FASD. Half

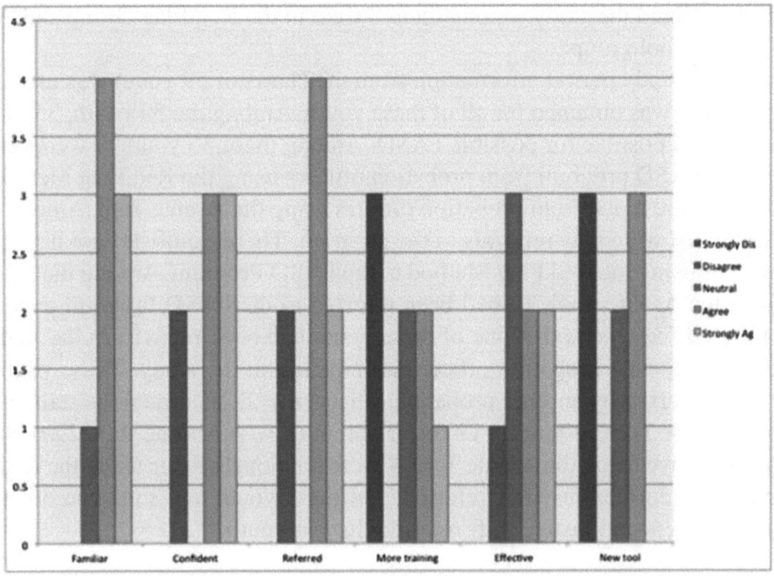

Fig. 7.2 Survey results of Red Flag Group

the group declared that they would strongly disagree to using a tool/form to guide them in referring youth with possible FASD to the FASD Youth Justice Program and half of the group stated they would agree that using a tool/form would be helpful.

The majority of probation officers using the Asante Survey Tool agreed that the tool was user friendly, that they had enough information on youth to fill out the tool effectively, that it could be filled out in 20 min, and that it was an effective tool (see Fig. 7.3). The majority of probation officers were neutral when asked if they would prefer to use the Asante Tool compared to the Red Flag Method, and if they referred more youth for assessment using the Asante Tool than they usually do using the Red Flag Method.

7.8.2.9 Discussion and Limitations

Although we do not have the results of the prospective evaluation of the sensitivity and specificity of the Asante Tool comparing it to a full diagnostic assessment, important conclusions can be drawn from surveys administered to probation officers at the end of the data collection period, as well as the challenges that arose throughout the study.

First, prospective use of the Asante Tool in screening for youth with potential FASD generates more referrals to the FASD program versus the Red Flag Method for probation officers. Analysis has shown that the Asante Tool generated 13 new referrals that had not been picked up previously by the Red Flag Method and 14

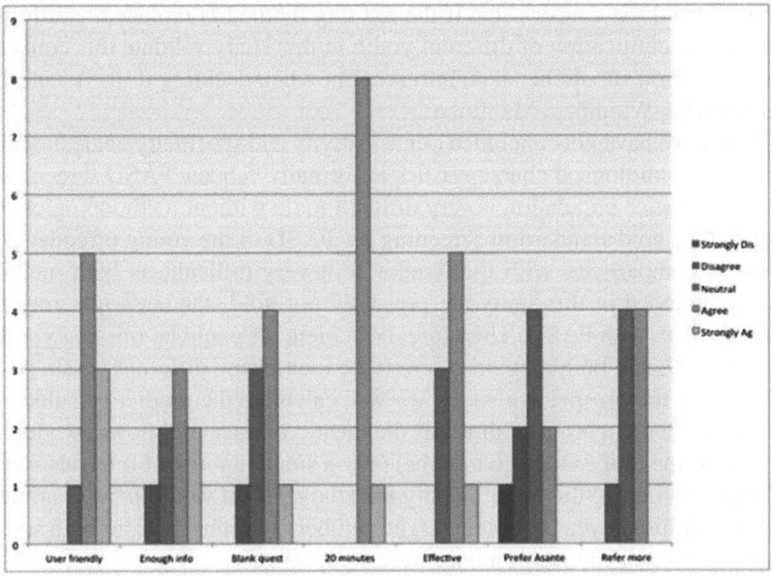

Fig. 7.3 Survey results of the Asante Tool Group

referrals that had been picked up by the Red Flag and the Asante Tool. However, the same probation officers making referrals using the Asante Tool did not recommend these youth for further assessment using the red flag method. This is an important finding, as probation officers do not seem to be the majority of personal referring youth to the program using the Red Flag Method. The addition of the Asante Tool brought these youth to the attention of these Probation Officers and resulted in a referral to the FASD Program by these probation officers.

This highlights the increased awareness of FASD symptoms that are brought to the attention of probation officers when using the Asante Tool that may be missed by the Red Flag Method. Furthermore, if these probation officers were not aware that a referral had been made to the program or that a youth on their caseload was at risk for FASD the needs of this youth may not be met. Further investigation should be done into the personnel making referrals to the program so that these staff can receive support for screening for youth with possible FASD. Furthermore, communication should be encouraged with other justice staff and probation officers to ensure that probation officers are aware of youth with possible FASD on their caseload.

Results from the retrospective and prospective study demonstrate that the two different screening methods identify different youth for possible FASD. This is extremely important in considering implementing this tool in the Manitoba Youth Justice System.

While the Asante Tool focuses on social/environmental and neurobehavioral factors, the Red Flag Method focuses on behaviors exhibited by youth. FASD Program staff have stated the concern that if the red flag method is replaced, youth may be missed. The identification of different youth in this study validate this concern and this consideration should be taken into account when deciding if the Asante Tool is implemented in Winnipeg, Manitoba.

Although we have not concluded our sensitivity and specificity analysis, calculating these epidemiological characteristics to formally validate FASD screening tools in the youth justice population is very difficult to do without methodological bias.

The lack of gold standard in screening for FASD in the young offender population makes comparisons with the Asante Tool very difficult, as both methods of screening included in this study are presently not gold standards in screening for young offenders with FASD. Therefore, both methods could be missing youth with possible FASD, and both methods seem to be identifying different youth. After the completion of the prospective study, we will calculate the predictive values of the Asante Tool by comparing with a full diagnostic assessment, however, due to the short time frame of the study (6 months) only a small amount of referrals were sent to the program during this time. Ideally the study period would have continued for at least an additional year to obtain larger numbers of referrals from both screening methods, and thus generate more accurate comparisons.

However, due to issues of feasibility such as probation officer workload, and the possibility of increased attrition of probation officers over longer time periods it was decided to limit the study to a practical 6-month time frame. In the real world, community based research in the youth justice population, it is difficult to discern ideal conditions to establish non-biased and valid epidemiologic sensitivity and specificity statistics (i.e., large sample sizes of youth with possible FASD and comparisons using gold standards). Until a true gold standard of screening is established for young offenders with possible FASD, this type of research will have its limitations.

Feedback generated from surveys was helpful in assessing the perspectives of probation officers using the Red Flag and Asante Tool. This information is important to take into consideration if implementation of the Asante Tool will be done in Winnipeg. The results of the surveys are highly representative of youth probation officers in Winnipeg, as it was estimated by program staff that approximately 25 probation officers worked in the four young offender sites in Winnipeg during the time the study was conducted, and 21 consented to participate in this study. While probation officers who participated in this study may have more awareness about FASD and may be more passionate about screening for young offenders with FASD versus those that did not participate, since the majority of probation officers across Winnipeg participated, this bias is less likely to influence results of this study. Results of this study may be extrapolated to other jurisdictions with similar programs and young offender populations as Winnipeg.

Most of the probation officers involved in this study are familiar with the Red Flag Method and are confident in their use with this method, however, there were inconsistent responses regarding further training in screening for potential FASD among youth offenders. This is an important finding that indicates probation officers may be interested in more training with FASD. Although probation officers may have received training screening for young offenders with possible FASD in a different position in the past, there was not a systematic and continuous training approach taken for all probation officers in the system. We do not know the proportion of officers who that have previously knowledge and training regarding FASD screening and those who do not. As well, new probation officers may have been hired who did not receive previous training. Resource should be allocated to set up consistent and mandatory training sessions for probation officers to screen for young offenders with possible FASD in the Manitoba Youth Corrections.

While the majority of probation officers feel the red flag is effective, half of them would prefer a standardized data form to screen for FASD. This finding demonstrates that probation officers may be willing to adapt to a more standardized screening tool. Probation officers who used the Asante Tool stated that it was user friendly, can be filled out in a timely manner. These findings are very important for implementation as a good screening tool is easy to administer and does not take much time. Despite this positive feedback, probation officers were neutral on stating if the tool was effective and if it leads to more referrals compared to the red flag method. This indicates that staff may be satisfied with their current method of referring youth with potential FASD and feel that the Red Flag Method is effective. However, there is the possibility of responder bias. Probation officers may not want to increase their workload by filling out another form and therefore, responses may be biased. This is common phenomenon seen in research when assessing new tools and instruments that should be taken into account. Further exploration of possible barriers to implementing the Asante Tool should be done with probation officers and justice staff before implementing the tool.

Recommendations

1. *Due to the higher number of referrals of young offenders with possible FASD to the MYJC program by the Asante Tool seen in the prospective study it can be concluded that the Asante Tool is effective at screening for youth with possible FASD.* As well, the tool increases awareness of probation officers to social and neurodevelopmental factors associated with FASD in young offenders on their case load. The Asante Tool generated more referrals than the Red Flag Method during the prospective study period. Furthermore, it increased awareness of youth with possible FASD who were on probation officers existing caseloads that had previous referrals made by other staff in the youth justice system. This demonstrates the Asante Tool's ability to increase awareness of FASD symptoms in the young offenders whom they serve. Mandatory, systematic screening of every youth with a history with the justice system on each probation officers case load using the Asante Tool will lead to increased referrals to the FASD program and less youth falling through system gaps. Implementing a tool/form that probation officers must fill out on all youth on their caseload who have a history with the justice system guarantees a place of definitive contact where youth will

be screened for FASD. At the moment this place of contact can be multiple staff throughout the youth's journey with the justice system. The implementation of this tool is a guarantee that the majority of young offenders who come through the MYC are screened for FASD and ensures less youth are missed. This process will ultimately improve appropriate sentencing, treatment and rehabilitation for young offenders with FASD.

2. *Results of both studies demonstrate that the two different screening methods identify different youth with possible FASD.* Therefore, the Asante Tool should be implemented in tandem with the Red Flag Method. Results of the retrospective study and prospective study show that the two screening methods are identifying different youth who may be at risk for FASD. This is an extremely important considering if the Asante Tool is going to be implemented in Winnipeg. FASD program staff have raised concern that if the red flag method is replaced by the Asante Tool, certain youth who display more behavior symptoms rather than have a history of social/environmental factors will be missed. *It is recommended that the Asante Tool be implemented with integration of the Red Flag Method.* Probation officers should be trained in using the Asante Tool for all youth on their caseloads that have a pre-sentence report or who they feel they have enough information to fill out the screen. They should also be trained to identify the behaviors classified as "red flags" for potential FASD in young offenders. If a youth who a probation officer believes displays red flags, but does not screen positive on the Asante screen, this youth should still be referred to the FASD program. Moreover, the Asante Screening Tool can only be used for youth who the probation officer has enough information to fill out the screen. In Winnipeg, this generally means youth who have existing pre-sentence reports are good candidates. The Red Flag method can be applied to youth who do not have a history with the justice system. Integrating both methods ensures that youth do not get missed using one method over another. In jurisdictions where there is no red flag method, the Asante Tool can be a helpful tool that will generate awareness of FASD in the young offender population.
3. *The Asante Tool should be implemented for use by probation officers only.* The Asante Tool was created for use by probation officers. Due to the family history, educational and neurobehavioral information required to fill out the tool effectively, we feel probation officers are in the best position to effectively use this tool to screen for young offenders with FASD. This tool may be adapted for use by other justice staff but this is beyond the scope of this study. Future work should be done in this area since other intuitional staff, families and community members also make referrals to the Manitoba FASD Youth Justice Program and the current formatting of the Asante Tool may not be applicable to them.
4. *Consistent and mandated FASD education sessions and screening training for FASD in young offenders for probation officers should be implemented throughout Manitoba Youth Justice.* There appears to be inconsistent knowledge in terms of the probation officers using the red flag method and for identifying youth with

possible FASD. A systematic approach to FASD education and screening tool training sessions should be created to enhance the capabilities of probation officers to screen for young offenders with FASD. Resources should be allocated to the Manitoba FASD Youth Justice Program to facilitate this additional training and to ensure training is continued in regular sessions throughout the future of this program. This will ensure that new probation officers who join the system are educated about FASD.

5. *Further exploration with probation officers must be done to address issues of time, workload and other barriers to implementation of a new screening tool.* Survey responses and feedback to study staff indicate there may be barriers to implementing the Asante tool in MYJC including issues of increased workload and time constraints. Probation officers are extremely busy front line personnel and are stretched for time and resources. The implementation of an additional tool may be resisted. Further discussion with probation officers should be done to elaborate on survey responses, for example why certain probation officers are strongly opposed to a new tool, while some see the value in it. The study team will have a session with probation officers who participated in this study to feed results back to participants and gain more context in interpreting these results.

Lessons Learned for Other Jurisdictions

It is our hope that this study will enhance the capabilities of probation officers and ultimately other staff at MYC and in other Youth Correction staff across Canada to accurately screen for Fetal Alcohol Spectrum Disorder. Below is a summary of the key lessons learned through this research process.

1. *Stakeholder buy-in is necessary when evaluating existing screening methods or new screening tools for identifying FASD in the young offender population.* The support of policy makers, judges, physicians and front line staff (i.e., probation officers) is key in conducting research in the youth justice system where time and resources are scarce. Including key stakeholders in the development of the research questions ensured that the projects priorities were aligned with the goals of the MYJC. Including the FASD program manager as part of the research team motivated study participations, i.e., to complete screening tools, return data collection forms in a timely fashion and take ownership of their participation in the research process as they had a familiar face as a point of contact to the study. This also increased their perception of the value in the study, as they were able to discuss the study with a fellow staff. Furthermore, the involvement of the program manager is invaluable in interpreting study results. The rich insight brought by the perspective of people running community programs answers many questions throughout the research process and ensures results are interrupted correctly and that few assumptions are made by researchers. The involvement of administrators, judicial leaders, program leaders and front line staff is highly recommended for other health care professionals or researchers looking to embark on community based research and evaluation in the youth justice system.

2. *Ethical issues of privacy and consent need to be taken into consideration.* Concerns from University Health Ethics Research Boards and the judicial system will need to be addressed when conducting research in this vulnerable and highly sensitive population. Background checks will be conducted by courts of research personal not affiliated with the justice system. Issues of consent will need to be taken into account for screening youth with possible FASD and may delay study goals by several months. These hurdles should be taken into account when planning the timeline for research projects and evaluations in the youth justice system.
3. *Conducting research in the youth justice system, particularly in the field of FASD is challenging versus conducting research in a controlled research setting.* Results will be biased due to lack of gold standard and systematic approaches to FASD screening and diagnosis. As stated, sensitivity and specific calculations that are not biased are impossible to achieve without a gold standard of screening FASD in the young offender population. Such a standard does not currently exist for screening young offenders with FASD. Furthermore, short study periods that are constrained due to issues of feasibility and workload of front line staff will generate small sample sizes. Despite these methodological issues, rich information can still be generated to assist local communities in evaluating current screening methods and deciding if the Asante Screening Tool should be implemented in their own jurisdictions.
4. *Amalgamation of screening methods may be necessary.* When considering implementing a screening tool or evaluating an existing method of screening in the youth justice system, healthcare professionals and researchers must assess what is currently working, and what is not working. Researchers and policy makers must be open to amalgamating portions of existing methods that are effective and familiar to justice staff in each region. This open mindedness and collaboration increases the capacity of accurate screening among youth in justice systems across Canada, and ensures that highest numbers of youth possible are identified for further diagnostic assessments.
5. *Capacity of the system must be taken into account when implementing screening for young offenders with FASD.* Screening for FASD among young offenders is only ethical and effective if the community has the capacity to offer these youth a full diagnostic assessment. The Manitoba FASD Program is an excellent example of an effective, cost-effective model that utilizes existing resources in the community to screen and facilitate diagnosis of FASD among youth offenders. The success of this program would not be possible without the expertise of a psychologist from the Manitoba Adolescent Treatment Centre and the physicians in the Manitoba FASD Diagnostic Clinic, which is the only provincially centralized clinic for diagnosing children with FASD. The capacity of Manitoba Youth Justice System to address the complex needs of young offenders with FASD is enhanced through collaboration with this clinic. This collaborative program is a model for all jurisdictions across Canada who can access these types of services.

7.9 Conclusions

This research has attempted to assess sensitivity and specific statistics for the Asante Screening Tool. It is difficult to calculate these statistics using existing screening methods, since none of these existing methods are "gold standards" in screening for FASD among the young offender population. When using full diagnostic assessments as the gold standard, issues of feasibility in conducting real world, community-based research are barriers and small sample sizes and system capacity to facilitate FASD diagnostic assessments need to be taken into account.

The Asante Tool is an easily administrated screening tool that probation officers can use to screen youth who they have a previous history with. This tool can be filled out in a timely manner and can facilitate further assessments for youth with possible FASD. In jurisdictions that do not have an existing method of referral the Asante Tool would be beneficial. In Manitoba where there is strong support for the Red Flag method, the tools should be integrated to ensure the highest proportion of youth who are at risk for FASD are identified and referred to the FASD program. Resources should be allocated to support ongoing and mandatory training for probation officers and corrections staff in identifying youth that have behavioral, social/environmental and neurobehavioral characteristics that place them at risk for FASD. FASD educational session should also be done to ensure a consistent knowledge base of this illness across the youth justice system.

Probation officers are an important point of contact for young offenders and are essential personnel that can identify possible FASD. To date there is no consistent and systematic way for staff at the Manitoba Youth Corrections to screen for young offenders at risk for FASD. Adolescents with FASD may fall through the gaps when being ushered through a fragmented legal, child welfare, educational and health system. Enhancing the capacity of probation officers to screen for FASD by implementing a systematic approach to education, training and screening will ensure the needs of these vulnerable youth will be met through a full diagnostic assessment. Youth who receive an FASD diagnosis are in the position to receive additional supports for treatment and management of their disorder. Ultimately, this will increase the well-being of young offenders afflicted with FASD by increasing the fairness and appropriateness of sentences, and tailoring the rehabilitation and treatment.

Acknowledgements We thank the probation officers and youth who participated in this study, and the senior management of Manitoba Corrections and the Manitoba Provincial courts for their support. Funding for this project was provided by the Canadian Association of Pediatric Health Centers FASD Screening Tool Initiative and the Public Health Agency of Canada.

The views and opinions expressed herein are those of the authors and do not reflect the views of the Manitoba Government or Manitoba Youth Corrections.

Appendices

Appendix 1: FASD Screening and Referral Tool for Youth Probation Officers

FASD Screening and Referral Tool for Youth Probation Officers

Screening Checklist

Please check all boxes in sections A and B that apply to this youth.

A. SOCIAL FACTORS

O Youth is adopted

O Youth has been in foster care or involved with child protection services

O Youth has a sibling with a documented diagnosis of FAS/pFAS/ARND

O There is documentation that youth is *suspected* of having FAS/pFAS/ARND

O Youth's mother has a history of alcoholism or known prenatal alcohol use

B. PERSONAL FACTORS

O Developmental delay in early childhood (e.g., required speech/language therapy, occupational therapy or child development services prior to school entry)

O School learning difficulties (e.g., required learning assistance, modified or special program, school failure or drop-out for academic reasons

O Growth deficiency (i.e., short height or low weight)

O Diagnosis of Attention Deficit Hyperactivity Disorder (ADHD or ADD)

O Other mental health diagnosis

oAnxiety	oPost Traumatic Stress Disorder
oDepression	oOppositional Defiant Disorder
oConduct Disorder	oSubstance Misuse Disorder
oAttachment Disorder	oUnknown
oOther ______________________	

Using the information in A and B previous, refer for an FASD assessment if youth meets the following criteria:

O One Social Factor (Section A) PLUS at least Two Personal Factors (Section B) **OR**

O No Social Factors (Section A) PLUS at least Three Personal Factors (Section B)

Is there documentation in medical, social service, and or court records that the youth already has a diagnosis of FAS/pFAS/ARND or FAE.

O Yes O No

If yes, who made the diagnosis: ______________________

Date of diagnosis: ______________________

Location: ______________________

To be used with the Youth Probation Officers' Guide to FASD Screening and Referral (2010)
Available for download at www.asantecentre.org
Page 2 of 4

THE ASANTE CENTRE
for fetal alcohol syndrome

Appendix 2: Survey for Study Participants Using the Red Flag Method

How easy and effective is the Red Flag Method for FASD Screening and Referral?

Thank you for taking out the time to fill out the following survey on your experience in referring youth with possible FASD to the FASD Youth Justice Program.

	Strongly Disagree	Disagree	Neutral	Agree	Strongly Agree
1. I am framiliar with the "red flag" method to screen for FASD in youth.	❑	❑	❑	❑	❑
2. I feel confident using the red flag method to reffer youth with possible FASD to the FASD Justice program.	❑	❑	❑	❑	❑
3. I have referred youth using this method in the past.	❑	❑	❑	❑	❑
4. I would like more training for screening youth with potential FASD.	❑	❑	❑	❑	❑
5. The Red Flag method is an effective way to screen youth with potential FASD.	❑	❑	❑	❑	❑
6. I would prefer to use a tool/form to help guide me in reffering youth with possible FASD to the FASD youth justice program.	❑	❑	❑	❑	❑

Please feel free to write down any comments you have about your experience using the "Red Flag Method" and it's effectiveness in screening youth with potential FASD:

Appendix 3: Survey for Study Participants Using Asante Centre Screening Tool

How easy and effective is the Asante Centre Youth Probation Officer's Tool to FASD Screening and Referral?

Thank you for taking out the time to fill out the following survey on your experience using the Asante Centre FASD Screening Tool.

	Strongly Disagree	Disagree	Neutral	Agree	Strongly Agree
1. The Asante Centre Screening Tool is user-friendly.	❑	❑	❑	❑	❑
2. I could answer the majority of the questions on the screen using the information I had.	❑	❑	❑	❑	❑
3. I left the majority of questions on the Asante Centre screening tool blank for most youth.	❑	❑	❑	❑	❑
4. The Asante Centre Tool can be filled out under 20 minutes.	❑	❑	❑	❑	❑
5. The Asante Centre Tool is an effective way to screen youth with potential FASD.	❑	❑	❑	❑	❑
6. I would prefer to use the Asante Cetnre tool compared to the current way to reffer youth to the FASD Youth Justice program.	❑	❑	❑	❑	❑
7. I reffer more youth for further FASD assessment using the Asante Centre Screening tool than I usually do	❑	❑	❑	❑	❑

References

Burd, L., R. Selfridge, M. Klug, and T. Juelson. 2003. Fetal alcohol syndrome in the Canadian corrections system. *The International Journal of FAS* 1: e14.

Burd, L., R. Selfridge, M. Klug, and S. Bakko. 2004. Fetal alcohol syndrome in the United States corrections system. *Addiction Biology* 9 (2): 169–176. Discussion 177–178.

Chudley, A.E., J. Conry, J.L. Cook, C. Loock, T. Rosales, and N. LeBlanc. 2005. Fetal alcohol spectrum disorder: Canadian guidelines for diagnosis. *CMAJ: Canadian Medical Association Journal = Journal de l'Association Medicale Canadienne* 172 (5 Suppl): S1–S21.

Conry, J.L., D.K. Fast, and C.A. Loock. 1997. *Youth in the criminal justice system: Identifying FAS and other developmental disabilities*. Vancouver: Final Report to the Ministry of the Attorney General.

Conry, J.L., BK, R. Wilier. 2009. *Cognitive profiles and social risk factors in youth justice clients with FASD*. Paper presented at: 3rd international conference on fetal alcohol spectrum disorder.

Cook, J.L., C.R. Green, C.M. Lilley, S.M. Anderson, M.E. Baldwin, A.E. Chudley, J.L. Conry, N. LeBlanc, C.A. Loock, J. Lutke, B.F. Mallon, A.A. McFarlane, V.K. Temple, T. Rosales, and Canada Fetal Alcohol Spectrum Disorder Research Network. 2016. Fetal alcohol spectrum disorder: a guideline for diagnosis across the lifespan. *Canadian Medical Association Journal = Journal de l'Association Medicale Canadienne* 188 (3): 191–197.

FAS Diagnostic & Prevention Network [Internet]. 2014. *FAS facial photographic analysis software*. https://depts.washington.edu/fasdpn/htmls/face-software.htm. Accessed Mar 21 2014.

Fast, D.K., and J. Conry. 2004. The challenge of fetal alcohol syndrome in the criminal legal system. *Addiction Biology* 9 (2): 161–166. Discussion 167–168.

———. 2009. Fetal alcohol spectrum disorders and the criminal justice system. *Developmental Disabilities Research Reviews* 15 (3): 250–257.

Fast, D.K., J. Conry, and C.A. Loock. 1999. Identifying fetal alcohol syndrome among youth in the criminal justice system. *Journal of Developmental and Behavioral Pediatrics: JDBP* 20 (5): 370–372.

Goh, Y.I., A.E. Chudley, S.K. Clarren, et al. 2008. Development of Canadian screening tools for fetal alcohol spectrum disorder. *The Canadian Journal of Clinical Pharmacology = Journal Canadien de Pharmacologie Clinique* 15 (2): e344–e366.

Harvie, M., S. Longstaff, and A.E. Chudley. 2011. The Manitoba FASD Youth Justice Program: Addressing criminal justice issues. In *Fetal alcohol spectrum disorder – Management and policy perspectives of FASD*, ed. E.P. Riley, S.K. Clarren, J. Weinberg, and E. Jonsoon. Weinheim: Wiley-VCH Verlag GmbH & Co.

Loeber, R., and D.P. Farrington. 2000. Young children who commit crime: Epidemiology, developmental origins, risk factors, early interventions, and policy implications. *Development and Psychopathology* 12 (4): 737–762.

MacPherson, P., A.E. Chudley, and B.A. Grant. 2011. *Fetal alcohol spectrum disorder (FASD) in a correctional population: Prevalence, screening and characteristics*. Report to Corrections Services Canada.

Murphy, A., M. Chittenden, and The McCreary Centre Society. 2005. *Time out II: A profile of BC youth in custody*. Vancouver: The McCreary Centre Society.

Popova, S., S. Lange, D. Bekmuradov, A. Mihic, and J. Rehm. 2011a. Fetal alcohol spectrum disorder prevalence estimates in correctional systems: A systematic literature review. *Canadian Journal of Public Health = Revue Canadienne de Sante Publique* 102 (5): 336–340.

Popova, S., B. Stade, D. Bekmuradov, S. Lange, and J. Rehm. 2011b. What do we know about the economic impact of fetal alcohol spectrum disorder? A systematic literature review. *Alcohol and Alcoholism (Oxford, Oxfordshire)* 46 (4): 490–497.

Rojas, E.Y., and H.M. Gretton. 2007. Background, offence characteristics, and criminal outcomes of aboriginal youth who sexually offend: A closer look at Aboriginal youth intervention needs. *Sexual Abuse: A Journal of Research and Treatment* 19 (3): 257–283.

Streissguth, A.P., H. Barr, K. Kogan, and F. Bookstein. 1997. Primary and secondary disabilities in fetal alcohol syndrome. In *The challenges of fetal alcohol syndrome: Overcoming secondary disabilities*, ed. A.P. Streissguth and J. Kanter. Seattle: University of Washington Press.

Streissguth, A.P., F.L. Bookstein, H.M. Barr, P.D. Sampson, K. O'Malley, and J.K. Young. 2004. Risk factors for adverse life outcomes in fetal alcohol syndrome and fetal alcohol effects. *Journal of Developmental and Behavioral Pediatrics: JDBP* 25 (4): 228–238.

Zara, G., and D.P. Farrington. 2010. A longitudinal analysis of early risk factors for adult-onset offending: What predicts a delayed criminal career? *Criminal Behaviour and Mental Health: CBMH* 20 (4): 257–273.

Part III
Characteristics of People with FASD

Chapter 8
Social Incompetence of FASD Offenders: Risk-Awareness as a Factor in Criminal Culpability

Stephen Greenspan and George Woods

Abstract People with Fetal Alcohol Spectrum Disorders (FASD) have a greater incidence of criminal justice contact, most often for petty offenses but sometimes for serious crimes. There is a growing consensus, as reflected in criminal statutes and bar association recommendations that FASD may decrease culpability for guilt and may be a mitigating factor in sentencing. The rationale usually noted is that the brain damage associated with FASD affects judgment, reasoning and self-control. Such a rationale, while undoubtedly true, would be more understandable and convincing if it could be embedded within a theory of social behavior and potentially impaired capacity and incompetence. In this paper, we describe a model of both static and dynamic social comptence and apply it to concrete criminal offenses engaged in by individuals with FASD or related neuro-developmental disorders.

Keywords Violence · Culpability · Incompetence · Mitigation

8.1 Introduction

A central assertion in this paper is that many criminal acts can be characterized as "foolish," in that they are committed by individuals who often fail to take into account the significant risks to the perpetrator, and—sometimes—to the target of the crime (Greenspan 2009). The notion of risk is central to Common Law theories of criminal culpability and punishment, as seen in legal philosopher

---

This chapter is dedicated to the memory of Scharlette Holdman, PhD, a pioneer in the field of culpability mitigation, and a founder of the profession of mitigation specialist.

S. Greenspan (✉)
Department of Educational Psychology, University of Connecticut, Storrs, CT, USA

Department of Psychiatry, University of Colorado, Denver, CO, USA
e-mail: stephen.greenspan@gmail.com

G. Woods
University of California-Berkeley, CA, USA
e-mail: gwoods@georgewoodsmd.com

E. Jonsson et al. (eds.), *Ethical and Legal Perspectives in Fetal Alcohol Spectrum Disorders (FASD)*, International Library of Ethics, Law, and the New Medicine 75,
https://doi.org/10.1007/978-3-319-71755-5_8

H.L.A. Hart's (1968) definition of a crime as "an act which puts at risk some legally protected interest." In Hart's definition, an "act" is a volitional bodily movement. Thus, harming someone while sleep-walking or having a seizure is not a crime because it is not volitional. A legally protected interest could be health (put at risk by assault or homicide) or wealth (put at risk by theft or fraud). Given the centrality of risk to such a definition of a crime, and the requirement that it be volitionally (consciously) carried out, factors which impair risk-awareness would appear to provide a strong rationale for determining possible mitigation of criminal culpability and sentence for offenders with a neurodevelopmental disorder such as FASD (American Bar Association 2013). That is because such disorders can be defined as "common sense deficit disorders" (Greenspan et al. 2011), with common sense defined as "awareness of obvious risk."

Although the concept of relative risk awareness is implicit in currently operative notions of criminal culpability, these notions were developed in the eighteenth and nineteenth centuries and obviously do not reflect a sophisticated or multifaceted model of human behavior. In this paper, we explore—in a preliminary fashion—the implications of current thinking about risk-awareness, foolishness and brain pathology, for development of a systematic rationale and method for determining if, when and how offenders with FASD should be eligible for reduced or alternative sentences.

8.2 Criminal Behavior as a Socially Incompetent Outcome

The term "incompetence" describes behavior which fails to achieve some desired end. Such failure could be practical (e.g., failure to build a coat rack that stands up), academic (e.g., failure to complete a course of studies) or social (e.g., failure to win and hold a job or a romantic relationship). The types of incompetence often overlap. Thus, while inability to master practical job tasks is often cited as the reason for keeping or losing a job (Gurwitch 2006), inability to avoid rubbing people the wrong way will get one fired in all settings, from executive suites (Barak 2013) to supported employment arrangements (Greenspan and Shoultz 1981). Social competence is perhaps even more important for people with marginal intelligence or cognitive deficits, as persons with higher intelligence are better able to adapt to marginal social circumstances and are more likely to have boorish behavior excused as a sign of eccentricty.

Social competence can be approached in two ways: (a) particular outcomes, or (b) traits which contribute to those outcomes. Outcomes that are looked at vary in terms of the age of the individual; for children, the most widely-used social outcome is popularity (measured typically through peer nominations or ratings), while for adults, social competence outcomes involve such things as holding a job and staying out of jail. Popularity is important for people across the age span, however, as almost everyone desires friends and feels pain when these are lacking. In childhood, rejected children are considered at risk of mental illness (Cowen and Work 1988).

In adulthood, absence of "normal" friends is a risk factor for criminal conduct. This is seen in the cases of people with FASD (who are often socially rejected from childhood on), who are often befriended by deviant individuals who prey on the naïve trust typically exhibited by people with brain impairments, a naïveté which makes them vulnerable to being talked into participating in crimes from which they have little to gain and much to lose (Belik 2012).

Being incarcerated, or facing the prospect of being convicted of a crime, can be considered an incompetent outcome, in that being locked up is an outcome desired by almost no one, unless they have become "habituated" due to a lack of familiarity with life outside of prison. People with FASD are reported (the exact size of the difference has not been reliably determined) to have much higher rates of arrest and incarceration than normally developing peers (Streissguth and Kanter 1988). While a single arrest incident is not in itself conclusive, the combination of cognitive impairment and a pattern of repeated arrests or incarcerations, especially for the same class of acts, is *prima facie* evidence of social incompetence. Our purpose in this paper is to explore the relationship between social incompetence and criminal behavior.

We have thus far discussed social competence in terms of outcomes (popularity in childhood, staying employed or jail-free in adulthood). In the next section, we want to discuss it mainly in terms of inputs: skills or behavioral tendencies which facilitate or sabotage good social outcomes. First, we discuss a static model of social competence developed a number of years ago, and then we discuss a dynamic model of social competence developed more recently. The dynamic model is more useful as a guide to understanding criminal behavior, as it focuses on the specific act which got the person (or could have gotten him or her) in trouble, rather than on the person as a "criminal." This is especially important when looking at offenders with FASD, as their criminal careers tend to involve (with exceptions—having brain damage does not rule out the possibility of also being nasty) very poor judgment in handling occasional situations of temptation, pressure, or challenge, most often novel or stressful (Godefroy 2003).

8.3 Static and Dynamic Models of Social Incompetence

The concept of social competence was much talked about in the 1970s, when evaluations of early educational intervention projects proved unsuccessful in raising IQ and researchers started casting about for alternative outcomes to measure (Ziger and Trickett 1978). A tripartite model (Greenspan 1981, depicted in Fig. 8.1) attained some traction in the special education and disability professional community. It has three components: Temperament, Character, and Social Intelligence. Temperament refers to self-regulatory traits, such as attention, ability to inhibit, and emotion; Character refers to personality traits such as assertiveness and niceness; while Social Intelligence refers to awareness skills such as interpersonal sensitivity, understanding of context, and judgment.

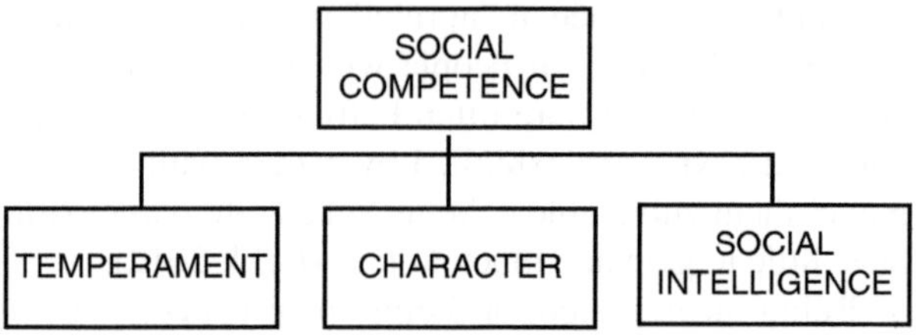

Fig. 8.1 Static model of social competence (From Greenspan 1981)

People with a neurodevelopmental disorder, such as FASD, are likely to have impairments in all three domains. Two of these—Temperament (attention and self-regulation) and Social Intelligence (reading other people and anticipating social consequences)—are primary deficits, in that they are direct consequences of the brain damage, while the third—Character (suggestibility and lack of ego strength)—is a secondary outcome, as it is a form of adaptation that an individual makes to the fact that he/ she has a lifetime of failure, and finds it usually useful (but sometimes catastrophically mistaken) to imitate and follow along with others. However, suggestibility and poor ego strength may also be by-products of cognitive impairment, as inability to withstand social pressure reflects both failure to give sufficient weight to social danger as well as failure to appeciate one's own right to say "no."

A limitation of a static content model of social competence is that each of the three factors can describe a person as he or she generally functions, but they do not operate in combination to explain the person's "stream of behavior" as a function of those traits operating in tandem. A related limitation is that the model focuses purely on the person, with no place for environmental input. In fact, one cannot fully understand any social (or non-social) behavior without looking at the context in which it occurs. Furthermore, few human behaviors can be explained by a single factor; most often two or more play an inducing role, and there may also be some forces operating in a countervailing direction (an example would be someone counseling an actor to stop and think, as opposed to someone urging him to act on dangerous impulses). For this reason, the behavior (gullible or not gullible, for example) is not fully predictable, as the strength of the factors in a given situation can never be fully known, and—in line with chaos or catastrophe (bifurcation) theory—a very small change in the valence of one factor can push one from an adaptive to a non-adaptive course of action (Stewart and Peregoy 1983).

A dynamic model of social competence contains the three domains (Temperament, Character and Social Intelligence) in the static model, but frames them less in terms of traits that apply to all situations, and more as forces that contribute to behavior (competent or incompetent) in a given specific situation. A situational component must, therefore, be one of the forces in such a model.

The dynamic model portrayed in Fig. 8.2 was first (Greenspan et al. 2001) framed as a theory of gullibility (induced socially risk-unaware behavior), then as a model of "foolish" (all forms of risk-unaware) behavior (Greenspan 2009), and here is being framed as a general theory of socially incompetent behavior, with or without involvement of risk. The three domains in the static model are included: social intel-

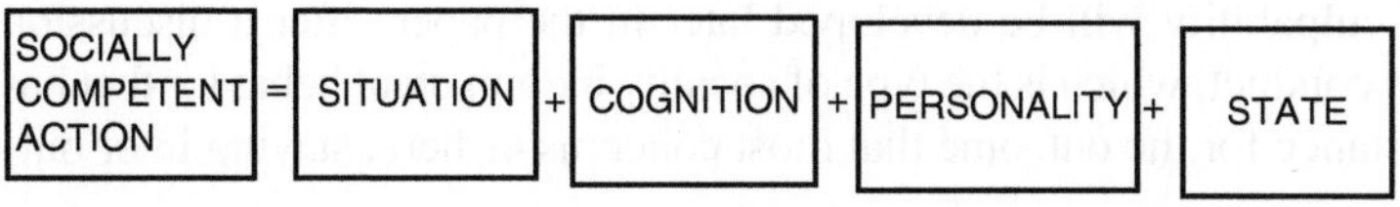

Fig. 8.2 Dynamic model of socially competent action (Adapted from Greenspan 1998)

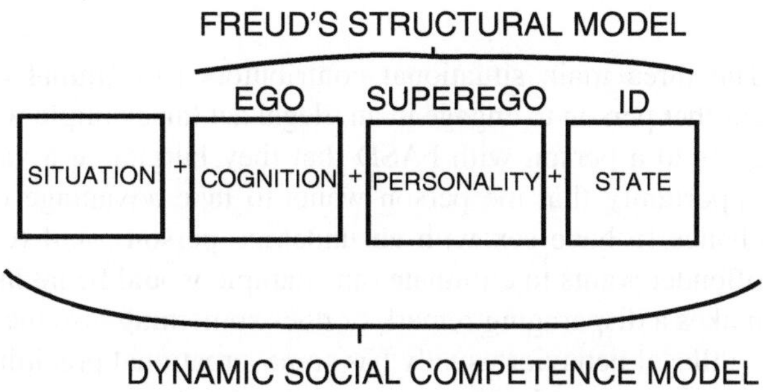

Fig. 8.3 Congruence between competence and Freudian models (Adapted from Greenspan et al. 2011)

ligence (renamed "cognition"), temperament (renamed "state") and character (renamed "personality"). In addition, there is a contextual component (termed "situations"). Behavior—whether competent or incompetent—is viewed as the result of the intersection of all four components, with the situational component grounding the behavior (with any attendant outcome, such as getting arrested) in the specific context surrounding the event. This model is loosely based on the motivational theory of Martin Ford (1992).

It has been pointed out (Robert Shilkret 2009 personal communication)—because of the role of multiple influences, in addition to the unpredictability of a given outcome—that this version of the social competence model is broadly psychodynamic, with similarities to Freud's "structural" (Id, Ego, Superego) theory. Two differences are that: (a) the outcome that mainly interested Freud was verbal parapraxes (slips of the tongue), while we address all forms of overt behavior, and (b) Freud, in line with other personality theorists, had little place in his model for the role of situations. The similarity between the two models can be seen in Fig. 8.3, with Id corresponding to state, Ego corresponding to cognition, and Superego corresponding to personality. As mentioned, Situation is included in our model but is missing in the Freudian model).

8.4 Relevance of Each Factor for Explaining Criminal Conduct

Each of the four factors in the dynamic social competence model will now be described, with a brief mention of how each of the factors might make people with FASD especially vulnerable to performing criminal offenses. This connection to criminal culpability will be developed later in the paper, after a discussion of risk-oblivious conduct, which is the type of socially incompetent behavior that has particular importance for the outcome that most concerns us here: staying in or out of jail.

8.4.1 Situational Contributors to Criminal Acts

The three main situational contributors to criminal acts are: (a) pressure from another person to engage in an illegal act (an example would be when someone suggests to a person with FASD that they burglarize a vacant or dark home), (b) an opportunity that the person wants to take advantage of (an example would be a chance to have sex with an underage person), and (c) a source of pain that the offender wants to eliminate (an example would be taking revenge on someone who makes a disparaging remark or does something else the person finds offensive).

Illegal behavior usually has some situational precipitant or antecedent, but these vary in terms of salience (the external pressure, temptation or precipitant may be strong or weak) and/ or ambiguity (the illegal nature of the act may be clear or unclear). People with neurodevelopmental disorders, such as FASD, do not require as much in the way of a situational precipitant, both because they are less likely to perceive the array of consequences or because they are more impaired in their decision-making style. In this way, situation always interacts with other factors, but situation itself is usually insufficient to explain an illegal action. (The one exception would be duress, where the actor is forced to do something at gunpoint or with a strong threat to the person or a loved one; in such a situation, many "normal" individuals would crumble, except of course where the threat is patently phony).

8.4.2 Cognitive Contributors to Criminal Acts

As mentioned in the above discussion of situations, contexts differ in the cognitive demands they pose for the offender. These demands can take various forms: (a) recognizing the illegality and criminal consequences of a particular act; (b) understanding the motives of someone who may be using deceptive pressure; (c) possessing verbal skills and diversionary mechanisms needed to escape from an uncomfortable situation, and (d) the ability to learn from past mistakes. People with FASD, and related neuro -developmental disorders, are deficient, to a greater or lesser degree, in all of these cognitive realms, and often lack the judgment, reasoning and problem-solving skills (including knowing when and how to seek help) to make intelligent decisions about acts that could get them in legal hot-water. In addition (a topic that will be addressed later), people with FASD—as measured in deficits in "executive functioning"—lack the cognitive ability to anticipate future consequences and, thus, are almost universally lacking in risk-awareness.

8.4.3 Personality Contributors to Criminal Conduct

People with FASD vary widely in their personalities (something true of all people, disabled or non-disabled), with some being introverted, some extroverted, some kind, others not so kind, etc. But there are compensations which people with FASD and other cognitive limitations make to get by in life, and these can and do contribute to illegal behavior. Among the most important of those compensations is a tendency towards interpersonal trust, credulity, and suggestibility (Brown et al. 2011). The reason for this is that people with cognitive impairments develop an "external" style (Switzky and Schultz 1988) in which they rely on others to provide clues as to how to behave in ambiguous situations. The cognitive impairments that are so often the core of a person with neurodevelopmental disorders create inabilities to see the big picture, understand emotionally complex circumstances, and respond effectively to social cues. These deficits are largely neurologically caused, but are exacerbated when the individual grew up in a family where perspective-taking was not encouraged or modeled.

We are thinking particularly of situations where the person with FASD has poor risk-awareness or limited understanding of the array of possible outcomes. This of course is also affected by the fact (discussed in the above section on situations) that people with FASD, because they are often not accepted by normally-developing peers, often are more accepted by peers with similar limited understanding of social mores. These marginally less impaired "friends" will often take advantage, consciously or unconsciously, of the FASD person's combination of social neediness, high trust and low social intelligence to induce them into criminal conduct that they might not engage in on their own. This does not rule out the possibility, of course, that the person with FASD can also have his or her own misanthropic tendencies which may need little encouragement. It is our experience, however, that "antisocial personality disorder" and other psychiatric labels are often inappropriately assigned to offenders with FASD and other neurodevelopmental disorders, as: (a) they lack the required poorly normed DSM criteria; and (b) their underlying brain-based condition is often missed or insufficiently understood as the cause of most of their difficulties.

8.4.4 State Contributors to Criminal Conduct

A universal characteristic of people with brain impairment, whether congenital or acquired, is a constellation of "temperamental" impairments. Included in this constellation are limitations in attention, behavior inhibition, affective stability, and other aspects of self-regulation. These tendencies are often exacerbated by the excessive use of intoxicants which characterize many young people with FASD. All of these factors interfere with the ability of individuals to control and reflect on their own behavior. Such a self-regulatory deficit increases the likelihood that an individual will engage in socially inappropriate and, often, illegal behavior. As with the two other intra-person contributors—Cognition and Personality—the contribution of State to criminal conduct does not stand alone, and should be considered in light of the situational context, as well as the possible role of the other two within-person factors. Like Cognition, but unlike Personality (which for the most part is a secondary accommodation to life as a brain-impaired person), State is largely an intra-individual characteristic mainly attributable directly to an FASD individual's cognitive deficits. An exception, however, would be when an individual's dysregulatory state is partly attributable to ingestion of alcohol or another psychoactive substance.

8.5 Risk-Obliviousness as a Type of Social Incompetence Found in FASD Individuals

FASD is a "disorder" (a brain-based medical condition), but many—assuming they meet arbitrary numeric criteria, especially a low-enough IQ score—also qualify for a "disability" label, such as Intellectual Disability" (ID; Salvador-Carulla et al. 2011). The term disability originated in the vocational rehabilitation system but today has much broader applicability. Essentially, it indicates that a particular bureaucracy (vocational, residential, educational, legal, social security, etc.) has determined that the person needs protections, subsidies or supports in order to function safely in various age-related social roles. Partly due to the recent celebratory emphasis on positive accomplishments and potential of people with disabilities when given appropriate supports (Bradley and Knoll 1995), there has been very little writing by disability theorists about what is likely to happen to people with disabilities when they do not receive such supports. At the risk of being seen as reactionaries who hark back to the days when virtually all of the emphasis was on what people with disabilities could not do, we feel that a balanced approach requires some discussion of the basic reason why the term disability is used, namely that without supports and protections, the majority of people given that label could experience catastrophically dangerous outcomes.

In a paper (Greenspan et al. 2011) focusing on ID, but with applicability to FASD (which we mention frequently in that paper) and other nerodevelopmental disorders, we argued that what makes people with these disorders "disabled" is a tendency to act in a manner that pays insufficient attention to social or physical risk. A developmental continuum (depicted in Fig. 8.4) was proposed; in terms of risk-awareness, that continuum ranged from "foolishness" (unawareness of obvious risk) through "common sense" (awareness of obvious risk) to "wisdom" (awareness of subtle and hidden risk). Most adults possess common sense (basic risk-awareness) but only a sub-set with unusual risk-discernment can be considered wise. People with brain-based cognitive disorders, however, are functioning at a younger developmental level in their inability to discern risks which to normally-developing peers would be fairly obvious.

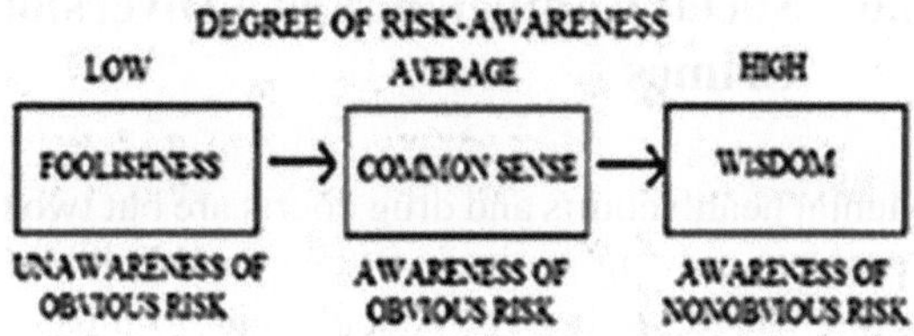

Fig. 8.4 Continuum of risk- awareness and unawareness (From Greenspan et al. 2011)

The continuum is developmental in two ways: (a) children, up until around age nine, lack even basic physical risk-awareness (which is why we do not allow youngsters to travel, cook, operate machinery or do many other daily living tasks independently, even if their motor and cognitive skills allowed them to) and (up until adolescence), lack social risk-unawareness (which is why we do not allow them to independently enter into contracts, whether monetary as in buying or selling property, or social, as in marrying or joining associations); (b) adults with significant developmental disabilities (who are essentially "fixated" at younger developmental ages) also lack important risk-awareness skills, which is why we put protective arrangements (e.g., staying at home long after others of their age-group have left, group homes, supported living or work arrangements, guardianships, etc.) into effect for their protection.

While the concept of risk-unawareness includes limitations in cognition, we are using the term to refer more broadly to observable behavior. As reflected in the dynamic social competence model, it is possible for someone to have some recognition of a risk in an action (such as illegal conduct) but to ignore it: (a) if the risk is not all that salient (situation), (b) if someone encourages him or her to participate in the action (situation), (c) if one is very motivated to engage in the behavior (state), (d) if one lacks the self-regulatory skills to resist the behavior (state), (e) if one is highly suggestible and dependent on the lead of others (personality), or (f) if one lacks moral concern about the rights or interests of others (personality). From a mitigation standpoint, risk unawareness, as reflected in impaired cognition, is undoubtedly most important, followed by state-based absence of self-regulatory control. But all factors can enter in; an example would be an offender who experienced abuse in childhood so horrendous that it elicited great empathy from jurors.

Many if not most illegal acts can be considered foolish, in that they pose unacceptable or unjustified risks both to the actor and/ or to the target of the act. (By characterizing a criminal act as foolish, we do not mean to minimize the possibility that it could also be very evil). Some illegal acts are undoubtedly more foolish than others: (a) because there is a high likelihood of being caught, (b) because the potential return to the actor does not justify running such a risk, (c) because the damage done to the target of the act is excessive or unjustified, or (d) because less, or non-risky, alternatives (such as verbal rebuke) is available to the actor. Lessened ability to assess risk has been cited as a rationale for reduced culpability and exempted or reduced sentences for youths (Steinberg 2013) and for individuals with ID (Baroff 2010).

8.6 Social Competence as a Diversion Rationale for Minor Crimes

Mental health courts and drug courts are but two manifestations of something called "problem-solving justice" (Berman and Feinblatt 2005). The idea behind this concept—which we believe is applicable to most offenders with FASD—is that correctional facilities are overcrowded with inmates who are incarcerated less because they have committed serious crimes than because they lack the ability to comply with social norms or with procedural (e.g., showing up) requirements of probation or parole. The idea is to keep the individual from a revolving door of unnecessay jail time by getting prosecutors, judges and probation officers to recognize and be more flexible when dealing with brain-affected defendants who have deficits (such as in memory and executive functioning) which allow one to reframe the offending behaviors as a sign of disability rather than responsibiity.

It can be useful to think of such diversionary interventions in terms of the social competence model described above. Here is an illustrative example involving "Donald," a young man with FASD and high functioning Intellectual Disability. Donald has been in and out of foster care and group home facilities, and these placements typically end badly when he violates rules or acts out emotionally. His most recent court appearance occurred when he kicked another group-home resident in the leg and the police were called. Initially, the prosecutor charged Donald with felony assault, but the charge was reduced, and ultimately dropped, when the prosecutor and judge were helped by one of us to understand that Donald has the mental age (and frustration tolerance) of a 10-year-old, and such a severe sentence is obviously excessive when applied to someone who behaves socially in a manner more typical of a child than an adult.

Here is an analysis of Donald's action as explained by the dynamic social competence model. Cognitively, Donald lacked the risk-awareness to understand the consequences (arrest, plus expulsion from the group home with resultant homelessness) of striking another resident, especially now that he qualifies as an adult. Donald's most salient personality trait is egocentrism, which makes it difficult for him to comply with requests or treat others with respect. State (temperament) is an area of special (brain damage-caused) difficulty, as reflected in extreme impulsivity and emotional reactivity. The Setting factor was residing in a place where other residents were also socially immature, and the immediate stimulus probably was a mutual exchange of insults which escalated quickly. Also contributing to Donald's penchant for conflict was that this group home, like many, provides little in the way of social skills training or supports, and is staffed by people who themselves lack skills for managing conflict. (Donald has since been accepted into a program specializing in people with neuro-developmental disorders, and he is doing much better). The dynamic four-factor social competence model provides, we believe, a way to recognize that an action (kicking someone) which technically qualifies as a crime, might better be viewed as the cumulative outcome of several incapacities, most of which reflect brain-based immaturity rather than that adult criminal intent.

8.7 Social Competence and Mitigation of More Serious Crimes

In criminal law, a mitigating factor is information regarding a defendant or the circumstances of his or her crime that might persuade a judge, jury or prosecutor to seek or impose a lesser sentence. The mitigation process is most formalized in capital cases, as part of a penalty phase where courts are required to allow introduction of such evidence (e.g., Lockett v Ohio 1978) or in support of an "Atkins v Virginia" proceeding, in which a judicial finding that a petitioner has intellectual disability will cause exemption from capital punishment (Polloway 2015). Mitigation evidence can also play an important part in the trying of lesser offenses as well, as it can provide a window into a defendant's state of mind or legal culpability at the time a crime was committed (Dudley and Leonard 2008).

The basic purpose of mitigation is to enable someone to be seen as an individual rather than defined by the alleged or proven offense; to create sympathy for and understanding of the defendant; and to establish the possibility that he or she fully or partially lacks *mens rea* (criminal intent) and thus deserves a lesser punishment. Mitigating information essentially comes mostly from an extensive social history investigation (Holdman and Seeds 2008; Olive and Stetler 2008), and can be of various kinds, including but not limited to: (a) the circumstances of the crime (role of the victim, role of the defendant, domination of the defendant by a co-participant); (b) mental state of the defendant at the time of the offense (extreme emotional disturbance; impaired capacity to appreciate right from wrong or to conform one's conduct to the law); (c) character of the defendant (future non-dangerousness; history of good deeds); (d) history of severe mental illness; (e) history of brain-based injury, abnormality or impairment; and (f) history of severe abuse, hardship or deprivation.

As a rule, mitigating factors cannot also serve as aggravators, but an exception would be when a mental health diagnosis takes the form of a character disorder which portrays the person in a negative (e.g., nasty) light. This is controversial, as some courts prohibit use of mental health information as aggravators, while others allow it. A specialized sub-type of clinical examination applies to so-called "Atkins" (death penalty exemption due to ID) cases in which the task is narrowly focused on collecting information, much of it from percipient witnesses (family members, teachers, peers), focused on the person's cognitive and social-cognitive (e.g., gullibility) functioning and limitations both in academic and community settings and roles to ensure that person meets the well-established clinical guidelines for Intellectual Disability .

Two limitations of the way in which the mitigation process is often conducted are: (a) a tendency to rely on specific mental health diagnoses rather than the symptoms which form the basis of the impairment, and (b) a tendency to collect information in a haphazard manner that can be both overly inclusive and yet which may miss important domains of functioning, without use of a comprehensive and systematic organizing framework. It is our belief that the four-factor social competence model, used both statically and dynamically to understand foolish criminal action can provide such an organizing framework. For example, knowledge of Situation can indicate the extent to which the individual behaved in a manner lacking full volition or reflection because of external pressure or inept response to some action (such as escape attempt) initiated by the victim. Cognition can indicate that an individual may not have appreciated the risk to a victim of a particular act, or may have lacked the skills to escape from an emerging dangerous situation. Personality may indicate that an individual was highly trusting and gullible, and was generally a kind and law-abiding person. State may indicate that a person may have been in a panic mode, or highly emotionally labile. Taken together, all of these factors could put together a picture of a defendant with FASD that helps judges, juries or prosecutors to understand why a lesser sentence is justified.

8.8 Social Competence and Adaptive Functioning

FASD is one of the leading causes of Intellectual Disability (ID) and ID is a diagnosis for which a sizeable minority (at least a quarter) of people with FASD are eligible, and this number should increase as the more liberal criteria for ID in DSM-5 are implemented (Greenspan and Woods 2014). It behooves any mental health evaluator who believes, in the course of his or her determination that a client might have FASD to also consider the possibility that he or she might qualify for a diagnosis of ID. This is especially important in capital cases in jurisdictions in the United States which still have capital punishment (a consideration that does not apply to Canada or most other countries), in that a judicial finding of ID will cause a defendant to be exempt from the death penalty under *Atkins v Virginia.*

The type of mental health evaluation needed to establish ID in so-called "Atkins" proceedings is different from standard (e.g., penalty phase) examinations in that many of the kinds of information (such as familial violence or future non-dangerousness) gathered in social histories are not particularly germane for Atkins purposes. Conversely, there are kinds of information (such as a history of gullibility) that are not typically gathered in standard mental health evaluations (but probably should be), that are essential in establishing a diagnosis of ID and, for that matter, FASD. So, it is important that a mental health examiner understands exactly what is the purpose of a particular neurodevelopmental examination, and gather information accordingly, rather than to use the same "one size fits all" approach in every case. A complication, of course, is that both forms of clinical information may be needed: Atkins-specific data for a hearing held (typically) before a trial to determine if death can be pursued, and a broader social history investigation and clinical examination in the event that the Atkins claim is denied and a capital (or any) trial will immediately take place.

Social competence comes into play in an Atkins proceeding in that one of the three legal prongs in both clinical and judicial definitions of ID is "adaptive functioning" (also referred to as "adaptive behavior"). Adaptive Functioning deficits are also diagnostically indicative of FASD. In fact, one argument for diverting defendants with FASD from harsh criminal punishments is that from an adaptive behavior standpoint, people with FASD function in a socially vulnerable manner indistinguishable from that of people who (because of slightly lower IQ scores) may have received the ID diagnosis.

The model of adaptive functioning/adaptive behavior that is described in clinical manuals, including the recent DSM-5 (American Psychiatric Association 2013) was proposed by the first author over three decades ago (Greenspan 1981) and takes thee forms: Conceptual (deficits in functional academics), Practical (deficits in daily living and work-related tasks) and Social (deficits in social competence, particularly social intelligence). The literature on social adaptive functioning makes clear that what is of interest is not maladaptive behavior (e.g., aggression and criminal behavior) but rather deficits in interpersonal judgment and reasoning. That is because people with ID (as well as FASD) may or may not be "nice" or "nasty," but they regularly manifest poor interpersonal judgment, as reflected in repeated episodes of gullibility (being duped) and foolishness (ignoring of very predictable social risks). A problem with the implementation (as in DSM-5) of the recommendation to emphasize the cognitive aspects of social adaptive functioning when diagnosing ID is that formal rating instruments until fairly recently, had virtually no gullibility or foolishness content. That is changing, however, as both the recently-published Vineland-3 (Sparrow et al. 2016) as well as the forthcoming Diagnostic Adaptive Behavior Scale (DABS; Tassé et al. 2016), contain some gullibility items. On the DABS, those items are reported to discriminate powerfully between ID and non-ID subjects at the adult level. (They do not discriminate as well at the child level, for the obvious reason that all children are relatively gullible, whether cognitively impaired or not).

8.9 FASD as an Automatic Criminal Sentence Mitigator

There are a small number of legal jurisdictions where courts are instructed by statutory guidelines to consider alternate sentence structures for offenders who have FASD. This is analogous to the "mental health/drug courts," mentioned earlier, that are intended to keep mentally ill and/ or substance-abusing individuals from cyclically going to jail, by responding flexibly and compassionately to non-serious offenses such as lacking the organizational skills (a near universal problem in mentally- and brain-based disorders) to keep court-mandated commitments such as periodic urine analyses. FASD advocates have been lobbying to get other jurisdictions to adopt similar provisions, but few have yet done so. Typically, such automatically mitigated sentences for FASD defendants are available only for misdemeanors or minor felonies, but are not available for serious felonies such as manslaughter, rape or aggravated assault.

A problem with the implementation of such an accommodation is that it is often not done, typically because an attorney lacks awareness of his or her client's disorder. Furthermore, adequate and supportive alternatives to incarceration are difficult to find, even if funds were available to have an individual evaluated (a problem for even serious offenses, let alone minor ones) and even if clinicians could be located who possess specialized knowledge and training in FASD (an even bigger problem). All of this is exacerbated by the fact that the largest subcategory of FASD—Alcohol-Related Neurodevelopmental Disorder (ARND)—is diagnosed functionally (cognitive/ neuropsychological, adaptive functioning, evidence of maternal drinking) with no requirement or expectation of finding biomedical indicia. Developing effective treatment programs for brain-based disorders that do not respond to pharmacological interventions is also an impediment to the implementation of these legal mandates.

Because FASD it is not always an easy or reliable diagnosis to make, there are some—such as in the UK (Michael Rutter 2014 personal communication), where more conservative criteria for diagnosing FASD are in place—who would argue that using a FASD categorical pathway to automatically mitigated sentence is a mistake. In fact, there is a more fundamental reason for resisting use of a categorical approach to seeking mitigated sentencing for defendants with FASD, and that is because the same kinds of brain impairments with related developmentally-evident cognitive and social disorders, can be found in dozens (if not hundreds) of other conditions. There is, thus, a fundamental issue of unfairness involved in providing accommodation for people in one sub-class of neurodevelopmental disorder, but not for others with nearly identical characteristics and vulnerabilities, but who do not have the benefit of belonging to a class that is better known or which has more politically effective advocates.

As example, we are aware of one young man who as a newborn was diagnosed with Meconium Aspiration Syndrome (caused by breathing a mixture of meconium [tar-like initial stool] and amniotic fluid into the lungs during the birth process), and who as a consequence was identified during infancy as someone with special needs, and has throughout his young life functioned in a manner indistinguishable (with developmental and special education supports) from how he would have functioned had he been diagnosed with FASD. It is our view that this young man (who got into trouble as a result of sexual involvement with a minor shortly after he turned 18) should be considered for the same degree of consideration from the court as he would if had been diagnosed with the more prevalent, visible and politically supported condition of FASD. This issue in fact came up during the Consensus Conference on Law and FASD out of which this book emerged, (Binnie et al. 2014). The resulting policy recommendation (for proposed changes to the national Canadian criminal code) emphasized brain-based developmental disorders which cause limitations in such things as risk-awareness and rational thinking, and did not specify any one particular syndrome or diagnostic label. The point here is not to focus attention solely on the plight of people with FASD in the criminal justice system, but rather to focus attention on the plight of people with brain-based cognitive disorders (including those who have FASD) in the criminal justice system.

8.10 Conclusion

Ending up on death row or in prison for a very long time (or facing that likelihood), is a goal sought by almost nobody, which makes it a form of social incompetence. What makes it also foolish is that the likelihood of getting away with a serious crime is typically very small, especially for offenders with ordinary or below-average intelligence. A four-factor causative model of social competence was described in this paper to illustrate its potential utility as a static framework for devising a greater understanding of FASD within a legal framework, and as a dynamic framework for explaining the relationship between the cognitive deficits in FASD (and related disorders) and criminal intent. This framework is especially useful for offenders who have FASD, but could eventually have broader applicability. That is because there are many brain-based disorders where symptoms (impaired executive functioning, failure to anticipate risk, impulsivity and emotional lability, suggestibility and gullibility) are the same as those that are found in people with FASD, and where an affected defendant is entitled to the same legal protections and accommodations. Furthermore, even people who lack pathology or maldevelopment often make foolish decisions affected by confusion, emotion and lack of reflection. When such factors place individuals in legal jeopardy, the cause of justice will be better served if various parties in the legal process come to better and more fully understand who they are and why they acted as they did. In this paper, we presented a very preliminary picture of how a static and dynamic model of social competence can assist in this process. We intend to develop the idea further in subsequent publications (e.g., Greenspan and Driscoll in press).

References

American Bar Association (2013). *Fetal Alcohol Spectrum Disorders: Legal issues*. Washington, DC.

American Psychiatric Association. 2013. *Diagnostic and statistical manual of mental disorders, 5th edition: DSM-5*. Alexandria: Author.

Barak, S. 2013, November 13. *Microsft's Sinofsky: Ambitious, abrasive, out of work* (embedded.com/print/330103).

Baroff, G.S. 2010. On the mitigating nature of Intellectual Disability (ID) in the offender with developmental disability. *NADD Bulletin* 8(1): Article 2.

Belik, V. 2012, April 13. Caring for people with FASD: From joy to pure "hell." *Yukon News*.

Berman, G., and J. Feinblatt. 2005. *Good courts: The case for problem-solving justice*. New York: The New Press.

Binnie, I., M. Trussler, and E. Jonsson, eds. 2014. *Legal Issues of FASD, Fetal Alcohol Spectrum Disorder. Proceedings from a consensus development conference*. Edmonton: Institute of Health Economics.

Bradley, V.J., and J. Knoll. 1995. Shifting paradigms in services to people with disabilities. In *Community rehabilitation services for people with disabilities*, ed. O.C. Karan and S. Greenspan. Boston: Butterworth-Heinemann.

Brown, N.N., G. Gudjonsson, and P. Connor. 2011. Suggestibility and Fetal Alcohol Spectrum Disorders (FASD): I'll tell you anything you want to hear. *Journal of Psychiatry and Law* 39: 39–71.

Cowen, E.L., and W.C. Work. 1988. Resilient children, psychological wellness, and primary prevention. *American Journal of Community Psychology* 16 (4): 591–607.

Dudley, R.G., Jr., and P.B. Leonard. 2008. Getting it right: Life history investigation as the foundation for a reliable mental health assessment. *Hofstra Law Review* 36: 963–988.

Ford, M.E. 1992. *Motivating humans: Goals, emotions, and personal agency beliefs*. Thousand Oaks: Sage.

Godefroy, O. 2003. Frontal syndrome and disorders of executive functions. *Journal of Neurology* 250 (1): 1–6.

Greenspan, S. 1981. Defining childhood social competence: A proposed working model. In *Advances in special education*, ed. B.K. Keogh, vol. 3. Greenwich: JAI Press.

Greenspan, S. 1998. A contextualist perspective on adaptive behavior. In *Measuring adaptive behavior*, ed. R. Schalock. AAMR: Washington, DC.

———. 2009. Foolish action in adults with Intellectual Disabilities: The forgotten problem of risk-unawareness. In *International review of research in mental retardation*, ed. L.M. Glidden. New York: Elsevier.

Greenspan, S., and J.M. Driscoll. in press. Naïve offenders: Violence and intellectual disability. In *Neuroscience and violence risk in criminal offender populations*, ed. J.M. Fabian. Portsmouth: Wiley.

Greenspan, S., and B. Shoultz. 1981. Why mentally retarded adults lose their jobs: Social competence as a factor in work adjustment. *Applied Research in Mental Retardation* 2: 23–38.

Greenspan, S., and G.W. Woods. 2014. Intellectual Disability as a disorder of reasoning and judgment: The gradual move away from IQ ceilings. *Current Opinion in Psychiatry* 27(2): 110–116.

Greenspan, S., G. Loughlin, and R. Black. 2001. Credulity and gullibility in persons with mental retardation. In *International review of research in mental retardation*, ed. L.M. Glidden, vol. 24, 101–135. New York: Academic Press.

Greenspan, S., H.N. Switzky, and G.W. Woods. 2011. Intelligence involves risk-awareness and Intellectual Disability involves risk-unawareness: Implications of a theory of common sense. *Journal of Intellectual & Developmental Disability* 36 (4): 1–33.

Gurwitch, A. 2006. *Fired!: Tales of the canned, canceled, downsized, and dismissed*. New York: Touchstone Publishing.

Hart, H.L.A. 1968. *Punishment and responsibility*. New York: Oxford University Press.

Holdman, S., and C. Seeds. 2008. Cultural competency in capital mitigation. *Hofstra Law Review* 36 (3): 883–922.

Lockett v Ohio. 1978. 438 U.S. 586, 605.

Olive, M.E., and R. Stetler. 2008. Using the supplementary guidelines for the mitigation function of defense teams in death penalty cases to change the picture in post-conviction. *Hofstra law Review* 36: 1067–1093.

Polloway, E.A., ed. 2015. *Intellectual disability and the death penalty*. Washington, DC: American Association on Intellectual and Developmental Disability.

Salvador-Carulla, L., G.M. Reed, L.M. Vaez-Azizi, S.A. Cooper, R. Martinez-Leal, et al. 2011. Intellectual developmental disorders: Towards a new name, definition and framework for "mental retardation/ intellectual disability" in ICD-11. *World Psychiatry* 10: 175–180.

Sparrow, S.S., D.V. Cicchetti, and D.V. Saulnier. 2016. *Vineland adaptive behavior scales, Third Edition* (Vineland-3). Antonio: Psychological Corporation.

Steinberg, L. 2013. The influence of neuroscience on U.S. Supreme Court decisions involving adolescents' criminal culpability. *Nature Reviews Neuroscience* 14: 513–518.

Stewart, I.N., and P.L. Peregoy. 1983. Catastrophe theory modeling in psychology. *Psychological Bulletin* 94 (2): 336–362.

Streissguth, A.P., and J. Kanter, eds. 1988. *The challenge of fetal alcohol syndrome: Overcoming secondary disabilities*. Seattle: University of Washington Press.

Switzky, H.N., and G.F. Schultz. 1988. Intrinsic motivation and learning performance Implications for Individual Educational Programming for learners with mild handicaps. *Remedial and Special Education* 9 (4): 7–14.

Tassé, M.J., R.L. Schalock, D. Thissen, G. Balboni, H. Bersani, S.A. Borthwick-Duffy, S. Spreat, K.F. Widaman, D. Zhang, and P. Navas. 2016. Developent and standardization of the Diagnostic Adaptive Behavior Scale: Application of item response theory to the assessment of adaptive behavior. *American Journal on Intellectual and Developmental Disabilities* 121: 79–94.

Zigler, E., and P.K. Trickett. 1978. IQ, social competence, and evaluation of early childhood intervention programs. *American Psychologist* 33 (9): 789–798.

Chapter 9
Understanding the Neurobehavioral Deficits and Psychologal Capacities of Individuals with FASD in the Criminal Justice System

Kaitlyn McLachlan and Carmen Rasmussen

9.1 Introduction

It has been well-documented that individuals with FASD are over-represented in the criminal justice system. Individuals with FASD display a variety of cognitive impairments (particularly in the areas of executive functioning and memory) that likely contribute to poor functional and adaptive outcomes, and ultimately legal issues. Unfortunately, these deficits may also impact their ability to competently navigate legal adjudication. Legal experts have questioned whether justice-involved individuals with FASD experience difficulties understanding and appreciating their legal rights and the nature of adjudication from arrest and interrogation through the criminal trial process. The following chapter provides a summary of both common neurobehavioral deficits observed in individuals with FASD, as well as the manner in which they may interact to impair legal capacities relevant to adjudication.

9.2 Executive Functioning and Memory in FASD

Individuals with FASD may present with a variety neurobehavioral impairments including difficulties with intelligence, attention, language, visual perception, learning and memory, behavior, and importantly executive functioning (Kodituwakku 2007). Impairments in executive functions (EF), which are higher-order cognitive abilities (Zelazo and Muler 2002) are pervasive in FASD (Rasmussen 2005), and

K. McLachlan
Department of Psychology, University of Guelph, Guelph, ON, Canada

C. Rasmussen (✉)
Department of Pediatrics, University of Alberta, Edmonton, AB, Canada
e-mail: carmen@ualberta.ca

E. Jonsson et al. (eds.), *Ethical and Legal Perspectives in Fetal Alcohol Spectrum Disorders (FASD)*, International Library of Ethics, Law, and the New Medicine 75,
https://doi.org/10.1007/978-3-319-71755-5_9

likely contribute to their poor functional outcomes. EF is an umbrella term encompassing many different complex cognitive processes. Individuals with FASD have been shown to display impairments on a range of EF tasks measuring cognitive flexibility, inhibition, planning, strategy use concept formation, verbal reasoning, working memory, and fluency (see Rasmussen 2005 for a review). These EF impairments are generally found to be more severe than would be expected based on their IQ (Connor et al. 2000; Kerns et al. 1997). The above EF may be considered 'cool EF' involving more cognitive-based tasks, which is in contrast to 'hot EF' which involve more emotion-based tasks and processing affective stimuli (Kodituwakku et al. 2001; Zelazo and Muller 2002).

Examining the various constructs of EF and understanding the cognitive skills involved in each type of task may help us understand how such impairments may be related to maladaptive behaviours and poor functional outcomes in FASD. For instance, impairments in inhibition have been well-documented in FASD (Rasmussen and Bisanz 2009; Mattson et al. 1999), typically with Stroop-like tasks where the participant has to inhibit a prepotent response. Difficulty inhibiting unwanted behavior could have serious consequences in FASD resulting them in engaging in undesirable behaviors, thus having implications for the legal system.

Another critical EF that may be impaired in FASD is planning, which is typically measured with 'Tower' tasks that require a participant to think ahead and plan (Mattson et al. 1999), although research on these 'Tower' tasks in FASD is not always conclusive (Rasmussen and Bisanz 2009). Nevertheless, difficulties with planning may result in an individual with FASD having difficulty making and achieving short and long-term goals, taking the appropriate sequence of steps to complete a goal, and overall difficulty adaptive to society.

Verbal reasoning which involves processing more complex verbal information is also difficult for those with FASD (Rasmussen and Bisanz 2009). Difficulty with complex verbal reasoning skills may render an individual with FASD particularly vulnerable as they may not fully process and understand legal statements with complex language. Furthermore, concept formation is another EF that may be impaired in FASD. Tasks that involve set shifting and thinking flexibly (e.g. card sorting tasks) (McGee et al. 2008; Rasmussen and Bisanz 2009) may be particularly difficult and may lead to difficulty with problem solving (Mattson et al. 2011).

Individuals with FASD also have significant difficulty with working memory (Mattson et al. 2011; Rasmussen 2005; Rasmussen and Bisanz 2011), which can be measured by remembering lists of numbers or words (verbal working memory) or remember visual spatial information or sequences. Moreover, they also have impairments in other components of memory that involve long-term memory (see Pei et al. 2011 for a review) as well as source memory (remembering the source for information) (Kully-Martens et al. 2012b). Such impairments in so many critical aspects of memory may lead to individuals with FASD to have difficulty remembering appointments, phone numbers, to-do lists, places, and also confusing where they learned the information or who said it (i.e., source memory). Consequently, these pervasive memory difficulties may have huge implications for their functioning in society.

It is also important to understand how EF impairments in FASD may be manifested with age. One study found that, among 8–16 year-olds with FASD, impairments on some components on EF (fluency, inhibition and switching, and verbal reasoning) became more pronounced with age (Rasmussen and Bisanz 2009). The scores did not necessarily decline with age, but rather standard scores worsened with age relative to the norm, indicating on some components of EF the gap between typical development and FASD may widen with age. The above research was not longitudinal, so one cannot infer that age is a causal factor, and other factors play a role in the adolescent group showing more impaired scores. However, the findings highlight the need for more longitudinal research to better understand how EF is manifested during adolescence in individuals with FASD. Adolescence is a time of vulnerability with higher environment demands requiring one to use complex EF skills (e.g., inhibition, planning, decision making etc.) and thus due to their EF impairments, adolescence may be a time of heightened vulnerability in FASD.

Far less research has been conducted on more 'hot EF' tasks in FASD that involve more emotional and affective stimuli. One well-researched measure of hot EF and decision making is the Iowa Gambling Task (IGT) (Bechara 2007). The IGT is sensitive to prefrontal cortex damage (Bechara et al. 1994), an area of the brain important for EF (Stuss and Knight 2002). Although the IGT has been well-research in other clinical populations, until recently, it had not been studied in individuals with FASD. Kully-Martens et al. (2013) administered the IGT to 62 children and adolescents both with and without FASD (aged 8–18 years) and found that. The FASD group performed significantly worse than the controls. Moreover, the control group showed a typical learning curve on the task, however the FASD group showed no learning curve. What's more, the control group showed increasing performance across age (as would expected with typical development), but the FASD group did not perform better with age. In fact, there was surprisingly little difference in performance between adolescents and 8-years-olds. Again, this study was not longitudinal so one cannot conclude that age caused these changes (or lack of) but it does highlight that impairments on some important components of EF appear to be more pronounced with age as individuals with FASD may fall further behind their peers. Intact decision making would clearly be important for functioning in society on many different levels. Difficulty making decisions, particularly when they involve emotional stimuli, could lead to individuals with FASD demonstrating maladaptive behaviours and ultimately getting into to trouble with the law.

There are also few research studies empirically linking the EF impairments in FASD to overall functional outcomes. Children and adolescents with FASD do show considerable impairments when EF is rated by their caregivers (see Mattson et al. 2011). One commonly used rating scale of EF is the Behavioral Rating Inventory of Executive Functioning (BRIEF) (Gioia et al. 2000), in which the reporter rates EF impairments presented with various real-word situations. Although this test may have more real-world applicability and ecological validity, it may not be measuring the same aspects of EF as traditional cognitive tests (Gross et al. 2014). Nevertheless, among children with FASD ratings on the BRIEF predict ratings of social skills and problem behaviors (Schonfeld et al. 2006), and there is some research linking performance on cognitive tests of EF to ratings of adaptive functioning in FASD (Ware et al. 2012).

Although there does not appear to be research specially linking EF impairments to criminal behaviour in FASD, it does not mean they are not associated, and thus research in this area is critical. There is, however, considerable research linking EF difficulties to maladaptive behavior in other populations. EF deficits are linked to antisocial behaviors (Morgan and Lilienfeld 2000 review) and specifically poor inhibition is associated with delinquency and high-risk behaviors (Kerr et al. 1997; Roussy and Toupin 2000). Furthermore, EF impairments have been documented in offender populations, with performance on measures of impulsivity, concept formation, and flexibility predicting frequency and severity of violent offences (Hancock et al. 2010). Finally, poor performance on the IGT is associated with both psychopathology (Blair et al. 2001) and recidivism (Beszterczey et al. 2013). In many of the studies conducted with offender populations PAE may not have been examined or was unknown, thus precluding the examination of any potential effects of PAE.

It is also important to note that the above literature reviewed is based on research conducted with groups of individuals with FASD, and may not reflect the entire FASD and alcohol-exposed populations. Furthermore, there is considerable heterogeneity within FASD and large individual differences in performance and not all individuals would necessarily have impairments in all areas described. Finally, it is important to consider exposure to the environmental adversities that tend to co-occur with FASD when examining cognitive functioning and criminal behaviour in FASD.

In summary, individuals with FASD can present with a host of EF and memory impairments which may contribute to their poor functional outcomes. In addition to these above cognitive impairments individuals with FASD also have difficulty with language (Mattson et al. 2011) social communication, and social skills (Kully-Martens et al. 2012a), which can further impact their understanding of the legal system. These deficits are often "invisible" in that there is no obvious outward indicator of impairment, making the condition difficult to identify by laypersons such as police and lawyers.

9.3 Psycholegal Abilities and FASD

Canadian legal tradition has a long-standing history of ensuring procedural protections for individuals who come into contact with the criminal justice system (Roach and Bailey 2010). Safeguards such as these are particularly important in cases where individuals are vulnerable, such as youth, and those with compromised cognitive functioning or mental illness (Grisso 2003). As outlined, many individuals with FASD experience considerable challenges in neurocognitive and behavioural functioning across the domains outlined in Fig. 9.1. These deficits have led experts to

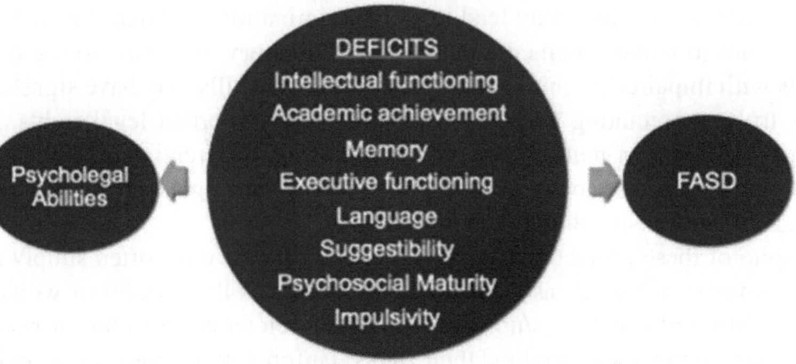

Fig. 9.1 The intersection between cognitive impairment and psycholegal abilities for offenders with FASD

identify offenders with FASD as a particularly vulnerable group in the criminal justice context (McLachlan et al. 2014; Roach and Bailey 2010; Binnie et al. 2014). Unfortunately, the risk for miscarriages in justice are great for vulnerable suspects, and might include legally invalid arrest/charter waivers; invalid statements and potentially false confessions, lack of necessary support for vulnerable suspects; and unrecognized deficits impacting legal competency for defendants standing trial or entering pleas (Conry and Fast 2000; Gagnier et al. 2011; Roach and Bailey 2010; Verbrugge 2003).

9.4 Police Questioning and Arrest

Legal safeguards are in place from the point when police initially approach and question an individual, right through the process of arrest, interrogation, and detention. All Canadians are guaranteed protections under the *Canadian Charter of Rights and Freedoms* (1982) including the right to silence, and the right to consult with a lawyer. Adolescents are also afforded a number of enhanced procedural safeguards owing to their relative developmental vulnerability, including the right to consult with a parent or other appropriate adult prior to giving a statement (*Youth Criminal Justice Act* 2003). In order for a suspect to validly waive his or her rights and make a statement or confession to police, he or she must both understand and appreciate each of these rights. It is not sufficient that a suspect is able to repeat a given right, or simply explain the meaning of that right. True appreciation requires that a suspect understand the relevance of a given right as it applies in his or her own situation. For example, it is not enough to understand that the right to silence means that one does not have to answer a police officer's questions, but additionally requires a complex level of understanding about the police interrogation process, including the idea that there is an adversarial relationship at play, that answering a police officer's questions may lead to self-incrimination, and that it is in one's best interests not to make statements that are incriminatory. It is easy to see how individuals with impaired cognitive and communication skills may have significant difficulty truly appreciating the significance of these important legal rights. Further, cognitive ability and maturity of judgment can be differentiated. Thus, even if a suspect understands the basic meaning of an arrest warning, he or she may nevertheless make a poor decision during interrogation.

In spite of these protections, in effect, police officers most often simply read the rights waiver to a suspect, ask if he or she understands those rights or would like to exercise them (all simply yes/no questions), and then request that the suspect to sign a form indicating they understood their rights. Unfortunately, both verbal and written arrest warnings are very complicated, and the extent to which even average adults can understand and thus meaningfully exercise their rights has been called into question.

It is not surprising then that research generally finds poor rights comprehension among both youth and adults, with significant impairment in vulnerable populations. It is well established that younger adolescents, particularly those with lower intellectual abilities, experience great difficulty understanding and appreciating their legal rights (Goldstein et al. 2003; Grisso 2003; McLachlan et al. 2011; Redlich et al. 2003; Viljoen and Roesch 2005). The content of arrest warnings read to suspects varies substantially across jurisdictions in terms of wording difficulty, readability, and linguistic complexity (Helms 2003; Helms and Holloway 2006; Rogers et al. 2007), with average required grade reading levels spanning far beyond the typical ability of individuals in the justice system. A recent Canadian study analyzed a sample of Canadian warnings and found their grade reading difficulty level varied from a grade 6 to grade 12 level (Eastwood et al. 2012).

The additional cognitive and behavioural challenges frequently seen in individuals with FASD may only serve to increase their risk of limited comprehension of both interrogation warnings and the waiver process. As shown in in Fig. 9.1, there is a high degree of overlap between the constellation of deficits frequently associated with FASD, and risk factors for impaired psycholegal abilities. At the most basic level, suspects with FASD are more likely to face substantial problems paying attention to written or oral warnings. Deficits in academic skills such as reading may render the tasks of understanding a written warning impossible without assistance, and they may not be able to concentrate long enough to grasp the significance of the waiver process. Beyond the basics, their level of cognitive impairment (including difficulties with verbal comprehension skills and reasoning) may predispose them to problems understanding the meaning of individual warnings, or appreciating their overall function within the context of a police investigation. Setting aside the issue of whether police have sufficient knowledge to competently evaluate the psycholegal capacities of suspects with FASD, the 'invisibility' of FASD in a suspect may render this task nearly impossible. Individuals with FASD often present an appearance of verbal and social facility that mask substantial underlying deficits (Abkarian 1992; Baumbach 2002; Williams 2006).

9.5 Confessions

Traditionally, police officers have been trained to approach the interrogation process from an adversarial standpoint. The most commonly used approach to interrogation and trained in both Canada in the United States is known as the Reid Technique (Inbau 2005; Leo 2008). Using this approach, the only goal of an interrogation is to elicit a confession from a guilty suspect. It has been criticized for being highly coercive. Confessions reflect one of the most powerful pieces of evidence resulting in convictions, and police officers are explicitly trained in coercive methods designed to extract statements (Kassin et al. 2010). Under these conditions, vulnerable suspects are at increased risk not only of making statements against their best interests, but also for producing false or inaccurate statements, including false confessions. Though the prevalence of false confession rates remains difficult to estimate, researchers agree they occur fairly often (Kassin et al. 2010). American studies using self-report methods to study false confession rates have shown rates ranging from 12% for adult prison inmates (Sigurdsson and Gudjonsson 2001) to 22% of offenders with mental health problems (Redlich et al. 2010). A recent large-scale study comprising 11,388 youth ages 14 to 24 found that hyperactivity significantly predicted reported false confessions across age groups, and that inattention was a significant predictor among youth ages 14–16 years (Drake et al. 2017).

A number of personal risk factors increase a suspect's vulnerability to coercive police tactics in interrogation, including younger age, impaired intellectual ability, and mental health problems (Appelbaum and Appelbaum 2004; Drizin and Leo 2004). Even the average adolescent may experience difficulty making sound decisions in the context of an interrogation due their relative developmental immaturity. For example, younger children and adolescents are generally less likely to think strategically about their decisions (Peterson-Badali and Abramovitch 1993), less future oriented, less likely to weigh the consequences of their decisions, and more often impulsive in their actions (Cauffman and Sternberg 2000; Halpern-Felsher and Cauffman 2001). Psychosocial and developmental immaturity is a commonly observed in individuals with an FASD, who are commonly described as functioning at much younger developmental level relative to same aged peers and have poor decision making skills (Kully-Martens et al. 2012a, b).

Suspects provide false confessions for a number of reasons, including factors internal to the suspect, such as those already described, as well as external factors. For example, Redlich et al. (2010) asked individuals to describe their reasons for providing a past false confession and found the most common reasons included: Wanting to stop the questioning or to go home (65%); protecting the true perpetrator (53%), and police pressure (48%). In the context of police interrogation, many suspects with FASD likely experience a number of challenges above and beyond normative developmental limitations. Individuals with FASD tend to present with immature interpersonal and social skills, such as the tendency to trust others, a strong desire to please persons in authority, and high levels of suggestibility (e.g.

Brown and Gudjonsson 2011; Conry and Fast 2000; Dagher-Margosian 1997; Fast and Conry 2004; LaDue and Dunne 1997; Streissguth and Kanter 1997), which may further increase their vulnerability to potentially manipulative or coercive tactics employed by police during interrogation.

9.6 Fitness to Stand Trial

Following arrest and questioning, additional formal safeguards protect an individual's rights during the pretrial, trial, and sentencing phases of the legal process.

Criminal defendants must be competent to proceed to adjudication in order for a trial to be fair. A defendant who is unable to meaningfully participate in his or her defence, due to mental disorder, is found unfit to stand trial if he or she is unable to (a) understand the nature or object of the proceedings, (b) understand the possible consequences of the proceedings, or (c) communicate with counsel. FASD has been accepted by Canadian courts in both adolescent and adult jurisdictions as a legally relevant condition in determinations about arrest rights comprehension, admissibility of statements, and fitness to stand trial (Roach and Bailey 2010; Chandler 2016). However, Canadian case law underscores a highly conservative standard of impairment in order for a defendant to be found unfit to proceed to trial. Provided his or her understanding of the requisite information and ability to communicate with counsel is sound, a defendant need not have the capacity to act in his or her best interests or make what others might judge to be a "good" legal decision (R v. Taylor 1992; R v. Whittle 1994). As a result, very few Canadian defendants are found unfit in the absence of active symptoms of a serious mental illness (Roesch et al. 1997).

Research findings in this area follows the pattern earlier described for compromised capacities in rights comprehension and waiver decisions. Specifically, younger adolescents, and individuals with impaired intellectual abilities show high rates of deficits in the legal capacities relevant to adjudication (Grisso et al. 2003; Peterson-Badali and Abramovitch 1993; Pirelli et al. 2011; Redlich et al. 2003; Viljoen and Roesch 2005). In addition, several forms of psychopathology have been associated with deficits in this area, including diagnosed learning disabilities, attention problems, psychosis, and externalizing behaviours (Grisso et al. 2003; LaVelle Ficke et al. 2006; Ryba and Zapf 2011; Viljoen and Roesch 2005; Warren et al. 2003). In addition to the overlapping risk factors and deficits previously described in the case of suspects with FASD, they also experience high rates of comorbid mental health problems, with estimates ranging as high as 90% (Famy et al. 1998; O'Connor et al. 2002; Streissguth et al. 1996). Rates of comorbid ADHD are exceptionally high among individuals with FASD (Peadon and Elliott 2010; Rasmussen et al. 2010). This is particularly troubling given the high level of attention and concentration needed to sit through lengthy legal meetings or proceedings in the courtroom and understand very complicated legal information.

The courtroom can be a strange and overwhelming environment as the suspect is the centre of attention and surrounded by officials and strangers. Legal jargon is complex and difficult to understand for laypersons at the best of times. The pace of action in the courtroom can range from a complete standstill to very fast. Further, it can be a noisy and busy place with little reprieve from sensory overload. Individuals with FASD often experience problems processing sensory information and can become easily overwhelmed in this type of environment (Jirikowic et al. 2008). Becoming overwhelmed may further hinder comprehension, and thus, meaningful participation at trial. This recipe may also result in impulsive and inappropriate behavior in the courtroom, which may be interpreted as hostile or purposeful by legal professionals, and potentially result in consequences.

Individuals with FASD experience substantial deficits in memory and communication skills (Wyper and Rasmussen 2010). This includes both expressive (the ability to general verbal output) and receptive (the ability to understand what is being communicated using verbal means) language deficits. During a trial, a suspect must be able to communicate clearly with his or her lawyer or judge to give the information required to mount a successful defence and participate in a legal hearing (e.g., entering a plea before a judge). Various learning strategies may prove helpful in improving comprehension and communication with legal professionals. For instance, a lawyer can spend more time with a suspect, or repeat, and carefully explain key or complex legal concepts. However, lawyers have very limited time to spend with clients, particularly those working under publicly funded legal aid programs. Further, the adult criminal courtroom operates at a fast pace, often without opportunity to spend sufficient time engaging in this type of task. For instance, a lawyer may not be able to "pause" a legal hearing to explain the meaning of a witnesses' lengthy or complex testimony. If that witness lied about key facts while a suspect with FASD was not paying attention or had difficulty understanding the witnesses' verbal testimony, he or she may meet the legal threshold for impaired communication under Canadian legal fitness standards. While there is limited data to inform how often this occurs, misunderstandings such as these may be frequent among defendants with FASD.

9.7 Research

Little research has been conducted on the subject of FASD in the context of the criminal justice system. To date, much of the work used to inform policy decisions has been descriptive in nature, and little reliable evidence is available to inform clinical practice with this population (Verbrugge 2003). The importance of undertaking empirical research in this area is also particularly critical because of the high standard at which criminal courts typically set the bar for admissibility standards of forensic evidence (R. v. Mohan 1994; Saunders 2001).

In a recent study, co-author, McLachlan et al. (2014), assessed the psycholegal abilities of adolescents and young adults with FASD. We compared the understanding, appreciation, and communication skills of 50 young offenders with FASD with 50 justice-involved adolescent offenders without FASD.

Participants were first asked to report on their waiver decisions in the context of their most recent interrogation experience with police (McLachlan 2012). In keeping with the general population of offenders and lay research participants, suspects with FASD did not often assert their rights, with only approximately half asserting their right to silence, 38% their right to a lawyer, and 18% their right to a parent or other adult. However, these rates were comparable in the control group. In assessing their rights understanding, more than half (60%) of young offenders with FASD had significantly impaired comprehension of at least one legal right, a proportion that was much higher compared to the control group. Participants were also asked to rate how well they felt they understood their rights, and how confident they would feel, based on their current level of understanding, making an informed waiver decision in a future interaction with police. Participants with FASD had relatively good appreciation for their own understanding of their legal rights, however, relative to the comparison group, they had higher confidence levels, which were not commensurate with their actual level of understanding. Put another way, a suspect with FASD who had poor comprehension of his or her rights may be more likely to waive them in a confident manner with police, thus failing to trigger outward warning signs that an officer may need to spend extra time helping that suspect providing a valid waiver based on sufficient understanding and appreciate of their rights.

Furthermore, and alarmingly, nearly 40% of participants with FASD acknowledged that they had made at least one false confession to police. While these data are self-report in nature and may be somewhat limited with respect to reliability, it is still concerning that such a high proportion of offenders indicated having a history of false confessions. Further, the comparison group reported similar rates (43.5%) of past false confession experiences, suggesting that the experience is not unique to offenders with an FASD (all participants in both groups were young, and thus a relatively vulnerable group with respect to false confession). Particularly troubling was participants' assertion that they were convicted of a given charge for which they entered a false confession in roughly two-thirds of cases, often resulting in serious sanctions including supervision in the community and community service orders, as well as time in custody.

Turning to fitness to stand trial, the FASD group also had significantly greater deficits in understanding, appreciation, and communication, relative to the comparison group, with particular impairment in understanding the relevant legal concepts at trial. This study did not assess communication or other neuropsychological deficits directly, but rather relied on the observations taken over a 3-h interview with participants. Thus, more research would be required to better understand functional links between observed psycholegal abilities and deficits relevant to the trial process. We also conducted the testing in a quiet and controlled environment with breaks as needed and a friendly examiner. Thus, rates of impairment likely represent an underestimation of the true capacities of such vulnerable defendants in the context of a real trial or interrogation. Overall, these results raise serious concerns about the ability of an "average" offender with FASD to competently navigate the adjudication process without additional supports. Across the entire study, 90% of participants with FASD showed significant deficits in at least one psycholegal ability canvassed. However, we also observed considerable variability in skills within the group, indicating that a "one-size fits all" approach to dealing with capacity and competency issues for offenders with FASD would not be appropriate. Indeed, some showed very good understanding and appreciation of their various legal rights, while others exhibited excellent communication skills. That being said, the vast majority showed high levels of impairment and it is likely that most would go undetected, or appropriately supported, in the real legal context.

Although it is beyond the scope of this chapter to talk about competency remediation in much detail, this is an important area for consideration in the context of impaired psycholegal abilities. The most common approach to addressing deficits leading to a finding of incompetence focuses on use of psychiatric medications (when the deficit is related to mental health symptomatology) and/or psychoeducation to teach the necessary skills (Zapf and Roesch 2011). Brief teaching approaches are typically not successful in remediating comprehension deficits in average populations (Cooper 1997; Viljoen et al. 2007). The question of whether a group of vulnerable suspects with organic brain damage and pervasive deficits in cognitive functioning can be returned to competency via intervention is a difficult one. It parallels the question asked in other populations with substantial intellectual deficits or intractable psychosis, for example. This has led some legal scholars to question the utility of raising competency related issues at trial, when the risk of lengthy detainment for assessments and remediation are at risk. On the flip side, the question of how our justice system should manage individuals who are so impaired that their competence cannot be restored (and thus cannot be tried, or detained indefinitely), but continue to offend, remains complex.

9.8 Promising Practices

Unfortunately, little evidence exists to support the efficacy of various programs and approaches that have been developed to support the needs of suspects with FASD as they circumnavigate the criminal justice system. Nevertheless, a number of approaches may prove useful in helping to overcome these challenges, and deserve future research attention to ensure appropriate safeguards are available for vulnerable suspects such as individuals with FASD. Here, we introduce a few potential practices that may prove helpful.

Training The responsibility for upholding these procedural safeguards and ensuring that vulnerable suspects have access to legal protections under the law falls to a variety of legal professionals, including police officers, lawyers, and judges. Unfortunately, it is unlikely that these professionals receive sufficient training to either recognize offenders with an FASD or help uphold legal safeguards in a meaningful way. They are also faced with the task of working in an overburdened criminal justice system that allows little time to provide the extensive supports necessary for especially compromised defendants. Increased access to training for legal professionals about FASD is a clear need (Binnie et al. 2014). Many good training programs have been developed and exist for a range of legal professionals including police, probation officers, judges, and lawyers. Examples include the Asante Centre's FASD Guidebook for Police Officers, available online at: http://www.asantecentre.org/_Library/docs/latestfasguide.pdf. Manitoba introduced a promising program whereby youth defendants with FASD were able to access a highly trained lawyer with expertise in FASD and related neurobehavioral deficits and needs during their defence (Legal Aid Accommodation Counsel for Youth with FASD Project). This lawyer was given a smaller caseload which translated into more time to spend with defendants and their families during a trial.

Identification In a related theme, the importance of identifying offenders with vulnerabilities and additional needs remains key. Under identification of offenders with FASD stems from a number of reasons, including limited access to assessment and diagnostic resources, historically limited knowledge of FASD among justice professionals, and limited presentation of sometimes generalized deficits among offenders themselves (e.g., there is often no "face" to FASD). Increased access to screening and diagnostic capacities, particularly in legal systems, for when capacity related issues are raised is necessary. However, it is not immediately clear whether "FASD-specific" or unique programs are needed to bridge this gap. Presently, there is a lack of appropriately trained professionals able to conduct assessments in this population. One potential resource may involve better levearing already existing systems that are in place to assess and treat the forensic mental health needs of offenders. This might involve specialty consultation teams within established forensic health programs (such as the Centrepoint program in Edmonton, a program that provides forensic mental health assessments for the courts to adolescent offenders and employs several specially trained professional who undertake FASD assessments in addition to evaluating other legally-pertinent mental or physical health needs). Or, expanding court-based screening programs for fitness to stand trial to include FASD-related impairments more specifically.

Alternative Approaches to Interrogation Alternative approaches to interrogation are used in other common law jurisdictions with much success. One example is the PEACE model, which stands for the five components of this method of interviewing suspects, including "Planning and Preparation," "Engage and Explain," "Account," "Closure," and "Evaluate" (Milne and Bull 1999). This protocol has been used in the United Kingdom, and more recently, has been used training Canadian police officers. The PEACE approach is substantially less confrontational and designed to elicit information rather than secure a confession (Bull and Milne 2004; Milne and Bull 1999).

Increased Supports During Interrogation and Trial All of the evidence presented above suggests that suspects with FASD may need access to improved supports during all aspects of the adjudicative process. This might include mandating the presence of counsel during police interrogation, though unfortunately, this is unlikely a practical solution given the overwhelming demand this would likely place on already strained publicly available defence systems. Research in the general population shows that allowing a parent or other supportive adult to attend police questioning may not result in practical advantages to an accused, and may sometimes have the opposite effect if said person pressures the suspect into cooperating with police (Woolard et al. 2008). The availability of appropriately trained "lay experts" who understand both the unique needs of suspects with FASD, as well as the law concerning rights in police questioning, might help to fill this gap without placing undue strain on the public defence system. However, this type of accommodation would clearly require research to assess its efficacy and practical impact.

Alternatively, providing environmental accommodations at trial may be a more practical solution to help ameliorate competency-related deficits for suspects in the courtroom. Modifications more easily made available in the less formal juvenile courts may be of benefit to vulnerable defendants. This might include conducting sessions at a slower pace, ensuring the necessary time for lawyers and judges to explain important legal concepts, allowing for frequent breaks, or closing the courtroom to observers. Ensuring that judges take additional time to question the understanding of defendants during plea bargaining might be particularly helpful, as a number of participants in the McLachlan et al. (2014) study informally indicated they had wrongfully plead guilty to charges.

9.9 Conclusion

Individuals with FASD who come into contact with the legal system are likely at increased risk for miscarriages in justice owing to their compromised neurobehavioral functioning. Deficits in communication, executive functioning, and memory, among a range of additional cognitive difficulties represent a constellation of risk factors salient to psycholegal abilities. Further research is needed to better understand the abilities of persons with FASD to competently interact with police officers, lawyers, and judges during the adjudicative process. Further, this population may be especially vulnerable to coercive and pressuring tactics during police interrogation, raising the risk for false confessions. Unfortunately, little evidence is available to inform policy change in this respect. However, it is likely that suspects and defendants with FASD require considerable additional support during the legal process.

References

Abkarian, G.G. 1992. Communication effects of prenatal alcohol exposure. *Journal of Communication Disorders* 25: 221–240. https://doi.org/10.1016/0021-9924(92)90017-Q.

Appelbaum, K.L., and P.S. Appelbaum. 2004. Criminal justice-related competencies in defendants with mental retardation. *Journal of Psychiatry and Law* 22: 483–503.

Baumbach, J. 2002. Some implications of prenatal alcohol exposure for the treatment of adolescents with sexual offending behaviors. *Sexual Abuse: A Journal of Research and Treatment* 14: 313–327.

Bechara, A. 2007. *Iowa gambling task professional manual*. Lutz: Psychological Assessment Resources.

Bechara, A., A. Damasio, H. Damasio, and S. Anderson. 1994. Insensitivity to future consequences following damage to human prefrontal cortex. *Cognition* 50: 7–15.

Beszterczey, S., P.G. Nestor, A. Shirai, and S. Harding. 2013. Neuropsychology of decision making and psychopathy in high-risk ex-offenders. *Neuropsychology* 27 (4): 491–497.

Binnie, I., M. Trussler, and E. Jonsson, eds. 2014. *Legal issues of FASD, fetal alcohol spectrum disorder: Proceedings from a consensus development conference*. Edmonton: Institute of Health Economics.

Blair, R., E. Colledge, and D. Mitchell. 2001. Somatic markers and response reversal: Is there orbitofrontal cortex dysfunction in boys with psychopathic tendencies? *Journal of Abnormal Child Psychology* 29: 86–99.

Brown, N., and G. Gudjonsson. 2011. Suggestibility and fetal alcohol spectrum disorders: I'll tell you anything you want to hear. *Journal of Psychiatry and Law* 39: 39–71.

Bull, R., and B. Milne. 2004. Attempts to improve the police interviewing of suspects. In *Interrogations, confessions, and entrapment*, 181–196. Springer US.

Canadian Charter of Rights and Freedoms. 1982.

Cauffman, E., and L. Sternberg. 2000. Immaturity of judgment in adolescence: Why adolescents may be less culpable than adults. *Behavioral Sciences and the Law* 18: 741–760.

Chandler, J.A. 2016. The use of neuroscientific evidence in Canadian criminal proceedings. *Journal of Law and the Biosciences* 2: 550–579. https://doi.org/10.1093/jlb/lsv026.

Connor, P.D., P.D. Sampson, F.L. Bookstein, H.M. Barr, and A.P. Streissguth. 2000. Direct and indirect effects of prenatal alcohol damage on executive function. *Developmental Neuropsychology* 18 (3): 331–354.

Conry, J., and D.K. Fast. 2000. *Fetal alcohol syndrome and the criminal justice system*. Vancouver: Law Foundation of British Columbia.

Cooper, D.K. 1997. Juveniles' understanding of trial-related information: Are they competent defendants? *Behavioral Sciences and the Law* 15: 167–180. https://doi.org/10.1002/(SICI)1099-0798(199721)15:2<167::AID-BSL266>3.0.CO;2-E.

Dagher-Margosian, J. 1997. Representing the FAS client in a criminal case. In *The challenge of fetal alcohol syndrome: Overcoming secondary disabilities*, ed. A. Streissguth and J. Kanter, 125–133. Washington, DC: University of Washington Press.

Drake, K.E., R.A. Gonzalez, J.F. Sigurdsson, I.D. Sigfusdottir, and G.H. Gudjonsson. 2017. A national study into temperament as a critical susceptibility factor for reported false confessions amongst adolescents. *Personality and Individual Differences* 111: 220–226. https://doi.org/10.1016/j.paid.2017.02.022.

Drizin, S.A., and R.A. Leo. 2004. The problem of false confessions in the post-DNA world. *North Carolina Law Review* 82: 891–1008.

Eastwood, J., B. Snook, and K. Luther. 2012. Measuring the reading complexity and oral comprehension of Canadian Youth Waiver Forms. *Crime and Delinquency*. https://doi.org/10.1177/0011128712453689.

Famy, C., A.P. Streissguth, and A.S. Unis. 1998. Mental illness in adults with fetal alcohol syndrome or fetal alcohol effects. *American Journal of Psychiatry* 155: 552–554.

Fast, D.K., and J. Conry. 2004. The challenge of fetal alcohol syndrome in the criminal legal system. *Addiction Biology* 9: 161–166.

Gagnier, K.R., T.E. Moore, and M.A. Green. 2011. A need for closer examination of FASD by the criminal justice system: Has the call been answered? *Journal of Population Therapeutics and Clinical Pharmacology* 18: e426–e439.

Gioia, G.A., P.K. Isquith, S.C. Guy, and L. Kenworthy. 2000. *Behavior rating inventory of executive function*. Psychological Assessment Resources: Lutz.

Goldstein, N.E., L.O. Condie, R. Kalbeitzer, D. Osman, and J.L. Geier. 2003. Juvenile offenders' *Miranda* rights comprehension and self-report likelihood of offering false confessions. *Assessment* 10: 359–369. https://doi.org/10.1007/s10979-009-9198-4.

Grisso, T. 2003. *Evaluating competencies: Forensic assessments and instruments*. 2nd ed. New York: Kluwer Academic/Plenum Press.

Grisso, T. Steinberg, J. Woolard, E. Cauffman, E. Scott, S. Graham, F. Lexcen, N.D. Reppucci, and R. Schwartz. 2003. Juveniles' competence to stand trial: A comparison of adolescents' and adults capacities as trial defendants. *Law and Human Behavior* 27: 333–363. https://doi.org/10.1023/A:1024065015717.

Gross, A.C., L.A. Deling, J.R. Wozniak, and C.J. Boys. 2014. Objective measures of executive functioning are highly discrepant with parent-report in fetal alcohol spectrum disorders. *Child Neuropsychology* 1: 1–8.

Halpern-Felsher, B., and E. Cauffman. 2001. Costs and benefits of a decision: Decision making competence in adolescents and adults. *Journal of Applied Developmental Psychology* 22: 257–273.

Hancock, M., J.L. Tapscott, and P.M. Hoaken. 2010. Role of executive dysfunction in predicting frequency and severity of violence. *Aggressive Behavior* 36 (5): 338–349.

Helms, J. 2003. Analysis of Miranda reading levels across jurisdictions: Implications for evaluating waiver competency. *Journal of Forensic Psychology Practice* 3: 25–37.

Helms, J.L., and C.L. Holloway. 2006. Differences in prongs of the Miranda warnings. *Criminal Justice Studies* 19: 77–84.

Inbau, F.E. 2005. *Essentials of the reid technique: Criminal interrogation and confessions*. Sudbury: Jones and Bartlett Publishers.

Jirikowic, T., H.C. Olson, and D. Kartin. 2008. Sensory processing, school performance, and adaptive behavior of young school-age children with fetal alcohol spectrum disorders. *Physical & Occupational Therapy in Pediatrics* 28 (2): 117–136.

Kassin, S.M., S.A. Drizin, T. Grisso, G.H. Gudjonsson, R.A. Leo, and A.D. Redlich. 2010. Police-induced confessions. *Law and Human Behavior* 34 (1): 3–38.

Kerns, K.A., D. Audrey, C.A. Mateer, and A.P. Streissguth. 1997. Cognitive deficits in nonretarded adults with Fetal Alcohol Syndrome. *Journal of Learning Disabilities* 30 (6): 685–693.

Kerr, M., R. Tremblay, L. Pagani, and F. Vitaro. 1997. Boys' behavioral inhibition and the risk of later delinquency. *Archives of General Psychiatry* 54 (9): 809–816.

Kodituwakku, P., W. Kalberg, and P.A. May. 2001. The effects of prenatal alcohol exposure on executive functioning. *Alcohol Research & Health* 25 (3): 192–198.

Kodituwakku, P. W. (2007) Defining the behavioral phenotype in children with fetal alcohol spectrum disorders: A review. *Neuroscience & Biobehavioral Reviews* 31 (2): 192–201

Kully-Martens, K., K. Denys, S. Treit, S. Tamana, and C. Rasmussen. 2012a. A review of social skills deficits in individuals with FASD and PAE: Profiles, mechanisms, and interventions. *Alcoholism, Clinical and Experimental Research* 36 (4): 568–576.

Kully-Martens, K., J. Pei, J. Job, and C. Rasmussen. 2012b. Source monitoring in children with and without fetal alcohol spectrum disorders. *Journal of Pediatric Psychology* 37 (7): 725–735.

Kully-Martens, K., S. Treit, J. Pei, and C. Rasmussen. 2013. Affective decision-making on the Iowa Gambling task in children and adolescents with fetal alcohol spectrum disorder. *Journal of International Neuropsychological Society* 19 (2): 137–144.

LaDue, R.A., and T. Dunne. 1997. Legal issues and FAS. In *The challenge of fetal alcohol syndrome: Overcoming secondary disabilities*, ed. A. Streissguth and J. Kantor, 146–161. Seattle: University of Washington Press.

LaVelle Ficke, S., K.J. Hart, and P.A. Deardoff. 2006. The performance of incarcerated juveniles on the MacArthur Competence Assessment Tool—Criminal Adjudication (MacCAT-CA). *Journal of the American Academy of Psychiatry and the Law* 34: 360–373. https://doi.org/10.1037/t02322-000.

Leo, R.A. 2008. *Police interrogation and American justice*. Cambridge, MA: Harvard University Press.

Mattson, S.N., et al. 1999. Executive functioning in children with heavy prenatal alcohol exposure. *Alcoholism: Clinical and Experimental Research* 23: 1808–0815.

Mattson, S., N. Crocker, and T.T. Nguyen. 2011. Fetal alcohol spectrum disorders: Neuropsychological and behavioral features. *Neuropsychology Review* 21: 81–101.

McGee, C.L., A.M. Schonfeld, T.M. Roebuck-Spencer, E.P. Riley, and S.N. Mattson. 2008. Children with heavy prenatal alcohol exposure demonstrate deficits on multiple measures of concept formation. *Alcoholism-Clinical and Experimental Research* 32 (8): 1388–1397.

McLachlan, K. 2012. *An examination of the abilities, risks, and needs of adolescents and young adults with Fetal Alcohol Spectrum Disorder (FASD) in the criminal justice system.* Doctoral dissertation, Simon Fraser University.

McLachlan, K., R. Roesch, and K. Douglas. 2011. Examining the role of interrogative suggestibility in *Miranda* rights comprehension in adolescents. *Law and Human Behavior* 35: 165–177. https://doi.org/10.1007/s10979-009-9198-4.

McLachlan, K., R. Roesch, J. Viljoen, and K. Douglas. 2014. Evaluating the psycholegal abilities of young offenders with fetal alcohol spectrum disorder. *Law and Human Behavior* 38: 10–22.

Milne, R., and R. Bull. 1999, August 1. *Investigative interviewing; psychology and practice*. Wiley, 240pp ISBN: 978-0471-98729-1.

R. v. Mohan. 1994. 2 S.C.R.

Morgan, A.B., and S.O.A. Lilienfeld. 2000. A meta-analytic review of the relation between antisocial behavior and neuropsychological measures of executive function. *Clinical Psychology Review* 20 (1): 113–136.

O'Connor, M.J., B. Shah, S. Whaley, P. Cronin, B. Gunderson, and J. Graham. 2002. Psychiatric illness in a clinical sample of children with prenatal alcohol exposure. *American Journal of Drug and Alcohol Abuse* 28: 743–754.

Peadon, E., and E.J. Elliott. 2010. Distinguishing between attention-deficit hyperactivity and fetal alcohol spectrum disorders in children: Clinical guidelines. *Neuropsychiatric Disease and Treatment* 6: 509.

Pei, J., K. Denys, J. Hughes, and C. Rasmussen. 2011. Mental health issues in fetal alcohol spectrum disorder. *Journal of Mental Health* 20 (5): 438–448.

Peterson-Badali, M., and R. Abramovitch. 1993. Children's knowledge of the legal system: Are they competent to instruct legal counsel? *Canadian Journal of Criminology* 34: 139–160.

Pirelli, G., W.H. Gottdiener, and P.A. Zapf. 2011. A meta-analytic review of competency to stand trial research. *Psychology, Public Policy, and Law* 17: 1–53. https://doi.org/10.1037/a0021713.

Rasmussen, C. 2005. Executive functioning and working memory in fetal alcohol spectrum disorder. *Alcoholism Clinical and Experimental Research* 29: 1359–1367.

Rasmussen, C., and J. Bisanz. 2009. Executive functioning in children with fetal alcohol spectrum disorder: Profiles and age-related differences. *Child Neuropsychology* 15 (3): 201–215.

Rasmussen, C., and J. Bisanz. 2011. The relation between mathematics and working memory in young children with fetal alcohol spectrum disorders. *The Journal of Special Education* 45 (3): 184–191.

Rasmussen, C., J. Benz, J. Pei, G. Andrew, G. Schuller, L. Abele-Webster, et al. 2010. The impact of an ADHD co-morbidity on the diagnosis of FASD. *The Canadian Journal of Clinical Pharmacology* 17: e165–e176.

Redlich, A.D., M. Silverman, and H. Steiner. 2003. Pre-adjudicative and adjudicative competence in juveniles and young adults. *Behavioral Sciences and the Law* 21: 393–410.

Redlich, A.D., A. Summers, and S. Hoover. 2010. Self-reported false confessions and false guilty pleas among offenders with mental illness. *Law and Human Behavior* 34: 79–90. https://doi.org/10.1007/s10979-009 -9194-8.

Roach, K., and A. Bailey. 2010. The relevance of fetal alcohol spectrum disorder and criminal law from investigation to sentencing. *University of British Columbia Law Review* 42: 1–68.

Roesch, R., J.R.P. Ogloff, S.D. Hart, R.J. Dempster, P.A. Zapf, and K.E. Whittemore. 1997. The impact of Canadian criminal code changes on assessments of fitness to stand trial and criminal responsibility. *Canadian Journal of Psychiatry* 42: 509–514.

Rogers, R., K.S. Harrison, D. Shuman, K.W. Sewell, and L.L. Hazelwood. 2007. An analysis of Miranda warnings and waivers: Comprehension and coverage. *Law and Human Behavior* 31: 177–192.

Roussy, S., and J. Toupin. 2000. Behavioral inhibition deficits in juvenile psychopaths. *Aggressive Behavior* 26 (6): 413–424.

Ryba, N.L., and P.A. Zapf. 2011. The influence of psychiatric symptoms and cognitive abilities on competence-related abilities. *International Journal of Forensic Mental Health* 10: 29–40.

Saunders, J.W. 2001. Experts in court: A view from the bench. *Canadian Psychology/Psychologie Canadienne* 42 (2): 109.

Schonfeld, A.M., B. Paley, F. Frankel, and M.J. O'Connnor. 2006. Executive functioning predicts social skills following prenatal alcohol exposure. *Child Neuropsychology* 12 (6): 439–452.

Sigurdsson, J.F., and G.H. Gudjonsson. 2001. False confessions: The relative importance of psychological, criminological and substance abuse variables. *Psychology, Crime and Law* 7 (1–4): 275–289.

Streissguth, A., and J. Kanter, eds. 1997. *The challenge of fetal alcohol syndrome: Overcoming secondary disabilities*. Washington, DC: University of Washington Press.

Streissguth, A.P., H.M. Barr, J. Kogan, and F.L. Bookstein. 1996. *Final report to the centers for disease control and prevention on understanding the occurrence of secondary disabilities in clients with fetal alcohol syndrome and fetal alcohol effects*. Seattle: University of Washington.

Stuss, D.T., and R.T. Knight, eds. 2002. *Principles of frontal lobe function*. New York: Oxford University Press.

R.v. Taylor. 1992 77 C.C.C. (3d) 551 (Ont.C.A.).

Verbrugge, P. 2003. *Fetal alcohol spectrum disorder and the youth criminal justice system: A discussion paper*. Ottawa: Department of Justice.

Viljoen, J.L., and R. Roesch. 2005. Competence to waive interrogation rights and adjudicative competence in adolescent defendants: Cognitive development, attorney contact, and psychological symptoms. *Law and Human Behavior* 29: 723–742. https://doi.org/10.1007/s10979-005-7978-y.

Viljoen, J.L., C. Odgers, T. Grisso, and C. Tillbrook. 2007. Teaching adolescents and adults about adjudicative proceedings: A comparison of pre- and post-teaching scores on the MacCAT-CA. *Law and Human Behavior* 31: 419–432. https://doi.org/10.1007/s10979-006-9069-1.

Ware, A., N. Crocker, J.W. O'Brien, et al. 2012. Executive function predicts adaptive behavior in children with histories of heavy prenatal alcohol exposure and attention-deficit/hyperactivity disorder. *Alcoholism: Clinical and Experimental Research* 36 (8): 1431–1441.

Warren, J.I., J. Aaron, E. Ryan, P. Chauhan, and J. Duval. 2003. Correlates of adjudicative competence among psychiatrically impaired juveniles. *Journal of the American Academy of Psychiatry and the Law* 31: 299–309.

R. v. Whittle. 1994. 2 S.C.R. 914.

Williams, S.J. 2006. Research brief: Is there justice in the juvenile justice system? Examining the role of fetal alcohol spectrum disorders. *Justice Policy Journal* 3: 2–15.

Woolard, J.L., H.M. Cleary, S.A. Harvell, and R. Chen. 2008. Examining adolescents' and their parents' conceptual and practical knowledge of police interrogation: A family dyad approach. *Journal of Youth and Adolescence* 37 (6): 685–698.

Wyper, K.R., and C.R. Rasmussen. 2010. Language impairments in children with fetal alcohol spectrum disorders. *Journal of Population Therapeutics and Clinical Pharmacology= Journal de la therapeutique des populations et de la pharamcologie clinique* 18 (2): e364–e376.

Youth Criminal Justice Act, S.c. 2003.

Zapf, P.A., and R. Roesch. 2011. Future directions in the restoration of competency to stand trial. *Current Directions in Psychological Science* 20: 43–47. https://doi.org/10.1177/0963721410396798.

Zelazo, P., and U. Müller. 2002. *Executive function in typical and atypical development*. Malden: Blackwell Publishers Ltd.

Chapter 10
FASD in Adult Populations: Clinical and Forensic Considerations

Jerrod Brown, Nikki Freeman, Hal Pickett, Erin Watts, and Aaron J. Trnka

Abstract Afflicting millions of individuals across the United States, Fetal Alcohol Spectrum Disorder (FASD) is a permanent disorder present from birth that results from prenatal alcohol exposure (PAE). FASD can consist of a wide range of physical (e.g., dysmorphia, sensory systems, musculoskeletal conditions), cognitive (e.g., intelligence and executive control), social (e.g., communication skills and empathy), and adaptive (e.g., independent living skills) symptoms. These impairments of FASD have important consequences across the lifespan including a predisposition to substance use issues and other co-occurring psychiatric disorders (e.g., behavioral, mood, and anxiety disorders). This complex interplay of co-occurring symptomatology complicates the identification and diagnosis of FASD, which often results in overlooked diagnosis and misdiagnosis of the disorder well into adulthood. To help familiarize clinical and forensic mental health professionals with this challenging, resource-intensive population, this chapter will provide an overview of FASD in adult populations. Red-flag indicators and common comorbid symptomatology as well as screening and intervention approaches will also be included. Further, the chapter will include a discussion of interviewing strategies and techniques that have the potential to improve screening, assessment, and treatment of

J. Brown (✉)
Concordia University, St. Paul, MN, USA

Pathways Counseling Center, Inc, St. Paul, MN, USA

The American Institute for the Advancement of Forensic Studies (AIAFS), St. Paul, MN, USA
e-mail: jerrod01234brown@live.com

N. Freeman
Hardy and Stephens Counseling Associates, 11070 183rd Circle NW, Suite C, Elk River, MN 55330, USA

H. Pickett
Headway Emotional Health, Richfield, MN, USA

E. Watts
Education Program Spec 2, CEHD Community Integration, Inst on Community Integration, University of Minnesota, 4201A Room 111, 150 Pillsbury Dr SE, Minneapolis, MN 55455, USA

A. J. Trnka
Lighthouse Psychological Services, Fridley, MN, USA

E. Jonsson et al. (eds.), *Ethical and Legal Perspectives in Fetal Alcohol Spectrum Disorders (FASD)*, International Library of Ethics, Law, and the New Medicine 75,
https://doi.org/10.1007/978-3-319-71755-5_10

the disorder, with an eye toward adult clinical and forensic mental health settings. This chapter will conclude with an examination of the current state of empirical research on FASD and identify the next steps for inquiry.

Keywords FASD · ND-PAE · Adult · Screening · Intervention

10.1 Introduction

Affecting millions of Americans, Fetal Alcohol Syndrome Disorder (FASD) is a life-course persistent disorder that is present from birth and caused by prenatal alcohol exposure (May et al. 2009). FASD can include a wide range of cognitive (e.g., intelligence, executive control, short- and long-term memory, and attention), social (e.g., communication skills and naivety), and adaptive impairments (e.g., independent living skills and basic self-care and preservation) (Green et al. 2009; Kodituwaku 2009; O'Connor et al. 2006; Paley and O'Connor 2011; Roozen et al. 2016). No universal set of FASD criteria fits all cases because the presentation and severity of these symptoms varies as a function of the prenatal exposure to alcohol. In addition, individuals with FASD often develop comorbid behavioral (e.g., ADHD and conduct disorder), mood (i.e., major depression and bipolar disorder), anxiety, and substance use disorders secondary to the symptoms of FASD (Famy et al. 1998; Glass et al. 2014; Streissguth et al. 1996; Streissguth 1997). While these disorders can co-occur as primary diagnoses, they are often developed secondary to or exacerbated by symptoms of FASD that are not recognized and appropriately treated. This complex interplay of comorbid psychiatric symptoms makes screening and assessment difficult which can increase the likelihood of missed or inaccurate diagnosis and contribute to negative long-term outcomes. In light of these pervasive difficulties, FASD is likely prevalent in adult inpatient and outpatient clinical and forensic mental health settings. To help combat these issues, the Diagnostic and Statistical Manual-5th Edition (American Psychiatric Association 2013) recently introduced Neurodevelopmental Disorder Associated with Prenatal Alcohol Exposure (ND-PAE) as a diagnosis in the Other Neurodevelopmental Disorder section. The DSM-5 also includes ND-PAE as a distinct disorder for future study.

The presence of FASD in an adult client may not be immediately clear during initial encounters (Benz et al. 2009; Elliott et al. 2008; Morleo et al. 2011; Sokol et al. 2003). There are several commonly assumed factors that require careful reconsideration by mental health professionals in order to contest this obfuscation. First, clinical and forensic mental health professionals who serve adult populations should not rely exclusively on intelligence measures in their assessment batteries. Intelligence tests may not accurately detect the adaptive functioning deficits of adults with FASD and clinicians should avoid assuming correlation of intelligence and adaptive functioning. Second, the manner by which a clinical or forensic mental health professional interviews adults with suspected or confirmed FASD is important. For example, FASD-related deficits may be masked by an over-reliance on simple yes/no questions, parroting the interviewer, or confabulated answers in hopes of pleasing the interviewer (Brown et al. 2017). Third, a clinical or forensic mental health professional must also keep in mind the impact of FASD symptoms on screening and assessment approaches. Memory-related impairments (i.e., memory loss, suggestibility, and confabulation) can result in misinformation that muddles the screening and assessment process (Brown 2017). For example, completing an assessment tool that requires the individual to rate symptoms over the past 2 weeks may be difficult if the individual struggles with memory issues. Consequently, the individual may rely on how he or she is currently feeling to respond to the questions. Finally, the accurate identification of FASD often necessitates nuanced differential diagnosis, which may be beyond the skill sets of some mental health professionals and require consultation with an FASD expert. The consequences of not accounting for these diagnostic complications is the missed and misdiagnosis of FASD in adult clinical and forensic populations. Misdiagnosis can result in the use of inappropriate treatments, decreased likelihood of treatment success, miscarriages of justice, and psychological harm to the individual (Brown et al. 2017).

Treatment plans for individuals with confirmed or suspected FASD should be individualized in a developmentally appropriate manner that considers the symptoms and difficulties of FASD unique to that client (Brown et al. 2016a, b). This conscientious consideration serves to maximize the possibility of treatment success and minimize the risk of harm from inappropriate treatment approaches for adults with suspected or confirmed FASD. Treatment plans should first and foremost evaluate any intervention or treatment approach in the context of the individual's brain function (Brown et al. 2016a, b). After considering brain function, most treatment plans will avoid the incorporation of insight-based therapeutic and group therapy approaches. In contrast, adults with FASD may benefit from the utilization of neurobehavioral and nurturing attachment-based approaches that emphasize the development of life-skills, self-advocacy, social skills, sleep improvement, behavioral regulation, emotional regulation, and, most importantly, a strong and compassionate support system that is educated about FASD and accepting of the person with FASD. A trauma-informed care approach coupled with a practical understanding of how PAE changes an individual's brain may also be particularly fruitful because the symptoms of FASD may predispose adults to higher rates of victimization and trauma than the general population (Thiel et al. 2011). Given the range of expertise such a treatment endeavor necessitates, clinical and forensic mental health professionals need to form and coordinate a network of FASD-informed professionals that could include health care, assisted living services, financial management, criminal justice officials, psychotherapy, and case management.

The primary goal of this chapter is to familiarize clinical and forensic mental health professionals who work with adults suspected or confirmed to have FASD. This chapter will highlight four key areas via an overview of relevant empirical research and clinical experience. First, we will examine key characteristics, symptoms, and outcomes associated with adult FASD populations. Particular focus will be given to the impact FASD has on adult clinical and forensic populations, including substance abuse treatment considerations. Second, we will discuss the best available screening and assessment practices by emphasizing the skills and strategies that can maximize the identification of adults with FASD. Third, we will highlight suggested interventions and treatment approaches most effective for adults with FASD. Fourth, we will highlight suggested areas for further research and study. Together clinical and forensic mental health professionals who have greater familiarity with FASD across these key areas are better equipped to increase recognition, accurate diagnosis, and improve intervention and treatment strategies for adults with FASD.

10.2 Adults with FASD

Precipitated by prenatal alcohol exposure (PAE), Fetal Alcohol Spectrum Disorder (FASD) is a form of permanent brain injury in that the brain and central nervous system are physically damaged as they are forming in the womb (Chasnoff et al. 2015; Currie et al. 2016; Nash et al. 2015; Stevens et al. 2012; Rojmahamongkol et al. 2015). It is worth pausing to consider that alcohol is solvent and, as such, the alcohol actually dissolves or damages the cells that are forming the brain and all other parts of the body. Consequently, the brain injury is at the cellular level and often cannot be seen in medical scans which makes it the epitome of an invisible physical disability. The PAE can contribute to a wide range of physical (e.g., physical abnormalities), cognitive (e.g., intelligence and executive control), social (e.g., communication skills and empathy), and adaptive (e.g., capacity to care for oneself, solve problems and make decisions) symptoms (Jirikowic et al. 2008; McMurtrie 2011; Stevens et al. 2015; Ware et al. 2015; Whaley et al. 2001). The presence and severity of these symptoms varies as a function of the timing and severity of PAE as well as other factors such as maternal nutrition during pregnancy and genetics. As such, individuals with FASD can present with very different constellations of symptoms, which decreases the likelihood of identification and accurate diagnosis. Complicating matters, physical abnormalities, which are often unrecognizable to the naked and untrained eye, are present in only 10–20% of individuals with FASD, and these physical abnormalities become less identifiable as an individual matures into adolescence and adulthood (Spohr et al. 1993, 1994). Furthermore, FASD was initially recognized in children and the presence of the designation fetal gives the impression to many that FASD is a childhood disorder rather than a lifetime disorder. Because of this, even clinicians that have a basic awareness of FASD neglect to consider the diagnosis in adults. These challenges often culminate with the failure to identify adults with FASD, which has dire consequences on the health, global functioning, and treatment of these individuals as well as their support systems (Brown et al. 2016a, b).

The cognitive, social, and adaptive impairments of FASD have important consequences across the lifespan. Specifically, co-occurring conditions and disorders such as substance use issues and affective disorders often worsen as an individual with FASD transitions from adolescence into adulthood (Famy et al. 1998; O'Malley

2007; Streissguth 1992). This may be because the developmental delays of FASD become more apparent as an individual matures leaving him or her vulnerable to further physical and psychological trauma. For example, a 24-year-old may have an average IQ and a high vocabulary and yet, have the adaptive and social functioning of a 10-year-old. Such impairments in functioning predispose adults with FASD to many negative outcomes including all types of abuse and trauma. According to available research, as many as 75% of adults with FASD have been exposed to emotional, physical, or sexual abuse (Conry et al. 1997; Streissguth et al. 1996; Thiel et al. 2011). Further, low self-esteem and self-injurious behaviors, and an increased risk for suicide are common concerns for many adults with FASD (Baldwin 2007; Merrick and Kandel 2007; O'Malley and Huggins 2005; Streissguth et al. 1996). To limit the impact of FASD symptoms and these co-occurring conditions, early and accurate identification is a necessary first-step to ensure that individuals with FASD receive effective interventions (Brown et al. 2016a, b).

FASD and these associated secondary conditions may negatively impact an individual's relationships with family, friends, co-workers, and professionals. Even in a stable, functional family environment, social dysfunction and sensory issues can impede the ability to establish and maintain attachment and strong relationships and can contribute to an unstable home life. An abusive, neglectful family environment further complicates attachment and general stability. For example, adults with FASD typically experience several household moves throughout their lifespan (Burd et al. 2010; Streissguth 2004). Frequent moves destabilize the development of social support, a key protective feature against negative life events and secondary conditions. As a result, adults with FASD may fall into dangerous relationships and peer groups (Thiel et al. 2011). This could result in exposure to a range of harmful experiences including substance use, domestic abuse, gang activity, and several forms of victimization. These perils emphasize the importance of ensuring positive and compassionate social support for adults with FASD.

FASD and related secondary conditions can also have deleterious effects on an individual's capacity to function as an adult. This includes an adult's ability to develop daily living skills (e.g., financial management; Clark et al. 2008) and obtain and maintain steady employment (Streissguth 1997). For example, longitudinal research has found that unemployment plagues adults with FASD, even when provided with job training programs (Spohr et al. 2007). As a result, many adults with FASD are incapable of independent living (Streissguth et al. 1996), and may spiral into a vicious cycle of poverty and homelessness without a dedicated system of support and care (Burns 2009; Rutman and Van Bibber 2010). Situations characterized by inadequate employment, poverty, weak or non-existent support systems, or homelessness may drive an adult with FASD to criminal behavior or involvement with those that would use them for criminal behavior. In light of impulsivity and deficits in decision-making ability, many adults with FASD are prone for entanglement in the criminal justice system (Streissguth et al. 1991). It is imperative for support system members to consistently support healthy choices and make them available to adults with FASD. Left unaddressed, these difficulties in global functioning likely exacerbate the symptoms of FASD and related secondary conditions (Popova et al. 2015) that become increasingly entrenched as time progresses.

The symptoms of FASD and related secondary conditions can become worse across the development of an individual in the absence of necessary treatment and social support (Streissguth 1992). Nonetheless, ensuring adequate treatment and support of adults with FASD is easier said than done. Many adults with FASD have been inaccurately diagnosed or underdiagnosed with behavioral (e.g., conduct disorder and ADHD), personality (e.g., borderline and antisocial personality disorders), mood (e.g., major depression), and psychotic (e.g., schizophrenia, bipolar) disorders rather than FASD. Adults with FASD typically have an extensive history of ineffective psychiatric and psychological treatment. Treatment may have included inpatient and outpatient settings with several different mental health professionals employing a variety of treatment approaches. To make matters worse, the symptoms of FASD make it difficult to take advantage of any available social welfare and disability services (Shankar 2015). This troubling situation emphasizes the need for greater awareness of FASD in the mental health and social welfare systems (Wedding et al. 2007).

10.3 Substance Use Treatment Considerations

Adults with FASD are disproportionately likely to suffer from substance use issues (Grant et al. 2013). This affliction is driven by the very symptoms of FASD (Yates et al. 1998). For example, the cognitive deficits of FASD (e.g., executive function and impulsivity) could result in adults with FASD being unable to resist the appeal of alcohol and drugs, even in inappropriate situations. Alternatively, the social impairments of FASD may result in the use of alcohol and drugs to either self-medicate social anxiety or impress or follow peers in social settings. Adults with FASD may even be unable to refuse alcohol or drugs when offered by someone else due to the suggestibility issues that plague many with the disorder (Brown et al. 2011; Douglas 2010; Greenspan and Driscoll 2015; Roach and Bailey 2009). From adaptive and executive functioning perspectives, individuals with FASD are simply prone to making poor decisions and have difficulty understanding how their actions lead to consequences, which could contribute to the persistent use of substances (Brown et al. 2017). In light of this susceptibility towards substance use, medical and mental health professionals are particularly likely to encounter adults with FASD in substance use treatment programs (Grant et al. 2013).

It is important to establish that individuals with FASD actually have a substance abuse disorder. For example, individuals who receive DWI/DUIs are often sent for substance abuse evaluations. In these evaluations, the individual with FASD may over-report substance use depending on how he/she is interviewed. Even if individuals report accurate substance use, it is imperative to evaluate if this use is consistent with the people they associate with. Sometimes individuals with FASD are only using substances at abusive levels because their peer group uses at abusive levels and no actual addiction is present. In these cases, traditional substance abuse treatment should be modified to focus primarily on building a sober support system as simply removing the individual with FASD from others who use may solve the problem. If a "true" substance abuse disorder is determined to be present, an individualized approach or curriculum would be wise in any setting with such an array of diversity among symptomatology or disability. Despite the substance use issues that are common in adults with FASD, substance use treatment programs typically do not offer specialized programming for this group (Grant et al. 2014). This is problematic because treatment modifications for adults with FASD may be necessary to increase the likelihood of success. For example, many substance use treatment programs necessitate skills such as metacognition and introspection. However, these activities may be hindered by the cognitive, social, and adaptive functioning impairments of FASD. Poor memory often makes it difficult for the individual to recognize the amount, duration, frequency, and intensity of substance use. Difficulty connecting cause and effect – and especially higher order cause and effect – hinders the ability to see substance use as a problem. Without the ability to gain insight into their substance use, the likelihood of successful treatment outcomes in the long-term is limited. Nonetheless, the scarcity of evidence-based practices in this area does little to assist medical and mental health professionals in the improvement of substance use treatment for adults with FASD (Grant et al. 2014).

Adults with FASD and co-occurring substance use problems may be particularly prone to involvement in the criminal justice system (Brown et al. 2017). The symptoms of the disorder (e.g., impulsivity and poor decision making) may make it hard to comprehend and abide by laws (Brown et al. 2011; Grant et al. 2014). As such, adults with FASD may inappropriately use alcohol (e.g., minor consumption of alcohol or drinking and driving) or consume illegal narcotics, or non-prescribed drugs without realizing the legality or long-term consequences of their actions. Unfortunately, substance use treatment programs in correctional settings do not frequently consider FASD as a need to be considered and addressed during treatment. The development of diversion programs (e.g., drug and DWI courts) tailored to addressing the needs and risks of adults with FASD may be a promising way forward.

10.4 Communication and Interviewing Approaches

In light of difficulties with identification and diagnosis of adults with FASD, clinical and forensic mental health professionals must maximize assessment opportunities through strong communication and interviewing approaches meant to accommodate FASD symptoms. Any approach must consider the impact of the cognitive, social, and adaptive functioning impairments of FASD on the capacity of an adult to respond to a question or perform a task. By recognizing and accommodating for weaknesses and employing strengths of adults with FASD, clinical and forensic mental health professionals can increase the reliability and validity of information needed to diagnose clients and develop their treatment plan. The D.E.A.R. (Direct

Language/Engage Support System/Accommodate Needs/Remain Patient) (Brown et al. 2014) framework may be particularly useful in guiding the interactions between mental health professionals and adults with FASD.

The consistent use of simple, concrete, and direct language has the potential to improve communication between mental health professionals and adults with FASD (Brown et al. 2016a, b). Mental health professionals should not utilize sarcasm, colloquialisms, idioms, or jargon because most adults with FASD have difficulty processing abstract concepts (Streissguth et al. 1991). Employing themes of concrete communication in treatment settings is an advisable practice. Any conversation must be conducted at a slow and leisurely pace to provide an adult with FASD with enough time to adequately process any information discussed (Brown 2017). Clinical and forensic mental health professionals should avoid leading and close-ended questions in favor of open-ended questions (Brown et al. 2017). Common FASD symptoms include short and long-term memory impairments and suggestibility (Fast and Conry 2004). Open-ended questions can help limit the potentially damaging effects of these symptoms (Brown et al. 2016a, b). If an adult with FASD appears confused or provides an answer that does not make sense, a mental health professional may try restating their question in simpler or different words. It is important to create a safe and comfortable setting along with rapport-building between the mental health professional and adult with FASD. These factors will assist in ensuring this communication exchange is effective. A mental health professional should monitor adults with FASD for comprehension throughout any conversation. This can be done by incorporating the use of strategies from motivational interviewing such as reflective listening, affirmations, and summaries. If an adult with FASD over-relies on the same answer or repeats the phrasing of the mental health professional, another approach could be asking the adult with FASD to put statements into their own words. The use of these direct language strategies can improve the quality and accuracy of any information obtained from an adult with FASD (Brown et al. 2016a, b, 2017).

Communication with adults who may have FASD can be vastly improved by engaging their support system team. One way for a mental health professional to do this is by including parents, family members, legal guardians, social workers, or legal representation during the process of consultation. Suitable members of the support system may be identified by inquiring if anyone accompanied them to their appointment or asking if they have the contact information of someone who typically adds assistance. Once identified, a mental health professional can reach out to the support system member to gain a better understanding of the client with FASD. If willing, the support system member could attend appointments to assist the client and even serve as an interpreter of sorts. During this process, any concerns brought forth by the support system member or client should be taken seriously by the mental health professional even if the adult denies the concern is an issue. This will avoid discouragement from participation and encourage further activation of the support system (Thiel et al. 2011).

The engagement of support systems is particularly salient in legal situations. Because adults with FASD typically have short- and long-term memory deficits, difficulty understanding cause and effect, and are prone to suggestibility and confabulation, forensic mental health professionals may consider interviewing an adult with FASD in the presence of a support system member or legal representation (Brown 2017; Brown et al. 2016a, b). In any case, the avoidance of confusing, repetitive, or leading questions, and intimidating situations can improve the accuracy of information collected from adults with FASD. Further, adults with FASD struggle to comprehend the seriousness of criminal justice situations and may falsely confess out of fear or to simply please the individual conducting the questioning. As such, the incorporation of support system members, particularly legal representation, is imperative to ensure that miscarriages of justice are prevented (Baumbach 2002; Brown et al. 2017; Fast and Conry 2004; Roach and Bailey 2009).

A mental health professional can improve the quality of communication with adults with FASD by accommodating their needs. Specifically, there are several cognitive (e.g., attention, impulsivity, and sensory sensitivity), social (e.g., receptive and expressive communication deficits, gullibility, and proneness to be intimidated or influenced), and adaptive functioning impairments of FASD that can impact the quality of communication (Brown et al. 2011; Burd et al. 2010; Gibbard et al. 2003). Several precautions can be taken by mental health professionals to improve the likelihood of good communication. First, all interactions should take place in calm and quiet locations that limit the impact of distractions on attention (Brown 2017; 2017). Second, because adults with FASD are sensitive to intimidation, mental health professionals should not invade an individual's personal space or resort to verbal confrontations, yelling or even firm tones of voice, and threats. Third, mental health professionals should avoid interrupting the person with FASD when they are accounting events. Often, interrupting causes people with FASD to lose their train of thought, which causes a need to start their story from the beginning in order to continue. This can be time-consuming and frustrating for both the client and the mental health professional. Instead, the mental health professional should jot down clarifying questions and inquire about them once the full story is told. Fourth, mental health professionals need to allow ample time for an adult with FASD to process a question and provide an answer to the best of their ability. The cognitive and social deficits of FASD, along with expressive language deficits, can make it difficult for adults with FASD to provide an answer in a socially expected amount of time. If an adult with FASD is struggling to provide an answer, mental health professionals should encourage them to take as much time as necessary. Fifth, rather than relying solely on verbal communication, mental health professionals can incorporate other methods of communication. The incorporation of written communication, drawing an event, conducting an interactive role play, or acting out what happened may render more accurate information than verbal communication alone. Sixth, as mentioned above, the inclusion of a support system member who knows the adult with FASD may serve as an interpreter. A support system members can assist in breaking down the barriers of communication deficits. Sometimes simply having the support system member present serves as a calming factor for people with FASD, allowing their brains to function more efficiently because stress and anxiety is reduced. Finally, being consistent in both word and action helps the client to feel safe and trusting in the professional relationship. A consistent approach can help achieve an efficacious outcome by maintaining healthy and productive communication. Adults with FASD respond well to routine and consistent messages. Together, this collection of approaches to accommodating the needs of adults with FASD can improve the quality of communications (Brown 2017; Brown et al. 2017).

Remaining patient can improve communication with an adult with FASD. In light of the impairments of FASD, interactions can be a challenging and frustrating process for a mental health professional, particularly in time-sensitive situations such as legal contexts. Nonetheless, mental health professionals should not rush through an interaction or assessment with an adult with FASD. Further, the use of loud, emotional, or threatening language should be avoided. If rushed or frightened, adults with FASD are likely to become overwhelmed or over-stressed, which may lead to a deterioration of executive control, emotional regulation, or communication skills. Mental health professionals might keep in mind that peculiar speech patterns, inconsistent statements, and repeating statements may not be deliberate attempts to obfuscate an assessment. Rather than be seen as a deliberate defiance or manipulation, such responses could simply be a manifestation of FASD symptoms (e.g., short- and long-term memory deficits, limited communication skills, confabulation, and suggestibility), a stressful or anxiety-provoking situation, or an attempt to conceal confusion and misunderstanding. As such, mental health professionals should make every effort to ensure that adults with FASD are provided with the best opportunity to tell their side of events by allowing adequate time for interactions (Brown 2017; Brown et al. 2017).

Improved communication with a mental health professional could be a lifeline for an adult with FASD. Information gained during such interpersonal exchanges has the potential to better enable a mental health professional to identify suitable interventions and advocate on behalf of the client. Once the lines of communication are firmly established, a mental health professional can help foster the development of strengths and skills that protect the adult with FASD. The D.E.A.R. framework is one promising opportunity for mental health professionals to increase the likelihood of positive short- and long-term outcomes for adults with FASD.

10.5 Assessment Considerations and Challenges in Screening Adult Populations

The process of identifying adults in need of FASD screening, assessment, and diagnosis is riddled with challenges (Boland et al. 2002; Fast and Conry 2004). Foremost amongst these difficulties is a dearth of screening and assessment instruments for adults with FASD. To make matters worse, the screening and assessment instruments that are available have limited evidence of reliability and validity. This situation is particularly dire for adults with FASD, as much of the limited clinical and research attention garnered for the disorder has been allocated to children. Another issue is that adults are often not screened at all because FAS is not even considered as a diagnosis. As such, very little empirical evidence exists to form a foundation of evidence-based practices in the assessment of FASD. This lack of empirical evidence has led some to call for the adaptation of FASD tools used for children for use with adults as a stopgap. In the meantime, medical and mental health professionals are often left to confront several of the diagnostic challenges of FASD without adequate resources.

One of the primary difficulties in the identification and diagnosis of FASD in adults is the verification of prenatal alcohol exposure (PAE) (Brown et al. 2017). Specifically, medical and mental health care professionals are often unable to obtain evidence that the mother of an adult with a suspected case of FASD consumed alcohol during the pregnancy. A contributing factor is that there are often historical gaps in medical records on PAE. An adult born prior to the identification of the condition of Fetal Alcohol Syndrome likely has no notation in medical records of maternal alcohol use during pregnancy because it was not officially recognized as detrimental at the time and, therefore, not screened. Further, adults with FASD commonly have a history of foster care placements and/or adoption and may have very little or no medical records; this is especially true in foreign adoptions (Landgren et al. 2010; Murawski et al. 2015). In foster and adoption situations, communication with the birth mother to inquire about alcohol use may not be possible. However, inquiring with any mother about alcohol consumption during pregnancy can be a challenging prospect if difficult family dynamics exist. A mother and other family members (father, siblings, aunts, uncles, etc.) may completely deny alcohol use during pregnancy even though the mother is or was known to be an alcoholic. Many dynamics may exist with the birth mother (e.g., guilt, shame, denial), which can add difficulty in ascertaining the level of PAE.

Without confirmation of PAE, medical and mental health professionals must turn towards other features of FASD during the assessment process. In a limited number of instances, the defining physical features of FASD can be relied upon in the identification and diagnosis of this disorder. That said, physical features of FASD such as facial dysmorphia are only present in 10–20% of cases (Spohr et al. 1993, 1994; Steinhausen et al. 1993). Even in the relatively few cases of FASD where such physical characteristics are present, facial features often change and become indistinguishable as individuals with FASD mature into adulthood. To combat these issues, medical and mental health professionals sometimes rely on baby pictures in the diagnostic process. Nonetheless, FASD remains difficult to identify and is often misdiagnosed or not detected in the vast majority of cases where physical characteristics of the disorder were never present (Streissguth et al. 1991).

When PAE cannot be confirmed and physical features are not present, the identification and diagnosis of adults with FASD is complicated by the presence of co-occurring psychopathology and other phenomena (O'Malley 2007). Typically, adults with FASD have a laundry list of comorbid psychiatric symptoms and conditions such as behavioral (e.g., Anti-Social Personality Disorder and ADHD), mood (e.g., major depression and bipolar disorder), anxiety, and substance use disorders. Many of these disorders share defining symptoms with FASD such as impulsivity and emotional dysregulation (Boe et al. 2003). Further, adults with FASD commonly have a history of adverse life events such as traumatic brain injuries along with physical and sexual abuse (Fast and Conry 2004; Burd et al. 2010). FASD characteristics also place these individuals at high risk for sexual perpetration and physical assault. In combination, the process of disentangling the underlying cause of this complicated interplay of symptomatology is difficult and time consuming for medical and mental health professionals, many of whom have limited if any expertise with FASD. Therefore, clinicians tend to diagnose and treat the conditions they are most familiar with, overlooking PAE simply because it cannot be confirmed and physical features are not present to justify a FASD or Neurobehavioral Disorder Associated With Prenatal Alcohol Exposure (ND-PAE) diagnosis. In these cases – and especially if maternal history indicates strong likelihood of PAE – it may be prudent to proceed with the likelihood of PAE in mind.

Complicating matters, the assessment and diagnosis of FASD in adults is limited by some of the symptoms of the disorder: verbal ability and memory issues. First, verbal intelligence and talkativeness often masks the cognitive (e.g., executive control) and adaptive functioning (e.g., decision-making) deficits that typify adults with FASD. In fact, adults with FASD may demonstrate adequate levels of intelligence on assessment tools, but great difficulty in school, work, and home settings. As such, over-reliance of intelligence measures in the assessment of FASD in adults can perilously mask the deficits of FASD (Streissguth 1997). Second, short- and long-term memory issues including confabulation and suggestibility are common in adults with FASD, which threatens the validity of self-reported information. Information provided by clients is integral in the assessment and diagnostic process. Medical and mental health professionals must incorporate collateral information from other sources to ensure the validity of any information provided by adults with a suspected case of FASD. Although this adds substantial time and resource burdens to the assessment process, such safeguards are necessary to ensure accurate diagnosis and, in turn, appropriate treatment that leads to more effective outcomes.

To combat these nuanced and difficult screening, assessment, and diagnostic issues, medical and mental health professionals need a greater awareness of FASD in adults, advanced training, and a network of FASD experts to serve as a support system (Brown 2017; Brown et al. 2017). Unfortunately, there are few options to obtain advanced education or training in FASD in adult populations (Boland et al. 2002). Further, FASD experts are few and far between. In the cases of both training and experts, existing resources usually focus on children and adolescents rather than adults. This is unfortunate because accurate diagnosis is a fundamental stepping stone in the development of an intervention plan. Without advancement in the assessment and treatment of FASD, adults with this disorder are destined not to receive the support they desperately need to avoid short- and long-term negative outcomes (Popova et al. 2015).

10.6 Treatment Considerations, Interventions, and Support Systems for Adults with FASD

Clinical and forensic mental health professionals typically have minimal understanding of FASD and limited expertise and experience in treating this debilitating disorder. As such, treatment and intervention for adults with FASD is often disorganized and piecemeal. Complicating matters, very few empirical research studies have examined interventions and support systems in adults with FASD (Temple 2012; Wheeler et al. 2013). The lack of research has resulted in a limited amount of evidence with which to develop clear recommendations for best practice with FASD adults. Until much needed research evaluates the potency of existing treatment programs and tailors programs to the needs of adults with FASD (Wheeler et al. 2013), any summary of available interventions must rely on the expertise of clinical and forensic mental health professionals who actively work to treat this population. To this end, this section highlights several concerns for clinical and forensic mental health professionals to consider. These concerns include the importance and difficulty of accurate diagnosis, evaluation of promising treatment techniques and programs, the impact of FASD symptoms on treatment performance, and the need to maintain and enhance support team systems.

Accurate diagnosis forms the basis of any responsive treatment plan. In the case of adults with FASD, clinical and forensic mental health professionals must (a) recognize the possibility of previous misdiagnosis and overlooked diagnosis and (b) disentangle the complex webs of diagnostic comorbidity. First, adults with FASD often have a long history of inaccurate and/or incomplete psychiatric diagnoses. This may be due, at least in part, to the traditional dismissal of FASD by many clinical and forensic mental health professionals. This possibility is encapsulated by the pervasive accounts of parents and caregivers who recall lobbying treatment professionals to consider and address the possibility of prenatal alcohol exposure (PAE) only to have these concerns ignored and dismissed. This delay exacerbates the difficulty of gathering the necessary evidence (e.g., confirmation of PAE) to accurately diagnose FASD. For example, it becomes more difficult to track down the birth mother and family members for confirmation of PAE as time passes, particularly in situations of adoption or foster care (Gindis 2014). Even if PAE may be noted in an adult's case history, FASD is still typically not diagnosed. As such, misdiagnosis and overlooked diagnosis is the rule rather than the exception.

Second, the accurate diagnosis of the varied and complex symptomatology of FASD is complicated by the high likelihood of comorbid psychiatric conditions. For example, adults with FASD frequently have co-occurring substance use issues, a history of trauma, issues associated with sleep, and mood disorders. This is further limited by the inherent difficulties in conducting a valid neuropsychological assessment. Failed attempts to disentangle FASD symptoms from secondary conditions commonly contribute to the misdiagnosis of FASD. To protect against this possibility, clinicians should evaluate the presence of symptoms across several sessions and keep re-evaluating if initial diagnoses are accurate. The impact of these issues may be alleviated if clinical and forensic mental health professionals become familiar with FASD and disorders that are likely to co-occur with FASD or develop secondary to FASD (Brown 2017; Brown et al. 2017).

In combination, a history of inaccurate diagnosis increases the likelihood of inappropriate and ineffective treatment. This can create future barriers to effective intervention such as anger, mistrust, and therapeutic pessimism among adults with FASD and their families. Further, inappropriate treatment may have an iatrogenic or harmful effect that exacerbates existing or creates new secondary conditions. If symptoms of a client worsen during treatment, false perceptions of an inability to treat may arise in the client, the client's family members, and even the clinician. As such, accurate diagnosis is a necessary first-step in the development of a potentially successful treatment plan.

After accurate diagnosis but before the development of a treatment plan, clinical and forensic mental health professionals should be aware of how the cognitive, social, and adaptive functioning impairments of FASD can impact treatment performance. First, the cognitive impairments of FASD can limit a client's information processing speed, which may require more time, patience, and persistence on the part of a clinician (Greenbaum et al. 2009). For example, the presence of short- and long-term memory problems may increase the difficulty of everything from assessment and skill building to treatment attendance and performance. Further, the sensory sensitivity of FASD may exacerbate the cognitive deficits and require that the session environment accommodate the individual's sensory needs. Consistent with common practice, most clinical sessions are held in a calm setting that minimizes distractions. However, accommodations for lighting, room temperature, color, sound, and smell may be needed. In short, the treatment of FASD requires that a clinician be flexible and understanding of how the cognitive impairments and sensory sensitivities of FASD impact an adult's capacity to participate in treatment (Brown 2017; Brown et al. 2017).

Second, the social and language deficits of FASD can limit the ability of adults with FASD to communicate during therapy. Clinicians must recognize that communication issues not only impact how well clients can express their thoughts and feelings to the clinician, but also the degree with which clients can understand the clinician and the content of the treatment program (Brown et al. 2016a, b). As such, the clinician must be sure to communicate in a manner that is simple, concrete and understandable for their client. It may take time, flexibility, a significant degree of creative perception, and trial and error for the clinician to learn how the client communicates most effectively.

Third, the adaptive functioning deficits of FASD decrease an adult's capacity to complete basic tasks such as showing up to appointments on time and completing treatment assignments (Baumbach 2002; Brown et al. 2011; Hofer and Burd 2009; Greenspan and Driscoll 2015). Even when attending appointments, adults with FASD may have inconsistent performance during the session or become fatigued faster than other patients. This lack of endurance may be partially due to the excessive cognitive toll it takes for adults with FASD to perform relatively simple tasks. To combat these issues, the incorporation of varied activities, frequent breaks, and shorter sessions may be integral in improving treatment efficacy along with treatment outcomes (Brown 2017; Brown et al. 2016a, b).

Awareness and consideration of the limitations imposed by FASD is an integral step when developing a treatment plan. Because FASD is such a rich continuum, clinicians should take care to treat each person as an individual and avoid assuming that successful interventions with some will be effective for others. The multitude of nuances in each individual requires the clinician to liberally build rapport and understanding of the individual and adjust the treatment plan accordingly. In most cases the treatment plan may become a living document as the minutiae of the individual with FASD are discovered throughout treatment.

Despite the limited base of intervention evidence for adults with FASD, the clinical experiences of professionals who actively treat FASD offers hope. In fact, the clinical expertise of the authors suggests several viable treatment options for adults with FASD. This includes a balanced combination of individualized therapy and, when indicated, an individualized medication routine. With modifications for developmental age (i.e., dysmaturity) and other brain-based symptoms (memory deficits, impulsivity, processing speed, generalization of information, etc.) specific to each individual with FASD, dialectical behavioral therapy (DBT), dual diagnosis treatment, targeted skills and attention training, and neurofeedback are potentially promising treatment options. A neurobehavioral family therapy approach currently evolving out of the neurobehavioral approach to FASD as developed by Diane Malbin has had encouraging success with adults with FASD. Families Moving Forward is a skills training program for families of children with FASD developed be Heather Carmichael Olson that could potentially be modified for the support system members of adults. Insight-based therapy may not be a good fit in adults with FASD because the cognitive (e.g., executive control and impulsivity) and adaptive functioning (e.g., decision-making and linking cause and effect) impairments of the disorder make it difficult for them to gain insight into their behavior. Group therapy may be problematic for many adults with FASD because the social impairments of the disorder make communication with others difficult, particularly with several people at once. Group therapy could also be counterproductive because of confabulation and suggestibility; people with FASD may take on or the stories others share as their own or confabulate stories from the details others share in the group. When treatment recommendations include group therapy, ensure the treatment plan is individualized and needs are taken into consideration (i.e. create a safety plan, or offer an option for a "timeout," etc.). Similarly, the effectiveness of talk therapy may also be limited by the communication deficits of FASD. To maximize the likelihood of success, a clinician must remain flexible yet vigilant in the identification of comorbid symptomatology as treatment techniques are selected and develop a thorough relapse prevention plan (Brown 2017; Brown et al. 2017).

Because the needs of adults with FASD are vast and debilitating, a successful treatment plan will likely require coordination between several care providers. For example, the adaptive functioning impairments of FASD (e.g., poor decision-making ability, abstract thought, and long-term planning) often necessitate assistance for a client with employment, money management, housing, transportation, and other daily needs. To adequately address these needs, a clinician may need to ensure that the client has educational and vocational support along with independent and supportive living services to compliment the client's psychological and psychiatric care. Further, clinicians may garner assistance in the areas of safety education, communication skills, behavioral control and self-advocacy. Regular communication among treatment team care providers is necessary to ensure that a client's diverse needs are met and the client does not slip through the cracks (Brown 2017; Brown et al. 2017).

To compliment these treatment options, there are several different intervention approaches that may benefit an adult with FASD. The primary goal of an approach should be to forge structure, routine, and stability in the life of a client to the degree that is most helpful for each individual. The incorporation of devices such as calendars and other organizational tools may be integral in ensuring the maintenance of structure, routine, and stability (Rutman and Van Bibber 2010). Once established, the clinician should work with the client to identify developmentally appropriate and reachable goals along with a clear step-by-step plan to reach them. Next, clinicians must ensure that clients have a resilient support system amongst their family, friends, and co-workers. This may require the clinician to teach members of the client's support system about the symptoms of FASD and how the support system can help prevent the development or exacerbation of secondary disabilities. A support system that understands FASD and how it personally affects an individual is perhaps the most vital piece of any treatment plan or intervention. In most cases, a modified form of family therapy is necessary to ensure the success of any treatment or intervention. In combination, appropriate treatment and a strong support system improve the likelihood of positive short- and long-term outcomes for adults with FASD (Brown 2017; Brown et al. 2017).

10.7 Suggestions for Further Research

There has been very sparse and limited empirical research investigating FASD in adults. To address the existing gaps in knowledge, a wealth of research is needed in at least six areas. First and foremost, research must establish prevalence estimates of FASD in adults in the general population as well as subpopulations (e.g., mental health, substance use, correctional, forensic, and other at-risk settings). Second, the applicability, reliability, and validity of ND-PAE criteria, the recent DSM-5 diagnosis, should be investigated in adults. Third, the development and validation of FASD screening tools for adults is imperative for the accurate identification of adults afflicted with this disorder. Fourth, assessment research should be careful to consider the potential impacts of confabulation and suggestibility, the presence of which is pronounced in FASD, on any FASD screening or diagnostic tools. Fifth, research must explore the effectiveness (e.g., completion rates, process outcomes, and short- and long-term outcomes) of existing and new treatment techniques and programs for adults with FASD. Sixth, by taking into consideration the treatment efficacy research described above, clinicians and researchers should endeavor to develop FASD education and training programs for psychiatrists, psychologists, and other mental health professionals who serve adult populations. In doing so, treatment professionals could aspire to identify empirically-based, best practice treatment modalities for adults with FASD. Overall, such a ranging and varied program of research has the potential to forge a body of evidence-based practices for adults with FASD.

10.8 Conclusion

This chapter offers an overview of communication strategies, screening and assessment techniques, and intervention and treatment approaches for adults with FASD. Individuals with FASD represent a group that is disproportionately likely to require treatment for mental health and substance use issues. As such, medical and mental health professionals in clinical and forensic settings are in a position to intervene on behalf of this at-risk group through identification and intervention. This is not a simple task because adults with FASD vary in the presence and severity of cognitive, social, and adaptive functioning impairments. To ease this process, medical and mental health professionals should become familiar with the red flags (e.g., foster care placements, adoption, and marked developmental dysmaturity) and commonly co-occurring disorders (e.g., ADHD, major depression, and substance use disorders) of FASD. If red flags or frequently comorbid conditions are present, clinicians should consider conducting an interview with the client and gathering information from collateral sources to screen for FASD (e.g., family members, medical history, legal history, and social services records). When coupled with an assessment of the client's strengths and coping strategies, these pieces of information will help guide the selection of appropriate interventions. Early identification and effective treatment have the potential to improve long-term outcomes for the client by limiting the exacerbation of FASD symptoms, preventing the further entrenchment of secondary conditions, and encouraging healthy behaviors.

References

American Psychiatric Association. 2013. *Diagnostic and statistical manual of mental disorders.* 5th ed. Arlington: American Psychiatric Publishing.

Baldwin, M. 2007. Fetal alcohol spectrum disorders and suicidality in a healthcare setting. *International Journal of Circumpolar Health* 66: 54–60.

Baumbach, J. 2002. Some implications of prenatal alcohol exposure for the treatment of adolescents with sexual offending behaviors. *Sexual Abuse: A Journal of Research and Treatment* 14 (4): 313–327.

Benz, J., C. Rasmussen, and G. Andrew. 2009. Diagnosing fetal alcohol spectrum disorder: History, challenges and future directions. *Paediatrics & Child Health* 14 (4): 231–237.

Boe, R., M. Nafeka, B. Vuong, R. Sinclair, and C. Cousineau. 2003. *The changing profile of the federal inmate population: 1997 and 2002*, Report Number R132. Ottawa: Research Branch, Correctional Service Canada.

Boland, F.J., A.E. Chudley, and B.A. Grant. 2002. The challenge of Fetal Alcohol Syndrome in adult offender populations. *Forum on Corrections Research* 14: 61–64.

Brown, N., G. Gudjonsson, and P. Connor. 2011. Suggestibility and fetal alcohol spectrum disorders: I'll tell you anything you want to hear. *The Journal of Psychiatry & Law* 1: 39–73.

Brown, J. 2017. Fetal alcohol spectrum disorder and confabulation: A clinical, forensic, and judicial dilemma. *The Journal of Special Populations* 1 (2): 1–11.

Brown, J., S. Herrick, and J. Long-McGie. 2014. Fetal alcohol spectrum disorders and offender reentry: A review for criminal justice and mental health professionals. *Behavioral Health* 1 (1): 1–19.

Brown, J., S.D. Rich, and N. Freeman. 2016a. Neurodevelopmental Disorder associated with Prenatal Alcohol Exposure (ND-PAE): A beginner's guide for clinical and forensic mental health professionals. *Behavioral Health* 4 (1): 1–6.

Brown, J., A. Wartnik, T. Aiken, et al. 2016b. Fetal alcohol spectrum disorder and suggestibility: Tips for criminal justice interviewers. *The Journal of Law Enforcement* 5 (4): 1–9.

Brown, J.M., J. Haun, P.A. Zapf, and N.N. Brown. 2017. Fetal Alcohol Spectrum Disorders (FASD) and competency to stand trial (CST): Suggestions for a 'best practices' approach to forensic evaluation. *International Journal of Law and Psychiatry* 52: 19–27.

Burd, L., D. Fast, J. Conry, and A. Williams. 2010. Fetal alcohol spectrum disorder as marker for increased risk of involvement with correction systems. *Journal of Psychiatry & Law* 38 (4): 559–583.

Burns, C. 2009. *Report on supportive housing opportunities for adults with FASD*. Cold Lake: Lakeland Centre for FASD. Available from http://lcfasd.com/wp/content/uploads/2013/05/Report-on-Supportive-Housing-Opportunities-foradults-with-FASD.pdf.

Chasnoff, I.J., A.M. Wells, and L. King. 2015. Misdiagnosis and missed diagnoses in foster and adopted children with prenatal alcohol exposure. *Pediatrics* 135 (2): 264–270.

Clark, E., P. Minnes, J. Lutke, and H. Ouellette-Kuntz. 2008. Caregiver perceptions of the community integration of adults with foetal alcohol spectrum disorder in British Columbia. *Journal of Applied Research in Intellectual Disabilities* 21: 446–456.

Conry, J.L., D.K. Fast, and C.A. Loock. 1997. *Youth in the criminal justice system: Identifying FAS and other developmental disabilities*. Final report to the Ministry of the Attorney General, Vancouver, BC.

Currie, B.A., J. Hoy, L. Legge, V.K. Temple, and M. Tahir. 2016. Adults with fetal alcohol spectrum disorder: Factors associated with positive outcomes and contact with the criminal justice system. *Journal of Population Therapeutics and Clinical Pharmacology/Journal de la thérapeutique des populations et de la pharamcologie clinique 23* (1): e37.

Douglas, H. 2010. The sentencing response to defendants with foetal alcohol spectrum disorder. *Criminal Law Journal* 34: 221–239.

Elliott, E., J. Payne, A. Morris, E. Haan, and C. Bower. 2008. Fetal alcohol syndrome: A prospective national surveillance study. *Archives of Disease in Childhood* 93 (9): 732–737.

Famy, C., A.P. Streissguth, and A. Unis. 1998. Metal illness in adults with fetal alcohol syndrome or fetal alcohol effects. *The American Journal of Psychiatry* 155: 552–554.

Fast, D.K., and J. Conry. 2004. The challenge of fetal alcohol syndrome in the criminal legal system. *Addiction Biology* 9: 161–166.

Gibbard, W.B., P. Wass, and M.E. Clarke. 2003. The neuropsychological implications of prenatal alcohol exposure. *The Canadian Child and Adolescent Psychiatry Review* 12: 72–76.

Gindis, B. 2014. Psychological characteristics of internationally adopted post-institutionalized children with Fetal Alcohol Spectrum Disorders. *The International Journal of Alcohol and Drug Research* 3 (1): 35–42.

Glass, L., D. Graham, B. Deweese, K. Jones, E. Riley, and S. Mattson. 2014. Correspondence of parent report and laboratory measures of inattention and hyperactivity in children with heavy prenatal alcohol exposure. *Neurotoxicology and Teratology* 42: 43–50.

Grant, T.M., N.N. Brown, J.C. Graham, N. Whitney, D. Dubovsky, and L.A. Nelson. 2013. Screening in treatment programs for Fetal Alcohol Spectrum Disorders that could affect therapeutic progress. *The International Journal of Alcohol and Drug Research* 2 (3): 37–49.

Green, C.R., A.M. Mihic, S.M. Nikkel, et al. 2009. Executive function deficits in children with fetal alcohol spectrum disorders (FASD) measured using the Cambridge Neuropsychological Tests Automated Battery (CANTAB). *Journal of Child Psychology and Psychiatry* 50: 688–697.

Greenbaum, L., S. Stevens, K. Nash, G. Koren, and J. Rovet. 2009. Social cognitive and emotion processing abilities of children with Fetal Alcohol Spectrum Disorders: A comparison with attention-deficit/hyperactivity disorder. *Alcoholism: Clinical and Experimental Research* 33: 1656–1670.

Greenspan, S., and J. Driscoll. 2015. Why people with FASD fall for manipulative ploys: Ethical limits of interrogators' use of lies. In *Fetal alcohol spectrum disorders in adults: Ethical and legal perspectives-An overview of FASD for professionals*, ed. M. Nelson and M. Trussler, 23–38. New York: Springer.

Hofer, R., and L.J. Burd. 2009. Review of published studies of kidney, liver, and gastrointestinal birth defects in fetal alcohol spectrum disorders. *Birth Defects Research Part A—Clinical and Molecular Teratology* 85: 179–183.

Huggins, J. 2005. Suicidality in adolescents and adults with fetal alcohol spectrum disorders. *Canadian Journal of Psychiatry* 50(2): 125.

Jirikowic, T., D. Kartin, and H.C. Olson. 2008. Children with Fetal Alcohol Spectrum Disorders: A descriptive profile of adaptive function. *Canadian Journal of Occupational Therapy* 75: 238–248.

Kodituwaku, P.W. 2009. Neurocognitive profile in children with fetal alcohol spectrum disorders. *Developmental Disabilities Research Reviews* 15: 218–224.

Landgren, M., L. Svensson, K. Strömland, and M. Andersson Grönlund. 2010. Prenatal alcohol exposure and neurodevelopmental disorders in children adopted from Eastern Europe. *Pediatrics* 125 (5): e1178–e1185.

Mattson, S.N., E.P. Riley, L. Gramling, et al. 1998. Neuropsychological comparison of alcohol exposed children with or without physical features of fetal alcohol syndrome. *Neuropsychology* 12: 146–153.

May, P.A., J.P. Gossage, W.O. Kalberg, L.K. Robinson, D. Buckley, M. Manning, and H.E. Hoyme. 2009. Prevalence and epidemiologic characteristics of FASD from various research methods with an emphasis on recent in-school studies. *Developmental Disabilities Research Reviews* 15: 176–192.

McMurtrie, J. 2011. The criminal justice system's disparate treatment of individuals with Fetal Alcohol Spectrum Disorders in cases involving sexual activity. *Journal of Psychiatry & Law* 39: 159–177.

Merrick, J., and I. Kandel. 2007. Fetal alcohol syndrome and suicide. A review. *International Journal on Disability and Human Development* 6 (3): 237–240.

Morleo, M., K. Woolfall, D. Dedman, R. Mukherjee, M.A. Bellis, and P.A. Cook. 2011. Underreporting of foetal alcohol spectrum disorders: An analysis of hospital episode statistics. *BMC Pediatrics* 11: 14.

Murawski, N.J., E.M. Moore, J.D. Thomas, and E.P. Riley. 2015. Advances in diagnosis and treatment of fetal alcohol spectrum disorders. *Alcohol Research L Current Reviews* 37 (1): 97–108.

Nash, K., S. Stevens, R. Greenbaum, J. Weiner, G. Koren, and J. Rovet. 2015. Improving executive functioning in children with fetal alcohol spectrum disorders. *Child Neuropsychology* 21 (2): 191–209.

O'Connor, M.J., J. McCracken, and A. Best. 2006. Under recognition of prenatal alcohol exposure in a child inpatient psychiatric setting. *Mental Health Aspects of Developmental Disabilities* 9: 105–108.

O'Malley, K. 2007. Fetal alcohol spectrum disorders: An overview. In *ADHD and Fetal Alcohol Spectrum Disorders (FASD)*, ed. K. O'Malley, 1–23. New York: Nova Science Publishers, Inc.

O'Malley, K., and J. Huggins. 2005. Suicidality in adolescents and adults with fetal alcohol spectrum disorders. *Canadian Journal of Psychiatry* 50 (2): 125.

Paley, B., and M. O'Connor. 2011. Behavioral interventions for children and adolescents with fetal alcohol spectrum disorders. *Alcohol Research and Health* 34: 64–75.

Popova, S., S. Lange, L. Burd, and J. Rehm. 2015. The economic burden of fetal alcohol spectrum disorder in Canada in 2013. *Alcohol and Alcoholism* 51 (3): 367–375. https://doi.org/10.1093/alcalc/agv117.

Roach, K., and A. Bailey. 2009. The relevance of fetal alcohol spectrum disorder and the criminal law from investigation to sentencing. *University of British Columbia Law Review* 42: 1–68.

Rojmahamongkol, P., A. Cheema-Hasan, and C. Weitzman. 2015. Do pediatricians recognize fetal alcohol spectrum disorders in children with developmental and behavioral problems? *Journal of Developmental & Behavioral Pediatrics* 36 (3): 197–202.

Roozen, S., G.J.Y. Peters, G. Kok, D. Townend, J. Nijhuis, and L. Curfs. 2016. Worldwide prevalence of fetal alcohol Spectrum disorders: A systematic literature review including meta-analysis. *Alcoholism: Clinical and Experimental Research* 40 (1): 18–32.

Rutman, D., and M. Van Bibber. 2010. Parenting with Fetal Alcohol Spectrum Disorder. *International Journal of Mental Health and Addiction* 8: 351–361.

Shankar, I. 2015. The making of a medical disorder: Tracing the emergence of fetal alcohol Spectrum disorder in Alberta. *Social Work in Public Health* 30 (1): 38–50.

Sokol, R., V. Delaney-Black, and B. Nordstrom. 2003. Fetal alcohol spectrum disorder. *JAMA* 290 (22): 2996–2999.

Spohr, H.L., J. Willms, and H.C. Steinhausen. 1993. Prenatal alcohol exposure and long-term developmental consequences. *Lancet* 341: 907–910.

———. 1994. The fetal alcohol syndrome in adolescence. *Acta Paediatrica* 404: 19–26.

———. 2007. Fetal alcohol spectrum disorders in young adulthood. *The Journal of Pediatrics* 150 (2): 175–179.

Stevens, S.A., D. Major, J. Rovet, and M. Desrocher. 2012. Social problem solving in children with fetal alcohol spectrum disorders. *Journal of Population Therapeutics and Clinical Pharmacology* 19: 99–110.

Stevens, S.A., J. Dudek, K. Nash, G. Koren, and J. Rovet. 2015. Social perspective taking and empathy in children with fetal alcohol spectrum disorders. *Journal of the International Neuropsychological Society* 21 (01): 74–84.

Streissguth, A. 1992. Fetal alcohol syndrome and fetal alcohol effects: A clinical perspective of later developmental consequences. In *Maternal substance abuse and the developing nervous system*, ed. I. Zagon and T. Slotkin, 5–25. San Diego: Academic.

Streissguth, A. 1997. *Fetal Alcohol Syndrome- A guide for families and communities*. Baltimore: Paul H. Brookes Publishing.

Streissguth, A.P., J. Aase, K. Sterling, M.D. Clarren, S.P. Randels, R.A. LaDue, et al. 1991. Fetal Alcohol Syndrome in adolescents and adults. *Journal of the American Medical Association* 25: 1961–1967.

Streissguth, A.P., H.M. Barr, J. Kogan, and F.L. Bookstein 1996. *Understanding the occurrence of secondary disabilities in clients with fetal alcohol syndrome and fetal alcohol effects*. Final Report to the Centers for Disease Control and Prevention (CDC), August, 1996 (Technical Report No. 96-06). Seattle: University of Washington.

Streissguth, A.P., F.L. Bookstein, H.M. Barr, P.D. Sampson, K. O'Malley, and J.K. Young. 2004. Risk factors for adverse life outcomes in fetal alcohol syndrome and fetal alcohol effects. *Journal of Developmental & Behavioral Pediatrics* 25 (4): 228–238.

Steinhausen, H.C., J. Willms, and H.L. Spohr. 1993. Long-term psychopathological and cognitive outcome of children with fetal alcohol syndrome. *Journal of the American Academy of Child and Adolescent Psychiatry* 32(5): 990–994.

Temple, V.K. 2012. *The Surrey Place Centre fetal alcohol spectrum disorders adult diagnostic clinic: Outcomes and service update*. Toronto: Surrey Place Centre.

Thiel, K., N. Baladerian, K. Boyce, O. Cantos, L. Davis, K. Kelly, K. Tavenner, K. Mitchell, and J. Stream. 2011. Fetal Alcohol Spectrum Disorders and victimization: Implications for families, educators, social services, law enforcement, and the judicial system. *Journal of Psychiatry & Law* 39: 121–157.

Ware, A., M. Infante, J. O'Brien, S. Tapert, K. Jones, E. Riley, and S. Mattson. 2015. An fMRI study of behavioral response inhibition in adolescents with and without histories of heavy prenatal alcohol exposure. *Behavioural Brain Research* 278: 137–146.

Wedding, D., J. Kohout, M.B. Mengel, M. Ohlemiller, M. Ulione, K. Cook, et al. 2007. Psychologists' knowledge and attitudes about fetal alcohol syndrome, fetal alcohol spectrum disorders, and alcohol use during pregnancy. *Professional Psychology: Research and Practice* 38 (2): 208.

Whaley, S.E., M.J. O'Connor, and B. Gunderson. 2001. Comparison of the adaptive functioning of children prenatally exposed to alcohol to a nonexposed clinical sample. *Alcoholism: Clinical and Experimental Research* 25: 118–124.

Wheeler, J.A., K.A. Kenney, and V. Temple. 2013. Fetal alcohol spectrum disorder: Exploratory investigation of services and interventions for adults. *Journal on Developmental Disabilities* 19 (3): 62–75.

Yates, W.R., R.J. Cadoret, E.P. Troughton, M. Stewart, and T.S. Giunta. 1998. Effect of alcohol exposure on adult symptoms of nicotine, alcohol, and drug dependence. *Alcoholism, Clinical and Experimental Research* 22: 914–920.

Part IV
Sentencing and Support of People with FASD

Chapter 11
Introduction; FASD and the Revolving Door of Criminal Justice

Fia Jampolsky

11.1 Introduction

Fetal Alcohol Spectrum Disorder ("FASD") has been used as an umbrella term for serious medical conditions involving central nervous system abnormalities including fetal alcohol syndrome (FAS), partial FAS, and alcohol-related neurodevelopmental disorder (ARND) (Brown et al. 2012). Revised Canadian Guidelines uses the term FASD diagnostically by defining it precisely and collapsing all FASD diagnosis into two categories: FASD with sentinel facial features and FASD without sentinel facial features (Cook et al. 2016).

Researchers have identified many adverse outcomes in those diagnosed with FASD who have not received optimized intervention: over 90% have mental health problems; 43% have interrupted school experiences as children, peaking at 70% in later years; 60% have been in trouble with the law; 50% have been or are in jail; 50% have engaged in inappropriate sexual activity; and, 30% have alcohol or drug problems early on and increasing as individuals become adults (Streissguth et al. 1997). While such secondary disabilities from FASD are well documented, the actual consequences of FASD with respect to the criminal justice system, both the risk of entering into and experiences within the system, have often been overlooked or disregarded.

A body of research is slowly being developed with respect to FASD and the law, including research into the effects of FASD within the criminal justice system. Much of the content of this chapter, however, comes from observation and deliberation of my earlier years of practice in legal aid and courts when little was written of the effects of FASD in the criminal justice system.

F. Jampolsky (✉)
Counsel, Aboriginal Law Group, Legal Services, Yukon Government, Whitehorse, YT, Canada
e-mail: f.jampolsky@northwestel.net

E. Jonsson et al. (eds.), *Ethical and Legal Perspectives in Fetal Alcohol Spectrum Disorders (FASD)*, International Library of Ethics, Law, and the New Medicine 75, https://doi.org/10.1007/978-3-319-71755-5_11

11.2 How FASD Became a Four-Letter Word in the System

A legal aid practice is frequently endowed with long hours, a high file load, and in general, the task of dealing with the most disadvantaged of clientele, almost always in crisis mode. In order to stay on top of your practice, it is necessary to fight daily fires and deal with the next most urgent matter in a pool of urgent matters. In doing so, one can miss obvious red flags. It is only when I stepped back from practice to reflect on my clients and files that I realized that I had the same questions for many of them:

- "Why do I keep dealing with this person again and again?"
- "Didn't I tell him last time that if he did this again, he would be back in court?"
- "Why are we dealing with the same kind of breach again?"
- "Why didn't she learn her lesson the last time?"
- "Why does she keep getting arrested for the exact same thing?"

After working at Legal Aid for over a decade, it became impossible to ignore certain anomalies, which seemed to occur within the criminal justice arena. There was always a population of offenders who were caught up in what I have commonly referred to, as the 'revolving door' of the criminal justice system.

While often picked up on what would be considered to be less significant substantive charges – such as minor theft or assault – these individuals could not seem to deal with those charges without accumulating an impressive roster of additional charges. They were mostly administrative charges, such as breaching the original release conditions or earlier probation orders. Such individuals would consistently fail to contact their bail supervisor, be caught drinking or miss their curfew over and over. There was often a disconnect between my communication and their comprehension. My clients would nod while I explained their charges, the evidence and their options. They would parrot back what I had explained to them and so I felt certain that they understood the circumstances, their options and the likely outcome of their case. Nevertheless, they would walk out of my office and repeat the exact same pattern of behavior that sent them into my office, and the court system, in the first place.

11.3 FASD and the Criminal Justice System

The criminal justice system in many jurisdictions is a complex maze which may confuse even the most assiduous of participants. The practical demands of court combined with budget constraints, limited resources and time pressures have resulted in a veritable processing plant for those charged with a criminal offense.

The foundation of the criminal justice system is based on an objective analysis of whether ones' intention and behavior fall outside legislated norms. It is designed to analyze and contextualize the behavior, not the person. Professor Kent Roach explains the criminal justice systems' confines: "The justice system is premised on assumptions that people act in a voluntary manner that is determined by free will and that they can make informed and voluntary choices both with respect to the exercise of their rights and the decision to commit crimes" (Roach and Bailey 2009, at p. 2).

As knowledge and awareness regarding FASD have increased, this premise becomes paradoxical in its application to FASD offenders. The justice system often requires what the FASD offender cannot provide. However, there are unique implications for individuals with FASD who find themselves before the criminal justice system (Roach and Bailey 2009).

11.3.1 Alarm

The mnemonic 'ALARM' describes the increased risk for individuals with FASD to interact with the criminal justice system (Fast and Conry 2004). ALARM refers to Adaptive behavior, Language, Attention, Reasoning and Memory. Fast and Conry found that as a result of impaired adaptive behavior, individuals with FASD cannot meet accepted societal standards of independence and social responsibility. Language deficits result in a disconnect between use and comprehension. Attention and impulsivity deficits result in actions regardless of consequence and reasoning deficits prevent an ability to learn from experience. Memory problems create a risk of confabulation. These deficits were seen to increase ones risk to enter the criminal justice system (Fast and Conry 2004).

Following identification of the ALARM mnemonic, ten specific brain domains have been identified as "critical to CNS diagnostic parameters for successful FASD identification and management" (Lang 2006). This compilation, and explanation of how these brain domains create a relationship between the central nervous system ("CNS") and FASD, examined in a criminal justice context, is jarring in its relevancy. There are few characteristics within these brain domains that do not put FASD individuals at risk of interacting with the criminal justice system, illustrating the need for urgent attention by criminal justice professionals.

11.3.2 Brain Domains

11.3.2.1 Achievement

Achievement refers to traditional academic skills. Despite the fact that many people with FASD have an IQ within a normal range (Streissguth et al. 1997), other brain domains affected by FASD can create barriers to academic success. Individuals with FASD may suffer from intellectual impairment, developmental delays, and/or learning disabilities, affecting their ability to achieve 'success'[1] within a traditional

[1] I have highlighted the term success because despite challenges to the ideology, most mainstream academic institutions still use traditional academic measurements as a way of measuring success in the education system.

classroom environment.[2] Individuals with FASD can have very literal processing skills that, without nuanced processing and comprehensive analytical skills, result in misunderstanding in both the relay and retrieval of instructions.

Attention deficits resulting in difficulty with concentration, impulsivity and hyperactivity, challenge the rote requirements of the education system, which requires focused attention. Children with such challenges risk being labeled with behavioral problems or as willfully disobedient. Noise and light sensitivity can also create a challenge in a classroom setting where teachers deal with large numbers of children, large noise levels and fast moving environments.

Difficulties in other domains such as adaptation, cognition, executive functioning, language, memory and social communication can all result in struggles within a traditional classroom setting that becomes magnified as the student progresses into higher grades (Streissguth et al. 1997).

11.3.2.2 Adaptation

Adaption refers to the ability to meet the challenges of daily living including self-care, managing money, getting and maintaining employment, and using leisure time in healthy and acceptable ways (Fast and Conry 2004). Individuals with FASD often lack adaptive living skills, particularly in terms of healthy and acceptable use of leisure time. Such challenges can be enhanced when individuals are vulnerable to suggestion and susceptible to external influence.

11.3.2.3 Attention

Attention refers to one's ability to have both sustained and flexible attention. This is reflected in behaviors such as reduced concentration, hyperactivity and impulsivity. Individuals with FASD commonly have attention deficit issues including all of the characteristics listed above.

11.3.2.4 Cognition

Cognition refers to general thinking ability. Intellectual impairment, and developmental delays may affect one's cognition. Even though many individuals with FASD have an IQ within a normal range, higher-level conceptual thinking can be challenging or absent which may, in turn, prevent someone from being able to process the consequence of their actions.

[2] Cognitive deficits and/or significant developmental delays in FASD manifest in learning disabilities, uneven cognitive skill profiles, significant discrepancies between verbal and nonverbal skills, and problematic information processing (Kodituwakku 2009; Streissguth et al. 2004).

11.3.2.5 Executive Functioning

Executive functioning refers to a set of mental processes that help connect past experiences with present action. This includes self-regulation, initiation, working memory, planning, organizing and self-monitoring (Fast and Conry 2004). People use executive functioning for strategizing, paying attention to and remembering details, and managing time and space. Individuals with FASD, who may lack memory, processing or management skills, can be challenged by such goal-directed behavior. Cognitive and executive functioning impairment may also result in an inability to understand the consequences of ones actions.

An inability to connect past experiences with present action, combined with the challenge of understanding the consequences of one's actions puts individuals with FASD of risk of entering into the criminal justice system and of repeating their actions or crimes over and over again.

11.3.2.6 Language Skills

Expressive and receptive language skills, refers to the ability to utilize grammar, sentence structure and words to convey meaning (Lang 2006). Individuals with FASD can have both expressive and receptive language deficits.

Individuals with FASD can use mimicry as a coping tool. They can appear to have greater language ability than they actually have. They may use a sophisticated vocabulary with little comprehension of their 'choice' of words (Lang 2006). Their ability to parrot language, including for example, legal advice, can lead to the false impression that they have understood a conversation requiring comprehension of the law, their options and a course of action. It can lead to further impressions that they understand what is happening in court or in conversation with a lawyer or judge.

11.3.2.7 Memory

Memory refers to a capacity to consolidate, store, and retrieve information for later use. Individuals with FASD may lack this capacity. In addition, the resulting sporadic memory-recall can be 'influenced by suggestion' (Fast and Conry 2004) resulting in a risk for confabulation. Details of a relevant event may be intermingled with previous or subsequent events. Fictional events may replace actual events. This, combined with poor concepts of time and sequencing, can result in unreliable accounting.

Law is hyper-focused on both the minutia and the grand. Fact-finding seeks specific detail about events that may have occurred months or in some cases, years before. Faulty recounting and impaired memory may result in credibility challenges or may increase the risk of false confession.

11.3.2.8 Motor Skills and Sensory/Soft Neurological

Motor skills refers to one's ability to use and coordinate both large and small muscles to allow for both physical skills, fine motors skills such as writing or eating and hand eye coordination. Sensory skills refer to one's ability to process incoming information. Individuals with an FASD can lack motor skills and have an increased sensitivity to their surroundings, which can affect other domains including academic and adaptive living skills.

11.3.2.9 Social Communication

Social communication includes our ability to relay information coherently and cohesively (Lang 2006). Social communication allows one to communicate in an appropriate and effective way to many social situations. Individuals with FASD who have difficulty relaying information in a consecutive sequence, can confuse relevant events with irrelevant ones, or reality with perception. An increased propensity to mimicry and suggestibility or diminished ability to understand acts and consequences, as discussed earlier, can severely impact one's social communication skills.

11.4 The Community, the Police and the Court System

The characteristics of FASD, as outlined above, put individuals at risk within their own communities, with potential police encounters and within the criminal justice system.

Negative outcomes and failure facing individuals as a result of deficits in language, memory, soft neurological, social communication, attention and adaptation are almost assured. From a very young age behavior labelled as 'willful' and 'oppositional' as opposed to 'incapable', 'unable' or 'needing assistance' sets the stage for an inevitable clash – first with caregivers, then with educators and ultimately with the criminal justice system.

The tendency toward suggestibility and/or mimicry opens vulnerable youth, and adults, to negative peer influences. This in combination with the inability to see consequences can result in risky, unlawful behavior. An inability to foresee consequences, combined with characteristics such as impulsivity or suggestibility, creates a high risk for those with FASD to come in conflict with the criminal justice system. Impulsivity combined with impaired judgment means that a jar of change on the edge of a hotel desk might be irresistible, a purse on a hook in a beauty salon may be grabbed without a second thought, and a car with open doors and loose change is a fleeting opportunity rather than a serious crime.

Without external information, police respond to situations as they appear and often have to make quick, sometimes forceful decisions. Often, these charged situations include the presence of drugs and alcohol. The presence of FASD, which can be invisible to the unknowing eye, in such situations creates a maelstrom for potential escalation.

What seems like a simple encounter can result in serious charges as the FASD offender reacts with an inability to process, comprehend, communicate effectively or regulate his/her behavior. One charge can quickly turn into many. Once police find or question someone with FASD they may, without malice or intention put that person at risk of confabulation or self-incrimination (Moore and Green 2004).

Coming to the attention of the police and escalating charges are just the start of where things can break down for individuals with FASD. Once ensconced in the system, the FASD offender must contend with decisions, choices and demand that are challenged by the very characteristics of FASD.

What seems like a simple act of showing up for a meeting with a lawyer can prove virtually impossible for someone with time impairment issues without an external support system. Lawyers, like all other players in the criminal justice system, are perpetually time crunched. They have limited opportunity to explain charges and options to their client. They expect clients to understand their initial explanation of the charges, their options and potential consequences. However, expressive and receptive language deficits may impede the ability for an FASD client to understand, process and instruct counsel. Further, the ability for an FASD client to parrot what the lawyer has just said means that this disconnect may not be detected.

It is difficult at the best of times to comprehend the language or the pace of court. The court process requires concentration and focus and can confound even those who know the system well. For those with affected brain domains, the ability to even focus, let alone comprehend the lawyer's or judge's words is challenged. As a result, an individual with FASD may act like they are paying no attention at all to the proceedings. This has the potential of attracting the ire of the court. Much like the willfully disobedient student, the FASD accused can be seen as uninterested or worse, oppositional.

In court, watching someone with FASD can be like watching a terrible situation comedy. Appearing to pay no attention to the judge, an accused may be more preoccupied with a friend sitting in the gallery than with the court proceedings. She/he can miss the entire proceeding in court, which may be going to the heart of his/her own liberty while frantically trying to wave at a familiar face.

Expressive language impairment can create misunderstanding between lawyer and client. A lawyer unfamiliar with a client may take his or her ability to parrot back what has been said as comprehension. Likewise, a judge who thinks she is speaking directly to and really getting through to an FASD accused might be surprised when the offender who has just been sentenced to jail says at the end of the proceedings, "Is that it? Can I go home now?"

Once an individual has come to the attention of the criminal justice system, the requirements of the system, in combination with the characteristics of FASD create a Kafkaesque effect. The criminal justice system requires of an individual exactly that which FASD characteristics prevent them from being able to provide. For example, the criminal justice system generally requires that an accused follow conditions while in the process of dealing with his or her offense. Conditions may include requirements for court appearances, meetings with probation officers, or curfews. Such conditions do not include external support mechanisms to ensure that people with deficits in adaptive or executive functioning, memory, or attention can meet such obligations.

The entire foundation of the criminal justice system is counter intuitive for the FASD offender. The goal of the criminal justice system is to get people out of the system as fast as possible. The criminal justice system is not seeking enduring relationships and as such does not provide ongoing support on an indefinite basis. The system is finite, whereas the deficits caused by FASD are not. That which the FASD individual requires to avoid remaining in the system ongoing, consistent support – the criminal justice system disallows in its very foundation.

The criminal justice system is also designed to become increasingly punitive. A failure to learn from past mistakes results in greater punishment with each progressive offense. The underpinning of criminal justice system, that one learns from their own mistakes or the mistakes of others, belie the characteristics of FASD. The emphasis of the criminal justice system to demand exactly that which individuals with FASD cannot provide ensures the 'revolving door' effect of the system.

11.5 Recommendations

What then can we do with individuals that, by the very nature of their disability are almost certain to become 'lifers' in a system that operates so antithetically to the needs of an FASD affected individual? There is much that can be done, both in the short and in the long term. The recommendations that I focus on fall into the following categories:

1. Keep individuals with FASD out of the system;
2. Deal with individuals with FASD justly once in the system;
3. Pursue legislative reform; and
4. Think outside the box – create a paradigm shift.

11.5.1 Keep Individuals with FASD out of the System

Based on irrelevant assumptions and impossible expectations, the entire criminal justice system is simply wrong for those with FASD. The most appropriate response then, to such individuals, is to keep them out of the system altogether. This is not contrary to the rules of civil society. Rather, it is in keeping with the morays of crime and punishment; that is, punish people who are culpable for their actions. This, of course, is not to suggest that no crime committed by individuals with an FASD belongs in the criminal justice system. Some crimes are so serious that no other venue will suffice.

The very nature of FASD means that some individuals have racked up an impressive roster of charges even when the originating charge is not very serious. As noted earlier, the court treats each ensuing charge more serious than the last. Time and time again, the Crown in my cases argued that jail was an appropriate response to administrative breaches because jail was the appropriate response the last time my client committed the very same breach. To my shame, time and time again, I agreed with them. It is exactly this scenario which warrants closer attention, and, it is my suggestion, a very different response. I see no moral or legal argument for littering a criminal record with dozens of process related charges in which the original substantive charge was minor and inconsequential. This may also be the case, in some instances where the original charge was a serious one. Padding records with administrative breaches that tell the tale of a disability is not the intention of our justice system, rather, the unintended consequence.

11.5.1.1 Diagnosis

An FASD diagnosis can keep individuals with FASD out of the criminal justice system. However, in order to funnel out individuals who do not belong in the system due to brain damage, it is fundamental to identify those individuals (Chartrand and Forbes-Chilibeck 2003). The legal arena is littered with legal and other roadblocks to obtain a proper FASD diagnosis. Judges have limited ability at the sentencing stage to obtain a diagnosis due to the constrictive nature of the Criminal Code. Those with knowledge and awareness in the system often lack the resources to make more than an educated guess regarding accused who display red flags. There is often a debate both inter-provincially and nationally over who should pay for diagnostic reports. A lack of resources is often used as a just response to inaction. It is, however, as unjust to ignore the potential presence of such a disability if there are indicia that it exists as it is to suspect a disability without obtaining a proper diagnosis.

11.5.1.2 Funding for Prevention

The criminal justice system is a multi-billion dollar industry in Canada. However, key funding directed at criminal justice may be better served if redirected into supportive, preventive services in other portfolios such as education, health and social services. If we know that ongoing, consistent support for individuals with FASD can increase positive outcomes, then an interdisciplinary, multi-sectoral approach to coordinated, integrated service delivery is clearly the best response. There are obvious challenges to the notions of funding prevention services rather than criminal justice services. Opponents of change might argue that justice is a 'fixed cost'. In addition, the very characteristics of FASD that make interaction with the criminal justice system inevitable also make it difficult to provide some individuals with successful, consistent ongoing support. The financial implications of providing multi-sectoral support loom large in government with limited life cycles.

The idea of diverting criminal justice funding away from a crime and punishment model towards a model that provides therapeutic responses requires a higher level of thinking. It requires a paradigm shift. Reduced costs to a criminal justice system, as a result of increased support to some of our most vulnerable citizens makes both financial and moral sense. FASD cannot be cured. It can, however, be managed and individuals with FASD can lead productive, pro-social lives. How we treat the most vulnerable members of our community is a reflection of our integrity as a society as a whole.

11.5.2 Deal with Them Justly Once in the System

Arguably, some criminal charges for reasons of public safety and public policy must proceed through the criminal justice system. What is the best way to proceed when this happens?

11.5.2.1 Mandate Education

It is fundamental for all professionals to have as much information and knowledge as possible about both the accused and FASD (Roach and Bailey 2009). While basic knowledge and understanding of FASD has increased in the last 10 years, education and training should still be a requirement for justice and corrections professionals. Anecdotally, in speaking with professionals from across the country, the level of knowledge and awareness of FASD appears to vary significantly across jurisdictions. Education and training would encourage justice professionals to look for red flags in repeat offenders; those offenders we have talked about that just don't seem to 'get it.' It would help create a greater understanding of what is a essentially a medical disability and would help allay concerns or misperceptions that we disrupt 'justice' when we divert FASD offenders from the criminal justice system. It could increase opportunities to create new policy, and seek alternative ways of dealing with FASD offenders. It could set the stage for much needed legislative reform.

11.5.2.2 Diversion/Alternate Measures

Diversion and other alternative measure programs are legitimate alternative justice routes presently implemented in varying degrees across Canada. A regionalized method of implementation, however, can result in a haphazard approach to justice. Funding pressures, differing political agendas and varied resource challenges contribute to an imbalanced approach to such programs nationally. A uniform, consistent approach to diversion and alternative measures, creates a more consistent, measured and just approach.

11.5.3 Pursue Legislative Reform

In 2013, Ryan Leef, the former Conservative MP for Yukon introduced a private members bill (Bill C-583) that had the support of all territorial political parties in Canada. One aspect of the bill considered FASD as a mitigating factor in sentencing. Bill C-583 was ultimately withdrawn and sent to a parliamentary committee for report. Though unsuccessful, the Bill, and the resulting report did raise the FASD and justice discussion to a national level. In 2016, the Liberal MP for Yukon, Larry Bagnall, introduced a 2nd private members bill (Bill C-235), which was also ultimately defeated. Bill C-235 proposed to establish a procedure for assessing individuals appearing before the criminal justice system who were suspected of having FASD as well as considering FASD a mitigating factor in sentencing.[3] While conversations have seemingly stalled in 2017, a review of the criminal justice system by the present Liberal government may invite discussion and debate once more.

11.5.3.1 Mandatory Minimums and Escape Clauses

Legislative changes in the mid-2000s introduced the sweeping use of mandatory minimums. Such changes have, no doubt ensured that more individuals with FASD end up in jail. Mandatory minimums, by their very nature, are antithetical to the needs of the FASD offender. Mandatory minimums have been described by the Supreme Court of Canada as follows:

> They function as a blunt instrument that may deprive courts of the ability to tailor proportionate sentences at the lower end of a sentencing range. They may, in extreme cases, impose unjust sentences, because they shift the focus from the offender during the sentencing process in a way that violates the principle of proportionality. (*R. v. Nur*, 2015 SCC 15 at para. 44)

Escape clauses have been used in other countries to prevent 'constitutional infirmity' where there are mandatory minimums, to "exempt outliers for whom the mandatory minimum will constitute cruel and unusual punishment" (*R. v. Lloyd*, [2016] SCC 13 at para. 36). The use of escape clauses allows judges to craft more just decisions based on the individual offender.

11.5.3.2 Sentencing

Legislative change affecting individuals with FASD has occurred in Alaska where FASD can be considered a mitigating factor in sentencing. Judges in Canada have been inconsistent, considering FASD as both a mitigating and aggravating factor if considered at all[4] (Chartrand and Forbes-Chilibeck 2003; Roach and Bailey 2009).

---

[3] See: https://openparliament.ca/bills/42-1/C-235

[4] The website fasdjustice.ca posts updated court decisions from across Canada on all issues affecting offenders with FASD including sentencing decisions.

In some instances, the court has found that the precise qualities of FASD increase the risk for breaching conditions making the offender a high risk and therefore not suitable for community supervision.[5] A more consistent, therapeutic approach is required to ensure that offenders are dealt with both fairly and equitably.

11.5.3.3 Utilize Elements of the Youth Criminal Justice System

The adult system, in comparison to the youth criminal justice system, is one that individuals are expected to navigate on their own. Utilizing the knowledge of brain domain deficits, the concept of support for individuals with FASD, would be well served by provisions and concepts present in the youth justice system, under the *Youth Criminal Justice Act* ("YCJA").[6] For example section 34 of the YCJA allows a youth justice to order an assessment by a qualified person if the court believes that that the person is suffering from a physical or mental illness or disorder, psychological disorder, emotional disturbance, learning disability or mental disability. Provisions which mimic section 34, to allow for FASD specific assessments could prove to be invaluable to the courts as well as to both the accused and his or her care providers. It would also end the debate of who pays for such assessments. Section 25 of the YCJA allows for counsel to be provided for by a legal aid program or by direction of the court (and appointment by the AG) should the youth be unable to obtain counsel. This ensures that no youth has to appear unrepresented in Court. Similar provisions for adults with FASD could ensure that such individuals have legal representation. Finally, section 19 of the YCJA, sets out that a number of players in the system can convene a case conference for the purpose of making a decision required under the act. What this means practically, is that important players can be brought together to work on what is best for a young person. This circle of care approach would allow for a supportive, unified approach to working with an FASD individual both during and potentially following his or her involvement with the criminal justice system.

11.5.3.4 Human Rights

The treatment of individuals with FASD outside of and within the criminal justice system is a human rights issue and should be expressly covered under Human Rights legislation. Other forms of legislation could also include the duty to accommodate FASD. The most obvious example is the *Corrections and Conditional Release Act,*[7] which deals with matters post conviction.

---

[5] R. v. J., [1996] B.C.J. No. 2754 (Prov. Ct. (Youth Ct.)) (QL); R. v.B.(I.D.), 2005 ABQB 421, [2005] A.W.L.D. 2863, [2005] A.J. No. 689 (QL).

[6] S.C. 2002, c-1.

[7] S.C. 1992, c.20.

11.5.4 Paradigm Shift

The criminal justice system is based on the normative assumption that a person acts in a voluntary manner, makes informed choices with respect to the decision to commit crimes and learns from their own behavior as well as the behavior of others (Roach and Bailey 2009). Brain damage that affects ones' ability to foresee consequences, or to learn from previous behavior, directly clashes with the normative assumption that defines the very basis of the criminal justice system. If the criminal justice system is premised on assumptions about individual understanding the consequences of their actions and learning from their mistakes, then the presence of a permanent brain damage that affects memory impulsivity and suggestivity challenges that very presumption (Roach and Bailey 2009). Research is still required to examine the concepts of 'mens rea', 'operating mind' and 'culpability' in the context of neurological conditions such as FASD. The discussion about FASD in the criminal justice system is not, and should not be, about how people can get out of criminal charges. The reality is however, that the criminal justice system is a historic system, developed long before there was any knowledge of this and other complex neurological conditions.

The fundamental precepts of our criminal law system are based on tradition and history from a time when the presence and characteristics of FASD were unknown. With the kind of knowledge we have now, as a result of scientific research, it is imperative that we make a paradigm shift.[8] The entire conversation regarding some of our most vulnerable members must be reframed. We need to see some individuals who 'cannot' as opposed to 'will not'. We need to understand the disability for what it is rather than what we expect adults to be.

11.6 Conclusion

The characteristics of FASD affecting each brain domain, increases the risk for both entry and entrapment within the criminal justice system. It is only through education and a dedicated attempt to think outside of the box and to move beyond the parameters of our traditional structures and systems that we are going to be able to effect positive change.

Refocusing our efforts in support and prevention will ultimately decrease the necessity to reflect on the process in the context of criminal justice. With the knowledge that there are instances we will still need to engage the criminal justice system, we need to reflect on how to do this in a way that ensure truly just outcomes.

[8] This is not a new concept in the FASD field. Experts caring for individuals recommend this approach in caring for individuals in general not just in criminal justice. For example the Manual for Community Caring – FASD by the former FAS/E support Network of B.C. includes a section on Paradigm Shifts and FASD.

References

Brown, N.N., P.D. Conner, and R.S. Adler. 2012. Conduct-disordered adolescents with fetal alcohol spectrum disorder: Intervention in secure treatment settings. *Criminal Justice and Behavior* 39: 770–794.

Canadian Bar Association. 2010. *Resolution: Fetal alcohol spectrum disorder in the criminal justice system*. Retrieved from http://www.cba.org/getattachment/Our-Work/Resolutions/Resolutions/2010/Fetal-Alcohol-Spectrum-Disorder-in-the-Criminal-Ju/10-02-A.pdf

———. 2013. *Accommodating the disability of FASD to improve access to justice*. Retrieved from http://www.cba.org/getattachment/Our-Work/Resolutions/Resolutions/2013/Accommodating-the-Disability-of-FASD-to-Improve-Ac/13-12-A-ct.pdf.2016

Chartrand, Larry N., and Ella M. Forbes-Chilibeck. 2003. Offenders with fetal alcohol syndrome. *Health Law Journal* 11: 35–67.

Cook, Jocelynn L., Courtney R. Green, Christine M. Lilley, Sally M. Anderson, Mary Ellen Baldwin, Albert E. Chudley, Julianne L. Conry, Nicole LeBlanc, Christine A. Loock, Jan Lutke, Bernadene F. Mallon, Audrey A. McFarlane, Valerie K. Temple, and Ted Rosales. 2016. Fetal alcohol spectrum disorder: A guideline for diagnosis across the lifespan. *Canadian Medical Association Journal* 188: 191–197.

Corrections and Conditional Release Act, S.C. 1992, c.20.

Fast, Diane K., and J. Conry. 2004. The challenge of fetal alcohol syndrome in the criminal legal system. *Addiction Biology* 9: 161–166.

Kodituwakku, P. 2009. Neurocognitive. *Profile in Children with Fetal Alcohol Spectrum Disorders* 15 (3): 218–224

Lang, J. 2006. Ten brain domains: A proposal for functional central nervous system parameters for fetal alcohol spectrum disorder diagnosis and follow up. *JFAS International* 4 (e12): 1–11.

Moore, Timothy, and Melvyn Green. 2004. Fetal alcohol spectrum disorder (FASD): A need for closer examination by the criminal justice system. *Criminal Reports* 19 (6): 99–108.

Roach, K., and A. Bailey. 2009. The relevance of FASD in Canadian criminal law for investigation to sentencing. *UBC Law Review* 42 (1): 1–68.

Streissguth, A., et al. 1997. Primary and secondary disabilities in fetal alcohol syndrome. In *The challenge of fetal alcohol syndrome: Overcoming secondary disabilities*, ed. A. Streissguth and J. Kanter. Seattle: University of Washington Press.

Streissguth, A.P., F.L. Bookstein, H.M. Barr, P.D. Sampson, K. O'Malley, and J. Kogan Young. 2004. Risk factors for adverse life outcomes in fetal alcohol syndrome and fetal alcohol effects. *Developmental and Behavioral Pediatrics* 25 (4): 228.

Study of the Subject Matter of Bill C-583: An Act to Amend the Criminla Code (Fetal Alcohol Spectrum Disorder). 2015, May. Report of the Standing Committee on Justice and Human Rights. 41st Parliament, Second Session.

Youth Criminal Justice Act, S.C. 2002, c. 1.

Chapter 12
FASD and Competency to Stand Trial (CST): An Exploratory Review

Jerrod Brown, Jeffrey Haun, Patricia A. Zapf, and Tricia Aiken

Abstract Fetal Alcohol Spectrum Disorder (FASD) has the potential to complicate an individual's involvement in the criminal justice system. This disorder is precipitated by prenatal alcohol exposure and results in life course persistent cognitive (e.g. executive function and memory), social (e.g. communication and suggestibility), and adaptive (e.g. decision making and problem solving) deficits. As a result of these deficits, individuals with FASD are disproportionately likely to become entangled in the criminal justice system. Complicating matters, the symptoms of FASD can profoundly impact an individual's capacity to navigate the criminal justice system. Although empirical research is limited, defendants with FASD may be less likely to demonstrate the abilities necessary to be found competent to stand trial, Competency to Stand Trial (CST) refers to an individual's ability to understand and rationally participate in court proceedings (i.e. pleas, trial, and sentencing). The goal of this exploratory review is to alert forensic evaluators about the manner in which FASD might impact a defendant's CST as it relates to criminal cases in the United States. To this end, we (a) review the limited empirical research on FASD and CST, (b) discuss how the common features of FASD can impact various competency domains, (c) highlight which CST models might be most informative for defendants with FASD, (d) provide clinical and media case studies that distinguish the complex relationship between FASD and CST, and (e) offer inter-

---

J. Brown (✉)
Concordia University, St. Paul, MN, USA

Pathways Counseling Center, Inc, St. Paul, MN, USA

The American Institute for the Advancement of Forensic Studies (AIAFS), St. Paul, MN, USA
e-mail: jerrod01234brown@live.com

J. Haun
Minnesota State Operated Forensic Services, St. Peter, MN, USA

P. A. Zapf
John Jay College of Criminal Justice, The City University of New York, New York, NY, USA

Consolidated Continuing Education and Professional Training, Lithia, FL, USA

T. Aiken
Minneapolis Forensic Psychological Services, Minneapolis, MN, USA

E. Jonsson et al. (eds.), *Ethical and Legal Perspectives in Fetal Alcohol Spectrum Disorders (FASD)*, International Library of Ethics, Law, and the New Medicine 75,
https://doi.org/10.1007/978-3-319-71755-5_12

viewing suggestions appropriate for individuals with suspected or confirmed FASD. We conclude by providing recommendations for future empirical research on the impact of FASD on CST.

Keywords Fetal alcohol spectrum disorder · Competency to stand trial · Criminal justice · Screening · Law

12.1 Introduction

Fetal Alcohol Spectrum Disorder (FASD) besets approximately 2–5% of the U.S. population, which translates into millions of Americans (May et al. 2009). Precipitated by prenatal alcohol exposure, FASD can result in vast and life course persistent impairments such as cognitive (e.g. executive control, short- and long-term memory, attention, and intelligence; see Brown et al. 2010; Mattson et al. 1997), social (e.g. awkwardness, immaturity, and verbal and non-verbal communication; see Fast and Conry 2009; Jirikowic et al. 2008), and adaptive deficits (e.g. problem-solving ability, abstract thinking, and learning from previous experiences; see Edwards and Greenspan 2010; Popova et al. 2011; Streissguth et al. 1988). This array of impairments is incredibly difficult to assess and diagnose, which often results in missed diagnoses, inaccurate diagnoses, and comorbid diagnoses. As such, many cases of FASD go unnoticed and untreated (Benz et al. 2009; Clarren and Lutke 2008; Morleo et al. 2011).

When untreated, individuals with FASD are disproportionately likely to become entangled in the criminal justice system (Brown et al. 2010; Mela and Luther 2013). In fact, some research has estimated that as many as 60% of individuals with FASD become involved in the criminal justice system (Streissguth et al. 1996). This may be the result of FASD symptoms interfering with an individual's capacity to comprehend and behave within the confines of societal norms (LaDue and Dunne 1995). Complicating matters, the symptoms of FASD (e.g. poor memory, suggestibility, confabulation, and communication deficits) can render a level of global functioning comparable to a child and profoundly impact an individual's ability to navigate the criminal justice system (Chartrand and Forbes-Chilibeck 2003; LaDue and Dunne 1996; McLachlan et al. 2014). As a result, many North American Courts have advocated on behalf of individuals with FASD, whether defendants or witnesses, who often have difficulty comprehending and participating in basic legal processes including police interviews, testimony, standing trial, and complying with the conditions of community supervision (e.g. probation and parole; see Cox et al. 2008; Conry and Asante 2010; Fast and Conry 2009; Roach and Bailey 2009).

Although empirical research is scarce, competency to stand trial (CST) is one area where defendants with FASD might be particularly likely to suffer. CST refers to an individual's ability to understand and rationally participate in court proceedings (i.e. pleas, trial, and sentencing) including developing and executing one's defense strategy (Pirelli et al. 2011; Zapf et al. 2004; Zapf and Roesch 2009; Zapf and Viljoen 2003). Only a judge can determine whether a defendant is incompetent and this legal decision is made on the basis of information obtained during a competency evaluation, usually conducted by a psychiatrist or psychologist (Stafford and Sellbom 2013). Such evaluations usually consist of a battery of measures that index constructs such as intelligence, memory, psychopathology, and legal knowledge. This can be difficult for individuals who have varied and pervasive FASD symptoms, which can be masked by superficial verbal and communication skills and often go undetected by standardized intelligence measures. The likelihood of incompetence is exacerbated by the diagnostic comorbidity that plagues FASD. Some have estimated that approximately 90% of individuals with FASD present with comorbid psychiatric disorders (Famy et al. 1998; Streissguth et al. 1996). Specifically, FASD has established links to psychotic, mood, behavioral, and learning disorders, all of which increase the likelihood of incompetency (Grisso 2003; Ryba and Zapf 2011; Viljoen and Roesch 2005). When found incompetent, defendants are typically mandated to attend treatment, which may include taking psychiatric medication, until competency is restored (Bullock 2002; Miller 2003; Pinals 2005; Stafford and Sellbom 2013). In light of the complexities of chronic neurodevelopmental disorders like FASD, the restoration process can be both lengthy and costly (Pirelli et al. 2011; Toofanian Ross et al. 2015). Alternatively, if the Court fails to detect incompetence when present, the defendant risks being unfairly prosecuted and having his constitutional rights violated (Bryant et al. 2015; Chauhan et al. 2015).

In light of these concerns, it is important that criminal justice professionals (i.e. law enforcement, lawyers, and judges) and forensic evaluators obtain an increased understanding of how FASD impacts an individual's ability to participate in the criminal justice system (Laporte et al. 2003; Malbin 2004; Thiel et al. 2011). As such, the goal of this exploratory review is to inform forensic evaluators about the manner in which FASD might impact a defendant's CST. To this end, we (a) review the limited empirical research on FASD and CST, (b) discuss how the common features of FASD can impact various competency domains, (c) highlight which CST models might be most informative for defendants with FASD, and (d) provide clinical and legal case studies that distinguish the complex relationship between FASD and CST. We conclude by providing recommendations for future empirical research including the development of criminal justice-based FASD screening tools and systematic investigations into the number of defendants with FASD referred for CST evaluations and/or found incompetent to stand trial.

12.2 Overview of Competency to Stand Trial

Forensic mental health professionals are often called upon to inform judicial determinations by examining a defendant's competency to stand trial abilities. The prohibition against adjudication of an incompetent defendant (i.e. competency doctrine) is rooted in English common law and has evolved to constitutional status in the

United States. The U.S. Supreme Court has described this principle as "fundamental to an adversary system of justice" (*Drope v. Missouri*, 1975, p. 172) and the conviction of an incompetent defendant as a violation of due process rights to a fair trial (*Pate v. Robinson*, 1966). Accordingly, trial courts are required to implement procedures to protect a defendant's right to not be subject to trial or conviction if incompetent.

The competency doctrine functions to ensure the dignity, reliability, and autonomy of proceedings (Bonnie 1992a, b). A defendant who is substantially impaired may lack the ability to effectively assist his or her counsel (e.g. communicate relevant information) or to make autonomous decisions (i.e. decisional competency; see Bonnie 1992a, b). Not only would subjecting an impaired defendant to trial be unfair to the individual, it would undermine the reliability of the proceedings and the accuracy of information presented at trial (Grisso 2014). Subjecting a defendant who lacks understanding of the nature and purpose of the proceedings to trial and punishment "offends that moral dignity of the process because it treats the defendant not as an accountable person, but as an object of the state's effort to carry out its promises" (Bonnie 1992a, b, p. 295). The competency doctrine ensures that a guilty defendant has a meaningful understanding of his or her wrongdoing and the basis for punishment (Bonne 1992a, b; Group for the Advancement of Psychology 1974). Grisso (2014) further argued that allowing defendants with serious mental impairments to proceed to trial impugns the integrity of the criminal process and runs the risk of undermining the public's respect for the criminal justice system.

The constitutional minimum standard for competency to stand trial was established by the U.S. Supreme Court in *Dusky v. U.S.* (1960):

> …the test must be whether he has sufficient present ability to consult with his lawyer with a reasonable degree of rational understanding – and whether he has a rational as well as factual understanding of the proceedings against him. (p. 402).

In *Drope v. Missouri* (1975), the Supreme Court appeared to expand upon *Dusky* by including a requirement that a defendant "…must be able to assist in preparing his defense" (p. 171). Various commentators have described important implications on the nature of competency to stand trial based upon the language of *Dusky* (Kruh and Grisso 2009; Melton et al. 2007):

(a) Competency is focused on present abilities and anticipated functioning in the immediate future;
(b) Emphasis is placed upon the defendant's ability/capacity to understand the proceedings and consult with defense counsel, as opposed to unwillingness to do so or unfamiliarity with the legal process;
(c) Terms like *sufficient ability* and *reasonable understanding* suggest that the threshold for competency is flexible as applied to a particular case (i.e. context relevant) and that unimpaired functioning or complete understanding is not required; and
(d) Understanding must go beyond rote factual understanding of legal concepts.

The definition of competency that was established in *Dusky* has been adopted as the standard in U.S. federal and state courts (Melton et al. 2007). Many jurisdictions use the verbatim language set forth in *Dusky*, whereas other have abbreviated or made changes to the wording that follow its basic components (Grisso 2014; Melton et al. 2007; Zapf and Roesch 2009). Although a minority of states have expanded their competency standard to delineate specific functional abilities (e.g. Utah, Florida), most statutes provide little guidance as to the specific abilities to be assessed (Zapf and Roesch 2009). However, various entities have attempted to operationalize specific functional abilities relevant to competency to stand trial (e.g. Mossman et al. 2007; *Wieter v. Settle*, 1961; Zapf and Roesch 2009). Grisso (2014) suggested that such lists of functional competency abilities share much commonality and tend to group functions similarly according to three broad domains:

(a) Understanding of the basic purpose and process of criminal trials;
(b) Abilities associated with consulting and assisting counsel; and
(c) Ability to apply information to his or her own trial and circumstances.

Most competency statutes require that competency-related deficits be the result of mental impairment; although, how impairment is defined varies somewhat across jurisdictions. Major mental disorders, developmental disabilities, and cognitive limitations are typically included (Grisso 2014; Zapf and Roesch 2009) in most statutes; however, the mere presence of a qualifying mental impairment or the need for treatment is insufficient for a finding of incompetency (Melton et al. 2007). This holds true in the case of potentially substantially impairing conditions, such as FASD. Rather, it must be demonstrated that the defendant, as a result of features of the qualifying condition, experiences significant impairments in functional competency-related abilities. Unfortunately, it remains common for competency evaluators to conflate diagnosis and competency without consideration of specific functional abilities (Frederick 2012).

Researchers have demonstrated the overall rate of incompetency among individuals referred for evaluation ranges from approximately 20–30% (Pirelli et al. 2011; Nicholson and Kugler 1991; Warren et al. 2006). Although these finding have suggested that some conditions are associated with greater likelihood of a finding of incompetency (e.g. psychotic-spectrum mental illness; intellectual disability), it remains true that a substantial portion of individuals across conditions will demonstrate sufficient abilities to be adjudged competent. No known studies have explicitly examined the rates of incompetency or functional legal abilities of adults diagnosed with FASD. However, McLachlan et al. (2014) found that youth offenders diagnosed with FASD scored significantly lower than youth offenders not suspected of having experienced fetal alcohol effects across domains assessed by the Fitness Interview Test – Revised (Roesch et al. 2006). Approximately three-quarters of the youths diagnosed with FASD demonstrated deficits in at least one psycholegal domain.

The U.S. Supreme Court has held that inquiry into a defendant's competency to stand trial must be undertaken by the trial court whenever there is a *bona fide* doubt as to the defendant's competency (*Pate v. Robinson*, 1966). The question of competency can occur at any stage during the adjudicative process and the threshold for raising the question of competency is low (Grisso 2014; Melton et al. 2007; Zapf and Roesch 2009). There are no fixed criteria for determining that a competency inquiry is necessary (*Drope v. Missouri*, 1975) and trial courts are instructed to consider any number of factors suggestive of mental impairment (Melton et al. 2007). Although any officer of the court (i.e. judge, prosecutor, defense counsel) may raise the issue of competency, it is most typically raised by defense counsel. This practice is unsurprising given that defense counsel would likely be most interested in ensuring the defendant is capable of meaningfully assisting in their defense (Zapf and Roesch 2009). Indeed, Poythress et al. (2002) reported that attorneys across several jurisdictions endorsed harboring concerns about the competency of their clients in 8–15% of cases.

Criminal proceedings are suspended upon adjudication as incompetent to stand trial. However, in some jurisdictions, non-serious charges are dismissed by statute upon a finding of incompetency. In most cases, the trial court must make a determination whether or not competency can be achieved and, if so, what treatment is necessary to remediate the defendant's competency-related deficits (Grisso 2014). Defendants adjudicated as incompetent are often committed to public mental health systems for treatment (Melton et al. 2007). In *Jackson v. Indiana* (1972), the U.S. Supreme Court held that commitment can only be justified by progress toward the goal of remediating incompetency:

> [A] person charged by a State with a criminal offense who is committed solely on account of his incapacity to proceed to trial cannot be held more than the reasonable period of time necessary to determine whether there is a substantial probability that he will attain that capacity in the foreseeable future. If it is determined that this is not the case, then the State must either institute the customary civil commitment proceeding that would be required to commit indefinitely any other citizen, or release the defendant. (p. 738)

Although the Court did not define what constitutes a "reasonable period of time," most states place statutory limits on the amount of time a defendant can be held for treatment to remediate competency (Grisso 2014; Zapf and Roesch 2009).

By safeguarding a mentally impaired defendant's right to a fair trial, the competency doctrine promotes the integrity, dignity, and reliability of the criminal justice process. Given the great weight that is placed upon the opinions of forensic mental health professionals by the courts when determining competency to proceed (Zapf et al. 2004), it is incumbent upon professionals conducting competency examinations to be knowledgeable of the legal underpinnings of the competency doctrine and best practice standards for evaluating competency to stand trial (e.g. Kruh and Grisso 2009; Mossman et al. 2007; Zapf and Roesch 2009). Best practice requires examination of the direct link between the features of a mental impairment and areas of deficient psycholegal abilities. Accordingly, competent assessment of individuals diagnosed with FASD requires foundational knowledge of the myriad of impairments that can be resultant from fetal alcohol exposure, how these features manifest across individuals, valid and reliable assessment methods, and the ways in which the condition might impact various functional legal abilities.

12.3 FASD-Related Deficits Complicating the CST Evaluation Process

The symptoms of FASD are typically not well understood by laypersons and professionals alike (Blackstock 2011; Brown et al. 2010; Petrenko et al. 2014). As mentioned earlier, FASD is caused by prenatal alcohol exposure and consists of a variety of cognitive, social, and adaptive issues (Bishop et al. 2007; Brown et al. 2012; Fagerlund et al. 2012). Cognitive deficits can include executive control, attention capacities, short- and long-term memory, emotion regulation, information processing, sensory integration, and long-term planning (Bishop et al. 2007; Conry and Fast 2011; Kully-Martens et al. 2012). Social deficits may negatively impact communication skills, attachment patterns, verbal and non-verbal information processing, capacity to withstand the influence of peers and authority figures, and expressing situation-appropriate emotions (Gralton 2014; Thiel et al. 2011; Westrup 2013). Adaptive impairments can affect decision making ability, problem solving, linking actions to consequences, and the completion of multi-step tasks (Roach and Bailey 2009; Wartnik and Carlson 2011). These symptoms often co-occur with other serious mental illnesses and substance use issues as well as histories of victimization, traumatic brain injuries, and adoption (Burd et al. 2007; Conry and Lane 2009; Fast and Conry 2004; Thiel et al. 2011).

Complicating matters is the possibility that the FASD symptoms may predispose individuals to suggestibility and confabulation (Brown et al. 2011; Burd et al. 2010; Mela 2015). Suggestibility refers to the vulnerability of incorporating the views or information of others into your personal narrative of an event. A related issue is confabulation, which can be described as the development of false memories (Brown et al. 2011; Gudjonsson and Clark 1986). These false memories can be drawn from personal experience, popular media, and the suggestion of other people among other sources. Such predispositions can be dire in criminal justice settings because it calls into question the reliability of information obtained from individuals with FASD. Further, a proneness to suggestibility and confabulation increases the likelihood of false confessions, false testimony, and wrongful convictions (Brown et al. 2010; Cox et al. 2008; Roach and Bailey 2009).

Although few empirical studies exist on this topic, research in the area of cognition may hint at the negative impact of FASD on competency. Specifically, several aspects of cognitive functioning have been intrinsically linked to competency to stand trial (Kirkish and Sreenivasan 1999; Melton et al. 2007; Nestor et al. 1999), including: executive functioning, short- and long-term memory, attention, and intelligence. Each of these aspects of cognitive functioning has been repeatedly identified as a core deficit of FASD (Kodituwakku 2009; Kully-Martens et al. 2012; Mattson et al. 2011).

Competency concerns are relevant throughout the legal process including at arrest, during police interviews and interrogations, and during trial or other legal proceedings (Burd et al. 2010; Mela 2015; Wartnik et al. 2015). Upon arrest, FASD symptoms can hinder an individual's understanding of the arrest process, which may result in misinterpretation of constitutional rights including Miranda rights and the right to an attorney (Brown et al. 2010; Burd et al. 2010; Wartnik and Carlson 2011). Concerns persist as individuals are interviewed and interrogated by police (Brown et al. 2011; Greenspan and Driscoll (2015). Here, individuals with FASD may have difficulty comprehending the consequences of potential charges and distinguishing what information should be shared with authorities and attorneys. As the legal process progresses to the trial phase, concerns over FASD are only exacerbated (McLachlan et al. 2014). Individuals with FASD have difficulty standing trial in general, and this includes difficulty establishing a working relationship with defense attorneys, making sound and informed legal decisions, serving as a witness before the court, conforming behavior to courtroom standards, and filling out legal paperwork (Brown et al. 2015a, b; Wartnik et al. 2015). These tasks can be challenging for any adult, but are particularly difficult for someone with cognitive (i.e. attention and memory), social (i.e. communication), and adaptive (i.e. completion of complex tasks) deficits. These difficulties will likely continue after sentencing as the defendant transitions to a custodial placement or community supervision (i.e. probation and parole) (Chartrand and Forbes-Chilibeck 2003; Douds et al. 2012; Gagnier et al. 2010; Verbrugge 2003). Such potential difficulties highlight the importance of increased recognition, evaluation, and treatment of individuals with FASD.

Individuals with FASD will likely be undiagnosed or misdiagnosed upon initial contact with the criminal justice system (Brown et al. 2015a, b). One potential reason for this pervasive under-diagnosis is that individuals with FASD are quite effective at masking their deficits in global functioning. Many individuals with FASD can achieve average to above average scores on intelligence tests, but still suffer from poor day-to-day functioning. Further, the superficial verbal skills of individuals with FASD may result in professionals overlooking the presence of global functioning deficits. Despite these masks of normalcy, individuals with FASD can still suffer from the cognitive, social, and adaptive deficits that deleteriously impact competency. In fact, individuals with FASD could very well appear competent, but exhibit global functioning levels of someone much younger (Wartnik et al. 2015). As such, systematic screening for FASD holds great promise in curtailing the under-identification of FASD in criminal justice settings.

Competency evaluations are one of the last lines of defense against the mistreatment of defendants with FASD in the legal system. To maximize the utility of this opportunity, competency evaluations must consider an individual's cognitive, social, and adaptive functioning. This should include a systematic assessment of psychopathology, intelligence, medical and mental health records, family history, victimization, traumatic brain injury, and legal history (White et al. 2014; LaDue and Dunne 1996). Throughout this process, evaluators must be sure to consider the impact of any deficits on the defendant's insight into his or her behavior and the legal process. That said, this process is typically difficult, as defendants with suspected or confirmed FASD may behave in a challenging and confusing manner. Evaluators will have to consistently decipher whether the defendant is lying, malingering, confabulating, or simply confused. An accurate competency evaluation is essential for informing the court on how to proceed. Information collected can guide the development of restorative treatment plans, if necessary, and protect the constitutional rights of the defendant.

To increase the accuracy of competency evaluations and help combat the mistreatment of individuals with FASD in the criminal justice system, advanced education is needed for criminal justice and mental health professionals. Few professionals involved in CST evaluation and determination have specialized training or advanced knowledge in FASD. This gap in education is readily apparent in undergraduate- and graduate-level education programs. Further, potential training opportunities to develop expertise in FASD are limited in criminal justice settings. Training opportunities must be expanded to increase the likelihood that legal professionals and CST evaluators can identify and ensure the adequate treatment of defendants with FASD. Such educational opportunities must highlight the difficulty of disentangling intelligence, communication, and adaptive functioning deficits among individuals with FASD. Advanced training along these lines has the potential to improve the accuracy of CST evaluations and judgments.

12.4 Competency to Stand Trial (CST) Frameworks

Fetal Alcohol Spectrum Disorder (FASD) can have a debilitating impact on a defendant's competency to stand trial (CST) and the judicial process as a whole. FASD is characterized by a constellation of cognitive deficits (e.g. problem solving, attention, emotion regulation, and language-processing), social difficulties (e.g. awkwardness, maturity, susceptibility to manipulation), and poor adaptive functioning (e.g. perseveration of thoughts or actions, ability to link actions to outcomes and learn from prior errors; Fast and Conry 2009; Greenspan and Driscoll 2015; Mela and Luther 2013). These varied deficits in functioning can significantly impair an individual's ability to competently participate in the criminal trial process (McLachlan et al. 2014). Although the role of FASD in CST has been understudied, researchers have established that individuals with Intellectual Disability (ID) and other cognitive impairments, which are common amongst individuals with FASD, are disproportionately likely to be found incompetent to stand trial (Cochrane et al. 2001; Morris and DeYoung 2012; Warren et al. 2006). As with other mental and developmental conditions, the presence of FASD does not guarantee the presence of incompetence. For example, individuals with significant intellectual disabilities are often still found competent to stand trial (Cochrane et al. 2001; Chauhan et al. 2015). To convey the complexities of assessing CST in the presence of intellectual disabilities, organic brain diseases, and other psychiatric conditions, two theoretical models of CST are presented here. Although not conceptualized specifically for FASD, these models can be of assistance when evaluating the competency of defendants who have suspected or confirmed cases of FASD.

12.4.1 Bonnie's Reconceptualization of Competence

Bonnie's reconceptualization of competence (1992a, b) model advanced the understanding and assessment of adjudicative competence by focusing on two distinct aspects (Zapf et al. 2005). The first component of this model centers on a defendant's capacity to assist counsel in the development and execution of their own legal defense. This component requires that the defendant demonstrate the capacity to comprehend and appreciate the criminal charge(s) against them, understand the severity of potential sentence(s) for the charge(s), and actively help their defense counsel throughout the trial. Unfortunately, a defendant's capacity to actively participate in legal processes and proceedings can be limited by FASD-related symptoms such as cognitive deficits (e.g. attention and language-processing), social difficulties (e.g. awkwardness and susceptibility to manipulation), and poor adaptive functioning (e.g. problem solving and inability to link behavior to consequences; Wartnik et al. 2015; McLachlan et al. 2014).

The second focal point of Bonnie's reconceptualization of competence (1992a, b) model is the defendant's ability to make competent decisions (Bonnie 1992a, b; Zapf and Roesch 2009). This decisional competence consists of the knowledge, skills, and abilities (KSAs) that are necessary to make competent legal decisions independent of assistance from defense counsel (Zapf and Roesch 2009). Bonnie asserted that decisional competence becomes especially relevant for defendants who are entangled in adjudication that involves complex decisions (e.g. waiving the right to counsel, a jury trial, facing one's accuser, and a speedy trial; Bonnie 1992a, b; Zapf and Roesch 2009). The capacity to competently make such legal decisions may be hindered by the cognitive dysfunction and global functioning issues of FASD. In particular, individuals with FASD often have difficulty regulating their behavior and emotion across a variety of settings including during legal proceedings (Wartnik et al. 2015). As such, individuals with FASD may have a fundamental disadvantage in criminal justice settings. This includes the risk of poor and misinformed legal decision making as a result of the cognitive, social, and adaptive impairments of FASD (McLachlan et al. 2014).

Just like other potentially impairing conditions (e.g. intellectual disabilities), inquiries into the functional legal abilities of criminal defendants diagnosed with FASD are a necessity (McLachlan et al. 2014; Mela 2015; Wartnik et al. 2015). Ensuring that only competent defendants are prosecuted protects the "dignity, reliability, and autonomy of proceedings" (Bonnie 1992a, b; Zapf and Roesch 2009). That said, Bonnie (1992a, b) asserts that competence should be considered continuously at integral points throughout the legal process, with the finding of competence a temporary decision at each point of assessment. The consideration of this formulation is imperative because it is possible to prosecute individuals who were found competent by a single assessment (Zapf and Roesch 2009), but may be found incompetent by a subsequent assessment at a later point in time. Such situations emphasize the utility of the Bonnie's delineations of competency.

12.4.2 Grisso's Conceptual Model

Grisso (1986, 2003) developed an influential theoretical model to improve understanding and guide thought on the assessment of different legal competencies such as competency to stand trial. The most recent iteration of Grisso's (2003, 2014) model is composed of five components: (1) functional, (2) causal, (3) interactive, (4) judgmental, and (5) dispositional. Together, these interconnected components guide the competency evaluations through the assessment of different abilities that are required to successfully navigate the legal process.

The *functional component* focuses on the defendant's current functional capacities that are outlined in the legal standard for competency to stand trial (Grisso 2014). This includes "what the person understands, knows, believes, or can do that is directly related to the competency construct" (Grisso 2003, p. 25). For example, when evaluating the factual understanding aspect of this standard as outlined in *Dusky v. United States* (1960), an examiner should describe the defendant's comprehension of the adjudicative process. Another consideration could include describing the defendant's capacity to succeed in the use of requisite knowledge, concept, or belief (Denney and Tyner 2010; Grisso and Appelbaum 1998; Piel et al. 2015). In the presence of a documented impairment or intellectual deficit, the contextual factors of the legal situation are an integral aspect of any functional assessment (Grisso 2003). Conversely, in the absence of a documented impairment or other deficit, context becomes less relevant because the probability of being found incompetent to stand trial is greatly diminished.

The *causal component* refers to the inferential explanations of a defendant's competency-related abilities and deficits (Grisso 2003). For individuals with FASD, this component can include the discussion of FASD features that may cause observed deficits in competency abilities. Specifically, individuals with FASD may achieve average to above average performance on intelligence tests (Mattson et al. 2011) yet still suffer from neurocognitive deficits (e.g. executive control, attention, short- and long-term memory) that limit global functioning (Fryer et al. 2007; Guerri et al. 2009). This makes the process of ruling out other potential causal factors of incompetency important. If not, erroneous assumptions about client participation and underlying motivation can occur. For example, damaging assumptions have been made in cases where a defendant's intellectual disabilities were misinterpreted as malingering during a competency evaluation. This resulted in the subjection of individuals mistakenly identified as competent to legal proceedings in which they were unable to adequately participate (Gottfried and Carbonell 2014).

The *interactive component* weighs the defendant's functional abilities against the situational demands of the case (e.g. attorney-client circumstances; trial demands; Grisso 2003). Depending on the case's situational demands, a defendant's deficits may be more or less important. For example, the length and complexity of trial (e.g. defense strategies, complexity of evidence, number of witnesses, etc.) is quite different for a defendant accused of homicide than a defendant charged with the possession of an illicit drug. These situational demands can be difficult to manage in light of the symptoms of FASD (e.g. cognitive, social, and adaptive), which can leave the defendant functioning at a much lower developmental level than their chronological age would suggest (Wartnik et al. 2015). In support of this concern, McLachlan et al. (2014) found that youthful offenders with FASD had higher levels of psycholegal impairment (i.e. comprehension of legal processes of arrest, interrogation, and trial) than youthful offenders without FASD.

The *judgmental component* evaluates whether the gap between functional abilities and situational demands is sufficient enough to require a legal finding of incompetency (Grisso 2003). In competency to stand trial evaluations, the crux of this opinion is whether or not the legal standard for competency has been met. As described by Grisso (2014), many states permit forensic mental health examiners to offer ultimate issue opinions in competency to stand trial cases. Nonetheless, this practice has remained a topic of debate amongst forensic mental health professionals for many years (see Melton et al. 2007; Rogers and Ewing 1989, 2003; Slobogin 1989).

Finally, the *dispositional component* relates to the legal disposition regarding competence (Grisso 2003). To this end, information regarding prognosis for remediation of competency-related deficits is required by many jurisdictions and best practice guidelines (competency restoration; Mossman et al. 2007; Zapf and Roesch 2009). Such considerations could include the extent to which the identified deficits are treatable, the likelihood of restoration, potential interventions, an estimate of time needed to restore competency, preferred treatment setting (i.e. outpatient versus inpatient), and necessary restrictions (e.g. secure programming; Grisso 2014; Zapf and Roesch 2009). For a defendant with FASD, these considerations should be based upon the nature and severity of the FASD symptoms that were identified as barriers to competency, the extent to which these symptoms may be remediated, and the available intervention methods. Cognitive and intellectual impairments that can be associated with FASD are one particularly salient consideration. For example, in a study of 8416 evaluations of competency to stand trial in Virginia over a 12 year period, Warren et al. (2006) found that defendants with organic or intellectual/learning disorders were more likely to be opined as incompetent and non-restorable at the time of examination. Similarly, individuals with irremediable cognitive impairments such as intellectual disabilities have been associated with a lower probability of successful competency restoration (Anderson and Hewitt 2002; Morris and Parker 2008). Nonetheless, the likelihood of restoration varies widely in different samples of defendants who were committed for competency restoration. For example, Anderson and Hewitt (2002) demonstrated a restoration rate of 18% for individuals diagnosed with mental retardation (intellectual disability). In contrast, Morris and Parker (2008) found restoration rates of 61.1% and 75.9% following 6 months and one-year of competency restoration treatment, respectively, for defendants diagnosed with mental retardation. To a large extent, the likelihood of successful restoration varies widely as a function of impairment (Salekin et al. 2010).

12.4.3 ND-PAE/FASD, Bonnie's Reconceptualization of Competence & Grisso's Conceptual Model

Both Bonnie's (1992a, b) reconceptualization of competence and Grisso's (1986, 2003) conceptual model are well suited for identifying, describing, and recognizing the myriad of issues involved with cognitive and mental health conditions. These models can aid in assessing the array of considerations relevant to a defendant's competency, which go well beyond the presence or absence of a diagnosis. As such, Bonnie's reconceptualization of competence and Grisso's conceptual model may be particularly well suited to FASD, a complex disorder with many features at varying levels of magnitude. This is reinforced by the fact that FASD has been established as a condition for further study under the Neurobehavioral Disorder Associated with Prenatal Alcohol Exposure (ND-PAE) classification in the most recent edition of the Diagnostic and Statistical Manual of Mental Disorders-Fifth Edition (DSM-5; American Psychiatric Association 2013). The increased recognition and prominence of ND-PAE within the DSM-5 could be motivational in steering legal professionals and law-enforcement personnel toward increased awareness and better understanding of FASD. This includes forensic mental health examiners who are charged with conducting competency to stand trial evaluations. These professionals now have the ND-PAE diagnosis as a framework for better understanding the issues and challenges facing defendants with this disorder.

In the absence of Bonnie's reconceptualization of competence and Grisso's conceptual model, the accurate assessment of the competence of a defendant with ND-PAE/FASD may be more difficult. The United States Supreme Court has ruled that intelligence test scores alone cannot be relied upon for determining capital punishment eligibility (*Hall v. Florida*, 2014). By virtue of this ruling, identifying the functional capabilities of individuals with ND-PAE and relying less on intelligence test scores is imperative. This becomes more significant to the court for issues involving competency to stand trial, sentencing, and other key aspects of the trial process (Wartnik et al. 2015). As such, accurately assessing the competence related abilities of a defendant with FASD may limit the likelihood of violating constitutional rights and the possibility of wrongful conviction.

12.5 FASD & CST: Composite Case Example

Ms. Smith[1] was a 29-year-old woman who had resided in supported/supervised settings the entirety of her adult life due to limitations secondary to a diagnosis of FASD. She was court-ordered to undergo examination of her competency to stand

[1] The current case is collection of various features of FASD and potential impacts on functional legal abilities that was created as a composite example. All aspects of the described individual and history are fictitious. Any resemblance to real persons is purely coincidental.

trial. She was charged with Assault in the Third Degree after she allegedly struck another group home resident during an argument, causing an orbital fracture. This event represented her first contact with the criminal justice system, though she had some experience with the civil courts (e.g. guardianship proceedings).

Ms. Smith had a well-established history of developmental disability that had been attributed to fetal alcohol exposure. Medical records and collateral interviews indicated that her mother had a significant history of chemical dependency and regularly consumed alcohol during pregnancy. She was born 8 weeks premature and remained hospitalized for several weeks following her birth. She was delayed in meeting many early childhood milestones and was always small for her age. She required special education services throughout school due to speech and language impairments, learning difficulties, and disruptive behaviors. She was able to obtain a GED with the assistance of learning support services. Formal assessments conducted at various points throughout her teens and adulthood revealed mild intellectual disability, mild to moderate impairments in various cognitive domains (e.g. attention, executive functioning, memory), and mild to moderate adaptive functioning deficits. Descriptions of her recent functioning were indicative of social immaturity, poor impulse control, and emotional volatility.

Ms. Smith's court-appointed attorney indicated that he had raised the issue of competency after two meetings with Ms. Smith. He reported that she appeared markedly confused about her circumstances and did not understand the legal process. He described spending a significant amount of time trying to explain concepts and options with little success.

An interview of Ms. Smith was conducted on an outpatient basis. Her presentation was consistent with that described in records and by collateral sources. In addition to gathering information about her background and current mental status, focused inquiry into her psycholegal functioning was undertaken via semi-structured interview. Significant impairments were identified in several competency domains that were primarily attributable to intellectual and cognitive impairments. Areas of functional deficit included:

(a) *Understanding and appreciation of the charges and penalties*: For example, although she was able to describe the gist of the alleged offense, she was unaware of the formal charge and potential penalties. She could not identify relevant evidence. She lacked appreciation of the seriousness of the charge, the potential for conviction, and possibility of further punishment.
(b) *Factual understanding of the legal process*: Although she was knowledgeable about a few basic legal concepts (e.g. that the judge was in charge during court), her understanding was limited with respect to many topics (e.g. the purpose and adversarial nature of trial, roles within the courtroom, the adjudicative process, plea bargaining, testifying, available pleas, etc.). She struggled to learn legal concepts when provided education and was often unable to accurately recall novel information after moving on to new topics.
(c) *Ability to engage in a rational discussion of her case and options*: For example, Ms. Smith had tremendous difficulty addressing case specific questions. She

was unable to identify potential legal strategies or to meaningfully discuss the risk and benefits of various options identified by the examiner. She struggled when asked to engage in various hypothetical decision making scenarios specific to her case, particularly with more complex concepts (e.g. plea bargaining). She often failed to attend to or fully consider information relevant to decision making. If given options, she was quick to pick a choice. However, when queried about her choice, it was often apparent that she had not fully considered/understood the options. She was often unable to explain her basis/reasoning for various decisions. When she was able to do so, her decision making was significantly concrete and her appreciation for the implications of some choices was lacking (e.g. overvaluing short-term benefits and undervaluing long-term consequences).

(d) *Ability to meaningfully assist/engage during proceedings (e.g. track events as they unfold, appreciate the content of discussion, challenge witnesses, etc.)*: Consistent with reports of collateral sources, Ms. Smith demonstrated significant difficulty sustaining focus during interview and was easily confused. She believed her role with her attorney and at trial was to remain quiet and to acquiesce to authority, irrespective of the circumstance (e.g. if a witness were to tell a lie).

In light of her history of intellectual disability, Ms. Smith was also administered a structured competency assessment instrument developed for use with individuals with intellectual disabilities (Competency Assessment for Standing Trial for Defendants with Mental Retardation; CAST*MR; Everington and Luckasson 1992). Her performance on this instrument placed her understanding of basic legal concepts and skills to assist in her defense in a range similar to that demonstrated by individuals in the normative samples who had been adjudicated incompetent to stand trial.

Based upon the nature and extent of impairments across several competency domains that were attributable to features of FASD, it was the examiner's opinion that Ms. Smith did not possess a factual and rational understanding of the proceedings against her, nor did she possess sufficient present ability to rationally consult with and assist her attorney.

12.6 FASD & CST: Media Case Studies

Examples of popular news stories describing the impact of FASD on competency to stand trial can be found across the globe from North America to Australia. The selection of popular media accounts presented here highlights how FASD can limit an individual's competence to stand trial in both youths and adults. Further, FASD can have an impact in cases of severe crimes (e.g. murder) as well as less severe crimes (e.g. car theft). Of course, these news stories are not peer-reviewed publications or examples of case law. As such, each news story may not be a comprehensive representation of a case and could contain inaccuracies. Nonetheless, popular news stories are a powerful source of information regarding the links between FASD and competency to stand trial, which remains an understudied area.

12.6.1 Media Case Study 1

FASD may contribute to serious criminal behavior at a very young age. For example, an 11-year-old boy with FASD faced charges of assault and murder in California (Bartolow 2012; Littlefield 2013). When pregnant, the defendant's mother drank alcohol and used illicit substances to the point of blacking out. This resulted in physical, developmental, intellectual, and mental health issues consistent with FASD. Combined with a traumatic brain injury at 26 weeks of age, these symptoms may have played a role in the murder of a 12-year-old boy, who died after being stabbed in the chest with a kitchen knife. Further, the defendant's FASD symptoms made it difficult for him to comprehend his legal proceedings and adequately assist his attorneys in mounting a legal defense. As a result, the judge found him incompetent to stand trial. The boy has been placed in a residential treatment facility for psychiatric treatment to restore his competency, which will cost an estimated $160,000 per year (Littlefield 2013). His competency will be evaluated annually until he is able to stand trial or turns 21-years-old, whichever comes first.

12.6.2 Media Case Study 2

Inappropriate sexual contact is a common charge that some people with FASD face. For example, an 18-year-old male with FASD was charged with inappropriately touching two underage boys in Texas (Ortega 2011). Adopted at 4 months old, the defendant suffered from FASD, ADHD, and other impairments. From a young age, he exhibited impulsivity and explosive behavior, which led to behavioral issues in and out of school along with numerous psychiatric placements. The cognitive symptoms of FASD made it difficult for the defendant to comprehend why he was incarcerated. As a result, the defendant was found incompetent to stand trial. The judge ordered his placement in a maximum-security state hospital for restorative treatment but wait lists have left the defendant languishing in jail until bed space opens up. In the meantime, his incarceration has resulted in his psychological and physical deterioration, including losing 30 pounds. Should the youth's competency be restored, he will stand trial on these charges.

12.6.3 Media Case Study 3

Competency to stand trial evaluations by different experts can often provide conflicting opinions. For example, competency to stand trial was a contentious issue in the trial of a 13-year-old male with FASD who was charged with sexually assaulting a four-year-old boy (CBC News 2012). Specifically, expert witnesses could not agree in their evaluations of the defendant's competency. One doctor reported that the defendant had an IQ of 56 and the mental age of a six-year-old. In contrast, another expert concluded that the defendant was competent to stand trial. Ultimately, the judge concluded that the defendant may not be mentally fit, but he was still aware of his actions and, as a result, was competent to stand trial. Without any further psychiatric treatment, the defendant chose to plead guilty and awaits sentencing. This case emphasizes how the fates of defendants can vary widely based on competency to stand trial decisions.

12.6.4 Media Case Study 4

Competency to stand trial decisions can play a strong role in the legal cases of psychiatric patients. This includes the case of a 20-year-old with FASD who was accused of strangling his roommate in a residential treatment facility (Ramsey 2012). The defendant had been diagnosed with FASD and suffered physical and sexual abuse before the age of 2. As early as the age of 7, the defendant would fly into aggressive fits of rage characterized by kicking, hitting, and biting others. Despite his adoptive parents struggling for 20 years to get their son the treatment that he needed, the defendant cycled in and out of psychiatric facilities. In light of these pervasive and well-established difficulties, the court found the defendant incompetent to stand trial and dismissed the criminal charges. His adoptive parents argue that improving accessibility to mental health services prior to criminal behavior will be the key in preventing horrible things from happening in the future.

12.6.5 Media Case Study 5

Competency to stand trial was a hot topic in the case of a 21-year-old Florida man who was charged in the murder of his adoptive father ("Man accused of shooting father in SE Volusia camper to get new mental health exam," 2012). Although details are sketchy, the defendant is accused of shooting the man who adopted him when he was 10-years-old. The defendant had a history of psychiatric hospitalizations and life course persistent issues like FASD and other developmental disabilities that medication alone could not fix. In light of these issues, the defendant spent 6 months in a state hospital for restorative treatment. Afterward, his defense attorney was still not convinced that his client was competent to stand trial. Specifically, the defense attorney believed that the hospital did an inadequate job of improving the likelihood that the defendant could meaningfully help develop his own legal defense. As a result, additional competency evaluations were scheduled. With the defendant facing as many as 30 years in prison, his future hangs in the balance of these competency evaluations.

12.6.6 Media Case Study 6

FASD has impacted legal cases with varying ranges of seriousness. This includes the plight of a man in Texas on death row for killing a grandmother (Hunt 2012). When pregnant, the defendant's mother consumed alcohol, drugs, and sniffed paint, which led to a partial diagnosis of FASD. Things only got worse for him as he was neglected and abandoned throughout his childhood. As a result, he quickly became entangled in the legal system as a child including theft at 8-years-old and psychiatric hospitalizations beginning at 10-years-old. In fact, only a few months after his release from prison on a previous charge, he went on an eight-day crime spree and drug binge that concluded with him killing an elderly woman. The presence of FASD resulted in appeals to commute his death sentence. Some advocate that individuals with brain damage such as FASD should be excluded from the death penalty like people with mental retardation (intellectual disability), which was considered cruel and unusual punishment by the Supreme Court (*Atkins v. Virginia*, 2002). Despite these concerns, his initial appeal was denied and he remains on death row.

12.6.7 Media Case Study 7

When individuals with FASD are found incompetent to stand trial, adequate treatment services are often not available. As a result, these defendants are left in jails for indefinite periods of time. For example, an Aboriginal woman in her mid-twenties stole and then crashed a car in Australia (Stewart 2014). She had an official diagnosis of FASD along with other intellectual disabilities. Without inpatient hospitalization or other accommodations available, she was jailed for over 20 months without trial or conviction after a judge found her incompetent to stand trial. In response to a petition signed by 120,000 Australians, she has been placed in a staffed residential facility that employs a community-based support model. Understandably, this incident in Western Australia created a great deal of controversy and concern over the treatment of individuals with mental illnesses and FASD within the criminal justice system.

12.6.8 Media Case Study 8

The ability of psychiatric treatment to restore competency to stand trial is not certain in all cases. Such is the case for a man in his mid-twenties with an official diagnosis of FASD who was accused of arson (Tumilty 2010). Although typically nice and fun to be around, he had symptoms of impulsivity, aggression, low intelligence, and substance use. His comorbid psychiatric disorders included ADHD and Antisocial Personality Disorder (APD). He has a dense history of psychiatric hospitalizations and group home placements, including an extended stay in a psychiatric inpatient facility that ended a month prior to the act of arson. In fact, evidence indicates that he actively sought re-hospitalization in the time between his release and the act of arson. Unfortunately, he did not receive the help he desperately needed. He was charged with arson of a home, which had the potential to take someone's life. Police arrested him at the scene of the crime, where he was under the influence of drugs and in possession of lighters. The court found him incompetent to stand trial in light of his inability to assist his legal counsel or make informed legal decisions. He has been remanded to a psychiatric hospital and his psychiatrist is uncertain whether treatment will ever restore his competency.

12.6.9 Conclusions

These popular news stories highlight how the cognitive, social, and adaptive symptoms of FASD threaten an individual's competency to stand trial. As seen throughout these cases, this is particularly problematic in children and adolescents, but remains a problem well into adulthood. Perhaps most troubling is the fact that psychiatric treatment is not guaranteed to restore competency. In cases where restoration of competency is unlikely, individuals with FASD are prone to spending indefinite periods of time in jail or hospitals with no end in sight. Not only does this consume very limited and expensive resources with little benefit, but also such situations may violate the constitutional rights of individuals with FASD. In light of these serious consequences, there is a substantial need to move beyond popular news accounts of this issue and fund scientific research to empirically examine the role of FASD in competency to stand trial.

12.7 D.E.A.R.: An FASD Interviewing Approach

Because FASD is a nuanced and varied condition, Brown et al. (2014), relying on their clinical experience, created the D.E.A.R. guide. The D.E.A.R. guide provides forensic professionals with suggestions and guidance on how to assess and treat individuals who may have FASD. When employed effectively, D.E.A.R. has the potential to enhance the quality of interactions between individuals with FASD and forensic professionals. This is incredibly important because the vast majority of forensic professionals have not received advanced training or specialization in FASD. Each aspect of the D.E.A.R. acronym will be described below.

The "D" ("Direct Language") refers to the need to use direct language when communicating with individuals who may have FASD. As discussed above, verbal and non-verbal communication deficits are common in FASD. To limit the impact of such deficits, forensic professionals should use simple and concrete language while avoiding colloquialisms and sarcasm. Short, open-ended questions may be more effective than leading or complicated closed-ended questions. Forensic professionals should avoid using the same terms or questions over and over because individuals with FASD often begin mimicking others to compensate for confusion. The importance of such an approach is emphasized by the propensity for suggestibility and confabulation in individuals with FASD. Any interactions should be characterized as a slow-paced conversation that is appropriate for an individual's developmental capabilities and include frequent confirmations of comprehension. Such an approach has the potential to limit the impact of FASD's communication deficits.

The "E" ("Engage Support System") emphasizes the need to engage the support systems of individuals with FASD. In legal settings, individuals with FASD are disproportionately likely to suffer from confusion, suggestibility, confabulation, and a lack of understanding of basic legal rights. As a result, individuals with FASD may make false confessions or be incompetent to stand trial. To help combat these FASD-related difficulties, forensic professionals should help facilitate contact between individuals with FASD and their legal guardians, family, friends, and social workers. Members of an individual's support system may be an integral source of tips and strategies that can improve the validity of an evaluation. If such support systems are engaged, short- and long-term outcomes may be improved and the likelihood of miscarriages of justice can be decreased.

The "A" ("Accommodate Needs") highlights the importance of considering and addressing each individual's complex needs. Because individuals with FASD can be plagued by impulsivity and inattentiveness, a series of shorter assessments may be more effective than a single longer evaluation. Additional time may be needed for individuals with FASD to fill out forms and questionnaires or to respond to interview questions. For any assessment, forensic professionals should secure quiet locations with limited distractions for evaluations. Further, forensic professionals should also avoid making physical contact or gestures that could be interpreted as threatening, given that individuals with FASD can be easily intimidated. As such, the accuracy of any assessment will likely be improved in quiet and familiar settings.

The "R" ("Remain Calm") recommends that forensic professionals should act calm and non-threatening towards individuals with FASD. As discussed earlier, individuals with FASD are often characterized by affective dysregulation, which can include intense emotions ranging from anxiety to anger. To limit the impact of affective dysregulation, forensic professionals should employ a smooth and easy flowing interview-style. Such a strategy should decrease the likelihood of eliciting extreme emotional reactions from individuals who may have FASD.

The use of the D.E.A.R. strategies by forensic professionals can enhance the validity of CST evaluations. The effectiveness of these approaches can be improved by increased knowledge of the red flags and symptoms of FASD, which should include familiarity with the DSM-5's proposed ND-PAE criteria. Ultimately, if an individual with FASD continues to have difficulty with the CST evaluation under the conditions suggested by the D.E.A.R. strategies, there should be little confidence that their performance will improve under trial conditions.

12.8 Summary and Suggestions for Future Research

FASD and its related deficits in cognitive, social, and adaptive functioning have the potential to complicate a defendant's involvement in the criminal justice system and result in competence-related deficits and the concomitant inability to adequately understand and assist counsel in one's defense. These competence-related deficits may impact a defendant's ability to adequately participate at any point in the proceedings, from arrest and arraignment, to plea entry, trial, and sentencing. This chapter reviewed the limited empirical research on FASD and CST and provided a review of the ways in which FASD might impact a defendant's competence-related abilities. Models of competence provided by Bonnie and Grisso were presented to provide a framework for evaluators that can assist in evaluations of individuals with FASD. Legal and media cases were provided as examples of the myriad ways in which FASD and its related deficits might impact a defendant's functioning within the criminal justice system and the D.E.A.R. interviewing approach was presented as a heuristic to assist evaluators in working with defendants who present with FASD- or ID-related symptoms and deficits. Finally, we conclude with a few ideas for future research in this area.

Future empirical research over the next five areas is imperative to advance the treatment of individuals with FASD in the criminal justice system. First, reviews of case law hold promise in improving our understanding of the recent impact of FASD on CST in legal settings. Second, there is a dearth of information on how many defendants with FASD receive competency evaluations and are subsequently found incompetent. This research is necessary to contextualize the magnitude of FASD's impact on competency. Third, there is a dire need for an FASD screening tool that is appropriate for use in criminal justice settings. Such a tool would be even more beneficial if it were developed and validated in criminal justice settings, where pretrial and forensic evaluations are conducted, rather than psychiatric settings. Until such a measure is developed, research should evaluate the comparative validity of CST instruments in individuals with FASD. Fourth, the development of such an FASD screening instrument could be improved by nuanced experimental research on how different domains of CST are impacted by FASD, particularly with an eye towards the DSM-5's ND-PAE diagnostic criteria. Investigations that evaluate differences between adults and adolescents as well as between men and women will be particularly beneficial. Fifth, survey research that investigates the current level of familiarity with FASD in attorneys, judges, and forensic evaluators is imperative. This has the potential to inform the development of FASD awareness campaigns. Empirical research along these lines of inquiry can help ameliorate the impact of FASD on CST in future years.

References

American Psychiatric Association. 2013. *Diagnostic and statistical manual of mental disorders*. 5th ed. Washington, DC: Author.

Anderson, S.D., and J. Hewitt. 2002. The effect of competency restoration training on defendants with mental retardation found not competent to proceed. *Law and Human Behavior* 26: 343–351.

Atkins v. Virginia, 536 U.S. 304, 122 S. Ct. 2242, 153 L. Ed. 2d 335 (2002).

Bartolow, S. 2012, August 22. 11-year-old boy accused of fatally stabbing friend found mentally incompetent to stand trial. *Santee Patch*. Retrieved from http://patch.com/california/santee/mental-competency-hearing-for-12-year-old-boy-accused2783aea134

Benz, J., C. Rasmussen, and G. Andrew. 2009. Diagnosing fetal alcohol spectrum disorder: History, challenges and future directions. *Paediatrics & Child Health* 14 (4): 231–237.

Bishop, S., S. Gahagan, and C. Lord. 2007. Re-examining the core features of autism: A comparison of autism spectrum disorder and fetal alcohol spectrum disorder. *Journal of Child Psychology and Psychiatry* 48: 1111–1121.

Blackstock, C. 2011. Wanted: Moral courage in Canadian child welfare. *First Peoples Child and Family Review* 6 (2): 35–46.

Bonnie, R.J. 1992a. The competence of criminal defendant with mental retardation to participate in their own defense. *Journal of Criminal Law and Criminology* 81: 419–446.

———. 1992b. The competence of criminal defendants: A theoretical reformulation. *Behavioral Sciences and the Law* 10: 291–316.

Brown, N.N., A.P. Wartnik, P.D. Connor, and R.S. Adler. 2010. A proposed model standard for forensic assessment of fetal alcohol spectrum disorders. *The Journal of Psychiatry & Law* 38 (4): 383–418.

Brown, N.N., G. Gudjonsson, and P. Connor. 2011. Suggestibility and fetal alcohol Spectrum disorders: I'll tell you anything you want to hear. *Journal of Psychiatry & Law* 39 (1): 39–71.

Brown, N.N., P.D. Connor, and R.S. Adler. 2012. Conduct-disordered adolescents with fetal alcohol spectrum disorder intervention in secure treatment settings. *Criminal Justiceand Behavior* 39 (6): 770–793.

Brown, J., S. Herrick, J. Long-McGie, et al. 2014. Fetal alcohol spectrum disorders and offender reentry: A review for criminal justice and mental health professionals. *Behavioral Health* 1 (1): 1–19.

Brown, N.N., L. Burd, T. Grant, W. Edwards, R. Adler, and A. Streissguth. 2015a. Prenatal alcohol exposure: An assessment strategy for the legal context. *International Journal of Law and Psychiatry* 42: 144–148.

Brown, J., M. Mitchell, A. Wartnik, and A. Russell. 2015b. Fetal alcohol spectrum disorder and the courts: An introduction for legal professionals. *Behavioral Health* 3 (1): 1–13.

Bryant, A., G. Matthews, and B. Wilhelmsen. 2015. Assessing the legitimacy of competence to stand trial in juvenile court the practice of CST with and without statutory law. *Criminal Justice Policy Review* 26 (4): 371–399.

Bullock, J. 2002. Involuntary treatment of defendants found incompetent to stand trial. *Journal of Forensic Psychology Practice* 2: 1–34.

Burd, L., D. Roberts, M. Olson, and H. Odendaal. 2007. Ethanol and the placenta: A review. *The Journal of Maternal-Fetal & Neonatal Medicine* 20 (5): 361–375.

Burd, L., D.K. Fast, J. Conry, and A. Williams. 2010. Fetal alcohol spectrum disorder as a marker for increased risk of involvement with correction systems. *The Journal of Psychiatry & Law* 38 (4): 559–583.

CBC News. 2012, November 5. *Calgary teen fit to stand trial in sex assault of young boy*. Retrieved from http://www.cbc.ca/news/canada/calgary/calgary-teen-fit-to-stand-trial-in-sex-assault-of-young-boy-1.1276813

Chartrand, L.N., and E.M. Forbes-Chilibeck. 2003. The sentencing of offenders with fetal alcohol syndrome. *Health Law Journal* 11: 35–70.

Chauhan, P., J. Warren, L. Kois, and J. Wellbeloved-Stone. 2015. The significance of combining evaluations of competency to stand trial and sanity at the time of the offense. *Psychology, Public Policy, and Law* 21 (1): 50–59.

Clarren, S.K., and J. Lutke. 2008. Building clinical capacity for fetal alcohol spectrum disorder diagnoses in western and northern Canada. *The Canadian Journal of Clinical Pharmacology* 15 (2): 223–237.

Cochrane, R.E., T. Grisso, and R.I. Frederick. 2001. The relationship between criminal charges, diagnoses, and psycholegal opinions among pretrial federal defendants. *Behavioral Sciences and the Law* 19: 565–582.

Conry, J., and K. Asante. 2010. *Youth probation officers' guide to FASD screening and referral*. Maple Ridge: The Asante Center for FASD Fetal Alcohol Syndrome.

Conry, J., and D.K. Fast. 2011. Mental health issues for people with fetal alcohol spectrum disorders in the criminal justice system. *Canadian Journal of Community Mental Health* 29 (2): 65–70.

Conry, J.L., and K.A. Lane. 2009. *Characteristics of youth with FASD on adjudicated probation orders*. Final report to the Department of Justice Canada and British Columbia Ministry of Children and Family Development.

Cox, L.V., D. Clairmont, and S. Cox. 2008. Knowledge and attitudes of criminal justice professionals in relation to fetal alcohol spectrum disorder. *Canadian Journal of Clinical Pharmacology* 15 (2): 306–313.

Denney, R.L., and E.A. Tyner. 2010. Criminal law, competency, insanity, and dangerousness: Competency to proceed. In *The handbook of forensic neuropsychology*, ed. A.M. Horton Jr. and L.C. Hartlage, 2nd ed., 211–233. New York: Springer.

Douds, A., H. Stevens, and W. Sumner. 2012. Sword or shield? A systematic review of the roles FASD evidence plays in judicial proceedings. *Criminal Justice Policy Review* 24 (4): 492–509.

Drope v. Missouri, 420 U.S. 162 (1975).

Dusky v. United States, 362 U.S. 402 (1960).

Edwards, W.J., and S. Greenspan. 2010. Adaptive behavior and fetal alcohol spectrum disorders. *The Journal of Psychiatry & Law* 38 (4): 419–447.

Everington, C.T., and R. Luckasson. 1992. *Competence assessment for standing trial for defendants with mental retardation: Test manual*. Worthington: International Diagnostic Services.

Fagerlund, A., I. Autti-Ramo, M. Kalland, P. Santtila, E. Hoyme, S. Mattson, and M. Korkman. 2012. Adaptive behaviour in children and adolescents with foetal alcohol spectrum disorders: a comparison with specific learning disability and typical development. *European Child & Adolescent Psychiatry* 21: 221–231.

Famy, C., A.P. Streissguth, and A.S. Unis. 1998. Mental illness in adults with fetal alcohol syndrome or fetal alcohol effects. *American Journal of Psychiatry* 155: 552–554.

Fast, D.K., and J. Conry. 2004. The challenge of fetal alcohol syndrome in the criminal legal system. *Addiction Biology* 9: 161–166.

Fast, D.K., and J. Conry. 2009. Fetal alcohol spectrum disorders and the criminal justice system. *Developmental Disabilities Research Reviews* 15 (3): 250–257.

Frederick, R.I. 2012. Criminal competency of adults. In *Coping with psychiatric and psychological testimony*, ed. D. Faust, 6th ed., 511–518. New York: Oxford University Press.

Fryer, S.L., S.F. Tapert, S.N. Mattson, M.P. Paulus, A.D. Spadoni, and E.P. Riley. 2007. Prenatal alcohol exposure affects frontal–striatal BOLD response during inhibitory control. *Alcoholism: Clinical and Experimental Research* 31 (8): 1415–1424.

Gagnier, K.R., T.E. Moore, and M. Green. 2010. A need for closer examination of FASD by the criminal justice system: Has the call been answered? *Journal of Population Therapeutics and Clinical Pharmacology = Journal de la therapeutique des populations et de la pharamcologie clinique* 18 (3): e426–e439.

Gottfried, E., and J. Carbonell. 2014. The role of intelligence on performance on the inventory of legal knowledge (ILK). *The Journal of Forensic Psychiatry & Psychology* 25 (4): 380–396.

Gralton, E. 2014. Foetal alcohol spectrum disorder (FASD)–its relevance to forensic adolescent services. *Journal of Intellectual Disabilities and Offending Behaviour* 5 (3): 124–137.

Greenspan, S., and J.H. Driscoll. 2015. Why people with FASD fall for manipulative ploys: Ethical limits of interrogators' use of lies. In *Fetal alcohol spectrum disorders in adults: Ethical and legal perspectives*, 23–38. Cham: Springer.

Grisso, T. 1986. *Evaluating competencies: Forensic assessments and instruments*. New York: Plenum.

———. 2003. *Evaluating competences: Forensic assessments and instruments*. 2nd ed. New York: Kluwer Academic/Plenum Publishers.

———. 2014. *Competence to stand trial evaluations: Just the basics*. Sarasota: Professional Resource Press.

Grisso, T., and P.S. Appelbaum. 1998. *Assessing competence to consent to treatment: A guide for physicians and other health professionals*. New York: Oxford University Press.

Group for the Advancement of Psychiatry. 1974. *Misuse of psychiatry in the criminal courts: Competency to stand trial*. New York: Mental Health Materials Center.

Gudjonsson, G.H., and N.K. Clark. 1986. Suggestibility in police interrogation: A social psychological model. *Social Behaviour* 1: 83–104.

Guerri, C., A. Bazinet, and E.P. Riley. 2009. Fetal alcohol spectrum disorders and alterations in brain and behavior. *Alcohol and Drug Research* 44: 108–114.

Hall v. Florida, 134 S. Ct. 1986 (2014).

Hunt, D. 2012, July 15. *Fetal alcohol syndrome may spare a murderer*. The Seattle Times. Retrieved from: http://old.seattletimes.com/text/2018683861.html

Jackson v. Indiana, 406 U.S. 715 (1972).

Jirikowic, T., H.C. Olson, and D. Kartin. 2008. Sensory processing, school performance, and adaptive behavior of young school-age children with fetal alcohol spectrum disorders. *Physical & Occupational Therapy in Pediatrics* 28 (2): 117–136.

Kirkish, P., and S. Sreenivasan. 1999. Neuropsychological assessment of competency to stand trial evaluations: A practical conceptual model. *Journal of the American Academy of Psychiatry and the Law Online* 27 (1): 101–113.

Kodituwakku, P.W. 2009. Neurocognitive profile in children with fetal alcohol spectrum disorders. *Developmental Disabilities Research Reviews* 15 (3): 218–224.

Kruh, I., and T. Grisso. 2009. *Evaluation of juveniles' competence to stand trial*. New York: Oxford University Press.

Kully-Martens, K., J. Pei, J. Job, and C. Rasmussen. 2012. Source monitoring in children with and without fetal alcohol spectrum disorders. *Journal of Pediatric Psychology* 37 (7): 725–735.

LaDue, R., and T. Dunne. 1995. Legal issues and the fetal alcohol syndrome. *The FEN Pen* 3 (4): 6–7.

———. 1996. Capacity concerns and fetal alcohol syndrome. *The FEN Pen* 4 (1): 2–3.

Laporte, A., T. McKee, Z. Lisakowski, A.E. Chudley, and J. Conry. 2003. *Fetal alcohol spectrum disorder: FASD guidebook for police officers*. Ottawa: R.C.M.P.

Littlefield, D. 2013, April 18. Boy in fatal stabbing bound for treatment. *The San Diego Union Tribune*. Retrieved from http://www.sandiegouniontribune.com/news/2013/apr/18/boy-fatal-stabbing-treatment-ryan-carter/

Malbin, D.V. 2004. Fetal alcohol spectrum disorder and the role of family court judges in improving outcomes for children and families. *Juvenile and Family Court Journal* 55 (2): 53–63.

Man accused of shooting father in SE Volusia camper to get new mental health exam. 2012, April 15. The Daytona Beach News Journal. Retrieved from: http://www.news-journalonline.com/article/20120410/ARTICLES/304109985

Mattson, S.N., E.P. Riley, L. Gramling, D.C. Delis, and K.L. Jones. 1997. Heavy prenatal alcohol exposure with or without physical features of fetal alcohol syndrome leads to IQ deficits. *The Journal of Pediatrics* 131 (5): 718–721.

Mattson, S.N., N. Crocker, and T.T. Nguyen. 2011. Fetal alcohol spectrum disorders: Neuropsychological and behavioral features. *Neuropsychology Review* 21 (2): 81–101.

May, P.A., J.P. Gossage, W.O. Kalberg, L.K. Robinson, D. Buckley, M. Manning, and H.E. Hoyme. 2009. Prevalence and epidemiologic characteristics of FASD from various research methods with an emphasis on recent in-school studies. *Developmental Disabilities Research Reviews* 15 (3): 176–192.

McLachlan, K., R. Roesch, J.L. Viljoen, and K.S. Douglas. 2014. Evaluating the psycholegal abilities of young offenders with fetal alcohol Spectrum disorder. *Law and Human Behavior* 38: 10–22.

Mela, M. 2015. Medico-legal interventions in management of offenders with Fetal Alcohol Spectrum Disorders (FASD). In *Fetal alcohol spectrum disorders in adults: Ethical and legal perspectives*, 121–138. Springer International Publishing.

Mela, M., and G. Luther. 2013. Fetal alcohol spectrum disorder: Can diminished responsibility diminish criminal behaviour? *International Journal of Law and Psychiatry* 36: 46–54.

Melton, G.B., J. Petrila, N.G. Poythress, and C. Slobogin. 2007. *Psychological evaluations for the courts: A handbook for mental health professionals*. 3rd ed. New York: Guilford.

Miller, R.D. 2003. Hospitalization of criminal defendants for evaluation of competence to stand trial or for restoration of competence: Clinical and legal issues. *Behavioral Sciences and the Law* 21: 369–391.

Morleo, M., K. Woolfall, D. Dedman, R. Mukherjee, M.A. Bellis, and P.A. Cook. 2011. Underreporting of foetal alcohol spectrum disorders: An analysis of hospital episode statistics. *BMC Pediatrics* 11: 14.

Morris, D.R., and N.J. DeYoung. 2012. Psycholegal abilities and restoration of competence to stand trial. *Behavioral Sciences & the Law* 30 (6): 710–728.

Morris, D.R., and G.F. Parker. 2008. *Jackson*'s Indiana: State hospital competence restoration in Indiana. *Journal of the American Academy of Psychiatry and Law* 36: 522–534.

Mossman, D., S.G. Noffsinger, P. Ash, R.L. Frierson, J. Gerbasi, M. Hackett, et al. 2007. AAPL practice guidelines for the forensic psychiatric evaluation of competence to stand trial. *The Journal of the American Academy of Psychiatry and the Law* 35: S3–S75.

Nestor, P.G., D. Daggett, J. Haycock, and M. Price. 1999. Competence to stand trial: A neuropsychological inquiry. *Law and Human Behavior* 23 (4): 397.

Nicholson, R.A., and K.E. Kugler. 1991. Competent and incompetent criminal defendants: A quantitative review of comparative research. *Psychological Bulletin* 109: 355–370.

Ortega, J. 2011, October 15. 18-year-old's jailing reveals huge hole in mental health system, advocates say. *Victoria Advocate*. Retrieved from https://www.victoriaadvocate.com/news/2011/oct/15/jo_criminilization_ill_101611_154115/

Pate v. Robinson, 383 U.S. 375 (1966).

Petrenko, C.L., N. Tahir, E.C. Mahoney, and N.P. Chin. 2014. Prevention of secondary conditions in fetal alcohol spectrum disorders: Identification of systems-level barriers. *Maternal and Child Health Journal* 18 (6): 1496–1505.

Piel, J., M.J. Finkle, M. Giske, and G.B. Leong. 2015. Determining a criminal defendant's competency to proceed with an extradition hearing. *Journal of the American Academy of Psychiatry and the Law Online* 43 (2): 201–209.

Pinals, D.A. 2005. Where two roads meet: Restoration of competence to stand trial from a clinical perspective. *New England Journal of Criminal Civil Confinement* 31: 81–108.

Pirelli, G., W.H. Gottdiener, and P.A. Zapf. 2011. A meta-analytic review of competency to stand trial research. *Psychology, Public Policy, and Law* 17: 1–53.

Popova, S., S. Lange, D. Bekmuradov, A. Alanna Mihic, and J. Rehm. 2011. Fetal alcohol spectrum disorder prevalence estimates in correctional systems: A systematic literature review. *Canadian Journal of Public Health* 102 (5): 336–340.

Poythress, N.G., R.J. Bonnie, J. Monahan, R.K. Otto, and S.K. Hoge. 2002. *Adjudicative competence: The MacArthur studies*. New York: Kluwer Academic/Plenum.

Ramsey, K. 2012, December 24. Parents plead for easier route to help mentally ill kids. *The Cincinnati Inquirer*. Retrieved from http://www.usatoday.com/story/news/nation/2012/12/24/mental-health-violent-outbursts/1789147/

Roach, K., and A. Bailey. 2009. The relevance of fetal alcohol spectrum disorder and the criminal law from investigation to sentencing. *University of British Columbia Law Review* 42: 1–68.

Roesch, R., P.A. Zapf, and D. Eaves. 2006. *Fitness interview test—revised: A structured interview for assessing competency to stand trial*. Sarasota: Professional Resource Press.

Rogers, R., and C.P. Ewing. 1989. Proscribing ultimate opinions: A quick and cosmetic fix. *Law and Human Behavior* 13: 357–374.

———. 2003. The prohibition of ultimate opinions: A misguided enterprise. *Journal of Forensic Psychology Practice* 3: 65–75.

Ryba, N.L., and P.A. Zapf. 2011. The influence of psychiatric symptoms and cognitive abilities on competence-related abilities. *International Journal of Forensic Mental Health* 10: 29–40.

Salekin, K.L., J.G. Olley, and K.A. Hedge. 2010. Offenders with intellectual disability: Characteristics, prevalence, and issues in forensic assessment. *Journal of Mental Health Research in Intellectual Disabilities* 3: 97–116.

Slobogin, C. 1989. The "ultimate issue" issue. *Behavioral Sciences and the Law* 7: 259–266.

Stafford, K., and M. Sellbom. 2013. Assessment of competence to stand trial. In *Handbook of psychology: Forensic psychology*, ed. R.K. Otto and I.B. Weiner, vol. 11, 2nd ed., 412–439. Hoboken: Wiley.

Stewart, J. 2014, June 25. Rosie Fulton to be freed after 21 months in jail with no conviction. *ABC*. Retrieved from http://nationalunitygovernment.org/content/rosie-fulton-be-freed-after-21-months-jail-no-conviction

Streissguth, A.P., R.A. LaDue, and S.P. Randels. 1988. *A manual on adolescents and adults with fetal alcohol syndrome with special reference to American Indians*. 2nd ed. Albuquerque: University of Washington.

Streissguth, A.P., H.M. Barr, J. Kogan, and F.L. Bookstein. 1996. *Understanding the occurrence of secondary disabilities in clients with fetal alcohol syndrome (FAS) and fetal alcohol effects (FAE)*. Final report to the Centers for Disease Control and Prevention (CDC), 96-06.

Streissguth, A.P., F.L. Bookstein, H.M. Barr, P.D. Sampson, K. O'Malley, and J.K. Young. 2004. Risk factors for adverse life outcomes in fetal alcohol syndrome and fetal alcohol effects. *Journal of Developmental and Behavioral Pediatrics: JDBP* 25 (4): 228–238.

Thiel, K.S., N.J. Baladerian, K.R. Boyce, O.D. Cantos, L.A. Davis, K. Kelly, et al. 2011. Fetal alcohol spectrum disorders and victimization: Implications for families, educators, social services, law enforcement, and the judicial system. *The Journal of Psychiatry & Law* 39 (1): 121–157.

Toofanian Ross, P., C.B. Padula, S.R. Nitch, and D.I. Kinney. 2015. Cognition and competency restoration: Using the RBANS to predict length of stay for patients deemed incompetent to stand trial. *The Clinical Neuropsychologist* 29 (1): 150–165.

Tumilty, R. 2010, December 15. Distressed mind with no place to go. *St. Albert Gazette*. Retrieved from http://www.stalbertgazette.com/apps/pbcs.dll/article?AID=/20101215/SAG0801/312159981/distressed-mind-with-no-place-to-go

Verbrugge, P. 2003. *Fetal alcohol spectrum disorder and the youth criminal justice system: A discussion paper*. Department of Justice Canada, Youth Justice Research.

Viljoen, J.L., and R. Roesch. 2005. Competence to waive interrogation rights and adjudicative competence in adolescent defendants: Cognitive development, attorney contact, and psychological symptoms. *Law and Human Behavior* 29 (6): 723–742.

Warren, J.I., D.C. Murrie, W. Stejskal, M.A. Colwell, J. Morris, P. Chauhan, and P. Dietz. 2006. Opinion formulation in evaluation the adjudicative competence and restorability of criminal defendants: A review of 8000 evaluations. *Behavioral Sciences and the Law* 24: 112–132.

Wartnik, A.P., and S.S. Carlson. 2011. A judicial perspective on issues impacting the trial courts related to fetal alcohol Spectrum disorders. *The Journal of Psychiatry & Law* 39 (1): 73–119.

Wartnik, A.P., J. Brown, and S. Herrick. 2015. Evolution of the diagnosis of fetal alcohol spectrum disorder from DSM-IV-TR to DSM-5: The justice system in the United States—time for a paradigm shift! In *Fetal alcohol spectrum disorders in adults: Ethical and legal perspectives*, 151–167. Cham: Springer.

Westrup, S. 2013. Foetal alcohol spectrum disorders: As prevalent as autism? *Educational Psychology in Practice* 29 (3): 309–325.

White, A.J., S. Meares, and J. Batchelor. 2014. The role of cognition in fitness to stand trial: A systematic review. *The Journal of Forensic Psychiatry & Psychology* 25 (1): 77–99.

Wieter v. Settle, 193 F.Supp. 318 (1961).

Zapf, P.A., and R. Roesch. 2009. *Evaluation of competence to stand trial*. New York: Oxford University Press.

Zapf, P., and J. Viljoen. 2003. Issues and considerations regarding the use of assessment instruments in the evaluation of competency to stand trial. *Behavioral Sciences and the Law* 21: 351–367.

Zapf, P.A., K.L. Hubbard, V.G. Cooper, M.C. Wheeles, and K.A. Ronan. 2004. Have the courts abdicated their responsibility for determination of competency to stand trial to clinicians? *Journal of Forensic Psychology Practice* 4: 27–44.

Zapf, P.A., J.L. Skeem, and S.L. Golding. 2005. Factor structure and validity of the MacArthur competence assessment tool—criminal adjudication. *Psychological Assessment* 17: 433–445.

Chapter 13
Clinical and Ethical Issues When Completing Decision-Making Capacity Evaluations with People Diagnosed with FASD

Arlin Pachet and Avril J. Keller

Abstract Decisional Capacity is a complex socio-legal construct, and is commonly conceptualized as an individual's ability to use cognitive processes to understand and identify options, to appreciate the consequences of choosing or not choosing the various options identified, and to either personally follow through with the chosen option, or to direct a surrogate to follow through with the chosen option on his or her behalf. Due to the multiple legal, ethical, medical, social, and cultural factors involved, decisional capacity issues are challenging for all affected parties. Similarly complex, Fetal Alcohol Spectrum Disorders (FASD), which involve neurodevelopmental impairment second to prenatal alcohol exposure can manifest in profound disabilities along a spectrum of disorders. Within the FASD population, in general, those afflicted tend to exhibit impairments that are likely to interfere with capable decision-making, such as impaired social and adaptive functioning and impulse control issues. As such, consideration of the interplay between decisional capacity and FASD is warranted. This chapter aims to highlight the vital tenants integral to the conscientious conceptualization of decisional capacity, to discuss decisional capacity assessment from a best-practice perspective, and finally, to provide a broader context for some of the clinical nuances within the decisional capacity evaluation process, in particular, how the practice of decisional capacity assessment looks within the context of assessing individuals who carry a FASD diagnosis.

A. Pachet (✉)
Board Certified in Clinical Neuropsychology Pachet Assessment & Rehabilitation Services, University of Calgary, Calgary, AB, Canada
e-mail: arlin.pachet@gmail.com

A. J. Keller
Pachet Assessment & Rehabilitation Services, University of Calgary, Calgary, AB, Canada

E. Jonsson et al. (eds.), *Ethical and Legal Perspectives in Fetal Alcohol Spectrum Disorders (FASD)*, International Library of Ethics, Law, and the New Medicine 75,
https://doi.org/10.1007/978-3-319-71755-5_13

13.1 Decisional Capacity Defined

Decisional Capacity[1] is a complex socio-legal construct, and is commonly conceptualized as an individual's ability to use cognitive processes to understand and identify options, to appreciate the consequences of choosing or not choosing the various options identified, and to either personally follow through with the chosen option, or to direct a surrogate to follow through with the chosen option on his or her behalf (Grisso and Appelbaum 1998; Schulman et al. 2007; Silberfeld and Checkland 1999; Weisstub 1990). Due to the multiple legal, ethical, medical, social, and cultural factors involved, decisional capacity issues are challenging for all affected parties. Similarly complex, Fetal Alcohol Spectrum Disorders (FASD), which involve neurodevelopmental impairment second to prenatal alcohol exposure (Burd et al. 2007; Kodituwakku 2007; Weinberg et al. 2008; Riley et al. 2004), can manifest in profound disabilities along a spectrum of disorders (Burd et al. 2010; Abel 2006; Adams et al. 2002; Streissguth et al. 2004; Mattson et al. 2007), with the severity of the cognitive and functional impairment of each afflicted individual falling along a vast continuum. However, while heterogeneity of presentation is notable within the FASD population, in general, those afflicted tend to exhibit impairments that are likely to interfere with capable decision-making, such as impaired social and adaptive functioning (Conry and Fast 2000) and impulse control issues (Peadon and Elliott 2010). As such, consideration of the interplay between decisional capacity and FASD is warranted. This chapter aims to highlight the vital tenants integral to the conscientious conceptualization of decisional capacity, to discuss decisional capacity assessment from a best-practice perspective, and finally, to provide a broader context for some of the clinical nuances within the decisional capacity evaluation process, in particular, how the practice of decisional capacity assessment looks within the context of assessing individuals who carry a FASD diagnosis.

Of note, decisional capacity is not a medical diagnosis. Medical and mental health practitioners provide a clinical opinion of decisional capacity to the courts. The term competency, which has been removed from the Personal Directives Act (PDA) and the Adult Guardianship and Trusteeship Act (AGTA), has more commonly become associated with the legal rendering of a determination (Reid-Proctor et al. 2001). Therefore, in order to ensure that the clinical opinion provided is able to be used by the courts, it is important that all clinical proceedings adhere to legal standards.

There are a few guiding principles considered essential by those who work in the area of decisional capacity evaluation. The first is that of presumed capacity. Alberta legislation (i.e., Adult Guardianship and Trusteeship Act [AGTA] & Personal Directives Act [PDA]) states that every individual who has attained the age of majority (i.e., 18 years of age) is presumed to be entirely capable from a decision-

[1] While the term "capacity" is typically used in most literature and legislation, there has been a relatively recent movement to more aptly refer to the construct as "decisional capacity" in order to avoid confusion with other uses of the term "capacity" (e.g., mental capacity, building capacity). As such, the term "decisional capacity" will be used throughout to refer to "capacity" from a decision-making perspective.

making perspective. Any consideration of the possibility that the individual lacks capacity requires thorough evaluation, and the onus is on those involved in the decisional-capacity assessment to provide overwhelming evidence to the contrary. If, at the completion of the decisional capacity assessment, equal evidence exists to both support and refute an individual's decisional capacity abilities, the evaluator is required to provide the determination that the individual continues to retain decisional capacity (AGTA; Pachet et al. 2007).

Bearing this in mind, a situation that occasionally occurs where this principle may be called into question, and which may be particularly relevant within the population of those inflicted with FASD. This situation is comprised of an individual who has been diagnosed with significant developmental delay, associated pervasive functional impairment, complete and total reliance on caregivers, and a blatantly compromised ability to make decisions independently, approaches the age of majority. In these situations it seems illogical to entertain the assumption that this individual will magically sprout the requisite skills to be able to make capable decisions, simply by turning 18 years of age. However, if a decisional capacity assessment is not completed, the individual will legally be considered to poses decision capacity as of his or her 18th birthday. Of note, a decisional capacity evaluation can be carried out up to 6 months prior to an individual's 18th birthday (AGTA 2008).

Another guiding principle involves the concept of autonomy. Given that we live in a society built on the values of individualism and choice, the possibility that a decisional capacity evaluation might be needed introduces notable tension, which stems from the conflict between two ethical principles: autonomy/self-determination versus beneficence/the need to protect vulnerable individuals. Rendering an incapable determination is a serious endeavour that has implications not only for the person being evaluated, but also for the family of the individual being assessed, and possibly even for society at large (Moberg et al. 2012). As aptly stated by Pepper-Smith and Nelson (1996), a finding of incapacity "remains one of the most significant mechanisms in our society for the removal of a person's fundamental rights and freedoms." With this in mind, the AGTA states "the adult's autonomy must be preserved by ensuring that the least restrictive and least intrusive form of assisted or substitute decision-making that is likely to be effective is provided" (AGTA 2008). Further, practitioners, such as medical doctors, who are instructed to "Consider first the well-being of the patient" (Canadian Medical Association 2004), and psychologists who are ethically obliged to honour an individual's right to autonomy (Canadian Psychological Association 2000), are duty bound to balance their ethical and legal obligations with protecting individuals and others from harm. For this reason, many practitioners choose not to include decisional capacity assessments as part of their regular practice; this is also one of the reasons, the remainder of which will be discussed in greater detail below, it is vital that only seasoned experts engage in the assessment of decisional capacity.

A guiding principle that that will be briefly touched upon is that declaring someone incapable must be in that person's best interests. Specifically, once a healthcare practitioner opines that an individual lacks decisional capacity, it is up to the court to grant a guardianship order, which effectively rescinds that adult's decisional capacity. According to Alberta legislation, the court must be satisfied that this guardianship order will be in the adult's best interests and will result in substantial benefit to the adult. The AGTA does state that in attempting to determine the adult's best interests, the following should be considered: "any wishes known to have been expressed by the adult while the adult had capacity" and "any values and beliefs known to have been held by the adult while the adult had capacity" (AGTA 2008). However, operationalizing the concept "substantial benefit" can vary based on the source consulted, but according to my clinical experience, it ideally is someone who is willing to accept the support and guidance provided by a guardian, the results of which facilitates the decision making process and results in substantial positive change to the individual's well-being.

Further to the principle of acting in a person's best interest, a construct that is not discussed enough within the field of decisional capacity evaluation involves the sociocultural construct of capacity. In undertaking an evaluation to determine if an individual continues to possess decisional capacity, it is vital that the practitioner develop an awareness of the individual's cultural background, especially with respect to how an individual's cultural background influences decision making. For example, an elderly woman of Vietnamese origin, only in Canada for the past 3 years, presents with possible challenges to her decision-making abilities. She lacks any knowledge of federal or provincial legislation, and is not even able to provide the definition of "guardian." When asked to relay to the examiner her understanding of capacity, she states, "my family will come help me if I start having problems." This example illustrates that introducing informal supports to shore up capacity is common in certain cultures. In this situation, would proceeding with a capacity evaluation be warranted? The answer is no. In the event that the issues can be mitigated through the dedicated provision informal supports, effectively shoring up capacity, an evaluation is not required. And for her, they did so dramatically: she had a lot of family members willing to jump in and help manage what we call triggers or areas of concern.

Similar to the varying degrees of cognitive, behavioural, and adaptive challenges that individuals with FASD exhibit, decisional capacity also exists on a continuum. While some individuals retain full capacity, some require a moderate amount of support and guidance to shore up their decision-making abilities, and still others require more hand-over-hand assistance. Recent revisions to the provincial legislation involve modification to previous law aimed at better accommodating the amount of assistance required, and with this there has been a movement away from the dichotomization of this continuous construct. It should also be noted that decisional capacity abilities can fluctuate over time, and in some instances, determinations of incapacity are temporally limited (Grisso and Appelbaum 1998). To illustrate, in cases of delirium, acute intoxification, psychiatric disturbance, or the early stages of recovery from traumatic brain injury or stroke, the individual in question is likely to be experiencing a marked and transient decline in cognitive functioning that improves with treatment over time. As will be described in more detail below, these types of temporary or reversible changes in cognitive ability are typically identified during the pre-assessment phase of the evaluation, and decisional capacity assessment is postponed until resolution of the afflicting circumstance is achieved.

Finally, it is important to revisit the definition of decisional capacity for the purpose of demonstrating what it is not. An individual who maintains decisional capacity has an understanding of the necessary information needed to make the decision in question, possesses an appreciation of the possible choices at hand, and is aware of the conceivable outcomes of each choice. Sometimes people make choices that appear risky, eccentric, or quirky, but if they posses the requisite understanding and appreciation for said decision, there is no cause for the consideration of incapacity. Just because a person presents with a very atypical or eccentric behaviour does not mean that he or she is incapable. Also, a risky decision is not necessarily an incapable decision. Stockbrokers, soldiers, doctors, and patients make risky decisions everyday. Taking risks or being different does not necessarily equal a lack of capacity. Are their behaviours due to deficits in executive functioning, or are these individuals fully capable eccentrics/risk takers? To learn the answer we have to examine their behavioural patterns, and take a closer look at their history of decision-making and problem solving. This is achieved through the process of decisional capacity evaluation.

13.2 Decisional Capacity Assessment

Decisional capacity is a complex construct, and by extension, the assessment of decisional capacity is also extremely complicated. Due to the significant implications of possible outcomes, it was discussed above that a clinician with ample clinical experience and strong clinical acumen is best suited to take on evaluations of capacity. In fact, few clinicians actually specialize in decisional capacity assessment and only receive this type of referral sporadically. In a study measuring the degree of agreement between clinicians assessing for decisional capacity, it was demonstrated that poor reliability is the norm; this finding has been attributed to clinician's knowing the theory of capacity assessment, but lacking the skills to adequately and consistently put it into practice (Mukherjee and Shah 2009). Oppositely, clinician's with more *practical* experience in decisional capacity assessment showed higher agreement (Fassassi et al. 2009). It should be noted that no professions specifically provide for the development of expertise in capacity assessment as a sub-specialty of their profession, and few professionals become specialized in decisional capacity assessment through indirect routes (i.e., training under someone who has some experience, didactic study/research, policy development, and extensive practice; Silberfeld and Checkland 1999). Within the province of Alberta, with the introduction of the AGTA, physicians and psychologists are legally entitled to act as capacity assessors. Additionally, specified health care practitioners (e.g., occupational therapists, registered nurses, registered psychiatric nurses, nurse practitioners, and social workers) who complete the required capacity assessment training course offered by the Office of the Public Guardian are also eligible to complete capacity assessments in Alberta.

A key concept of capacity assessment is that decisional capacity is domain-specific. In the past, capacity had a tendency to be conceptualized as global, all embracing, and “all or nothing.” However, more recently this conceptualization has shifted to a more specific condition restricted to a particular realm or realms of decision-making (Checkland and Silberfeld 1995; Faden et al. 1986; Appelbaum et al. 1987). As such, a person may have capacity with regard to health care decisions, but lack capacity with regard to financial matters. Not only is decisional capacity now conceptualized as domain-specific but sometimes even decision-specific. For example, decisions within the health care domain can be further subdivided into decisions specifically about participating in health care treatments. This subgroup of decisions can be further broken down into whether or not an individual can make a capable decision about one treatment in particular. Of course, when considering this, it is important to keep in mind the complexity of the specific decision.

Another key concept in the evaluation of decisional capacity is that capacity assessment focuses on the functional ability of the individual. The premise intrinsic to this concept is that an individual’s diagnosis is not in itself suggestive of a particular level of capacity. This concept is especially salient when considering individuals with FASD, or dementia, or any other diagnosis with associated cognitive, behavioural, and/or adaptive implications, most notably when the range of impairment is extremely broad. It is typically understood that a diagnosis is clinically useful because it provides a general, albeit stereotyped, understanding of one’s challenges; however, to attach a determination of incapacity to an individual based solely on a pre-existing diagnostic classification, is to attempt to bridge the “inferential gap”, or to infer a certain degree of capability based entirely upon one’s diagnosis (Silberfeld and Checkland 1999). As such, while a diagnosis can always provide a useful starting point in terms of gaining a general understanding of the individual, to truly gain a sense of that person’s decision-making capacity, the practitioner must examine his or her functional abilities in regard to understanding information relevant to a decision, and appreciating the consequences of the presenting options. And again, it is necessary to reiterate that this examination needs to occur with consideration of the individual’s culture, values, and beliefs.

It is important to emphasize that a capacity assessor must also consider the quality of the decision-making process, not simply the actual course of action in which a person engages. The evaluation should focus on investigating an individual’s ability to rationally manipulate information, and not only that the individual compare/contrast the options and predict consequences of the same, but that individual employs a sound method for doing so. The assessor should consider what process the individual used to come to his or her decision? Take, for example, an individual who carries a diagnosis of FASD and who has a history of impulsivity (Peadon and Elliott 2010). An impulsive person might decide to do something in the spur of the moment without following a methodical step-by-step process, whereas capable decision makers are aware of the choices, understand the foreseeable consequences and effects, and make a decision after weighing the relative pros and cons of the choices. Impulsivity may preclude an individual from going through a step-by-step process. For individuals with FASD, it can be a struggle to effectively weigh pros and cons.

Finally, clinicians who commonly carry out decisional capacity evaluations need to maintain a solid understanding of their own values and risk tolerance. Proper insight into their own preconceived ideas about behaviour and cognition, in addition to their ability to identify their potential triggers, will increase the likelihood of an unbiased appraisal.

13.2.1 The Process of the Decisional Capacity Assessment

The first question that commonly comes to mind when discussing the process of decisional capacity assessment is, "How does one know when a capacity evaluation is necessary?" In order to initiate the capacity assessment process, there must be an established need, or a "trigger." These triggers can take many different forms, and are most easily identified by posing the questions: "What has changed to suggest that decision making might be compromised?" (i.e. "What's different?") and, "Why now?" (Pachet et al. 2007).

Anecdotally, our experience with individuals who carry an FASD diagnosis is that they commonly arrive on our radar when there has been as issue with adaptive (or rather, maladaptive) behaviour (Conry and Fast 2000; Sood et al. 2001; Streissguth et al. 2004), as opposed to something like low IQ (Thomas et al. 1998). The answers to the questions: "What's different" and/or "Why now" involve such scenarios as: they've recently been exploited – to a negative end, they've made decisions that have placed themselves or others at risk, or perhaps now someone is questioning their ability to make choices or decisions autonomously. Also important to keep in mind at this stage is that provincial legislation states anyone who is concerned with an individual's decision-making abilities can initiate the assessment process by contacting a capacity assessor and expressing concern. Common referral sources for this type of assessment include receive physicians, family members, case workers, and of course, self-referral. Once the process is initiated, it is then up to the capacity assessor to determine if there is likely an established need to proceed with the capacity assessment (AGTA 2008).

Once a potential established need has been identified, the capacity assessor then proceeds with the pre-assessment process. While this is always an important stage in any assessment, it is particularly important in the decisional capacity assessment process. A great deal of the assessment process, in fact, likely more time than is spent interviewing the person in question, is allocated to the pre-assessment process (Pachet et al. 2007). This stage in the evaluation is spent gathering information to determine if there in fact is a determined need to assess the person in question, and ascertaining a more in-depth and comprehensive understanding of the adaptive difficulties the individual might be experiencing.

At this point it is also important to query the possibility that the recent challenges with decision-making might be the result of a temporary or reversal condition (AGTA 2008). As previously described, occasionally individuals may demonstrate challenges with capable decision making that is secondary to a transient condition such as delirium or acute intoxication. This must be ruled out, and if it is possible that a temporary or reversible condition might be playing a role, the formal capacity assessment should be postponed.

If there is significant evidence to suggest the possibility that the individual in question might be having difficulty with capable decision-making, the next step is to identify where his or her challenges lie. As previously discussed, decisional capacity is currently conceptualized as domain-specific. Broadly, decisions are separated into two overarching categories: Financial Decisions and Personal Decisions (AGTA 2008). Financial Decisions are decisions which include any decision that involves money, while the Personal Decisions category includes all other, non-monetary, decisions. The Personal Decisions category is typically broken down into: Health Care, Choice of Accommodation, Choice of Associates, Choice of Social Activities, Education, Vocation, and Legal decisions (AGTA 2008). A domain where individuals with FASD commonly demonstrate challenges with decision capacity is Choice of Accommodation. In consideration of the fact that individuals diagnosed with FASD have an increased likelihood of demonstrating impaired adaptive functioning and decreased social responsibility (Conry and Fast 2000), an inability to generalize socially learned lessons (D'Onofrio et al. 2007; Thomas et al. 1998), poor interpersonal boundaries (Streissguth et al. 2004; Sood et al. 2001), and a high level of suggestibility (Kassin et al. 2010; Perske 1994; Fast and Conry 2009), it is not surprising that one of the main domains problematic for FASD clients is the Choice of Associates domain. Once sufficient information has been gathered and a need for the capacity evaluation has been thoroughly established, the capacity interview is scheduled.

The capacity interview begins with the informed consent process. When assessing decisional capacity is that the client understands that realization that their capacity is being challenged, and that they not only understand that they have a right to defend their capacity but also that they have an opportunity to demonstrate their capacity. This information, which embodies a crucial facet of the informed consent process, is a legislative requirement. Additionally, and perhaps not in keeping with typical assessment situations, the individual being assessed is permitted to have someone present to provide support and comfort during the assessment. It is not uncommon, in our experience working with individuals who carry an FASD diagnosis, for support workers or friends to attend the interview with the client. Inclusion of a third person can assist by helping the client to relax, by encouraging the development of rapport between examiner and client, and also by potentially providing collateral information that could benefit the assessment process; however, a cautionary note is indicated, as individuals who carry a diagnosis of FASD can be easily suggestible (Kassin et al. 2010; Perske 1994; Fast and Conry 2009), and as such, it is important to consider and potentially examine the motives of those accompanying the client.

Upon completion of informed consent, the clinical interview ensues. The clinical interview is aimed at evaluating an individual's functional abilities pertaining to the domains of decisional capacity that, during the pre-assessment phase, were identified as potentially problematic. The interview, which consists largely of posing scenarios to the examinee based on either client-specific information provided by collateral sources, or hypothetical situations designed to elicit real-time problem solving and decision making abilities, provides further clarification of the individual's decisional capacity, and also allows for the opportunity to identify additional areas where the client may be struggling.

Employing a semi-structured clinical interview to obtain a determination of patient's decision-making capacity is typically viewed as the gold standard when making a capacity determination (Grisso et al. 1998; Silberfeld 1994; Pachet et al. 2007; Wyszynski and Garfein 2005; Lai and Jason 2007; Mohahan 1993; Moye et al. 2005). And, while there is no overwhelming consensus with regard to what cognitive constructs underlie these "functional" decisional abilities, it is evident that executive functioning plays a prominent role in this multidimensional construct. Occasionally, when additional clarification is thought necessary, brief assessment tools that emphasize executive functioning, such as the Montreal Cognitive Assessment (Nasreddine et al. 2005) and the Frontal Assessment Battery (Dubois et al. 2000), might be administered, for the provision of a more comprehensive picture of a person's decision-making abilities.

13.3 Decisional Capacity and Persons with FASD: Conclusions

While it is important to be well aware of the dangers of bridging the inferential gap between diagnosis and decisional capacity, it is still important to note that knowledge of an individual's diagnostic classification(s) can provide a useful starting point for the evaluation of decisional capacity. Decisional capacity, like FASD, exists on a continuum and knowledge of the potential diagnosis, such as FASD, will provide the assessor useful background knowledge and areas for specific query related to behaviour and adaptive functioning.

Many details have been provided in this chapter regarding the clinical nuances related to capacity evaluations, including the necessity to complete a thorough pre-assessment, as well as the common process to consider when completing the actual assessment. It is apparent that the field of capacity assessment is very complex and that clinician's actively completing work in this area will need to be well abreast of the grand results of such assessment; this is, potential removal of decisional autonomy. Unfortunately, formal academic training in the capacity assessment process remains quite limited, and an area that requires further growth for upcoming practitioners.

References

Abel, E.L. 2006. Fetal alcohol syndrome: A cautionary note. *Current Pharmaceutical Design* 12: 1521–1529.

Adams, J., P. Bittner, H.S. Buttar, C. Chambers, T. Collins, G.P. Daston, and J. Ploifkam. 2002. Statement of the public affairs committee of the teratology society on the fetal alcohol syndrome. *Teratology* 66: 344–347.

Adult Guardianship and Trusteeship Act. 2008.

Appelbaum, P.S., C.A. Lidz, and A. Meisel. 1987. *Informed consent: Legal theory and clinical practice*. New York: Oxford University Press.

Burd, L., D. Roberts, M. Olson, and H. Odendaal. 2007. Ethanol and the placenta: A review. *Journal of Maternal-Fetal & Neonatal Medicine* 20: 361–375.

Burd, L., M.G. Klug, Q. Li, J. Kerbeshian, and J.T. Martsolf. 2010. Diagnosis of fetal alcohol spectrum disorders: A validity study of the fetal alcohol syndrome checklist. *Alcohol* 44: 605–614.

Canadian Medical Association. 2004. *CMA code of ethics*. Ottawa: Canadian Medical Association.

Canadian Psychological Association. 2000. *Canadian code of ethics for psychologists*. 3rd ed. Ottawa: Canadian Medical Association.

Checkland, D., and M. Silberfeld. 1995. Reflections on segregating and assessing areas of competency. *Theoretical Medicine* 16: 375–388.

Conry, J.L., and D.K. Fast. 2000. *Fetal alcohol syndrome and the criminal justice system*. Vancouver: Fetal Alcohol Syndrome Resource Society.

D'Onofrio, B.M., C.A. Van Hulle, I.D. Waldman, J.L. Rodgers, P.J. Rathouz, and B.B. Lahey. 2007. Causal inferences regarding prenatal alcohol exposure and childhood externalizing problems. *Archives of General Psychiatry* 64: 1296–1304.

Dubois, B., A. Slachevsky, I. Litvan, and B. Pillon. 2000. The FAB: A frontal assessment battery at bedside. *Neurology* 55: 1621–1626.

Faden, R.R., T.L. Beauchamp, and N.M.P. King. 1986. *A history of informed consent*. New York: Oxford University Press.

Fassassi, S., Y. Bianchi, F. Stiefel, et al. 2009. Assessment of the capacity to consent to treatment in patients admitted to acute medical wards. *BMC Medical Ethics* 10: 15.

Fast, D.K., and J.L. Conry. 2009. Fetal alcohol spectrum disorders and the criminal justice system. *Developmental Disabilities Research Reviews* 15: 250–257.

Grisso, T., and P.S. Appelbaum. 1998. *Assessing competence to consent to treatment: A guide for physicians and other health professionals*. New York: Oxford University Press.

Kassin, S.M., S.A. Drizin, T. Grisso, G.H. Gudjonsson, R.A. Leo, and A.D. Redlich. 2010. Police-induced confessions. *Law and Human Behavior* 34 (1): 3–38.

Kodituwakku, P.W. 2007. Defining the behavioral phenotype in children with fetal alcohol spectrum disorders: A review. *Neuroscience and Biobehavioral Reviews* 31: 192–201.

Lai, J.M., and K. Jason. 2007. Assessing the capacity to make everyday decisions: A guide for clinicians and an agenda for future research. *The American Journal of Geriatric Psychiatry* 15: 101–111.

Mattson, S., A. Schonfeld, and E. Riley. 2007. *Teratogenic effects of alcohol on brain and behavior*. Washington, DC: National Institute on Alcohol and Alcoholism, National Institutes of Health.

Moberg, P.J., and S. Shah. 2012. Ethical issues in capacity and competency evaluations. In *Civil capacities in clinical neuropsychology: Research findings and practical applications*, ed. G.J. Demakis, 264–289. New York/Oxford: Oxford University Press.

Mohahan, D.J. 1993. Assessment of dementia patients and their families: An ecological-family-centered approach. *Health Social Work* 18: 123–131.

Moye, J., J.C. Armesto, and M.J. Karel. 2005. Evaluating capacity of older adults in rehabilitation setting: Conceptual models and clinical challenges. *Rehabilitation Psychology* 50: 207–214.

Mukherjee, S., and A. Shah. 2009. Capacity to consent: Issues and controversies. *Hospital Medicine* 62: 351–354.

Nasreddine, Z.S., N.A. Phillips, V. Bedirian, et al. 2005. The Montreal cognitive assessment, MoCA: A brief cognitive impairment. *Journal of the American Geriatric Society* 53: 695–699.

Pachet, A., A. Newberry, and L. Erskine. 2007. Assessing capacity in the complex patient: RCAT's unique evaluation and consultation model. *Canadian Psychology* 48: 174–186.

Peadon, E., and E.J. Elliott. 2010. Distinguishing between attention-deficit hyperactivity and fetal alcohol spectrum disorders in children: Clinical guidelines. *Journal of Neuropsychiatric Disease and Treatment* 6: 509–515.

Pepper-Smith, R., and M. Nelson. 1996. *The assessment of capability in parts two and three of the Adult Guardianship Act: A project to help determine interim standards of practice, with a focus on the mid-Vancouver Island region*. Unpublished government document, Nanaimo.

Perske, R. 1994. Thoughts on the police interrogation of individuals with mental retardation. *Mental Retardation* 32: 377–380.

Personal Directives Act.

Reid-Proctor, G.M., K. Galin, and M.A. Cummings. 2001. Evaluation of legal competency in patients with frontal lobe injury. *Brain Injury* 15: 377–386.

Riley, E.P., C.L. McGee, and E.R. Sowell. 2004. Teratogenic effect of alcohol: A decade of brain imaging. *American Journal of Medical Genetics* 127C: 35–41.

Schulman, K.I., C.A. Cohen, F.C. Kirsh, et al. 2007. Assessment of testamentary capacity and vulnerability to undue influence. *The American Journal of Psychiatry* 164: 722–727.

Silberfeld, M. 1994. Evaluating decisions in mental capacity assessments. *International Journal of Geriatric Psychiatry* 9 (5): 365–371.

Silberfeld, M., and D. Checkland. 1999. Faulty judgement, expert opinion, and decision-making capacity. *Theoretical Medicine and Bioethics* 20: 377–393.

Sood, B., V. Delaney-Black, C. Covington, B. Nordstrom-Klee, J. Ager, T. Templin, and R.J. Sokol. 2001. Prenatal alcohol exposure and childhood behavior at age 6–7 years: I. Dose-response effect. *Pediatrics* 108 (2): e34.

Streissguth, A.P., F. Bookstein, H.M. Barr, P.D. Sampson, K. O'Malley, and J.K. Young. 2004. Risk factors for adverse life outcomes in fetal alcohol syndrome and fetal alcohol effects. *Journal of Developmental and Behavioral Pediatrics* 25: 228–238.

Thomas, S.E., S.J. Kelly, and S.N. Mattson. 1998. Comparison of social abilities of children with fetal alcohol syndrome to those of children with similar IQ scores and normal controls. *Alcoholism: Clinical and Experimental Research* 22: 528–533.

Weinberg, J., J.H. Sliwowska, N. Lan, and K.C.G. Hellemans. 2008. Prenatal alcohol exposure: Foetal programming, the hypothalamic-pituitary-adrenal axis and sex differences in outcome. *Journal of Neuroendocrinology* 20: 470–488.

Weisstub, D.N. 1990. *Enquiry on mental competency: Final report*. Submitted to the Canadian Minister of Health on September 18.

Wyszynski, A.A., and C.F. Garfein. 2005. Assessing decisional capacity and informed consent in medical patients: A short, practical guide. In *Manual of psychiatric care for the medically ill*, ed. A.A. Wyszynski and B. Wyszynski. Washington, DC: American Psychiatric Publishing, Inc.

Chapter 14
Legislative Impediments to Judicial Consideration of Moral Blameworthiness in Sentencing FASD Affected Offenders – A Canadian Perspective

Jonathan Rudin

Keywords FASD · Sentencing · Proportionality · Mandatory minimum · Conditional sentence

14.1 Introduction

The fundamental principle behind sentencing in most (or many) jurisdictions is the idea of proportionality. Although the concept of proportionality is found in the Criminal Code, it existed as touchstone for judges well before it was formally placed in the Code in 1996 as part of a comprehensive set of sentencing principles in Bill C-41.

What is proportionality? Section 718.1 of the Criminal Code, a section headed "fundamental principle" states: "A sentence must be proportionate to the gravity of the offence and the degree of responsibility of the offender."

The notion that a proportionate sentence has two aspects to it is often missing from popular discourse. For many people, the only issue that should weigh on the sentence someone receives is the gravity of the offence. Expressions like "if you do the crime, you do the time" reflect this viewpoint. Objections are often raised to perceived disparities in sentencing because it is not always clear to the general public why person A received a sentence that seems to be so different from that received by person B even though the offence was the same.

J. Rudin (✉)
Aboriginal Legal Services, Toronto, Canada

Faculty of Liberal Arts and Professional Studies, Osgoode Hall Law School Graduate Program, York University, Toronto, Canada

FASD Justice Committee, Toronto, Canada
e-mail: cglane@telus.net; clanegoodfellow@gmail.com

E. Jonsson et al. (eds.), *Ethical and Legal Perspectives in Fetal Alcohol Spectrum Disorders (FASD)*, International Library of Ethics, Law, and the New Medicine 75,
https://doi.org/10.1007/978-3-319-71755-5_14

A large part of the explanation for such apparent disparities is the second branch of proportionality, namely the degree of responsibility of the offender. While focusing on the nature of the offence may push towards harsher sentences, a look at responsibility can exercise a moderating trend. In 2012, in R v. Ipeelee,[1] the Supreme Court of Canada said:

> …the principle of proportionality ensures that a sentence does not exceed what is appropriate, given the moral blameworthiness of the offender. In this sense, the principle serves a limiting or restraining function and ensures justice for the offender.[2]

The notion of moral blameworthiness explains why two people charged with the same offence, even as co-accused may receive different sentences. It may be that one of the individuals was the directing mind, the other was the follower. One person may have an extensive criminal record and an apparent disregard for rules and the other may have been under particular stress that led to one significant slip.

Moral blameworthiness helps to inform what an appropriate sentence might be in an instrumental sense as well. If an offender has no prior record, a supportive environment and if the offence can be placed in a context to allow a judge to think that there is little reason to think the behaviour will reoccur, then it is reasonable to think that the sentence for this individual will be different than for someone with a long record and no apparent interest in changing their behaviour. Why jail someone who has no need for jail and whose behaviour can be controlled in the community?

The Criminal Code recognizes that proportionality will dictate different sentences because the range of sentence for many offences is quite broad. Manslaughter (section 232 of the Criminal Code of Canada), which is committed by someone who causes the unlawful death of someone without intending to cause death, thus with less intent to cause harm than murder, is punishable by up to life imprisonment. There is however no minimum sentence for manslaughter.[3] A judge in a manslaughter case therefore has the broadest possible range to choose from in trying to determine a sentence. How can such a wide range of sentence occur? Because even though this is among the most serious offences that can be committed, the circumstances in which the offence takes place and the level of responsibility of the offender can vary tremendously.

Criminal law assumes that people who commit offences intend their actions. The legal definition of 'not criminally responsible" – what was previously referred to as not guilty by reason of insanity – has little to do with medical notions of insanity. According to the Canadian Department of Justice:

[1] R v. Ipeelee (Supreme Court of Canada) (http://canlii.ca/t/fqq00).

[2] Ipeelee at para. 37.

[3] However, if a firearm is used in the commission of the offence then there is a 4 year mandatory minimum – Criminal Code section 236(a).

> If a person is found to have committed the act that constitutes an offence, but lacked the capacity to appreciate what they did, or know that it was wrong, due to a mental disorder at the time, the court makes a special verdict of Not Criminally Responsible on Account of Mental Disorder.[4]

The bar to being found NCR is then clearly set very high. Many people who commit crimes while suffering from a mental disorder know what they are doing and know it is wrong – but for any number of reasons they do it anyway. These individuals are not NCR, but their responsibility for their actions will likely be much less than someone who commits the same crime to inflict pain or for personal gain.

Canadian criminal law also recognizes that when people are younger they have a harder time determining what is and is not appropriate behaviour. For this reason Canada has a separate youth justice system that applies to those between the ages of 12 to 18. One of the principles of the Youth Criminal Justice Act is that the youth justice system "must be based on the principle of diminished moral blameworthiness."[5]

14.2 Proportionality and the FASD Affected Offender

People who are FASD affected commit crime; in fact there is reason to believe that these individuals are over-represented in the criminal justice system.[6] While some of this crime is of a very minor nature and can be dealt with extra-judicially, sometimes the offences are quite serious and require the full attention of the judicial system. In those cases, and where the judge has an awareness both of FASD generally and how it manifests itself in the offender specifically, it is the consideration of moral blameworthiness that results in the crafting of a sentence that is truly proportionate.

In R v. Harper,[7] Judge Lillies of the Yukon Territorial Court stated:

> The Code's two-pronged proportionality consideration, which takes into account both the harm or potential harm occasioned by an offence and also the moral blameworthiness of the offender, is critical to the Canadian understanding of fundamental justice. It is moral blameworthiness that justifies the stigma and punishment of a criminal sanction and that animates the determination of a "just" sentence.

---

[4] Accessed from: http://www.justice.gc.ca/eng/news-nouv/nr-cp/2013/doc_32899.html

[5] YCJA s. 3(b), see also R v D.B. (Supreme Court of Canada) (http://canlii.ca/t/1wxc8) at para. 41, 45.

[6] Recommendation 17 from the Consensus Statement on Legal Issues of Fetal Alcohol Spectrum Disorder (FASD) states: "The Supreme Court of Canada has recognized that the overrepresentation of Aboriginal persons among the inmate population constitutes a crisis in the criminal justice system. In the jury's view, the over-representation of people with FASD in correctional facilities and in care of child protection agencies is of overlapping and equal concern" (Binnie et al. 2013, at p. 13).

[7] R v. Harper (Yukon Territorial Court) (http://canlii.ca/t/22pqx).

> Where FASD is diagnosed, failing to take it into account during sentencing works an injustice to both the offender and society at large. The offender is failed because he is being held to a standard that he cannot possibly attain, given his impairments. As noted by Judge Barry Stuart in R. v. Sam, FASD takes away someone's "ability … to act within the norms expected by society" and it is manifestly unfair to make an individual pay for their disability with their freedom. Society is failed because a sentence calculated for a "normal" offender cannot serve the same ends when imposed on an offender with FASD; it will not contribute to respect for the law, and neither will it contribute to the maintenance of a just, peaceful and safe society.[8]

An example of how courts deal with the sentencing of an FASD affected offender can be found in the 2012 case of R v. Soosay.[9] In that case, Justice Anderson of the Alberta Provincial Court grappled with the implications of the diminished moral blameworthiness of a young FASD offender when balanced against the fact that he committed two robberies and a break and enter. Justice Anderson stated "FASD presents a huge and unique challenge to sentencing courts. It is a bit like the elephant in the room."[10]

Given the gravity of the offences, the crown was seeking a penitentiary sentence of almost 3 years.[11] While acknowledging that such a sentence might be justified in some circumstances, Justice Anderson found that in this case it:

> ignores the accused's personal circumstances, particularly his cognitive deficiencies and the challenges presented by a pre-natal brain injury, all of which are clearly part and parcel of the offender's involvement in these offences.[12]

For the judge, in order to craft a proportionate sentence it was necessary to take into account the offender's diminished capacity and thus reduced moral blameworthiness. With respect to the robberies he received a 2 month sentence on top of time served, primarily to allow him to work with staff to develop a release plan.[13] For the break and enter he received a 4 month conditional sentence which allowed him to serve the sentence in the community under particular conditions.[14]

These cases, and many others,[15] illustrate how the notion of proportionality, particularly the concept of moral blameworthiness, can be used to find a fit sentence for an FASD offender. These individuals are in law, criminally responsible, but to act as though they have the same capacity as everyone else to make decisions is to ignore the reality of FASD in their lives.

---

[8] Harper at para 34, 38.

[9] R v. Soosay (Alberta Provincial Court) (http://canlii.ca/t/fs6vd).

[10] Soosay at para 26.

[11] Soosay at para 38.

[12] Soosay at para 29.

[13] Soosay at para 47.

[14] Soosay at para 48.

[15] A comprehensive list of cases dealing with the sentencing of FASD affected offenders and be found in the case law section of the FASD and the Justice System website: http://fasdjustice.ca/cases.html

Recent changes to the Criminal Code however are making it harder to arrive at truly proportionate sentences and are focused almost totally on the perceived gravity of the offence. The problem with disproportionate sentences is that they not only do not take into account the realities of the offender, but they do not necessarily contribute to community safety, and in fact, may make things worse.

14.3 The New Sentencing Landscape

The 1996 sentencing amendments in Bill C-41 marked a conscious move by Parliament away from a reliance on incarceration to deal with criminal offending. One practical way in which Bill C-41 attempted to accomplish this goal was through the creation of a new type of sanction – the conditional sentence. As noted in the discussion earlier regarding R v. Soosay, conditional sentences essentially allow offenders to serve what would otherwise be jail sentences in the community under tighter scrutiny and with more conditions than would be possible in a traditional probation order.

This new direction in sentencing was remarked upon by the Supreme Court of Canada in a number of cases, including R v. Gladue[16] in 1999 and R v. Proulx[17] in 2000. However, soon after these decisions, Parliament began a retreat from the principles of restraint in sentencing. This retreat appears to have culminated in 2012 with the passage of the Bill C-10, the Safe Streets and Communities Act.

In 1996, when C-41 was enacted, there were very few mandatory minimum sentences in Canada. The ones that were most well known and widely relied upon were the sentences for first and second degree murder which were life sentences with mandatory jail for 25 and 10 years respectively.[18] After the passage of C-10 there are now approximately 50 mandatory minimum sentences in the Criminal Code and the Controlled Drugs and Substances Act. Most mandatory minimum sentences now deal with the use of firearms, drugs and sexual offences involving those under 16.

The purpose of a mandatory minimum sentence is to take discretion in sentencing away from the judge. The judge is still required to arrive at a proportionate sentence, but the floor for that sentence is now set by Parliament. Mandatory minimum sentences are generally not required for hard core repeat offenders as they would likely receive jail in any event, rather their impact is felt most directly on what has been described as "the best offender", the person who may have the best opportunity for a rehabilitative and restorative sentence that would otherwise avoid prison (Roach 2001, at p. 390).

---

[16] R v. Gladue (Supreme Court of Canada) (http://canlii.ca/t/1fqp2).

[17] R v. Proulx (Supreme Court of Canada) (http://canlii.ca/t/527b).

[18] Although there was an opportunity for those convicted of first degree murder to apply for earlier parole after 15 years through the use of what is referred to as the faint hope clause. Access to the faint hope clause has been reduced over the years.

The rise in mandatory minimum sentences can have a particular impact on the sentencing of an FASD affected offender. There are many possible examples that could be provided but consider sections 151 and 152 of the Criminal Code – sexual interference and invitation to sexual touching. Both these offences target those who engage or seek to engage in sexual activity with a person under 16. The definitions of both offences are very broad and in the case of sexual interference can include kissing and fondling. The mandatory minimum sentence for both offences is 90 days if prosecuted summarily and 1 year if by indictment.[19]

Because adolescents engage in consensual sexual activity the Code provides for age exceptions. Where the victim in the offence is under 14 (but over 12) then consent is allowed as long as the other party is less than 2 years older than the victim. If the victim is over 14 and under 18, then the age gap is expanded to under 5 years.[20]

For an FASD affected individual however, chronological age is but one, and a very imprecise, measure of the person's ability to understand and appreciate the nature of their actions. Many FASD affected individuals are more comfortable and prefer the company of people who are chronologically younger than they are. A 19 year old FASD affected person might well have a 13 year old boy friend or girl friend.[21] What might be seen as an exploitative relationship if the 19 year old were not cognitively impaired, might not be viewed in the same light if the person has cognitive impairments. Without a mandatory minimum, the sentencing judge could take the cognitive impairment into consideration in fashioning a proportionate sentence. With a mandatory minimum the judge has no choice; the FASD affected person would automatically be going to jail.

While much of the focus in terms of sentencing amendments post 1996 has focused on the proliferation of new mandatory minimums, the increased restrictions on the use of conditional sentences may be more significant. In 1996, when they were introduced, conditional sentences applied to any offence for which there was no mandatory minimum and where the judge determined that the appropriate jail sentence, were one to be imposed, would be under 2 years. Since 2000, this expansive approach to conditional sentences has been continually whittled way until now the conditional sentence can only be applied in very few situations and almost none where there has been any physical harm or where the target of a property crime was a residence or the theft of a car.

---

[19] There will more discussion of the election between summary and indictable offences later in this article.

[20] Criminal Code of Canada 150.1 (2) and (2.1).

[21] If the issue in the case is whether or not the offender took reasonable steps to determine the age of the victim, then expert evidence on the impact of FASD on the decision-making capabilities of the accused person can be provided to a jury – see R v. Sinclair (2013, Alberta Queen's Bench) (http://canlii.ca/t/g2jtl).

Preventing judges from relying on conditional sentences does not require that the offender be sent to jail. The judge still has the option of jail or a non-custodial probationary sentence. The problem is, that with the more directive and specific options available in a conditional sentence off the table, it will be more likely that judges will opt for jail.

This too will likely have a negative impact on FASD affected offenders. Previously a well crafted plan that identified individuals and programs that could assist the offender in living in the community could result in a conditional sentence. Such a sentence would be a proportionate response that addressed concerns for public safety and moral blameworthiness. Without that option, FASD affected individuals are more likely going to find themselves sent to jail.

As noted earlier, the rise in mandatory minimums and also the taking away of conditional sentences is really an attempt to restrict the exercise of discretion by judges. This does not mean that discretion in the criminal justice system is removed, it is simply transferred from judges to crown attorneys. Criminal offences do not come labeled with clear lines around them that distinguish one offence from another.

The offence of robbery, which is not eligible for a conditional sentence, is comprised of a theft and an assault each of which individually are eligible. The decision as to what offence to prosecute rests exclusively with the crown attorney. While robbery is seen as a more serious offence than theft and assault, as the maximum sentence is higher for the former, when conditional sentences were available, at the end of the day, it was the judge who determined the fit and proportionate response. The decision by the crown could impact the upper range of sentence, but everything was on the table. That is not the case now where theft and assault can be the subject of a conditional sentence but robbery cannot.

The same is true, to some extent, with respect to mandatory minimum sentences. The decision by the crown attorney as to what offence to prosecute will determine whether there will or will not be a mandatory minimum sentence at play. As noted earlier with respect to the offences of sexual interference and invitation to sexual touching, the mandatory minimums in those cases depend on whether the crown chooses to prosecute the offences summarily or by indictment. If the crown chooses to go by way of indictment the judge has no choice but to start the sentencing discussion at 1 year imprisonment.

When judges exercise discretion their decisions are made in public, with reasons, and are subject to appellate review. When crowns exercise their discretion they need not explain why they did what they did, and for the most part, their decisions are immune for any review at all. The other significant difference between the way discretion is exercised between judges and crowns is that when passing a sentence the judge has all the information before him or her that the parties wish to have considered. When crowns exercise their discretion as to which offence to prosecute, they often have little information with which to make an informed and full decision.

14.4 Options for Change

Legislative initiatives to fetter judicial discretion and to vest more of it with crown attorneys obviously reflect a degree of political will. Just as Parliament was entitled to encourage judicial restraint with respect to the use of imprisonment in Bill C-41, they can turn their back on that approach as they have done with C-10. There are problems with this approach however both judicially and legislatively.

From the judicial perspective, none of the provisions of Bill C-41 have been repealed. Proportionality remains the fundamental principle of sentencing, but yet the ability to determine proportionate sentences is now compromised by an increasing number of mandatory minimums and a restriction on the availability of conditional sentences (Healy 2013).

Legislatively it appears that despite recent amendments to the Criminal Code, many politicians agree that jail is not the place for people with cognitive impairments. In May 2011, Vic Toews, then the Minister for Public Safety[22] and a strong proponent of the law and order agenda, spoke in Calgary at Building Bridges: Mental Health and the Justice System, a Symposium to Promote Collaboration. The Symposium was the result of an initiative by federal, provincial and territorial ministers of justice to look at the issue of mental health and justice.

In his remarks, Minister Toews spoke of the need to move people with mental illnesses out of the prison system and to "stop relying on prisons to act as a parallel health care system to provide care for individuals with mental illness after a crime has been committed."[23] That Bill C-10 was passed subsequent to this address suggests that for whatever reasons these concerns got lost as the legislation was developed.

We are at a point in time where judges and lawyers know more about the realities of FASD and the ways in which it can diminish the moral blameworthiness of offenders before the court than ever before. At the same time, there are fewer opportunities for judges to apply this knowledge in determining a proportionate sentence. So what is to be done? There are basically two sets of options – challenges under the Charter of Rights and Freedoms to mandatory minimum sentences and restrictions on conditional sentences and legislative amendments to the Criminal Code. The former is time consuming and expensive but bypasses political roadblocks. The latter is quicker but requites political will that appears to be absent.

To the limited extent that Charter challenges to mandatory minimum sentences have succeeded, they have been based on s. 12 of the Charter which protects against cruel and unusual punishment.[24] Cruel and unusual punishment has been interpreted by the court as a sentence that is grossly disproportionate to the harm that has

[22] And now a judge on the Manitoba Court of Queens Bench.

[23] See: http://www.hsjcc.on.ca/Resource%20Library/Mental%20Health%20and%20Justice%20Reports/Building%20Bridges%20-%20Mental%20Health%20and%20the%20Justice%20System%20-%20a%20Symposium%20to%20Promote%20Collaboration%20-%202011.pdf at p. 4.

[24] See R. v. Smith 1987 (Supreme Court of Canada) (http://canlii.ca/t/1ftmr).

occurred.[25] Many of the newer mandatory minimums are not likely to be found to be grossly disproportionate as they are not very long periods of incarceration.

It may be possible to argue that what might not be cruel and unusual punishment for someone who has no cognitive impairments is cruel for someone with FASD. There certainly is evidence that FASD affected individuals have a harder time in the prison system. Rather than being grounded in s. 12, such an argument would likely be based on a s. 15 equality rights analysis. The argument would be that while on its face the particular mandatory minimum being challenged treats all offenders in the same way, the law has a disproportionate and discriminatory impact on FASD affected offenders – those with physical and mental disabilities.

There is not a long history of s. 15 challenges to mandatory minimum sentences and none have been launched with FASD as the ground of discrimination. It is impossible to determine at this point whether such a challenge would or would not be successful. What is clear however is that such a challenge would take a great deal of time to litigate, both before the sentencing judge and then during the inevitable appeal(s).

Political change is, theoretically, a more immediate response. There are any number of ways in which a measure of proportionality can be reintroduced into the sentencing process even with mandatory minimums. Most jurisdictions in the world which have mandatory minimums also allow for an escape clause or safety valve where a judge can, in exceptional circumstances, depart from the mandatory minimum (Roberts and Bebbington 2013). Such departures would be subject to appellate review, and in a short while there would likely be a body of case law that would emerge to guide the use of such escape clauses.

It is possible to conceive of more targeted legislative responses. The Consensus Statement on Legal Issues of Fetal Alcohol Spectrum Disorder has two recommendations in this area. With respect to mandatory minimums recommendation 40 states:

> Parliament should craft a statutory exemption that allows judges to justify departures from mandatory sentences where such exemptions are necessary to provide a fit sentence on an offender with a mental disability such as FASD. Such an amendment would allow the courts to develop an appropriate and case-sensitive sentencing jurisprudence for offenders with FASD. (Binnie et al. 2013, at p. 25)

With respect to conditional sentences Recommendation 41 states:

> Parliament should consider greater availability of conditional sentences for persons with an intellectual impairment or neurological disorder such as FASD by allowing exceptions, with reasons, from the statutory exclusions that presently exist. Conditions should be crafted in such a way that they take into account the special challenges faced by those with FASD. (Binnie et al. 2013 at p. 26)

These recommendations, coming about after a 3 days intensive examination of the issue are due great respect and deference. There are however, two potential problems with them.

---

[25] Smith at para 56.

First, the reality is that most FASD affected offenders come before the court without a diagnosis and obtaining such a diagnosis is often very difficult if not impossible within the time that a matter is before the court.[26] If only those with an FASD diagnosis can benefit from legislative amendments, then there will be deserving individuals who will be left behind.

Second, it is not clear why FASD affected individuals and those with other similar mental disabilities (whatever those might be) should be allowed to escape mandatory minimums and/or obtain conditional sentences if others are not. There are other offenders who for any number of reasons should be allowed the opportunity to put forward a case as to why their personal circumstances and diminished moral blameworthiness might mean that a mandatory minimum not apply to them.

It can be argued that perfection in sentencing, while a lofty goal is fundamentally unattainable. It can also be maintained that legislative amendments such as the ones proposed above are best seen as a starting point rather than an end point.

While this is a useful and important discussion to have, whatever actions that might mitigate the deleterious impact caused by preventing judges from arriving at truly proportionate sentences for FASD affected offenders should begin immediately. No individual or societal interest is maintained by jailing someone with a cognitive deficit such as FASD if such imprisonment is not warranted.

References

Binnie, I., M. Trussler, and E. Jonsson. 2013. Legal issues of FASD. Fetal alcohol spectrum disorder. In *Proceedings from a consensus development conference*. ISBN 978-1-897443-36-1. www.ihe.ca

Healy, P. 2013. Sentencing from there to here and from then to now. *Canadian Criminal Law Review* 17 (3): 291–304.

Roach, K. 2001. Searching for smith: The constitutionality of mandatory sentences. *Osgoode Hall Law Journal* 39: 367–412.

Roberts, J., and H. Bebbington. 2013. Sentencing reform in Canada: Promoting a return to principles and evidence-based policy. *Canadian Criminal Law Review* 17 (3): 327–347.

[26] A Private Member's Bill C–583 – An Act to Amend the Criminal Code (Fetal Alcohol Spectrum Disorder) would allow for court ordered assessments for FASD. http://www.parl.gc.ca/HousePublications/Publication.aspx?Language=E&Mode=1&DocId=6497442

Chapter 15
The Alberta Youth Criminal Defence Office - A Model of Advocacy for Youth with FASD

Cathy Lane Goodfellow

Abstract This article describes the advocacy model used by the Youth Criminal Defence Office, a program of Legal Aid Alberta situate in Edmonton and Calgary, Alberta. The model focussed on creating a wrap-around legal approach to young people impacted by FASD that are in conflict with the criminal and quasi-criminal law. Further, the unique staffing dynamic, purposeful training and community invovlement highlight the breadth of knowledge found within the offices and the need to take a multi-disciplinary approach to assist this client group. Last, the artilce discusses gaps in the justice continuum and makes suggestions going forward.

Keywords Specialized advocacy · FASD youth · YCJA

15.1 Introduction

Many jurisdictions have created special rules and legislation to carve out distinctly different management systems for youth who are in conflict with the law. However, when compared to the history of legally regulated society, youth criminal justice appears to be in its infancy.

The first Children's Court in the world was established in Adelaide, South Australia, in 1890. (Newman 1991) In Canada, we saw the start of the youth justice journey in 1857 with An Act for establishing Prisons for Young Offenders – for the better governance of Public Asylums, Hospitals and Prisons, and for the better construction of Common Goals.[1] Although not defined in the enactment, it was clear that it applied to persons 21 years of age and under who were sentenced to a period of incarceration. The Act allowed such persons to be sent to "Reformatory Prisons" instead of the regular Provincial Penitentiaries and differentiated the length of the term of incarceration in a Reformatory for persons over and under the age of 16. Notably, one section of the Act allowed a Ship to be designated a Reformatory

[1] Statutes of the Province of Canada, 2nd Session, Fifth Parliament of Canada, 1857, c.28.

C. Lane Goodfellow (✉)
Formerly Senior Counsel at the Alberta Youth Criminal Defence Office, Calgary, Canada
e-mail: clanegoodfellow@gmail.com

E. Jonsson et al. (eds.), *Ethical and Legal Perspectives in Fetal Alcohol Spectrum Disorders (FASD)*, International Library of Ethics, Law, and the New Medicine 75,
https://doi.org/10.1007/978-3-319-71755-5_15

Prison for those offenders "...as may desire a seafaring life…". Although this may offer some insight into the living conditions found in the Provincial Penitentiaries of that time but one might also speculate as to the lifespan of a seafarer in the 1800s. One hundred and fifty one years later, the Supreme Court of Canada gave a name to the underlying philosophy for the separate system: there is a presumption of diminished moral culpability for young persons and that presumption is a principle of fundamental justice.[2]

This chapter focuses on the Youth Criminal Defence Office (YCDO), which has been a program of Legal Aid Alberta (LAA) since 1993. It examines the YCDO advocacy model, as it has developed over time, and how it is well-positioned to assist FASD affected youth and their families to navigate the justice system. The YCDO is a truly unique system, there is no such a facility elsewhere in Canada, and therefore it has no comparator in a potential scientific assessment of its success.

15.2 Staffing

The YCDO model is comprised of administrative staff, 16 lawyers and 6 youth workers as of 2014. It has offices in both Edmonton and Calgary.

Each of the two offices present themselves as a distinct law office with a primary focus on youth in conflict with the law. Any person who has committed a crime between the ages of 12 and 17 is eligible to be a client. The flow of assigned file work comes through the application filter of LAA. A youth, charged with a criminal offence, applies to LAA for counsel. In Alberta, the right to counsel under s. 25 of the Youth Criminal Justice Act (YCJA)[3] has been interpreted as universal which results in a youth receiving either counsel at the YCDO or, in the case of conflict, from a roster of lawyers prepared to receive files and be paid according to the LAA tariff. Any youth charged with homicide has choice of any counsel – YCDO or roster.

The YCDO administrative staff manage the data flow of files that are forwarded through a successful application for counsel with LAA, provide administrative assistance to lawyers and youth workers and are the vital first contact with youth and their families as they commence the navigation of the justice process. Systems and liaisons established with other stakeholder groups: courthouse, probation and correctional institution staff for instance, have developed over time to create an effective coordination of information that allows the lawyers and youth workers to know which youth is in court, how many youth are without assigned counsel, whom is appearing in and out of custody and the status of all charges. The administrative staff is also the first contact for members of the public seeking information or for walk-in youth looking for assistance, often both professional and personal.

---

[2] R. v. D.B., (2008] 2 S.C.R .3.

[3] S.C. 2002, c. 1 as amended.

Anecdotally, often these youth present as hungry, dirty, homeless, dissociative and emotionally distraught. Working in a specialized office, administrative staff take advantage of both internal and external training opportunities to learn skills to assist in communicating with and de-escalating youth (and sometimes their parents, supporters and friends).

Lawyers working at the YCDO have developed a specialized expertise in the area of youth criminal justice. The author is unaware of any Canadian Law School that includes in its curriculum a course dedicated to the youth criminal justice process and resultant legal issues. Therefore, specialized competency in this area has come as a result of practice, internal leadership identifying areas of skills and knowledge development and the strategic dedication of training dollars.

15.2.1 Promising Practices

In 2012, all YCDO staff met as a group and put to writing a working philosophy of promising practices,[4] which is described in the following.

15.2.1.1 YCDO Lawyers

- Are committed to providing necessary legal services to young persons in Edmonton and Calgary who come into conflict with the law, including Brydges service[5] (on a rotational basis 24 h, 7 days a week) and duty counsel services. Where the young person is charged with homicide, Brydges service also includes personal attendance at the place of detent ion. Duty counsel will attempt to obtain bail for young persons who are detained, engaging where appropriate the services of a youth worker to help establish the plan/conditions that will facilitate release and compliance with release conditions. YCDO lawyers will communicate the status of clients served as Brydges/duty counsel to the client's assigned counsel in order to help ensure that clients receive timely service and lawyers are informed of significant developments in their clients' matters;
- Are familiar with and employ all available resources in pursuit of the objectives of the Youth Criminal Justice Act[6] and the best outcomes for clients. Examples include Extra-judicial Sanctions, diversion programs (e.g., mental health), s. 19

[4] The YCDO was under the leadership of then Senior Counsel Greg Francis who is largely responsible for the synthesis of ideas and information from the meeting. Mr. Francis left the YCDO in December 2012 and is now General Counsel for the Calgary Board of Education.

[5] Infra footnote 48.

[6] s.c. 2002, c. 1.

conferences (which includes FASD conferencing), Gladue reports[7] and sentencing circles;

- Facilitate a multi-disciplinary, holistic and therapeutic approach to addressing client needs, recognizing that conflict with the law is an acute indicia of more complex and ongoing challenges in a young person's life. We therefore look for opportunities to engage appropriate support services to address these challenges, starting with YCDO youth workers;
- Look for opportunities to influence developments in the law by identifying and preparing significant cases at trial or on sentence, advancing appeals (when instructed by the client) and by making submissions to government and law reform bodies;
- Work as a team when defending complex cases at trial, advocating policy changes, and advancing significant cases on appeal;
- Contribute significantly to the efficient operation of docket court, arriving on time and prepared to conduct cases;
- As duty counsel, ensure that those youth needing assistance receive adequate information to understand the process and adequate assistance commensurate with the jeopardy faced in court that day. Youth in custody must be connected with counsel capable of addressing bail at the earliest opportunity.

YCDO lawyers are assigned files and represent accused young persons at every stage of the justice process from first appearance to appeal. YCDO lawyers have appeared before the Supreme Court of Canada twice.[8] Furthermore, if a youth reoffends, that youth, barring a conflict, continues with the same lawyer. This is another way in which continuity of legal care occurs.[9]

What makes the YCDO unique in Canada is the addition of youth workers to the advocacy model. The youth workers are the relationship builders. They support young people when they are in crisis, through pre-trial, and potentially post-trial or sentencing. For example, in March, 2014, a young person in Calgary charged with first degree murder was supported by a youth worker throughout her multi-week trial. The youth worker met with the client continuously in the correctional institution, sat in court with the youth's family and provided emotional and debriefing support. That kind of support may be of great importance, considering both the anxiety, fear and stress before and during the appearance in front of a judge in a courtroom, and of the physical and brain developments that continues during adolescence.

[7] In R. v.Gladue (1999]1 S.C.R.688, the Supreme Court of Canada interpreted s.718.2(e) of the Criminal Code of Canada. That section requires a sentencing court to consider all available sanctions other than imprisonment that are reasonable in the circumstances with particular attention to the circumstances of Aboriginal offenders. Sentencing courts have requested reports to be prepared for aboriginal offenders that contain, inter alia, a culturally sensitive and relevant background investigation. These reports are referred to as "Gladue Reports".

[8] B..v. D.((.): .B..v.K.CC.D.l. (2005) 3 S.C.R. 668 as appellants and .B... v.P.CB.W.l: R. v. N. (B.V.l.(2006) 1S.C.R. 941 as intervenors.

[9] "Legal care" to the author means more than legal representation in court. It includes support and relationship building with the client.

Traditionally lawyers tell their clients to not talk about the details of their offences pre-trial. Add to this mix the reality of adolescence – the developing brain and with it, an individualized moral code. Youth workers provide a confidential outlet that fills a huge gap that traditionally and typically exists in the criminal justice process. In another example, throughout 2013, youth workers provided support through personal contact to a First Nations youth from Northern Alberta serving a sentence in Edmonton as he had very limited access to his immediate family or community.

Youth workers have a role at every entry point of the justice system. They create relationships with government departments, justice stakeholders, youth focused agencies, caregivers, and parents. They assist with duty counsel, assigned counsel, roster lawyers, and private counsel and their professional training is very specific which allows them to identify and respond to risk and crisis. Lastly, the youth workers engage in resource development where there are gaps. This will be discussed in greater detail below.

15.2.1.2 Youth Workers

According to the YCDO Best Practices document, youth workers work closely with lawyers to help clients overcome their challenges and create the conditions necessary for healthy development and success in avoiding conflict with the law. Youth workers:

- Understand the fundamental principles of the Youth Justice system, especially judicial interim release and sentencing;
- Help the client to identify and communicate the client's own, self-identified issues–making sure the client's voice is heard;
- Assist the client in negotiations or negotiate on behalf of the client where the client is unable to do so;
- Where appropriate, mediate conflict in the client's life;
- Maintain high standard of integrity and professionalism, and behave at all times as if an officer of the Court. Youth workers are seen as trusted and reliable professionals by Judges and Crown Prosecutors, essential to the effective operation of Youth Court;
- Advocate for clients to receive required services, including shelter, appropriate adult support and supervision, education, psychological and medical treatment, addictions treatment;
- Assist with interviewing clients, parents and guardians, and witnesses in the preparation of legal proceedings;
- Make referrals to appropriate services and assist clients with transportation;
- Create release plans for youth in custody that assist in generating results in judicial release and sentencing hearings.

The philosophy of legal care at the YCDO creates a wrap-around competency to assist young people. The coordination and management of that resource, at this point in time, is based on client need and flexible prioritization.

15.3 Justice Entry Points and Continuity of Legal Care

The touch or entry points into the justice system include the following:

- Police investigation and arrest;
- Interview of youth by police (depending on the seriousness of the charge, may
- include a telephone call to a lawyer for advice, referred to as a Brydges call[10]);
- Judicial interim release by a Peace Officer, before a Justice of the Peace or Judge;
- First appearance in docket court for plea;
- Diversion to Extrajudicial Sanctions[11] 12 or a Mental Health Diversion program;
- Application for counsel to Legal Aid Alberta (under s. 25 of the YCJA);
- Sentencing after guilty plea;
- Trial;
- Sentencing after finding guilt;
- Appeal.

Typically there would be no or very little continuity of legal care for an accused until there is either a successful application to LAA private counsel retained. The areas in which the YCDO offer services create a non-traditional continuity that seeks to honour the statements of principle found in s. 3 of the YCJA which speaks to preventing crime by addressing the circumstances underlying a young person's offending behavior, emphasizing rehabilitation and reintegration, enhanced procedural protection and timely intervention.

The following explains, in more detail, some of the specific functions of the YCDO.

15.3.1 Brydges Calls

Each YCDO office has a cell phone dedicated to receiving these calls. Every day of the week, Monday to Sunday, a lawyer is assigned to receive any call that comes in. Although some calls are received during business hours, most are received between the hours of 5 pm and 8 am. The significance of the work performed is not ascertainable by simply looking at the bare number of calls received. A single call always involves a discussion with the client but may prompt several other calls not captured

[10] This refers to the case of & v. Brydges (1990), 74 C.R. (3d) 129 which established, inter alia, the duty of the police to expressly tell detainees about any Legal Aid and duty counsel services in existence and available at the time of detention.

[11] Extrajudicial sanctions refers to a post-charge process that allows for a diversion outside of the justice process. That diversion includes an acknowledgement of accountability and completion of a consequence that is assigned. Upon successful completion the criminal charge is withdrawn in court. See sections 4–12 of the YCJA. In adult court this process is referred to as Alternative Measures and is referred to in s. 717 of the Criminal Code of Canada R.S.C. 1985, c. C-46 as amended.

by the statistics. Collateral calls include those to parents, caregivers, youth workers, social workers, police, probation and may include participation in a hearing before a Justice of the Peace via teleconference. If the youth is charged with a homicide the general practice is to personally attend where the youth is being held regardless of the hour of the day. The call may also prompt email communication with other members of the office who are already assigned counsel for the youth on other matters or who are duty counsel in court the next day. During 2013 there were 4159 calls managed by YCDO staff.

15.3.1.1 Duty Counsel Service

Each office provides duty counsel services to Youth Justice Court. In Edmonton there is one docket court[12] in operation and in Calgary there are two. Each day lawyers are assigned to this role and youth workers also attend to assist both counsel and clients. Again, the significance of the work performed is not reflected by the number of assists. Duty counsel service includes:

- Interviewing the client out of custody;
- Interviewing the client in custody at the courthouse;
- Interviewing the client via closed circuit television from their custodial placement;
- Obtaining information from caregivers, guardians, probation officers, youth workers or other collaterals;
- Directing clients to Legal Aid Alberta Legal Services Officers for intake;
- Speaking to the crown regarding early case resolution or reviewing disclosure;
- Referring to the YCDO youth worker for assistance when personal or social issues are identified;
- Obtaining information from court personnel – reviewing Informations or other court documents;
- Setting trial dates;
- Making referrals to Child and Family Services either directly or by requesting an order of the Court under s. 35[13] of the YCJA;
- Entering guilty pleas and speaking to sentence;
- Debriefing with the youth.

Every day lawyers come into contact with youth who have complex personal or social issues, some of which are mentally and/or physically ill, cognitively impaired,

---

[12] Docket courts are courtrooms specifically designated to hear preliminary matters such as judicial interim release hearings, adjournments and initial pleas or where matters are deal with summarily by guilty plea. They are called "docket" courts because there is a docket list or schedule of pending cases for that particular court per juridical day. Youth charged with criminal or provincial offences (or both) appear in Youth Justice docket court.

[13] S. 35 reads: "In addition to any order that it is authorized to make, a youth justice court may, at any stage of proceedings against a young person, refer the young person to a child welfare agency for assessment to determine whether the young person is in need of child welfare services."

intoxicated or unfit. Some youth can present as naive, vacant, confused, scared, histrionic, anxious or belligerent. These factors complicate the interviewing and information sharing aspects for the lawyers who strive to provide information in a meaningful way, using language that is appropriate to their age and understanding. A total of 5524 youth were assisted by YCDO duty counsel in the two cities during 2013.

15.3.2 Attendance Court

The YCDO also provides duty counsel service to young people facing civil contempt applications under the School Act[14] in the Court of Queen's Bench. This service is not reflected in the YCDO data collecting system. Generally, the process involves providing legal information to youth who are under 16, the statutory school-leaving age, and, where needed, making recommendations to the court. This service occurs approximately four times per year. In Edmonton the hearings tend to occur over a 1 day period where 8–12 youth are assisted. In Calgary, the hearings tend to cover a one to 3 day period where 8–20 youth are assisted. If necessary, referrals are made to the YCDO youth workers. An effort is made to determine if any youth on the docket list for this court are also clients of the YCDO so that there can be continuity of care. One can easily see that the consequences available to the Justice: an adjournment, fine or probation order, are often woefully inappropriate for a youth who's chronic school absenteeism is often a longstanding social, emotional or family of origin issue that has gone unaddressed. Given the very specific knowledge base concerning adolescent behavior and available ameliorating resources that has come from years of practical application and experience, YCDO staff are well placed to provide meaningful input and suggest novel approaches in this civil environment. As an example, in one case the author successfully persuaded the presiding Queen's Bench Justice to order an assessment to determine if the youth fell on the FASD spectrum. Knowledge of Youth Justice Court practices resulted in finding a funding source. After several weeks the diagnosis was confirmed, provided new insight to the school board for the young person's educational management and opened up more resources for the youth and his family going forward.

15.3.3 Extrajudicial Sanctions Support

Extrajudicial sanctions is a diversion program that, if completed by the youth, results in criminal charges being withdrawn. A youth worker in each office is tasked with explaining the program, offering assistance to the youth during the process, liaising with program personnel and advocating for re-referrals. The goal, of course,

[14] R.S.A. 2000, c. S-3, as amended.

is successful completion. This service is offered to clients of the office and to youth managed by duty counsel. In Calgary, the assigned youth worker keeps statistics, which shows that 354 youth were assisted by her during 2013.

Once charged, the crown prosecutors' office decides, based on policy and subjective analysis, whether a youth can be referred to this program. Experience tells that sometimes this gatekeeping decision has been influenced by an assessment of the cognitive or behavioural ability of the youth to be successful given the programs or tasks typically asked of referred youth to complete. In early 2014 the Calgary youth worker assigned to this area participated at an organizational meeting that included the Calgary FASD Coordinator, and the Extrajudicial Sanctions Coordinator, both with Alberta Justice and Solicitor General (Ministry of Justice), to develop a referral plan to a newly formed youth justice committee designed to support youth who are low functioning or either have or suspected of having an FASD diagnosis. This new committee is comprised of volunteers that are supported by the FASD Coordinator. YCDO staff plays a pivotal role in the process by liaising with the crown prosecutor in docket court, flagging youth for this specialized committee, being available to offer additional support and reporting the outcomes to either assigned counsel or duty counsel. This diversion opportunity seems to have the ability to impact the over-representation of FASD affected youth in the justice system.

15.3.4 Traffic Court

The YCDO lawyers in Edmonton attend to Traffic Court on the second and fourth Wednesdays of every month. This service is reflected in the previously mentioned statistics for duty counsel. It should be noted that although this service is a natural extension of the philosophy of care for youth in conflict with the law, a young person with a traffic ticket is not eligible for Legal Aid coverage unless the ticket relates to a criminal charge.

Again, YCDO staff are well placed to provide meaningful input. Also, identifying risk factors for criminal behavior at this stage allows for referrals to youth workers and community resources that may impact the perpetuation of anti-social behavior.

15.3.5 "First Appearance Resource Individual" or "FAR" Court

Since 2010, a youth or social worker from YCDO Calgary has attended the Calgary Courts Center, First Appearance Court, on the first Thursday of every month to assist youth charged with city by-law infractions (for example graffiti tickets) or provincial offences. A strong working relationship has developed with the City's crown prosecutor's office that has resulted in unique, novel and individualistic approaches to resolving matters with youth. More recently a partnership has developed with the University of Calgary's Faculty of Law so that law students can receive some practical experience by attending and offering summary advice to these youth. The YCDO Calgary social worker assigned to this role has also developed working relationships with School Resource Officers, Probation Officers and Non-Profit organizations who call her for information or referrals. The following illustrates the impact of having a specialized advocate appearing at this court level:

In March of 2013, the YCDO social worker met a young person named D.Q. at First Appearance Court. She immediately became aware of his cognitive challenges during their initial conversation. D.Q. had several tickets, some of which were at warrant status or where convictions had been entered in absence of appearance. His seven tickets included transit fare violations, graffiti, skateboarding on transit property, loitering on transit property and urinating in public. D.Q. owed hundreds of dollars. The YCDO social worker contacted some collaterals in his life and discovered that his program placement seemed exhausted by his behavior and unaware of resources that may have been of assistance. Given his disability, D.Q. had only a marginal ability to find or maintain employment and to pay for or successfully work off outstanding fines. Without assistance D.Q. would be at risk of cycling through the warrant process when fines are unpaid continuously. It was discovered that while D.Q. had a bus pass, he would forget to take it and forget to come to court. The YCDO social worker adjourned the court process for the live tickets, spoke to a crown prosecutor with the City of Calgary, and enlisted the assistance of a YCDO lawyer to reverse the tickets where a conviction had been entered. The City of Calgary crown prosecutor had a personal conversation with D.Q. with an emphasis on conveying the reason these laws exist and a go-forward plan for D.Q. to consider, in an appropriate and meaningful language. The tickets were withdrawn. The YCDO is unaware of any further offending behavior and D.Q, now 18, does not have the burden of what would seem an insurmountable sum of fines. This is not to say that youth who commit these types of nuisance behaviours should, en masse, be forgiven without consequence. Advocacy at this court level allows for accommodation where there seems to be no advantage to prosecute and every reason to consider a different approach to behaviour – the goal always being to ameliorate it.

15.3.6 Edmonton Young Offender Centre – Legal Information

Once every 4 weeks a lawyer from YCDO Edmonton attends at the Edmonton Young Offender Centre to provide information, *inter alia*, to youth who have been sentenced about review and appeal processes. This process has the potential of assisting youth from other jurisdictions where there is no specialized counsel available.

15.4 Purposeful Training on FASD

The YCDO's experience with training around the diagnosis of FASD began in 2002 with a 2 day conference in Calgary entitled "Fetal Alcohol Spectrum Disorder Training for Legal Professionals" which was funded in part by the Alberta Law Foundation and the Government of Alberta. The YCDO contributed in kind by providing copies of written materials to all participants.[15] Members of the judiciary, lawyers and members of other stakeholder groups attended. This conference was replicated in Edmonton in April 2005. As an understanding of the diagnosis grew, staff at the YCDO participated in seminars and conferences[16] that linked the diagnosis with criminal behaviour which then informed a best practice approach that could be used at each of the touch points of the justice system. The YCDO's depth of knowledge in this particular area continues to evolve and the offices have a high level of credibility within the legal community, the judiciary and all associated stakeholder groups.

The training YCDO staff have had exposure to makes them better able to identify the red flags raised by a potential or actual diagnosis of FASD. However, being aware of a young person's disability without having a legislative framework that specifically allows for accommodation means always to be in conflict with traditional criminal law concepts, particularly when assisting an adult accused. This has been properly identified as an access to justice issue by the Canadian Bar Association[17] in Resolution 10-02-A from August 2010.[18] By contrast, the rehabilitative and reintegrative approach of the YCJA's framework has allowed inroads towards accommodation to be made which it comes to young people. Two cases

[15] The writer was a member of the organizing committee with Her Honour Judge Cook-Stanhope, member of the Alberta Provincial Court Bench, and Dr. Margaret Clarke and was the proposal writer for funding from the Law Foundation.

[16] Both the writer and Edmonton YCDO colleague Patricia Yuzwenko have presented or attended many conferences including: The 3rd International Conference on Fetal Alcohol Spectrum Disorder, "Integrating Research, Policy and Promising Practice Around the World: A Catalyst for Change" March 11–14, 2008; "Building on our Strengths: Stone by Stone" – International Conference on FASD. May 21–23, 2008 Banff, Alberta; Fourth National Biennial Conference on Adolescents and Adults with Fetal Alcohol Spectrum Disorder, Vancouver, B.C. April 15–17, 2010. Educational outreach in this area continues.

[17] The Canadian Bar Association is a professional organization that provides educational and networking opportunities for lawyers.

[18] BE IT RESOLVED THAT the Canadian Bar Association:

1. Support the initiative of Federal, Provincial and Territorial Ministers responsible for justice with respect to access to just ice for people w ith FASD and urge all levels of government to allocate additional resources for alternatives to the current practice of criminalizing individuals with FASD;
2. Urge the federal, territorial and provincial governments to develop policies designed to assist and enhance the lives of those with FASD and to prevent persistent over-representation of FASD affected individuals in the criminal justice system; and
3. Urge the federal government to amend criminal sentencing laws to accommodate the disability of those with FASD.

decided by the Supreme Court of Canada highlight the difference in approach between the two systems. First, in R. vs. B.D.[19] the Supreme Court found that "it is a principle of fundamental justice that young people are entitled to a presumption of diminished moral blameworthiness or culpability. This flows from the fact that, because of their age, they have heightened vulnerability, less maturity and a reduced capacity for moral judgement."[20] Next in the case of R. v. H.(L.)[21] the Court clarified that when a young person is being interviewed by a person in authority, for their inculpatory statement to be admissible, the crown must provide that reasonably steps were taken to ensure that the youth was capable of understanding the rights that were explained to him. A personalized inquiry as to the level of a young person's understanding must be done and a rights explanation given in language that is appropriate having regard to that context prior to the taking of a statement. Both of these cases interpret legislation and result in accommodation.

15.5 Putting the Pieces Together

The criminal justice system is a complex, multidimensional procedural process starting with arrest and ending with adjudication. A diagnosis of FASD often affects the ability of young people, or any accused person, to assert and protect their rights throughout the process.

The physicality of the arrest process itself is complex for a person with FASD: Why does that officer have to touch me? Why are they putting handcuffs on me? And why are they shouting? Further, the language of the criminal justice system is arcane. On arrest peace officers typically say: "You have the right to retain and instruct counsel without delay," In addition, visualize an accused with FASD, and think about all the doors they encounter in the process: the police vehicle, the interview room, the courtroom, the duty counsel room, the lawyer's office, the police station, the cell, the closed circuit television room, and the Legal Aid office. Imagine them going through that next door still wondering what the first room was for. Then, to what we know about FASD add the dimension of adolescence. The result is, and quite apart from criminal behavior, a youth who is dependent due to age, at risk of homelessness, immature, socially vulnerable, distractible, suggestible, cognitively vulnerable, with addiction issues, mental illness, school failure, and raging hormones. Lastly, add the prospect of two legal worlds colliding: youth criminal justice and child protection. FASD children very often have complex needs and struggle to

---

[19] (2008) 2 S.C.R. 3.

[20] The Consensus Statement on Legal Issues of Fetal Alcohol Spectrum Disorder (FASD) states that: "A more refined approach to diminished responsibility might properly be considered by Parliament under its policies to assist people with disabilities, or by the courts under their powers under s. 8(3) of the Criminal Code to create new common law defences that are not inconsistent with statutes" (Institute of Health Economics 2013).

[21] (2008) 2 S.C.R. 739.

stay on task or consistently comply with directions or connect poor behavior with negative consequences. Tragically, when residential placements are limited in number, they are given to the most compliant. As a result, when the child with FASD has complex needs and cannot comply, they are not appropriately housed. These children stay in a cycle of instability which puts them at risk of involvement with the criminal justice system.

With this as a backdrop and knowing the many facets to the YCDO advocacy model, the FASD affected youth is assisted through the justice system as mechanisms for continuity of care exist. It may be assumed that continuity of care aids in the early detection of disability, informs and accommodates assistance through a complex process and heightens the potential for meaningful or just outcomes. A young person gets arrested and is connected by phone to a YCDO lawyer. That lawyer provides advice about the process and, if necessary or appropriate, advises the arresting officers about any known disabilities. The lawyer is able to represent the young person by phone in a judicial interim release hearing with a Justice of the Peace. If the matter is adjourned and the young person appears in court the next day, the YCDO lawyer on call can inform the YCDO lawyer in court about the young person's particular needs. The duty counsel then can involve the youth workers. All of this information can then be provided to the lawyer who is assigned to the young person, whether it is staff from the YCDO, a member of the private bar, or a roster lawyer. The YCDO retains and files all FASD assessments and pre-sentence reports centrally so that if the young person reoffends that information can be accessed quickly. Barring a conflict the same lawyer would be assigned again as they know the context and can provide continuity both to the client and the court.

15.5.1 Using the YCJA as an Advocacy Tool with FASD Affected Youth

The YCDO has a history of using the YCJA as an advocacy tool. Generally speaking, the statement of principles found in the Act give ample opportunity for counsel to expand on concepts of proportionality, rehabilitation, diminished moral blameworthiness, respect for societal values, reparation of harm to victims and meaningful consequences, all words and phrases found in section 3. Section 34 of the YCJA empowers the court to order psychological or psychiatric reports. YCDO staff use that section to also request FASD assessments.[22]

[22] See also Recommendation 29 in the Consensus Statement on Legal Issues of Fetal Alcohol Spectrum Disorder(FASD): "Judges in the adult system should have similar powers as are available under s. 34 of the Youth Criminal Justice Act to order assessments of accused, especially when there are reasonable grounds to believe that the accused suffers from FASD or any other intellectual impairment or neurodevelopmental disorder" (Institute of Health Economics 2013).

Section 19[23] of the YCJA has been specifically used to address the special needs of FASD affected youth. Used most often in the context of sentencing, a Youth Justice Court would be asked to convene a conference under s. 19. The referral would go to the FASD Justice Support Project for Youth. The conference membership includes Alberta Justice and Solicitor General,[24] the YCDO,[25] Alberta Health Services, CFAN (Calgary Fetal Alcohol Network) or EFAN (Edmonton Fetal Alcohol Network), public or private school boards, Child and Family Services, Youth Probation services or other appropriate stakeholder agencies and guardians. The purpose of the conference is to develop a plan that would identify available resources that may reduce the likelihood of further involvement in the criminal justice system. The goals generally include developing meaningful support plans, identify supports needed, collaborate with relevant service providers, document case plans and forward same to the court and probation services. The written reports are well received by the court and their recommendations often adapted within the sentence given. The s.19 committee is available to follow up with the attending partners after the fact. There has been discussion for the project to seek funding for post-conference case management – to close the circle of care. Since two of the YCDO youth workers are co-facilitators, support, knowledge and training is continuously available to the rest of the staff.

15.6 Other Projects

Another YCDO project is the development of plain-language probation conditions. The members of the bench have developed a list of conditions, all of which are very legalistic in their wording, from which they craft release or probation orders. YCDO staff have found over the years that, because of the sophisticated language, these conditions are not meaningful to many young persons, especially those with a disability. A focus group was established that included staff of YCDO, a diagnostician, crown prosecutor, correctional staff, court administrator, City FASD Coordinator and youth probation. A center for Disability Services and Research was retained to translate the list of conditions into a plain language version and conduct audience testing. YCDO staff are now in a position to advocate for plain language conditions to be used in probation orders or release documents. That advocacy has to be done

[23] S. 19(1) A youth justice court judge, the provincial director, a police officer, a justice of the peace, a prosecutor or a youth worker may convene or cause to be convened a conference for the purpose of making a decision required to be made under this Act. (2) The mandate of a conference may be, among other things, to give advice on appropriate extrajudicial measures, conditions for judicial interim release, sentences, including the review of sentences, and reintegration plans. S. 19(3) and (4) concern the establishment and application of rules.

[24] In Calgary this position is filled by the FASD Coordinator previously mentioned.

[25] In both Calgary and Edmonton youth workers are co-facilitators.

on a case by case basis with the final decision-maker being the court. Although a slow evolution, s. 19 conference reports and some s. 34 reports, in which a youth is diagnosed with FASD, contain recommendations urging the plain language version to be used.

15.7 Looking to the Future – What Gaps Need Filling

Recommendation 30 of the IHE Consensus Statement on Legal Issues of FASD reads as follows:

> Consideration should be given to the establishment of special processes within the existing court structures to bring to bear the combined expertise and training of judges, prosecutors and defence counsel knowledgeable about FASD. This would service the interest of fairness as well as efficiency. (Binnie et al. 2013)

The YCDO has the infrastructure and the mandate to continue to provide continuity of legal care to youth impacted by an FASD diagnosis who come into conflict with the law. Looking to the future, in order to achieve a fairer and more efficient system which both meets the needs of the accused and recognizes the protection of society, there is work to be done. It is proposed here that the following issues are important for improvements in the future:

- Undertake robust research and analysis to assess whether the YCDO advocacy model is effective and provides desired outcomes;
- Consider whether this model can or should be replicated in other jurisdictions. It is an unfortunate reality that youth in Calgary and Edmonton receive specialized legal service when those a short distance away from those centres do not;
- Consider whether this model can or should be replicated within the adult criminal justice system;
- Undertake research to assess whether the FASD Justice Support Projects are effective and provide desired outcomes;
- Work towards sustainable funding for Legal Aid plans to provide specialized staff lawyer offices;
- Simplify language throughout the criminal justice process to improve access to justice;
- Establish training for all justice players so that the impact of impaired executive functioning, such as in FASD, is understood and that this knowledge is applied in the justice system;
- Increase access to diagnostic services, especially for adult accused;
- Work towards achieving sustainable funding to create a team approach to identifying and supporting youth and adults at the docket court stage to navigate the system and to provide resource support that is centrally located;

- Build on the success of community resources to create a team approach to post-criminal process support;
- Amend the Criminal Code in the area of sentencing and fitness to accommodate the reality of organic brain function impairment;
- Continue all efforts to educate in the area of prevention of FASD and in preventing people with FASD to come in conflict with the law.

It is time to change the way we think about the practice of criminal law. Justice, and access to it, needs to inform the process. When it comes to people living with FASD and in conflict with the law, access to justice does not mean trying to fit them into the criminal process, it means finding a way to create a system that fits them.

References

Binnie, I., M. Trussler, and E. Jonsson. 2013. Legal Issues of FASD. Fetal alcohol spectrum disorder. In *Proceedings from a consensus development conference*. ISBN 978-1-897443-36-1. www.ihe.ca

Lane Goodfellow, C. 2011. The Youth Criminal Defence Office: A model approach to the right to counsel. In *Children and the law. Essays in honour of professor Nicholas Bala*, ed. S. Anand. Toronto: Irwin Law Inc.

Newman, K. 1991. Juvenile justice in South Australia: In need of tune up or overhaul? In *Official responses to problem juveniles: Some international reflections*, ed. J. Hackler. Oñati: The Onati International Institute For the Sociology of Law.

Tonry, M., and A.N. Doob, eds. 2004. Youth crime and youth justice: Comparative and cross-national perspectives. In *Crime and justice: A review of research*. Vol. 31. Chicago: University of Chicago Press.

Part V
Societal Issues

Chapter 16
Risk, Needs, Responsivity: Rethinking FASD in the Criminal Justice System

Jacqueline Pei and Andrew Burke

16.1 Introduction

The prevalence of Fetal Alcohol Spectrum Disorder (FASD) among youth in the criminal justice system is currently unknown, although early indications place it at higher incidence than in the nonoffending population (Burd et al. 2003). Limited screening and diagnostic resources are noted as being among current barriers to determining an accurate prevalence rate at this time (Popova et al. 2011). Nonetheless, professionals working within the justice system recognize that this is a population requiring closer examination. In particular, Justice Canada reports that offenders with an FASD are more vulnerable than most offenders in the system and that their disability may contribute to potential barriers to service access in the criminal justice system (Government of Alberta 2007). To address this concern, in 2007, Justice Canada and the Youth Justice Policy section set three goals: (1) reduce the risk for individuals with an FASD to become involved with the criminal justice system; (2) provide appropriate care, assessment, and intervention to offenders with FASD within the correctional system; and (3) provide FASD training to Royal Canadian Mounted Police (RCMP) members or other service providers to increase the awareness of FASD and develop community networks for individuals with FASD (Government of Alberta 2007). Increased understanding of how these goals might be met remains a need in both practice and research. With a focus on goal two, in this chapter, we will review a current dominant theory driven approach to risk assessment and treatment for offenders, explore considerations in the application of this model for use with offenders with an FASD, and make recommendations for continuing to advance practice in pursuit of these identified goals.

J. Pei (✉) · A. Burke
University of Alberta, Edmonton, AB, Canada
e-mail: jpei@ualberta.ca

E. Jonsson et al. (eds.), *Ethical and Legal Perspectives in Fetal Alcohol Spectrum Disorders (FASD)*, International Library of Ethics, Law, and the New Medicine 75,
https://doi.org/10.1007/978-3-319-71755-5_16

16.2 Risk Needs Responsivity

Researchers examining interventions with juvenile offenders have demonstrated that punishment alone does not deter criminal recidivism or promote prosocial outcomes, and in some cases will actually increase recidivism (Gatti et al. 2009; Lipsey 2009). Interventions appear to be more successful when they: (a) base the intensity of treatment on the individuals specific level of risk, (b) identify the individuals risk factors and needs that contribute to and/or drive antisocial behaviour, and (c) manage or change those risk and needs factors though interventions that are tailored to the individual (Bonta and Andrews 2007). These principles are collectively defined as the risk-needs-responsivity (RNR) approach (Andrews and Bonta 2010), and is currently the most influential model for assessment and treatment of offenders (Blanchette and Brown 2006; Ward et al. 2007).

Based on current literature, it appears that RNR is a promising framework for reducing criminal offending behaviour. When implemented with strict fidelity, RNR has been reported to reduce subsequent recidivism by as much as 35% (Bonta and Andrews 2007). Conversely, researchers have also shown that nonadherance to RNR principles in service delivery is not only ineffective, but may also be harmful to juvenile offender outcomes (Lowenkamp and Latessa 2005). For example, Andrews et al. (2006) reported a significant negative correlation ($r = -.28$) between treatment and outcomes among programs that did not adhere to any of the RNR principles. For these reasons, fidelity in the implementation of this model is of critical importance, not only to maximize positive outcomes but also to minimize the potential of utilizing strategies that could unintentionally *increase* the possibility of criminal recidivism. This is particularly true for complex populations, such as individuals with an FASD, whose needs may be unique to the population and the individual, and the methods of diagnosing and responding to those needs may need to be specialized. Consequently it is essential that professionals have an understanding of diagnosis and risk assessment, what intervention strategies have been shown as most promising for ameliorating criminal behavior, and how the RNR model can be used as a framework to best understand risk and direct appropriate intervention. What follows is a brief description of the three fundamental principles that guide this approach and how they might be applied to the FASD population.

16.2.1 Risk

The risk principle holds that the level of service provided to juvenile offenders, which includes treatment interventions and supervision, should be matched to the individuals risk for re-offence. Accordingly, those offenders with the highest risk for reoffence are provided with the most intense services and management programs to help maximize positive outcomes, whereas lower risk offenders are matched with less intensive services/interventions. There are two fundamental assumptions that guide this principle. First, that risk for reoffence among juvenile offenders can be estimated with reasonable accuracy. Second, that matching the level of service to the level of risk actually reduces the probability of future offences.

16.2.1.1 Risk Prediction

In regards to forensic youth, risk assessment is a formalized process of estimating the probability that a youth will continue to offend or harm others if no interventions or management are attempted. Although many youth may exhibit problematic antisocial behaviors at some point in their development, few will continue a trajectory toward serious and persistent offending into adulthood (Steinberg and Scott 2003). Moreover, researchers have demonstrated that a small subset of juvenile offenders is responsible for the majority of crime in Canada. Carrington et al. (2005) observed that over 58% of all alleged criminal incidents were committed by only 16% of alleged offenders. Similarly, Loeber et al. (2003) reported that a mere 8% of male offenders were responsible for 70% of crimes committed by youth. Therefore, distinguishing those offenders who are most likely to reoffend from those who are less likely becomes an important task for treatment and supervision providers.

There have been several generations of risk assessment, the first being unstructured professional judgment where professionals relied on their impressions derived from their training and experience to form their impressions of risk (Andrews et al. 2006). This approach remains a widely used approach to risk assessment (Murray and Thomson 2010). However, this intuitive method of estimating risk has been heavily criticized for its lack of accuracy. Decision makers using such approaches may inappropriately weigh the importance of factors they consider predictive, make use of items that are not predictive in any way, may not attend to base rates, and may be influenced by causal attributions or spurious correlations (Andrews et al. 2006). Over a half-century of study has indicated that unstructured clinical opinion is often no more accurate than the flip of a coin for determining risk of reoffence (Grove et al. 2000; Monahan et al. 2001).

Fortunately, understanding of offending trajectories has helped researchers identify risk factors – individual psychological, social or behavioral characteristics – that contribute to the establishment and continuation of criminal offending. Hawkins et al. (2000), in a meta-analysis of available literature, demonstrated that the greater number of risk factors an individual offender accumulates in different domains, the higher the probability of subsequent offending. Moreover, those risk factors appear to have a cumulative and interactive effect on risk (Thornberry et al. 2004). As a result of these findings, there is a growing body of research dedicated to developing adolescent risk assessment instruments, which have shown notable superiority in their ability to predict risk compared to unstructured clinical opinion.

Schmidt et al. (2011) assessed the long-term predictive validity of three commonly used risk assessment instruments for young offenders, over a mean 10-year follow-up period. Their results demonstrated the substantial superiority of using structured risk assessment over clinical opinion. Likewise, Hilterman, Nicholls, and

Nieuwenhuizen (2011) examined the same three assessment instruments and reported that all three significantly predicted general, nonviolent, and violent recidivism with comparable degrees of accuracy, and were significantly better than unstructured clinical opinion.

Notwithstanding these promising findings, there has been very little research into the predictive accuracy of these types of instruments with FASD youth. A single unpublished study by Billie Joe Rogers et al. (2013) reported that FASD youth in their sample tended to be rated as high or very high risk, compared to non-FASD youth who tended to be rated as moderate or high risk. Interestingly, despite the impressive accuracy of the instruments with FASD youth, the authors suggested the FASD youth rating could reflect a possible ceiling effect beyond which further improvements in predictive validity cannot be achieved using the current psychological and social model of risk assessment. They also reported that FASD youth scored significantly higher than non-FASD youth on total scores and on several sub-scales that comprise those total scores on both instruments. In regards to the predictive power of each instrument, both demonstrated large effect sizes for general criminal recidivism.

In general, the scientific literature tells us that the most well researched risk assessment instruments perform significantly better than chance and clinical opinion, but that they do not have perfect accuracy. Most commonly used risk assessment instruments are based on factors derived from behavioral history, personality factors, attitudes and values, substance use, and social and community factors. In other words, although all the instruments have different individual risk factors in different combination, they are all structured to measure similar domains of functioning.

Like Billie Joe Rogers et al. (2013), others have also suggested that the predictive power of these instruments is limited. Specifically, researchers have found that when tools are combined, the accuracy of risk prediction does not tend to increase. Although the reasons for this outcome remain unclear, Kroner et al. (2005) suggested that adult instruments, upon which many of the above are based, may tap into shared dimensions of risk despite their varied formats. Using a factor analysis, the authors suggested the instruments were tapping into four overlapping dimensions: (a) criminal history, (b) irresponsible lifestyle, (c) criminal attitudes and psychopathic traits, and (d) substance abuse and related problems. Thus despite the varied item formats of the instruments, the current model of risk assessment may be measuring similar pools of variance, which may explain the limit of predictive validity beyond which they cannot improve. If this is the case, any instrument using a similar model will quickly reach a maximal point of predictive validity beyond which the addition of further items will show markedly diminishing returns. For example, in a review of over 1000 released adult offenders, Coid et al. (2011) observed that the majority of individual risk items included in risk assessment tools did not significantly predict violence. Indeed, when these items were removed, the remaining items that formed the reduced scales predicted violence as well, but not better than, the original full scales.

The results of these studies suggest that selection and combination of a few highly predictive risk factors may result in equally predictive power to more cumbersome instruments. In addition, as Kroner et al. (2005) suggested, an entirely new risk-based construct may help advance risk-prediction and provide more targeted areas for clinical intervention. In addition to anticipation of future behaviour, risk prediction is also a key component in matching service delivery to offenders in the system.

16.2.1.2 Level of Service to Risk Matching

Although it is well understood that interventions and management strategies may help mitigate the probability of offending, it is not as well known that inappropriate matching of services – that is providing high-intensity services to low-risk offenders or low-intensity services to high-risk offenders – may have deleterious effects. Studies that examined the impact of matching service level to risk with samples that included juvenile offenders reported between two and six times the positive effects compared to treatment programs that did not (Dowden and Andrews 2000; Lowenkamp and Latessa 2002). In those programs where the principle of risk-matching was not followed, outcomes for low-risk offenders actually worsened. A particularly clear illustration of the risk principle is seen in Lowenkamp and Latessas (2002) evaluation of treatment programs. Two of the programs among their sample that offered intensive services for offenders were able to reduce recidivism among high-risk offenders by over 30%. However, when those same programs were examined for their effects on low-risk offenders during the same time-period, it was observed that recidivism *increased* in one group by 7% and the other by 29%. In other words, the programs successfully reduced recidivism among high-risk offenders, but increased recidivism among low-risk offenders.

Though the reasons for these poor outcomes among low-risk offenders are uncertain, it has been hypothesized that low-risk offenders may become higher risk through association with and exposure to antisocial values and behaviors of high-risk offenders, and/or through disruption of factors related to their prosocial functioning when required to attend highly-structured and restrictive programs (Lowenkamp and Latessa 2004). This is particularly concerning in the case of FASD offenders who, as we discuss below, tend to be more easily influenced by peers and less able to evaluate their actions (Kully-Martens et al. 2012), which may increase the impact of any environmental risk factors they are exposed to while in custody. Irrespective of the reasons, the research indicates that appropriate matching of risk-level to service is imperative, both to improve outcomes and prevent harm.

16.2.1.3 FASD and Risk

Streissguth et al.'s (1996) finding that 60% of individuals in their study reported experiencing trouble with the law was the first to reveal that justice involvement is a significant concern for adolescents and adults with FASD. Moreover, offenders with an FASD may be vulnerable targets for victimization, end up committing more criminal acts without understanding why they are incarcerated in the first place, and often experience difficulty conforming to the custodial environment (Conry and Fast 2000). For example, in the young offender system, youth with an FASD tend to come into contact with the justice system earlier, with a higher number of charges than young offenders without an FASD, and have a greater risk of re-offending upon release (McLachlan 2012). Adult offenders also seem to pose an elevated risk, with a large number of young offender convictions, a higher number of adult convictions (relative to the average offender), a greater number of disciplinary problems during incarceration, and a faster rate of re-incarceration (6-months sooner) than offenders without an FASD (MacPherson et al. 2011). The reason for this elevated risk in the FASD group is as yet unclear, as there appear to be multiple factors playing a role. Also unclear are whether there are characteristics – or needs that can be changed – within the FASD group that can differentiate risk beyond diagnosis alone.

16.2.2 Criminogenic needs

The needs principle refers to the process of identifying criminogenic needs, those needs that have been empirically linked to an increased probability of criminal recidivism, and addressing them through intervention (Andrews and Bonta 2003, 2010). Often, the term *risk* is used interchangeably with *needs*. However, there is an important distinction between these two terms: all criminogenic needs are risks, but not all risks are criminogenic needs. Returning briefly to the previous principle, risk factors have been broadly classified in the literature as falling into one of two categories: static or dynamic (Borum 2003). Static risk factors primarily refer to those that are historical and do not change. Examples include the age at first offence, number of offenses, or victim type. By contrast, dynamic risk factors include typically individual, social or situational factors that can be changed or in the very least managed over time. Examples include peer associations, substance use, and beliefs and values about criminal behavior. Hoge and Andrews (1996) have defined these dynamic factors as *criminogenic needs*; namely those factors that the literature has related to offending that can be changed through intervention or management strategies (Stephenson et al. 2009). The importance of empirically linked needs must be emphasized. As in the case of other risk factors, many professionals mistakenly attribute criminal offending to factors that are not linked to recidivism (Ashford et al. 2001), and as such implement interventions that may not only be unhelpful but may sometimes be iatrogenic (Lowenkamp and Latessa 2004). However, by matching criminogenic needs, as identified on risk assessment instruments with interventions that align with these specific factors, researchers have demonstrated reductions of offending behavior of nearly 50% compared with youth whose criminogenic needs were not matched (Vieira et al. 2009).

Numerous studies with juvenile and adult offenders have identified antisocial personality features (e.g., impulsive, sensation seeking, low frustration tolerance), procriminal attitudes (e.g., rationalization of criminal behavior, negative attitudes toward convention), and antisocial peer group (e.g., isolation from prosocial friends, criminal peers) as dynamic risk factors that are strongly related to criminal recidivism (Andrews and Dowden 2007). Factors less strongly associated with criminal recidivism include substance use (e.g., alcohol or drug use), school and/or employment problems (e.g., difficulty in environment, low levels of satisfaction), family problems (e.g., inappropriate discipline, lack of supervision, relationship problems), and lack of prosocial leisure or recreational activities. Other risk factors, such as personal emotional stress, low self-esteem, presence of a major mental health disorder, and physical health issues appear to have virtually no relationship with criminal recidivism (Andrews and Bonta 2010).

16.2.2.1 FASD and Need

The separation of risk from need in FASD youth is muddied by the challenges identifying the extent to which risks in FASD may be dynamic or static – that is, which are factors that may be changed and which are not. FASD youth share many of the risk factors present among non-FASD youth, yet prenatal exposure to substances has been shown to increase vulnerability to criminal behaviour later in life (Heffron et al. 2011). For instance, Streissguth and Kanter (1997), reported that 94% of individuals with FASD have mental health issues, the most common of which are mood disorders including depression and anxiety, attention deficit hyperactivity disorder (ADHD), conduct disorder, and alcohol and drug addictions (Pei et al. 2011a, b). Additionally, family factors such as low caregiver supervision and warmth, and verbally aggressive family conflict have been shown to correlate with delinquency in youth with prenatal alcohol exposure (PAE) have been reported in FASD (Lynch et al. 2003). These findings parallel research in the general population implicating individual characteristics and negative family environment as risk factors for delinquency. However, it has been proposed that these environmental risks may be exacerbated by a biological vulnerability that exists in FASD – and thus the psychological factors reflect the meeting of biological vulnerability and environmental adversity, but are not fully explained by either (Pei et al. 2011a, b).

A core feature of FASD is disrupted neurocognitive development, as measured in formal testing settings (Mattson et al. 2011) as well as through functional description of behaviour provided in caregiver and teacher reports (Rasmussen et al. 2007). In particular, individuals with FASD struggle with higher-level tasks relying on complex Executive Functioning (EF) skills (Mattson et al. 2011) including inhibition (Burden et al. 2009), decision-making (Kully-Martens et al. 2013), working memory (Burden et al. 2005), integration of information (Pei et al. 2011a, b), and cognitive flexibility (Coles et al. 1997). These brain based risk factors form the foundation for the needs to be addressed as the presence of intense emotions, illogical thoughts, antisocial urges, and anti-social associates tend to exacerbate self-regulation potential leaving FASD adolescents with difficulties controlling aggression and other maladaptive behaviors (Burden et al. 2009). Affective or "hot" EF impairments have also been documented with this population as youth with FASD have been shown to be impaired on decision-making and risk-taking tasks and, relative to non-exposed controls, appear unable to change their behaviour when faced with negative consequences to make more positive choices as they seem to focus on the perceived benefits of the award and rather than the potential negative consequences (Kully-Martens et al. 2013), again emphasizing the vulnerability to peer and environmental influences. These brain based factors therefore do not exist in isolation but rather contribute to environmental vulnerability. It is as yet unclear to what extent changing environments may change some of these underlying aspects, or how impactful interventions targeting these brain based issues may be – thus contributing to the uncertainty regarding what can really be considered a dynamic versus a static risk factor. Resolving this question over time will be crucial in the efforts to best target those needs that can be remediated in order to reduce likelihood of reoffending behaviour (i.e., appropriate responsivity).

16.2.2.2 Assessment of Criminogenic Needs and Diagnosis

The problem of appropriately identifying the criminogenic needs of offenders with an FASD is further complicated by the complexity in the assessment process and wide range of function and needs that falls within this broad diagnostic umbrella. Studies of both animals and humans have suggested considerable variability in the individual manifestations of prenatal alcohol exposure. This variability depends on several prenatal factors, including timing and pattern of exposure, dosage, maternal age, body mass index, and genetics, as well as postnatal factors such as nutrition, socioeconomic conditions, and environmental enrichment (Day and Richardson 2004; Downing et al. 2009; Hannigan et al. 2007; May et al. 2008).

FASD is a diagnostic term in common usage that reflects the entire continuum of effects associated with prenatal exposure. In addition to Fetal Alcohol Syndrome (FAS), this term also includes the conditions of partial FAS, alcohol-related neurodevelopmental disorder, and alcohol-related birth defects (Chudley et al. 2005). Although the diagnosis provides categorical value by determining whether the individual meets the necessary criteria, it lacks dimensional value whereby the individuals symptoms are described in a way that links to functional implications. Because diagnosis informs interventions, and FASD includes a broad spectrum of functioning, the lack of quantifiable information is a critical weakness in the value of this diagnosis. Nevertheless, the majority of diagnostic assessments use such an approach, which fails to answer specific questions about: (a) the exact nature of functioning and impairment, and (b) the best interventions needed to address specific functioning and impairment. Clearly to fully engage the RNR model in providing optimized intervention to offenders with an FASD these questions need to be addressed, with specific consideration given to how they may enhance understanding of risk and needs such that response and intervention strategies can be best implemented.

16.2.3 Responsivity

The responsivity principle refers to the tailoring of interventions to engage the interest and maximize learning of the offender (Andrews and Bonta 2003). The principle considers relevant characteristics of the individual such as learning style, cognitive ability, personality traits, and values. The literature has long held responsivity as a critical concept in structuring interventions with young offenders. For example, Grant (1965) examined the impact of treatment on two offender groups of juvenile offenders; those classified as amenable, who were assessed as being bright and verbally intelligent, and nonamenables, who were less so. Both offender groups were offered psychodynamic treatment, which relies on personal insight, ability to generalize concepts, and good verbal intelligence. The amenable group showed a significant reduction in offending behavior, presumably because they were able to generalize the abstract concepts and insight they gained in treatment to their offending, whereas the nonamenable group demonstrated a slight but nonsignificant increase in offending. It is important to note that the classification of offenders in Grants study held no relation to actual criminogenic needs. Rather, it is likely the method of responsivity that played a role in those outcomes. More recently, Ogloff and Davis (2004) reported similar trends among young offenders groups; when supported interventions were used there was a significant reduction in recidivism compared to groups who were administered unsupported treatment interventions who subsequently showed a slight increase in recidivism.

Despite these positive trends there has been very little research in the area of responsivity. What is known has focused on particular interventions that have shown the greatest promise for reducing recidivism, which include cognitive behaviour, behavioural, and social learning approaches (Andrews and Bonta 2010; Landenberger and Lipsey 2005). Although the results of those studies are encouraging, they have not explored individual factors, such as neurocognitive functioning, which may influence the effectiveness and delivery of interventions. Because all treatment is a learning experience and individual factors that interfere with or facilitate learning are undeniably responsivity factors, the absence of research in this area is surprising.

Perhaps one reason for the dearth of information on the subject is that neuropsychological factors are not in-and-of-themselves criminogenic treatment targets, and therefore have not been the focus of treatment. However, recall that the responsivity principle focuses attention on client characteristics that influence their ability to learn within a therapeutic situation. Indeed, some of these neuropsychological factors appear to interfere with currently well-supported interventions. From this perspective, any interference must be addressed before an FASD offender can be expected to respond to therapist direction. Thus, neuropsychological assessment of youth appears necessary in order to adjust treatment delivery in a way that maximizes learning.

16.2.3.1 FASD and Responsivity

As described above, justice interventions may be most effective in reducing recidivism when intervention approaches are informed and guided by the offenders risk to society, profile of needs, and responsivity to treatment. Most offender rehabilitation programs employ cognitive approaches, and assume that offenders have a strong degree of control over their own behaviour, particularly in terms of personal attitudes and abilities such as problem-solving, self-monitoring and evaluation, and resisting temptation (Day et al. 2011). However, as noted above, individuals with FASD show marked deficits in these areas, struggling with attention, EF, and adaptive functioning (MacPherson et al. 2011) and therefore they may not be receptive to treatment that places a substantial emphasis on cognitive therapy (Boland et al. 1998). Alternatively, or in conjunction with cognitive approaches, behavioural therapy is also a typical therapeutic modality in which offenders are supported in replacing maladaptive coping with appropriate behaviours. However, because behavioural shaping requires appropriate, predictable, and pre-planned caregiver responses (i.e., reinforcement schedules), improvements in self-regulation will be directly correlated with environmental structure and consistency (Baumbach 2002; Streissguth et al. 1988), which has also been identified as a vulnerability in individuals with an FASD.

Unfortunately, an alternative evidence-based approach for offenders with an FASD has yet to be clearly identified in the research. Brown et al. (2012) have suggested that successful work with this population will necessitate programs that are highly structured, consistent, predictable, individualized, and involve behavioural reinforcement; targeting adaptive and social functioning; and avoiding peer group interventions. Basic behaviour therapies where long term environmental support is available are suggested as preferable to cognitive approaches. Reduction in dynamic risk factors is also encouraged, through management strategies such as removing youth from chaotic home environments and antisocial peer groups, building long-term individualized support and supervision plans for the future, and engaging a mentor to assist in transition back to the community. Other researchers have examined treatment strategies geared towards reduction of specific dynamic risk factors in young offenders with an FASD. In a survey of substance abuse service providers, McLachlan et al. (2013) found that strategies endorsed included: less use of insight-based, verbal, and highly attention/memory based approaches; more use of applied skill-building; extra support to ensure understanding of treatment content; integration of senses and physical learning; use of concrete rather than abstract concepts; and explicit teaching of memory strategies. Mela and Luther (2013) have added to these treatment recommendations noting adult offenders with FASD should have life-long supports that extend beyond the justice system, and are ideally coordinated by a mentor.

Responsivity often begins with sentencing. In Canada, section 72 of the Youth Criminal Justice Act (Youth Criminal Justice Act, S.C. 2002) directs the court to consider the offenders age, maturity, character, and his or her background when sentencing. Section 38(2)(c) states that the sentence must be proportional to the seriousness of the offence and the degree of responsibility of the young person regarding the offence. Therefore, the court must determine whether the youth with FASD is less able to restrain his or her behavior compared to other youth because of individual deficits associated with the disorder. The fundamental question in this matter is whether or not a youth with FASD is as responsible as other youth without similar deficits when he or she commits a criminal act. Under the Young Offenders Act (1985) the courts already found the presence of FASD to be a tenable mitigating factor (see *R. v M. [R.B.]* 1990; *R. v L. [J.G.]* 1996). Moreover, the purpose of sentencing is set out in Section 38(1) of the YCJA which states that the purpose of sentencing is to "hold a young person accountable for an offence through imposition of just sanctions that have meaningful consequences for the young person and that promote his or her rehabilitation and reintegration into society". Thus, one of the main objectives of the YCJA is rehabilitation. However, what may be assumed by the courts at sentencing if they are even aware that an offender may have an FASD, is that all FASD youth all share similar limitations. Yet as has already been discussed, there is a marked variability among youth diagnosed with FASD that may impact risk, needs, and consequent responsiveness to intervention which diagnosis alone does not clarify. Furthermore, also as already discussed, there are few evidence-based interventions that have been shown to be effective for offenders with an FASD.

Sentencing options under the YCJA are also made more complicated by the presence of FASD. For example, because unemployment is a common secondary disability among individuals with FASD (Clark et al. 2004; Streissguth et al. 2004), fines and other restitution orders may not be tenable options that allow the young person a reasonable chance of completing his or her order. Similarly, because of the self-regulation problems and difficulty complying with behavioral restrictions, probation or other community-based sentences that lack appropriate structural programming and monitoring may be equally unsuitable. Although custodial sentences offer the appeal of structure and supervision, which may provide these youth with the opportunity to attend programming to address their needs, the YCJA permits custodial sentences only under certain conditions. Moreover, the exposure to antisocial peers during incarceration may increase the probability of subsequent recidivism. Although Section 42(2)(r) of the YCJA provides for a special therapeutic sentence, intensive rehabilitative custody and supervision, it is available only under certain conditions and the youth must fully understand and consent to treatment, which some FASD youth may not be able to. Moreover, sentencing requires consideration of available programming, and availability may vary between regions. Thus, although responsivity often begins at sentencing, the range of sentencing options available under the YCJA and the provincial programs available to treat these youth may not address the specialized needs of FASD youth at this time.

16.3 Conclusions and Recommendations

The inability of the present system to effectively respond to the needs of offenders with FASD, combined with the increased vulnerability of this population to further victimization and antisocial influence within penal facilities provide strong impetus for the Canadian judicial system to closely examine the impact of the system on these offenders (Chartrand and Forbes-Chilibeck 2003). Traditional justice practices assume that an offender can understand the link between inappropriate behaviour and negative consequences (Malbin 2004), and even in the case of offenders with mental disorders, it is assumed that with treatment the disorder may be rectified (Roach and Bailey 2009). The current system fails to accommodate for FASD (Roach and Bailey 2009), and consequently for offenders with this disorder, the system falls short. That said, the RNR model provides a framework that may equip us to respond to this shortfall in a familiar way.

Current risk assessment instruments appear to reasonably estimate a youths level of risk, regardless of whether they may have an FASD diagnosis, and help identify some of the factors that may place them at a higher risk to reoffend. Through treatment and to a greater extent of management, the impact of these risk factors can be mitigated. However, those same instruments may fail to capture variance that is specifically related to FASD, which may result in underestimation of risk and misalignment in treatment and management plans that fail to account for specific needs that could be otherwise addressed. As a result, the development and subsequent addition of more specialized assessments is needed, which may be better able to identify the unique individual risk factors among FASD youth (e.g., neurocognitive functioning), including criminogenic needs that could be reduced through (or inform) treatment and/or intervention.

Although some judges have begun to consider the impact of FASD in their sentencing decisions, formal assessments for the disorder are rarely undertaken (Vidovic 2012). Because all treatment is a learning experience and individual factors that interfere with or facilitate learning are undeniably responsivity factors, assessment of individual neurocognitive abilities is imperative. Courts may not fully understand the unique individual needs that FASD youth present, and mistakenly treat those with the diagnosis with a uniform approach. Considering the importance of matching risk to treatment intensity, in terms of preventing reoffence, compilation of this information is crucial to accurate risk assessment – as poor matching is not benign, but in fact can *increase risk*.

Research exploring intervention strategies for offenders with an FASD is in its infancy, although growing understanding of the needs of the population is defining the starting points. For instance, although cognitive behavioural and social learning approaches are typically employed with offenders, these may not be optimal for individuals with an FASD. Instead concrete, applied, and where possible, environmentally supported strategies (e.g., mentorship) may be best employed, with consideration for *lifelong* application. Indeed, because FASD is a life-course persistent disorder, interventions of this nature will require support planning that extends beyond sentence expiry in order to facilitate continued success and reduce the probability of recidivism.

Unfortunately, in the absence of informed justice system approaches, the likelihood that an individual with an FASD may reoffend may increase. This knowledge alone must be a catalyst for careful examination of how risk is considered and how needs are identified and map this knowledge to intervention strategies in an informed way. Creating such a map may also require re-examination of the principles of the justice system in responding to the offender with an FASD. Recognizing that the presence of FASD results in increased vulnerability to environmental stressors and adversity, and that the brain injury caused by prenatal alcohol exposure may compromise an individuals ability to learn from their mistakes or fully understand the implications of the their actions, has created discussion around sentencing practices. Specifically, questions about the punitive nature of the justice system and the appropriateness of extended sentencing for this potentially less responsible group are raised. Thus, one may be inclined to argue that the justice system be more cognizant of the issue of responsibility when deciding upon appropriate punishments for the behaviours of those with FASD and sentence more leniently. However, the research evidence strongly suggests that reduced responsibility *does not* mean that the risk is lower for youth with an FASD. On the contrary, based on limited evidence, youth with an FASD appear to be at a higher risk to reoffend than nonFASD youths who have committed criminal offenses. Moreover, research evidence indicates that treatment response *must be* matched in intensity to the risk for the individual, which suggests that this is a group requires higher intensity support and intervention.

The RNR model provides a framework for conceptualizing the way in which the justice system might best respond to the needs of offenders with an FASD. An evidence based model, this approach underscores the necessity of matching risk and needs to intervention practices – regardless of the reasons for these needs. And consequently, as a high risk group of offenders, establishes that it is crucial that high levels of support and intervention be provided to the FASD population. That said, intervention and support, as directed through sentencing practices, does not necessarily mean incarceration, but rather intensive support. Possibly this may mean that funding for such support be redirected from expensive incarceration for shorter periods of time, towards community based intensive support, for extended periods of time. This may then satisfy the need to match risk and intensiveness of intervention, and also avoid further risk factors such as negative peer associations. It is only through further research and close monitoring that this and other creative approaches may be vetted to determine if they are effective. However, it is clear that to best manage this high risk group, in a feasible fashion, consistent with current evidence in the field, adaptive use of evidence supported approaches are warranted. As we move forward, the challenge may simply be to change the tone of our response – moving to a long term management perspective – while simultaneously ensuring that sentencing, and therefore treatment opportunities, are of sufficient intensity to potentially produce the desired effect – reduced reoffences.

References

Andrews, D., and J. Bonta. 2003. *The psychology of criminal conduct*. Cincinnatti: Anderson.

———. 2010. *The psychology of criminal conduct*. 5th ed. New Providence: LexisNexis/Matthew Bender.

Andrews, D., and C. Dowden. 2007. The risk–need–responsivity model of assessment and human service in prevention and corrections: Crime-prevention jurisprudence. *Canadian Journal of Criminology and Criminal Justice* 49 (4): 439–464.

Andrews, D., J. Bonta, and J. Wormith. 2006. The recent past and near future of risk and/or need assessment. *Crime & Delinquency* 52 (1): 7–27.

Ashford, J., B. Sales, and W. Reid. 2001. Aftercare and recidivism prevention. In *Treating adult and juvenile offenders with special needs*, ed. J. Ashford, B. Sales, and W. Reid, 273–290. Washington, DC: American Psychological Association.

Baumbach, J. 2002. Some implications of prenatal alcohol exposure for the treatment of adolescents with sexual offending behaviors. *Sexual Abuse: A Journal of Research and Treatment* 14 (4): 313–327.

Billie Joe Rogers, Kaitlyn McLachlan, and Ronald Roesch. 2013. Resilience and enculturation: Strengths among young offenders with fetal alcohol spectrum disorder. *First Peoples Child & Family Review*, Special Issue: Fetal Alcohol Spectrum Disorder (FASD) 8 (1): 62–80.

Blanchette, K., and S. Brown. 2006. *The assessment and treatment of women offenders: an integrative perspective*. Chichester: Wiley.

Boland, F., R. Burrill, M. Duwyn, and J. Karp. 1998. *Fetal alcohol syndrome: implications for correctional service*. Ottawa: Correctional Service Canada.

Bonta, J., and D. Andrews. 2007. *Risk-need-responsivity model for offender assessment and rehabilitation corrections research user report no. 2007–06*. Ottawa: Carleton University.

Borum, R., P. Bartel, and A. Forth. 2003. *Manual for the structured assessment of violence risk in youth (Version 1.1)*. Tampa: University of South Florida. Google Scholar.

Brown, N., P. Connor, and R. Adler. 2012. Conduct-disordered adolescents with fetal alcohol spectrum disorder: Intervention in secure treatment settings. *Criminal Justice and Behavior* 39 (6): 770–793.

Burd, L., R. Selfridge, M. Klug, and T. Juelson. 2003. Fetal alcohol syndrome in the Canadian corrections system. *Journal of FAS International* 1: 1–7.

Burden, M.J., S.W. Jacobson, R.J. Sokol, and J.L. Jacobson. 2005. Effects of prenatal alcohol exposure on attention and working memory at 7.5 years of age. *Alcoholism: Clinical and Experimental Research* 29: 443–452.

Burden, M., C. Andrew, D. Saint-Amour, E. Meintjes, C. Molteno, H. Hoyme, et al. 2009. The effects of fetal alcohol syndrome on response execution and inhibition: An event-related potential study. *Alcoholism: Clinical and Experimental Research* 33 (11): 1994–2004.

Carrington, P., A. Matarazzo, and P. deSouza. 2005. *Court careers of a Canadian Birth cohort*, Crime and justice research paper series. Ottawa: Canadian Centre for Justice Statistics.

Chartrand, L., and E. Forbes-Chilibeck. 2003. The sentencing of offenders with fetal alcohol syndrome. *Health Law Journal* 11: 35–70.

Chudley, A., J. Conry, J. Cook, C. Loock, T. Rosales, and N. LeBlanc. 2005. Fetal alcohol spectrum disorder: Canadian guidelines for diagnosis. *Canadian Medical Association Journal* 172 (5): s1–s21.

Clark, E., J. Lutke, P. Minnes, and H. Ouellette-Kuntz. 2004. Secondary disabilities among adults with fetal alcohol spectrum disorder in British Columbia. *Journal of FAS International* 2 (e13): 1–12.

Coid, J., M. Yang, S. Ullrich, T. Zhang, S. Sizmur, D. Farrington, and R. Rogers. 2011. Most items in structured risk assessment instruments do not predict violence. *Forensic Psychiatry & Psychology* 22 (1): 3–21.

Coles, C.D., K.A. Platzman, C.L. Raskind-Hood, R.T. Brown, et al. 1997. A comparison of children affected by prenatal alcohol exposure and attention deficit, hyperactivity disorder. *Alcoholism: Clinical and Experimental Research* 21 (1): 150–161.

Conry, J., and D. Fast. 2000. *Fetal alcohol syndrome and the criminal justice system*. Vancouver: Fetal Alcohol Syndrome Resource Society.

Day, N., and G. Richardson. 2004. An analysis of the effects of prenatal alcohol exposure on growth: A teratologic model. *American Journal of Medical Genetics Part C: Seminars in Medical Genetics* 127C (1): 28–34.

Day, A., T. Ward, and L. Shirley. 2011. Reintegration services for long-term dangerous offenders: A case study and discussion. *Journal of Offender Rehabilitation* 50 (2): 66–80.

Dowden, C., and D.A. Andrews. 2000. Effective correctional treatment and violent reoffending: A meta-analysis. *Canadian Journal of Criminology* 42 (4): 449–467.

Downing, C., C. Balderrama-Durbin, H. Broncucia, D. Gilliam, and T. Johnson. 2009. Ethanol teratogenesis in five inbred strains of mice. *Alcoholism: Clinical and Experimental Research* 33 (7): 1238–1245.

Gatti, U., R. Tremblay, and F. Vitaro. 2009. Iatrogenic effect of juvenile justice. *The Journal of Child Psychology and Psychiatry* 50 (8): 991–998.

Government of Alberta. 2007. *Federal government actions on Fetal Alcohol Spectrum Disorder (FASD)*. Retrieved from http://www.phac-aspc.gc.ca/hp-ps/dca-dea/prog-ini/fasd-etcaf/publications/pdf/factsheet10-fasd-etcaf-eng.pdf

Grant, J. 1965. Delinquency treatment in an institutional setting. In *Juvenile delinquency: research and theory*, ed. H.C. Quay, 263–297. Princeton: Van Nostrand.

Grove, W., D. Zald, B. Snitz, and C. Nelson. 2000. Clinical versus mechanical prediction: A meta-analysis. *Psychological Assessment* 12 (1): 19–30.

Hannigan, J.H., S.K. OLeary-Moore, and R.F. Berman. 2007. Postnatal environmental or experiential amelioration of neurobehavioral effects of perinatal alcohol exposure in rats. [Original]. *Neuroscience & Biobehavioral Reviews* 31 (2): 202–211.

Hawkins, J., T. Herrenkohl, D. Farrington, D. Brewer, R. Catalano, T. Harachi, and L. Cothern. 2000. *Predictors of youth violence*. Washington, DC: Office of Juvenile Justice and Delinquency Prevention, U.S. Department of Justice.

Heffron, W., S. Babalonis, M. Staton-Tindall, L. Molenaar, K. Lommel, A. Kazura, et al. 2011. Evidence-based practice in criminal justice settings. In *Handbook of evidence-based substance abuse treatment in criminal justice settings*, ed. C. Leukefeld, T.P. Gullotta, and J. Gregrich, 23–44. New York: Springer.

Ed L. B. Hilterman, Tonia L. Nicholls, and Chijs van Nieuwenhuizen. 2013 Predictive validity of risk assessments in Juvenile offenders: Comparing the SAVRY, PCL:YV, and YLS/CMI With unstructured clinical assessments. Assessment. Vol 21, Issue 3, pp. 324–339. First Published August 6, 2013 HYPERLINK "http://dx.doi.org/10.1177/1073191113498113" \o "https://doi.org/10.1177/1073191113498113" \t "_blank" https://doi.org/10.1177/1073191113498113.

Hoge, R., and D. Andrews. 1996. *The Youthful Offender: Issues and Techniques*. New York: Plenum.

Kroner, D., J. Mills, and J. Reddon. 2005. A coffee can, factor analysis, and prediction of antisocial behavior: The structure of criminal risk. *International Journal of Law and Psychiatry* 28 (4): 360–374.

Kully-Martens, K., K. Denys, S. Treit, S. Tamana, and C. Rasmussen. 2012. A review of social skills deficits in individuals with fetal alcohol spectrum disorders and prenatal alcohol exposure: Profiles, mechanisms, and interventions. *Alcoholism: Clinical and Experimental Research* 36 (4): 567–576.

Kully-Martens, K., S. Treit, J. Pei, and C. Rasmussen. 2013. Affective decision-making on the Iowa Gambling Task in children and adolescents with fetal alcohol spectrum disorder. *Journal of International Neuropsychological Society* 19 (2): 137–144.

Landenberger, N., and M. Lipsey. 2005. The positive effects of cognitive-behavioral programs for offenders: A meta-analysis of factors associated with effective treatment. *Journal of Experimental Criminology* 1: 451–476.

Lipsey, M.W. 2009. The primary factors that characterize effective interventions with juvenile offenders: A meta-analytic overview. *Victims & Offenders* 4 (2): 124–147.

Loeber, R., D. Farrington, and D. Petechuk. 2003. *Child delinquency: Early intervention and prevention*. Washington, DC: Department of Justice, Office of Justice Programs, Office of Juvenile Justice and Delinquency Prevention.

Lowenkamp, C., and E. Latessa. 2002. *Evaluation of Ohios community based correctional facilities and halfway house programs*. Technical report. Cincinnati: University of Cincinnati.

———. 2004. Understanding the risk principle: How and why correctional interventions can harm low-risk offenders (technical report). *Topics in community corrections*. Cincinnatti: U.S. Department of Justice, National Institute of Corrections.

———. 2005. Increasing the effectiveness of correctional programming through the risk principle: Identifying offenders for residential placement. *Criminology & Public Policy* 4 (2): 263–290.

Lynch, M.E., C.D. Coles, T. Corley, and A. Falek. 2003. Examining delinquency in adolescents differentially prenatally exposed to alcohol: The role of proximal and distal risk factors. *Journal of Studies on Alcohol* 64: 678–686.

MacPherson, P.H., A.E. Chudley, and B.A. Grant. 2011. *Fetal Alcohol Spectrum Disorder (FASD) in a correctional population: Prevalence, screening and diagnosis*, R-247. Ottawa: Correctional Service of Canada.

Malbin, D. 2004. Fetal Alcohol Spectrum Disorder (FASD) and the role of family court judges in improving outcomes for children and families. *Juvenile and Family Court Journal* 55 (2): 53–63.

Mattson, S., N. Crocker, and T. Nguyen. 2011. Fetal alcohol spectrum disorders: Neuropsychological and behavioral features. *Neuropsychology Review* 21: 81–101.

May, P., J. Gossage, A. Marais, L. Hendricks, C. Snell, B. Tabachnick, et al. 2008. Maternal risk factors for fetal alcohol syndrome and partial fetal alcohol syndrome in South Africa: A third study. *Alcoholism, Clinical and Experimental Research* 32 (5): 738–753.

McLachlan, K. 2012. *An examination of the abilities, risks, and needs of adolescents and young adults with Fetal Alcohol Spectrum Disorder (FASD) in the criminal justice system.* Dissertation, Simon Fraser University, Burnaby.

McLachlan, K., K. Wyper, and A. Pooley. 2013. *Promising practices in substance abuse treatment for justice-involved youth with FASD*. Maple Ridge: Asante Centre.

McLachlan, K., R. Roesch, J.L. Viljoen, and K.S. Douglas. 2014. Evaluating the psycholegal abilities of young offenders with fetal alcohol spectrum disorder. *Law and Human Behavior* 38: 10–22.

Mela, M., and G. Luther. 2013. Fetal alcohol spectrum disorder: Can diminished responsibility diminish criminal behaviour? *International Journal of Law and Psychiatry* 36 (1): 46–54.

Monahan, J., H. Steadman, E. Silver, P. Appelbaum, P. Robbins, E. Mulvey, et al. 2001. *Rethinking risk assessment: The MacArthur study of mental disorder and violence*. New York: Oxford University Press.

Murray, J., and M. Thomson. 2010. Clinical judgment in violence risk assessment. *Europes Journal of Psychology* 6 (1): 128–149.

Ogloff, J., and M. Davis. 2004. Advances in offender assessment and rehabilitation: Contributions of the risk-needs-responsivity approach. *Psychology, Crime and Law* 10 (3): 229–242.

Olver, M., K. Stockdale, and J. Wormith. 2011. A meta-analysis of predictors of offender treatment attrition and its relationship to recidivism. *Journal of Consulting and Clinical Psychology* 79 (1): 6–21.

Pei, J., K. Denys, J. Hughes, and C. Rasmussen. 2011a. Mental health issues in fetal alcohol spectrum disorder. *Journal of Mental Health* 20 (5): 438–448.

Pei, J., J. Job, K. Kully-Martens, and C. Rasmussen. 2011b. Executive function and memory in children with fetal alcohol spectrum disorder. *Child Neuropsychology* 17 (3): 290–309.

Popova, S., S. Lange, D. Bekmuradov, A. Mihic, and J. Rehm. 2011. Fetal alcohol spectrum disorder prevalence estimates in correctional systems: A systematic literature review. *Canadian Journal of Public Health* 102 (5): 336–340.

R. v. *L. (J.G.)*. 1996, 75 B.C.A.C. 227, (B.C.C.A).

R. v. *M. (R.B.)*. 1990. 54 C.C.C. (3d) 132 (B.C.C.A.).

Rasmussen, C., R. McAuley, and G. Andrew. 2007. Parental ratings of children with fetal alcohol spectrum disorder on the behavior rating inventory of executive function (BRIEF). *Journal of FAS International* 5 (2): 1–8.

Roach, K., and A. Bailey. 2009. The relevance of fetal alcohol spectrum disorder in Canadian criminal law from investigation to sentencing. *University of British Columbia Law Review* 42 (1): 1–68.

Schmidt, F., M. Campbell, and C. Houlding. 2011. Comparative analyses of the YLS/CMI, SAVRY, and PCL:YV in adolescent offenders: A 10-year follow-up into adulthood. *Youth Violence and Juvenile Justice* 9 (1): 23–42.

Steinberg, L., and E. Scott. 2003. Less guilty by reason of adolescence: Developmental immaturity, diminished responsibility, and the juvenile death penalty. *American Psychologist* 58 (12): 1009–1018.

Stephenson, M., H. Giller, and S. Brown. 2009. Effective practice in youth justice. *The Howard Journal of Criminal Justice* 48 (4): 432–438.

Streissguth, A., and J. Kanter, eds. 1997. *The challenge of fetal alcohol syndrome: Overcoming secondary disabilities*. Seattle: University of Washington Press.

Streissguth, A., R.A. LaDue, and S.P. Randels. 1988. *A manual on adolescents and adults with fetal alcohol syndrome with special reference to American Indians*. 2nd ed. Albuquerque: Indian Health Service.

Streissguth, A., H.M. Barr, J. Kogan, and F.L. Bookstein. 1996. *Understanding the occurrence of secondary disabilities in clients with fetal alcohol syndrome (FAS) and fetal alcohol effects (FAE)*. Final report to the centers for disease control and prevention. Seattle: University of Washington, Fetal Alcohol and Drug Unit.

Streissguth, A., F. Bookstein, H. Barr, P. Sampson, K. OMalley, and J. Young. 2004. Risk factors for adverse life outcomes in fetal alcohol syndrome and fetal alcohol effects. *Journal of Developmental and Behavioral Pediatric* 25 (4): 228–238.

Thornberry, T., D. Huizinga, and R. Loeber. 2004. The causes and correlates studies: Findings and policy implications. *Journal of the Office of Juvenile Justice and Delinquency Prevention* 9 (1): 3–19.

Vidovic, P. 2012. *Neuro-cognitive impairments and the criminal justice system: A case analysis of the impact of diagnoses of FASD and ADHD on the sentencing of offenders in the courts of three Canadian provinces*. Doctor of Philosophy, Simon Fraser University.

Vieira, T., T. Skilling, and M. Peterson-Badali. 2009. Matching court-ordered services with treatment needs: Predicting treatment success with young offenders. *Criminal Justice and Behavior* 36 (4): 385–401.

Ward, T., J. Mesler, and P. Yates. 2007. Reconstructing the risk–need–responsivity model: A theoretical elaboration and evaluation. *Agression and Violent Behavior* 12 (2): 208–228.

Young Offenders Act, RSC 1985, c Y-1. Available from: http://canlii.ca/t/kmfv.

Youth Criminal Justice Act, SC 2002, c 1. Available from: http://canlii.ca/t/527q5.

Chapter 17
Fetal Alcohol Spectrum Disorder and Firesetting: An Exploratory Review

Jerrod Brown, Anthony P. Wartnik, Sarah Herrick, Kathi Osmonson, Margaret R. Wimberley, and Patricia Jones

Abstract Fetal Alcohol Spectrum Disorders (FASD) are caused by prenatal alcohol exposure and characterized by lifelong cognitive, social, and adaptive deficits. This disorder can result in impaired executive functioning and other associated deficits (e.g., poor decision making, impulsivity, and an inability to comprehend cause and effect). These impairments place an individual at greater odds of becoming involved in the criminal justice system for illegal activities, possibly including firesetting.

To this point, only anecdotal evidence and case study accounts have suggested a link between FASD and firesetting behavior. These observations suggest the need for mental health, fire, and forensic professionals to acquire a basic understanding of FASD and its relationship with known firesetting risks and motivations. This chapter will review: (1) relevant caregiver and case study accounts (2) possible etiological origins of firesetting behaviors among youth with FASD; (3) overlap in descriptive characteristics of youth with FASD and youth who set fires; (4) approaches to better identify and screen youth with FASD who may be at risk to set fires; and (5) appropriate fire-safety strategies as well as intervention and treatment approaches for youth with FASD who set fires.

J. Brown (✉)
Concordia University, St. Paul, MN, USA

Pathways Counseling Center, Inc, St. Paul, MN, USA

The American Institute for the Advancement of Forensic Studies (AIAFS), St. Paul, MN, USA
e-mail: jerrod01234brown@live.com

A. P. Wartnik · S. Herrick
Concordia University, St. Paul, MN, USA

K. Osmonson
Minnesota Deputy State Fire Marshal, St. Paul, MN, USA

M. R. Wimberley
ABC-TV, New York, NY, USA

P. Jones

E. Jonsson et al. (eds.), *Ethical and Legal Perspectives in Fetal Alcohol Spectrum Disorders (FASD)*, International Library of Ethics, Law, and the New Medicine 75,
https://doi.org/10.1007/978-3-319-71755-5_17

The goals of this chapter are two-fold; to raise awareness of the potential link between FASD and firesetting behavior and to facilitate further research into the role of FASD in firesetting. Proactive research is necessary to understand the etiology, prevalence, and appropriate interventions for youth with FASD who set fires.

Keywords FASD · Fire · Forensic · Criminal justice · Youth

17.1 Introduction

Afflicting millions of individuals, Fetal Alcohol Spectrum Disorder (FASD), which is caused by prenatal alcohol exposure (PAE), has an estimated prevalence of 2–5% in the U.S. (May et al. 2009). FASD is characterized by a range of life-long cognitive (e.g., executive functioning, short- and long-term memory, attention, and intelligence) (Brown et al. 2014; Green et al. 2009; Mattson et al. 1997); social (e.g., awkwardness, immaturity, and verbal/non-verbal communication) (Fast and Conry 2009); and adaptive dysfunction (e.g., problem-solving ability, abstract thinking, and learning from previous experiences) (Edwards and Greenspan 2010). Because this complicated constellation of symptoms can vary greatly on a case-by-case basis, FASD is often very difficult to assess and diagnose (Clarren and Lutke 2008; May et al. 2009; Streissguth et al. 1996; Watkins et al. 2014). As such, many individuals with FASD do not receive an accurate diagnosis and/or adequate treatment and social support (Chasnoff et al. 2015; Thiel et al. 2011). This lack of diagnosis and treatment often results in individuals with FASD becoming involved in the criminal justice system (Burd et al. 2003; Fast and Conry 2004, 2009; McLachlan et al. 2014).

Anecdotal and case accounts from primary caregivers and professionals suggests individuals with FASD, particularly children, may be prone to atypically higher rates of firesetting compared to their non-FASD counterparts. Additional reviews of case literature began to expose an overlap in the behavioral, cognitive, and social correlation of the FASD and youth firesetting populations. Firesetters commonly have cognitive impairments (e.g., intellectual deficits, executive functioning issues, and learning disabilities) and/or mental health issues including, but not limited to: Attention-Deficit/Hyperactivity Disorder (ADHD), Conduct Disorder (CD), Autism Spectrum Disorder (ASD), mood disorders (i.e., Bipolar Disorder), and Reactive Attachment Disorder (RAD). Similarly, many of the same cognitive deficits (e.g., executive functioning, disinhibition, and intelligence) are symptoms consistent with FASD.

Typically, primary FASD caregivers attribute the firesetting behaviors of their wards to disinhibition, curiosity, absence of adequate parental supervision, and peer influence. These attributions mirror the classic description of youth firesetting. Similar to youth firesetting in the general population, motivation for firesetting varies by individual with FASD. The majority of cases in both groups appear to be perpetrated without intent to damage property or harm others. Fire and law enforcement professionals may be disproportionately likely to encounter individuals with FASD. The high correlation between FASD and criminal justice interaction makes it imperative to review and compare the broad areas of overlap in firesetting with and without FASD.

Comparison of characteristics with FASD and general population firesetters may help illuminate how these two issues can co-occur. Such a review may assist in avoiding the hyper-criminalization of firesetting for these individuals, as well as shed light on which FASD-related symptoms are most likely to increase the risk of firesetting behaviors for the purposes of education and prevention.

17.2 What Is Youth Firesetting?

Another area of challenge for the justice system, as well as public safety, is youth firesetting. The United States ranks as one of the most fire-prone nations in the industrialized world (Federal Emergency Management Agency 2011). Fire incidents within the US are reported to the National Fire Incident Report System, a system of data collection and reporting that is run by the Federal Emergency Management Agency (FEMA). The aggregate information is distributed to government agencies and made available to the public for the purpose of informing and enhancing public safety policies. For example, the data is used to identify various fire-related needs, risk assessment, and fire trends. An area of keen interest is intentional firesetting (Kolko 2002). Other aspects of fire and firesetting explored by these agencies include fires caused by children and juveniles.

In 2010, playing with fire was estimated to have caused 49,300 fires in the United States and another 260,600 fires were set intentionally (National Fire Protection Agency 2010). From 2005–2010, 46% of arson arrests were associated with juveniles (Federal Emergency Management Agency 2012). In 2010, 47.6% of those arrested were less than 16 years of age (Federal Emergency Management Agency 2012). In the United States, firesetting is the only major crime where adolescent offenders outnumber adults (Bartol and Bartol 2012). Juvenile firesetting behavior is seen in other countries as well. In the United Kingdom, 40% of firesetting involved individuals age 21 or younger and in New Zealand, the incident rate is 73% (Lambie and Randell 2011). It is conjectured the incident rate of juvenile firesetting, caused either deliberately or otherwise, is higher. In Massachusetts, a group of firesetting juveniles suggested only 11% of the fires they admitted to setting were reported (Zipper and Wilcox 2005).

Firesetting is a pervasive, largely hidden, and complex behavior that can occur in tandem with numerous mental health conditions and negative life situations. The many dangers associated with firesetting impacts not only the firesetter, but a wide range of others not necessarily known to the firesetter (Johnson and Jones 2014). As such, treatment and educational efforts should focus not only on the firesetter and their family/caregivers, but also the community in general (Zipper and Wilcox

2005). Any firesetting behavior, whether intentional or unintentional, can result in death, injury, and destruction of property. Unintentional firesetting may prove to be just as deadly as intentional setting. Many fires set by children and juveniles are done in secret, often by themselves, which can contribute to incendiary situations that become uncontrollable. A child's bedroom is where 40% of fires associated with at-home play are ignited (Federal Emergency Management Agency 2012). It is believed two out of five children who die by fire have set the fire that killed them (Huff 2014).

The high percentage of youth involvement in firesetting surprises many adults (Johnson and Jones 2014). This may contribute to the low parental monitoring of fire use by children and juveniles, a major factor contributing to firesetting behavior (Lambie et al. 2012). Furthermore, parents and caregivers may not consider a youth who is attracted to fire as being at-risk for firesetting (Johnson and Jones 2014). Although a juvenile might be considered chronologically old enough to be exposed to matches, candles, and objects that can start a fire, he/she may be in fact developmentally younger and incapable of handling the responsibility associated with access to firesetting material (Lambie et al. 2012). A juvenile firesetter motivated by curiosity may also have low impulse control, lack understanding of the danger involved, and suffer from cognitive deficits and/or disabilities such as ADHD (Kolko 2002). Consequently, these youth may have difficulties resisting firesetting experimentation.

Many children are inherently intrigued by fire. This perilous interest can be magnified as children often have difficulty linking their dangerous actions to the potentially disastrous consequences of firesetting.

A fascination with fire is seen as a normal part of childhood, with onset typically seen from five- to seven-years-old (Bartol and Bartol 2012). A child who continues to set fires by age ten, however, is considered as moving from playing with fire into the firesetting stage (Bartol and Bartol 2012). Fire is exciting, adding to its attraction. Given for some youth there is an awareness of the danger associated with starting a small fire, an element of defiance may be involved (Kolko 2002; Zipper and Wilcox 2005). Furthermore, fire is accessible and inexpensive to create (Kolko 2002).

Firesetting is commonly associated with aggression. When comparing levels of aggression within a selection of juveniles identified with rule-breaking behaviors, those who were firesetters demonstrated significantly higher aggression levels than the non-firesetters (Stickle and Blechman 2002). Children diagnosed with Conduct Disorder who participated in playing with matches and firesetting, have also been found to be more aggressive than their non-firesetting counterparts (Kolko and Kazdin 1991). Even within a group of randomly-selected Italian youths with no mental health disorders or law enforcement record, aggression and fire play were directly correlated, with these youths more likely to engage in delinquency unknown to their parents or caregivers (Del Bove et al. 2008).

Intentional firesetting by children has been associated with impulsivity/ADHD, adverse childhood experiences including violence at home, conduct disorder/criminality, social skill deficits, substance abuse, and suicidal ideation (Gelhorn et al. 2007; Lambie and Randell 2011; MacKay et al. 2009). Nineteen percent of children in mental health outpatient treatment programs and 35% of children hospitalized for psychiatric care have firesetting behavior (Huff 2014). It is conjectured the correlation of firesetting and any behavioral disorder may be typical to individuals whose symptoms are at the severe end of a spectrum of behavior, ranging from rare and minimally disruptive, to frequent and requiring immediate attention for the health and safety of self and others (Gelhorn et al. 2009; Watt et al. 2015). Intentional juvenile firesetting may also be categorized as a cry for help, a means to draw attention to an area of discord, or an act of aggression (Lambie and Randell 2011; Zipper and Wilcox 2005). Juveniles who intentionally set fires are typically found to have limited social skills, low self-esteem, and a preference for solitary or covert rule breaking behavior (Zipper and Wilcox 2005). When a child is experiencing abuse or bullying in some part of their life, playing with fire may be a means to experience control over something powerful (Kolko 2002). A sense of "control" may involve starting a small fire, and then, in theory, putting it out (Kolko 2002). Other negative aspects of the family environment such as a lack of parental supervision, poor behavioral modeling, and domestic violence, may also contribute to firesetting behavior (Johnson and Jones 2014). Research shows a positive correlation between firesetting and childhood abuse, neglect, and other maltreatment (Burnett and Omar 2014).

Historically, the overlap of childhood maltreatment and aggression has caused some confusion in determining the risk factors for juveniles and children who set fires. In the 1960's, a cluster of three behavioral characteristics, firesetting, cruelty to animals, and enuresis, were dubbed as the "MacDonald Triad" (MacDonald 1966; Sakheim and Osborn 1986). MacDonald hypothesized children who exhibited all three characteristics should be considered at risk for violence and predatory behavior when they reached adulthood (Hellman and Blackman 1966). Even though the MacDonald Triad hypothesis has been repeatedly debunked (Prentky and Carter 1984; Ryan 2009; Tallichet et al. 2005), a considerable number of individuals and organizations continue to postulate this triad is predictive of strong aggressive impulses and rule-breaking behaviors (Singer and Hensley 2004). The juvenile firesetting portion of the triad includes five specific social factors: maternal rejection, father abandonment, creation of conditions of control over adults through firesetting, sexual excitement, and a diagnosis of Conduct Disorder. These factors were found to strongly correlate with juvenile fire starters who became violent in adulthood, indicating deprivation and maltreatment in childhood were causative of adult violence (Sakheim and Osborn 1986). Another common misunderstanding often associated with firesetting behavior is the use of the term "pyromania." Pyromania is a rare mental disorder that differs from firesetting behavior in terms of both motivation (reason for setting the fire) and context (the situation in which the fire is set) (American Psychiatric Association 2013). The diagnosis of this disorder appears in only approximately .04% of the population (American Psychiatric Association 2013).

The frequency and magnitude of firesetting can be more pronounced in children with learning disabilities, who may be less likely to recognize the potential damaging results of their actions (Lambie and Randell 2011). As such, children with disorders characterized by cognitive and learning difficulties (e.g., FASD) may be disproportionately likely to set fires. Firesetting behavior has been positively correlated with medical and neurological disorders. These include, but are not limited to, epilepsy; brain tumors; Huntington's Chorea; Klinefelter's Syndrome and other chromosomal disorders such as cerebellar arachnoid cyst; infection-related disorders, particularly AIDS; reactive hypoglycemia; Moebius Syndrome (Huff 2014); focal brain lesions (Kanehisa et al. 2012); and Asperger's Syndrome (Barry-Walsh and Mullen 2003). The connection between FASD, known for neurological deficits with strong links to difficulties managing self-control and aggression and its anecdotal association with firesetting, needs to be fully explored.

17.3 How and Why FASD May Lead to Firesetting Behaviors

Individuals with FASD exhibit a number of symptoms, including behaviors, many of which are the direct result of permanent brain damage caused by prenatal alcohol exposure. These symptoms may predispose some individuals with FASD to firesetting behaviors, across all age ranges. Individuals with FASD commonly have a number of cognitive deficits (e.g., short-and long-term memory, learning ability, impulsive control, emotion regulation, and decision-making skills), as well as social dysfunction (e.g., poor interpersonal relationships, susceptibility to peer pressure, a vulnerability to manipulation by others, and a proneness to imitating others) (Alloway et al. 2009; Rasmussen and Wyper 2007; Thiel et al. 2011; Wheeler et al. 2012). In addition, many individuals with FASD function significantly below their chronological age emotionally, intellectually and behaviorally (Wartnik et al. 2015). In combination, this constellation of symptoms may increase the likelihood of actions without recognition of consequences, poor decision making, and a failure to link their initial act of firesetting to the subsequent consequences or damage caused by the fire.

In theory, the cognitive deficits of FASD could increase the likelihood of firesetting behaviors among some youth with FASD in several ways. Highlighted in this chapter are three important possibilities.

First, a key issue in FASD is difficulty thinking in an abstract manner (Brown et al. 2012). Individuals with FASD often think more concretely and experience great difficulty in generalizing something learned in one setting to another setting (Burnside and Fuchs 2013; Douglas 2010; Jeffery 2010). Such difficulties could have a profound impact on the likelihood some individuals with FASD will have difficulties distinguishing between situations where it is not appropriate to use fire. For example, a child with FASD may not comprehend why it is alright to light candles on a birthday cake in the kitchen, but inappropriate to light matches in a closet. Alternatively, a child with FASD might not realize it is safe to set fire to logs in a fire pit, but not a pile of brush in a forest. Most children eventually learn to understand the importance of context and safety, but children with FASD often have difficulty distinguishing these concepts across situations. As such, primary caregiv-

Table 17.1 Areas of shared concern in FASD and youth firesetting literature

Co-Morbid mental health issues	Poor emotional regulation
Deficits in understanding cause and effect	Poor family functioning
Emotional capacity deficits	Poor relationship skills
Impulsivity	Wide range of cognitive deficits

ers must take great care in ensuring children with FASD understand the when and whys to use fire.

Secondly, another contributing factor to firesetting incident is short- and long-term memory deficits, a cognitive symptom of FASD. Rather than malicious in nature, dangerous acts of firesetting may be the result of children with FASD forgetting how and when it is appropriate to use fire. For example, starting a campfire during a dry season and then fail to extinguish it is of course inappropriate; such a fire has the potential to result in a full-blown forest fire. Finally, a child with FASD, relative to children without FASD, may have difficulty learning from personal experiences and the consequences of their actions. For example, a child without FASD can usually learn and adhere to their parent(s) warnings (i.e., "don't leave your gaming device in the car, the heat will damage it"). The ability to generalize this knowledge from one situation to another is not the norm in children with FASD. As such, children with FASD could have a limited comprehension of perilous and destructive nature of fire.

The social dysfunction symptoms of FASD could be just as important to consider as cognitive symptoms. The communication difficulties of children with FASD could result in trouble conveying how one feels about what they are experiencing. For example, a child with FASD may have had a stressful day at school and not be able to express these difficulties in words. Instead of discussing their problems, these communication difficulties, in combination with emotional problems, can result in frustration, potentially causing some children to lash out in inappropriate ways such as angry outbursts or firesetting. Complicating matters are the impulse control and peer pressure issues characterizing many children with FASD. In fact, children with FASD may understand firesetting is dangerous and should be avoided, but they may not be able to control their actions, particularly in response to peer pressure. These dangers emphasize the importance of helping children with FASD to find ways to express their troubles in more pro-social ways.

Social deficits, which can include a diminished ability to exhibit compassion or empathy, characterize some individuals with FASD (Fernandes et al. 2015; Stevens et al. 2015). In some cases, empathy deficits may contribute to a lack of moral conflict or concern over potentially harming other individuals. This could be further complicated by a limited understanding of ownership and personal property. Because empathy and the principles of ownership simply may not register with some individuals diagnosed with FASD, the risk of destroying property and, even worse, hurting other people could be elevated.

A number of overlapping characteristics are prevalent in FASD and in documented firesetters. When comparing these characteristics (see Table 17.1) it supports the hypothesis that those with FASD are at high risk to set fires. As such, it is recommended those with FASD be involved in additional pro-active educational programs targeting fire safety. Fire professionals would also benefit from training to assist in early identification of FASD and the conjectured link(s) between FASD and firesetting. Specific fire safety tips for families with children affected with FASD are available for free from the corresponding author of this chapter.

17.4 Copycat Firesetting and FASD

The existing literature on juvenile firesetting has overlooked the possibility of copycat firesetting (Doley et al. 2013; Lambie et al. 2014). In relation to children and adults with FASD, the copycat phenomenon becomes an important consideration. Those impacted with FASD frequently have limited impulse control and lack the ability to appropriately consider the predictable cause and effect outcomes. Increased impulsivity, emotionality and social skills deficits are common traits among both the firesetters and those impacted by FASD.

The true prevalence rates of copycat firesetting events within the realm of FASD are currently unknown. As with other criminogenic behaviors, there are inherent difficulties present in determining, and then proving, the origins of firesetting, including copycat firesetting. When considering possible copycat behavior, an original event is needed, with associated media describing the event, which occured prior to the suspected copycat event. Furthermore, there needs to be a link between the media and additional firesetting events. Lambie et al. (2014) offered media presentation of criminal behavior to be a major factor in copycat behaviors.

Youth impacted by FASD are particularly vulnerable to repeating behaviors seen in the media or by demonstrated (role-modeled) by other youth. Children with FASD are also highly suggestible. Exposure to violent media may impact a child's behavior into adolescents and young adulthood (Hopf et al. 2008). This becomes particularly troubling for youth with FASD, for whom managing impulsivity and suggestibility is often a lifetime struggle. Although fire-related media content may not cause firesetting behavior, it may increase the incidence for at-risk youth (Doley et al. 2013; Surette 2011). Ongoing and consistent involvement with violent media results in decreased psychological reactivity, thus decreasing the probability a youth with FASD will recognize the inherent dangers of the firesetting in real-life (Krahe et al. 2011). Entertainment media is not the only concern in regard to copycat firesetting. FASD provides a uniquely ample set of vulnerabilities to poor choices related to peer-pressure and suggestibility (Brown et al. 2011). In the following three cases, these vulnerabilities had catastrophic outcomes for youth eventually diagnosed with FASD.

In the first case, a male high school junior impacted by FASD was approached by a well-regarded popular student and invited to socialize with the popular student and the popular student's friends. This group of students had been setting fires on campus as "practical jokes" resulting in tens of thousands of dollars in property damages and serious safety risks. This group encouraged the student with FASD to set a fire in the boys' bathroom, and recorded it on a cell phone. The recording was then turned into the authorities by the popular student as "the arsonist," in exchange for the reward being offered by the school.

In a second case a youth, with documented prenatal alcohol exposure and previously undiagnosed FASD, was witnessing multiple fires in a large-scale event burning thousands of acres of wild land and suburban areas around the youth's home. The youth was exposed to the fires non-stop in the barrage of social media, television news, and discussion for over 72 h. The youth set a small fire and was reprimanded. The youth went back outside the next day and started a second fire, which rapidly spread due to wind and debris from the other fires, leading to the loss of over a dozen structures and hundred more acres. During the law enforcement examination of the youth, much of the information presented by the officers was parroted back, a common occurrence when interviewing those impacted by FASD. This, in combination with the lack of a functional explanation for the youth's repetitive and dangerous behavior, led to a guilty verdict of felonious arson.

In a third case, copycat firesetting behavior exploded worldwide during the fall of 2014 as a result of the "fire challenge." The fire challenge was a social media epidemic where children and adolescents covered themselves or others with flammable liquids and lit themselves or others on fire. The behavior was videotaped and posted on YouTube. Luckily the fire challenge only lasted for 2 months, however many children were burned. It is unknown what percentage of these children had FASD, but given the nature and suggestibility of the activity, should at the very least be considered as a possibility.

As stated above, scientific documentation of copycat firesetting is very scarce (Lambie et al. 2014). Cases, such as those above, tend to be known only to those individuals working with the youth (Morgan et al. 1995). The correlations made by Doley et al. (2013) make a compelling case for copycat firesetting and an even more compelling case for the routine documentation of such cases. Documentation and further study is needed in order to empirically link copycat firesetting with FASD populations. Given the nature of FASD, the number of copycat firesetters in this population is likely to be high. Currently, fire departments hosting programs for firesetting intervention are just beginning to learn about the signs and symptoms of FASD. These programs will likely be referring more firesetters who are exhibiting signs of FASD to mental health professionals. It is also important for mental health professionals to learn about working with child firesetters.

17.5 Case Studies

Despite a number of case studies and media accounts linking some individuals with FASD to the phenomena of firesetting behaviors, this topic has not received a great deal of academic attention or empirical research. Nonetheless, these cases, both legal and clinical, are frequently seen by mental health and medical professionals who treat FASD as well as fire and legal professionals who investigate and prosecute the crime of arson. This section reviews numerous case studies where the symptoms of FASD may have contributed to firesetting behaviors. These case studies are drawn from clinical and legal cases along with the personal accounts of caregivers. When possible, the identifiable details of individuals involved in these case studies are masked to protect the anonymity of any involved individuals.

17.5.1 Case Law Example 1: Rompilla v. Beard, Secretary, Pennsylvania Department of Corrections (2005)

A closer look at case law indicates that FASD can have an influential impact in the legal system. For example, in Rompilla v. Beard, Secretary, Pennsylvania Department of Corrections (2005), concerns over the failure to consider FASD and related mental health symptoms during the penalty phase of a trial were brought to the attention of the United States Supreme Court. In the initial case (Commonwealth v. Rompilla 1995), the defendant was accused of murdering a bartender by repeated stabbings and then lighting the victim on fire. After the defendant was found guilty by the jury, the prosecution pursued the death sentence by presenting evidence of three aggravating factors during the penalty phase of the trial. These aggravating factors included: (a) the defendant's previous convictions for several felonies; (b) the current act of murder was perpetrated in conjunction with another felonious act; and (c) the present murder involved the use of torture. In response, the mitigating evidence presented by defense attorneys primarily consisted of pleas for mercy and claims of innocence by the defendant's family members, but not evidence of the defendant's difficult childhood experiences, the possible presence of FASD, other related mental health issues, and substance use problems. As a result, the jury sentenced the defendant to death.

The failure to thoroughly investigate and present mitigating evidence resulted in a series of appeals for sentencing relief on the grounds of inadequate representation. Specifically, the defendant's subsequent attorneys argued that their client's original defense attorneys neglected to sufficiently investigate the possible role of the defendant's FASD and other mental health is-sues. This appeal was initially denied by the Supreme Court of Pennsylvania, which found the defense had adequately explored the possibility of such mitigating factors (Commonwealth v. Rompilla 1998). In contrast, the Federal District Court, reversing this decision by the Supreme Court of Pennsylvania, found the original trial representation did not sufficiently explore clear evidence of childhood and mental health difficulties (Rompilla v. Horn 2000). In turn, a conflicted Third Circuit Panel, reversing the Federal District Court's decision, concluded the defense's efforts to uncover mitigating evidence had been adequate (Rompilla v. Horn 2004). Resolving this see-saw of legal decisions, the Supreme Court of the United States reviewed and reversed the decision of the Third Circuit Panel. In finding that the defendant's defense was inadequate, the Supreme

Court ultimately ruled that "...Pennsylvania must either retry the case on penalty or stipulate to a life sentence" (Rompilla v. Beard, Secretary, Pennsylvania Department of Corrections, 2005).

This case law review highlights two imperative points. First, FASD and related mental health concerns should be considered as potential causal contributors to violence, including fire-related criminal behavior. The case of Commonwealth v. Rompilla (1995) is just one of many examples where such mental health issues have been linked to firesetting behaviors. Second, failure to investigate and present evidence on the possible presence of FASD and related mental health issues is grounds for appeal in the United States. Such legal precedence has been firmly established in the case law by the Supreme Court of the United States in Rompilla v. Beard, Secretary, Pennsylvania Department of Corrections (2005). The consideration and active investigation of such possibilities on a client-by-client basis is a legal and ethical responsibility.

17.5.2 Case Law Example 2: State of Washington v. Scholler, Snohomish County Superior Court, (2008)

Scholler is another case of an individual with prenatal alcohol exposure who committed a series of arsons when he was 18-years-old. His biological mother had an IQ under 70 and admit-ted to heavy drinking during pregnancy. Shortly after birth, he experienced a seizure, potentially due to alcohol withdrawal. Moreover, Scholler was considered a "failure to thrive" baby. He was diagnosed with Atypical FAS and ADHD at age three and qualified for special education. When he was four-days-old, he was placed in foster care with a maternal aunt, although his mother also lived with this aunt for approximately 30 months. Scholler was later adopted by the maternal aunt and her husband who described him as very stable, nurturing and caring.

In school, Scholler's teachers described him as cheerful, social, outgoing, cooperative, and willing to try unfamiliar things. Intellectual assessments found that he fell two standard deviations below the mean for overall cognition and academic functioning. Academically, he had difficulty with writing and math, and remained at the second grade level for 3 years. His significant short term memory deficits exacerbated these difficulties. As he moved through elementary and middle school, he developed behavioral problems in the classroom and had ongoing difficulties with attention, hyperactivity, learning, and understanding social boundaries. In particular, Scholler had difficulty focusing and cooperating as the day wore on, had a tendency to blame others, and talk excessively in class. During elementary school, he was suspended for kicking the principal and threatening a peer. In addition, he was suspended three times in middle school for verbal and behavioral aggression. Nonetheless, there was no record of high school suspensions or other disciplinary actions.

Scholler suffered from many of the cognitive, social, and adaptive deficits of FASD. His cognitive impairments are documented in available records that describe on-going assessments. Issues include short and long term memory impairment, concentration deficits, and substantially below average intellectual functioning. In fact, he was diagnosed with a full scale IQ of 60. He had several other executive deficits including difficulties with perception, processing and retrieving information, disorganization, emotional dysregulation, and impulsivity. Complimenting these cognitive issues, he also exhibited significant social skills deficits such as difficulty reading social cues, limited boundary awareness, no sense of danger, and being overly friendly with strangers. Further, Scholler exhibited adaptive deficits like limited abstract thinking, difficulty linking cause with effect (anticipate consequences), incapacity to learn from experiences or generalize knowledge across situations, and the inability to complete tasks without external motivators such as frequent cues or guidance from others.

Although his adoptive father reported no significant behavioral problems with Scholler until the emergence of his preoccupation with fire at 18-years-old, the symptoms of FASD appear to have contributed to abnormal and antisocial behavior throughout his adolescence. For example, during his mid-teens, Scholler's adoptive parents reported compulsive masturbation and chronic sleep disturbances. Other times he simply told lies or made up stories for attention. He started smoking marijuana at age 15, which progressed to smoking every day. At no point did he have consensual and age-appropriate sexual experiences.

When Scholler was arrested at age 18 for setting two fires, he immediately waived his right to counsel. He promptly confessed to these crimes after receiving the *Miranda* Rights and Warning. He blamed the acts of arson on being sexual assaulted recently. Specifically, he claimed that he was sexually assaulted by "friends" 2–4 days prior to setting the first fire and then again before he set the second fire. Because he was upset about his sexual victimization, Scholler was drinking and using marijuana when he set the fires. He vandalized the first house, found a cigarette lighter on a table in the bedroom, and decided to set fire to clothing he found on the bed. Initially claiming that he set the fire to cover up his fingerprints, he thought the fire would extinguish itself. After the second sexual assault, he became extremely angry, frustrated, and felt powerless to stop the abuse. He set fire to the second house after determining it was unoccupied. Both homes became engulfed by flames, which he extinguished. During the investigation, he denied ever playing with fire or being fascinated by fire. He was never asked if he set the fires with the intent of burning the houses down or if he was using drugs before setting the fires.

The trial court judge found that Scholler was incompetent to stand trial. The judge said, "The defendant does have significant executive functioning deficits and does not have the ability to assist in his own defense due to his executive functioning deficits and his FAS." The judge concluded that Scholler would remain incompetent in light of the permanent nature of his brain damage, which was due to prenatal alcohol exposure.

17.5.3 Case Law Example 3: State of Texas v. Estrada (2008)

In another case, an 18-year-old man with pFAS committed robbery (money, credit cards and car keys), murder, and arson. Estrada's victim was an elderly woman who was the respected owner of a Mexican restaurant. She was the next door neighbor of Estrada and his family. He burglarized the house next door, shot the victim in the head with an arrow, and then set fire to the room where the victim's body was located.

Estrada's crime spree was characterized by a number of atypical criminal behaviors. This included providing his real name to neighbors, driving the victim's car to the gas station to purchase gas, and speeding through a school zone where he was seen by a police officer. Despite not having a driver's license, Estrada gave his real name to the officer, who in turn gave him traffic tickets. Further, he attempted to purchase merchandise using the victim's credit card at a store where he had interviewed for a job 2 days earlier, and went on to buy other products with the victim's credit cards. According to Estrada, his motive for the crimes was to obtain money to pay for his girlfriend's abortion, yet he did not give the girlfriend any of the stolen money. His actions were illogical, excessively aggressive, and impulsive. Finally, he immediately waived his rights and gave a guileless confession after his arrest. These peculiarities may have been contributed to by symptoms of FASD.

Not only did Estrada's mother drink heavily during pregnancy, but he was diagnosed with pFAS, along with ten functional life-long impairments on standardized testing. A neuro-psychological assessment determined that Estrada suffered from a developmental brain syndrome causing a mixed, widespread pattern of deficits in adaptive functioning which were the equivalent to mental retardation/intellectual disability. In fact, his cognition function was two and half standard deviations below the mean. Further, his attention, social skills, memory, learning, and executive functions all fell one standard deviation below mean. Estrada also suffered secondary disabilities, including mental health issues, disrupted school experiences, trouble with the law, confinement, substance abuse, dependent living, and employment problems.

In school, Estrada experienced many difficulties related to FASD symptoms. His teachers reported that he demonstrated the following: almost nonexistent self-control, inability to follow school rules, poor/inconsistent task completion, problems with working independently, frequent talking in class, and constant trouble with other students. His social skills were immature, with poor socialization with peers. His auditory attention tasks were below age level; he demonstrated a poor ability to follow oral instructions and comprehend class discussions and experienced poor recall.

During his school years, Estrada received discipline for approximately 100 infractions. One such infraction included a fistfight with another male student. Other serious infractions were for possession of marijuana, theft, and possession of prescribed medication belonging to another student. Additional infractions included tardiness, truancy, disrespect or insubordination, forging passes with teachers' signatures, lack of cooperation, sleeping in class, disrupting/disturbing class, and the use of profanity and/or gestures.

The family home lacked stability and structure. There was an absence of nurturing and protective parents during most of his childhood. His mother resisted Special Education and he received no special services. Estrada not only witnessed domestic violence during his child-hood, but also reported being a victim of physical and sexual abuse. Nonetheless, he did not demonstrate inappropriate sexual behaviors. During his trial, the defense alleged that Estrada lacked the biological capacity to premeditate and form the intent to kill due to mental defect. Specifically, the defense argued that (a) Estrada lacked the cognitive capacity to reflect, (b) this mental defect substantially impaired his capacity to appreciate the wrongfulness of his conduct, and (c) this resulted in his inability to self-regulate within the confines of the law. Based on the testimony of three forensic FASD experts, the jury struggled to consider the viciousness of the defendant's crimes and his medical and mental health conditions. Ultimately, the jury rejected the death penalty and rendered a verdict of life in prison without the possibility of parole.

17.5.4 Clinical Case Study 1

Despite never being officially diagnosed with FASD, Case Study 1 (CS1) is a male in his early twenties who experienced prenatal alcohol exposure. He exhibited many characteristics of FASD including cognitive (e.g., executive control deficits, impulsivity, and mood dysregulation), social (e.g., isolation and vulnerability to peer pressure and social manipulation), and adaptive (e.g., poor long-term planning, lacks good judgment, and low frustration tolerance) impairments. Accompanying these FASD symptoms are several secondary disorders, including antisocial personality disorder, substance use disorders, major depression, and anxiety. In addition to these diagnoses, CS1 has a history of suicidal thinking, low self-esteem, sleep difficulties, and racing thoughts. Many of these mental health disorders and symptoms often co-occur with FASD.

These cognitive, affective, and social impairments had a profound impact across CS1's life course. As is often the case for individuals who may have FASD, CS1 had difficulties in his home life and education that emerged during childhood. In terms of family background, CS1 felt ignored by his parents throughout his childhood. This was likely the result of the emotional absence of his father and his parents' divorce when he was an adolescent. Complicating matters, he was primarily raised by his birth mother, who has a history of substance use including alcohol use during pregnancy. These difficulties at home also manifested themselves at school, where CS1 spent much of his time in special education programs. As a result, CS1 never completed high school. This lack of academic success was primarily driven by a lengthy history of emotional and behavioral (including several fights) problems in school, which are also consistent with FASD.

Possible FASD symptoms may have also manifested in antisocial behavior including fire-setting. From childhood, CS1 repeatedly destroyed property, stole goods on over a dozen occasions, and resorted to hitting and kicking both objects and people when frustrated. In an effort to gain friendship, CS1 committed several inappropriate and illegal acts with the encouragement of peers, which is consistent with the social impairments of FASD. These acts included repeated acts of firesetting, which is an act that he later returned to as a way of venting anger. Worse yet, CS1 became preoccupied with firesetting behaviors as he grew into adolescence. This included setting small fires when overwhelmed and during times of great stress and anger, which was likely exacerbated by the cognitive and adaptive deficits of FASD.

17.5.5 Clinical Case Study 2

Case Study 2 (CS2) is an older female who exhibits many of the cognitive, social, and adaptive symptoms of FASD. CS2 demonstrated several cognitive symptoms including a limited attention span, short- and long-term memory issues, visuospatial reasoning deficits, and reading and comprehension difficulties. Further, she exhibited social deficits across her lifespan, as characterized by an inability to maintain close relationships, poor selection of peers and romantic partners, and repeated entry into abusive relationships. Last, but not least, CS2 has had adaptive functioning difficulties since childhood such as becoming easily overwhelmed. These difficulties continued into adulthood, where she still struggles with problem solving, performing complex tasks with multi-step instructions, and even utilizing public transportation. Nonetheless, it is difficult to discern whether her symptoms stem from her biological mother's documented alcohol issues or CS2's history of head injuries, accidents, physical abuse, and substance use.

CS2 also has a history of secondary mental health conditions stretching back into her childhood, requiring inpatient treatment. As a youth, CS2 was diagnosed with several disorders including Reactive Attachment Disorder, Attention Deficit/Hyperactivity Disorder, and Oppositional Defiant Disorder. More disorders emerged as CS2 developed into an adult, including Borderline Personality Disorder, Posttraumatic Stress Disorder, and traumatic brain injuries. Accompanying her disorders were co-occurring substance dependence issues, which have required "detox" on more than one occasion and resulted in the loss of custody of her child. Further complicating matters, CS2 has a history of low self-esteem, anger dysregulation, sleep difficulties, social isolation, sexual abuse, and suicide attempts, all of which are far too common in individuals with FASD.

Consistent with FASD, CS2 had many of the difficulties in her home, school, and work. Her biological father was absent and her biological mother had lifelong mental health and sub-stance issues, which resulted in the CS2's placement in the foster care system. CS2 was shuffled in and out of different homes and juvenile detention centers throughout her adolescence. Things did not go much better for CS2 at school or work. She never finished high school and has been fired from every job that she has ever held. As a result, CS2 had a long history of homelessness.

CS2's potential symptoms of FASD may have also contributed to her antisocial behavior. Her conduct issues began as a youth, when she was frequently truant, revealed a propensity for running away from home, and repeatedly got into fights. Her antisocial behavior also included firesetting, which she did as a means of obtaining vengeance and regulating emotions such as anger. As she entered adulthood, her criminal behavior escalated into substance use-related offenses, theft, and a history of assaults. The consequences of these actions included several incarcerations in juvenile detention, jail, and prison. CS2's ability to break this vicious cycle was likely limited by the cognitive, social, and adaptive impairments of FASD.

17.5.6 Clinical Case Study 3

Case Study 3 (CS3) is a male in his forties who has a confirmed diagnosis of FASD. Like many individuals with FASD, he was adopted at birth and has never had contact with his birth parents. He has manifested many of the cognitive (e.g., limited intellectual capacity and impulsivity), social, and adaptive symptoms of FASD. These FASD symptoms are accompanied by several co-occurring conditions including diagnoses of mood disorders (i.e., major depression and bipolar disorder), behavioral disorders (i.e., attention deficit hyperactivity disorder and antisocial personality disorder), substance use disorders, and learning disorders. Together, these mental health issues have contributed to several instances of self-injury, attempted suicide, and inpatient hospitalization.

CS3's FASD-related mental health struggles have prevented him from successfully maintaining employment and resulted in a long series of skirmishes with the legal system. During adolescence, CS3 began using illicit drugs and developed a significant history of fighting and thefts. Additionally, CS3 regularly engaged in thrill-seeking behaviors such as firesetting, which resulted in significant property damage. The antisocial behavior of CS3 persisted into adulthood, with some incidents of inappropriate sexual behavior. These sexual indiscretions led to prison time, and could very well be a function of the social impairments of FASD. It is probable that the adaptive, cognitive, and social skill deficits associated with FASD also contributed to his firesetting behaviors. As shown above, the symptoms of FASD and other co-occurring mental health ailments have made it increasingly difficult for CS3 to function within the confines of society.

17.5.7 Clinical Case Study 4

Case Study 4 (CS4) is an adolescent male with a documented medical history of prenatal alcohol exposure. Although he exhibits the classic cognitive and adaptive symptoms of FASD, he has excellent social skills and communicates with clarity. His bright, engaging, and friendly mannerisms frequently resulted in adults and authority figures assuming that he has no disabilities. These mistaken assumptions of his normative functioning led to a catastrophic fire that burned thousands of acres of wilderness and destroyed hundreds of homes.

Adopted shortly after pre-term birth at only 7 months gestation, CS4 was not expected to survive his first year due to the significant birth impairments, which were consistent with prenatal alcohol exposure. Despite regular hospitalizations for complications due to a weakened immune system, fainting spells, and seizure activity, he frequently participated in sporting events and enjoys time with his family. His adoptive mother calls him their "little Spartan" because of his strong will to survive and desire to conquer obstacles.

At home, CS4 experiences mood swings arising from extreme sensitivity and is very de-pendent on his family. At school, he makes acquaintances, but has difficulty developing deeper and more meaningful friendships. He began to fall behind in math and reading starting in the sixth grade. A year before the incident, a psychological assessment found significant concerns in processing speed, short term memory, and attention span were documented. To maximize his academic potential, kinesthetic learning was recommended.

At the time of the firesetting incident, lightening striking a tree had recently initiated a fire in a nearby field that burned down a neighbor's house. CS4's household and neighbors discussed this fire at length for several consecutive days. Everyone was very concerned about the potential for another fire because the area was heavily populated with brush. CS4 repeatedly questioned family and others in person and on social media about the concerns, especially about the fire's extinguishment. After receiving an answer he thought was satisfactory, he went into the lot next door and set a small fire. A neighbor ran over and put it out, chastising him for having lit the fire. The neighbor did not inform CS4's parents. Prompted by hearing his family talking about the fire on the following day, CS4 went back to the field and set another small fire. Wind caught the embers and they landed in a neighboring dry field. The fire burned for four and a half days. The young man was charged with, and found guilty of felony arson. The impact of FASD on his reasoning was never raised at the trial.

17.5.8 Case Studies Conclusion

As illustrated in these legal and clinical case studies, individuals with prenatal alcohol exposure can exhibit a wide range of deficits, challenges, and behaviors. Firesetting, no matter what the motive, can result in property damage and even death. Prenatal alcohol exposure often results in a wide range of executive and cognitive deficits including impulsivity, poor emotional regulation, co-morbid mental health issues, poor relationship skills, family difficulties, and impairments in understanding cause and effect. These FASD-related concerns have also been identified as characteristics consistent with firesetting. As such, some individuals with FASD may be at higher risk to set fires. Both legal and clinical environments would benefit from considering these implications.

Table 17.2 Possible red flag indicators of FASD

FASD symptoms
Impulsivity
Inattentiveness/hyperactivity
Immaturity
Poor decision making
Learning disabilities
Communication deficits including confusing or inconsistent responses to questioning
Difficulty linking past behavior to consequences, which may contribute to an individual not responding to punishment

In summary, there is substantial indirect evidence (for a review, see: Gelhorn et al. 2007; Lambie and Randell 2011; MacKay et al. 2009; Huff 2014; Gelhorn et al. 2009; Watt et al. 2015; Lambie and Randell 2011; Zipper and Wilcox 2005; Kolko 2002; Johnson and Jones 2014; and Burnett and Omar 2014) (including several case studies) for a link between FASD and tendencies of firesetting, and therefore an important challenge for future research in this field is to focus on direct evidence to accept or reject this hypothesis.

Appendix: Some Practical Advice to Fire Professionals and Forensic Mental Health Professionals

Per the anecdotal evidence presented here, there is an indication that youth with FASD may be predisposed to the risks of social interactions and behavioral inhibitions frequently seen as precursors and co-occurring concerns in youth firesetting. This suggests contact with fire professionals is likely. Fire professionals should become familiar with FASD to aid in both fire preventions and investigations. There are several red flags of FASD (i.e., symptoms, family background, and history of rule-breaking behavior) which fire professionals can use to identify youth who would potentially benefit from referral to screening for the disorder. (A template for this is available upon request from the corresponding author of this chapter). The importance of recognition is two-fold. First, the suspicion of FASD may necessitate fire professionals employ an interview style and investigative approach that is cognizant of the deficits of FASD (e.g., cognitive and communication deficits). Second, fire professionals have the opportunity to identify youth in need of additional screening for FASD. Any assistance offered by fire professionals in identifying youth with FASD has the potential to decrease the societal costs of firesetting and improve the projected quality of life youth with FASD (Table 17.2).

FASD and other disorders characterized by cognitive and developmental deficits are complicated to assess and treat, especially in the absence of appropriate training and understanding of the disorder. An added layer of complexity in the intervention and treatment of youth with FASD is when firesetting behaviors are present. An important step towards developing and utilizing appropriate intervention strategies with those impacted by FASD and who have engaged in fire-related activities is appropriate assessment. This assessment should consider possibly comorbid disabilities (e.g., ADHD, CD, anxiety, depression, attachment disorders, and substance misuse conditions). Further, any goal or treatment plan must incorporate considerations of development (i.e., mental versus physical age), communication ability (i.e., receptive and expressive language), and learning and memory disabilities. Such roadblocks can impede successful treatment efforts if not adequately addressed in the intervention plan. As such, medical, mental health, and fire professionals will often require the assistance of specialists with advanced training in the area of FASD. An evaluation from a neuropsychologist may also prove beneficial, especially in identifying specific brain impairments and determining the most effective means to communicate the intervention strategies. The most successful interventions likely begin in childhood, with early diagnosis, strong and consistent case management, and individualized services tailored across developmental stages from childhood to adulthood. Although impulsivity is difficult to directly address, the identification of environmental stressors contributing to impulsive actions may be key in reducing firesetting behaviors.

Additionally, many environmental considerations must be made including the identification of supportive caregivers, development of a strong supervision structure, and the limitation of influence by negative peers. To maximize the potential of success, treatment may need to include an individualized medication regimen along with targeted skills training, which could incorporate a combination of several approaches such as FASD-informed case management and therapy approaches, anger and stress management, Attention Awareness Training, pro-social skill teaching, sleep-improvement strategies, and neurofeedback. In light of these complexities, increased supervision and extended care may be the rule rather than the exception in this population.

As a result of the multitude of difficulties and comorbid conditions often present among many individuals with FASD, fire intervention specialists and forensic mental health professionals without advanced training in FASD are likely ill-equipped to deal with firesetting behavior in this population. In an effort to assist fire professionals, the first author of this chapter developed the D.E.A.R. guide (available upon request to the corresponding author of this chapter) on how to interact with individuals with suspected or confirmed FASD. D.E.A.R. is an acronym that emphasizes the use of (D.) direct language during interactions with the individual, (E.) engagement of the individual's support system, (A.) accommodating the individual needs of the individual, and (R.) remaining calm and non-threatening during interactions with the individual. With these recommendations in mind, fire and forensic mental health professionals have the potential to improve not only interactions and developmentally modified fire safety approaches, but also long-term outcomes in youth with FASD who are involved in firesetting behaviors. Although FASD is an incurable lifelong condition, many of these comorbid psychiatric conditions can be successfully treated and managed with appropriate psychiatric care and case management. This positive aspect emphasizes the essential nature of early identification, diagnosis, and treatment of FASD.

Nonetheless, fire professionals should still be aware that individuals with FASD are prone to providing false information and confabulation. In fact, individuals with FASD may be disproportionately likely to confess to illegal activities committed by other people. The veracity of statements may be particularly questionable when obtained in stressful situations (i.e., sirens, loud noises, and busy rooms), which can exacerbate the confusion and poor decision making of individuals with FASD. To help protect against these possibilities, fire professionals should corroborate any information provided by individuals who may have FASD with other available sources including family members, witnesses, and physical evidence. In conclusion, fire professionals should be aware that the presence of FASD impacts not only how they should communicate with an individual, but how much faith should be placed in the information provided by an individual with FASD.

References

Alloway, T.P., S.E. Gathercole, H. Kirkwood, and J. Elliott. 2009. The cognitive and behavioral characteristics of children with low working memory. *Child Development* 80 (2): 606–621.

American Psychiatric Association. 2013. *Diagnostic and statistical manual of mental disorders: DSM-5*. 5th ed. Alexandria: American Psychiatric Association.

Barry-Walsh, J.B., and P.E. Mullen. 2003. Forensic aspects of Asperger's syndrome. *The Journal of Forensic Psychiatry & Psychology* 15: 96–107.

Bartol, C.R., and A.M. Bartol. 2012. *Introduction to forensic psychology*. Thousand Oaks: Sage.

Brown, N.N., G. Gudjonsson, and P. Connor. 2011. Suggestibility and Fetal Alcohol Spectrum Disorders: I'll tell you anything you want to hear. *The Journal of Psychiatry & Law* 39 (1): 39–71.

Brown, N.N., P.D. Connor, and R.S. Adler. 2012. Conduct-disordered adolescents with Fetal Alcohol Spectrum Disorder intervention in secure treatment settings. *Criminal Justice and Behavior* 39 (6): 770–793.

Brown, J., S. Herrick, and J. Long-McGie. 2014. Fetal alcohol spectrum disorders and offender reentry: A review for criminal justice and mental health professionals. *Behavioral Health* 1 (1): 1–19.

Burd, L., R.H. Selfridge, M.G. Klug, and T. Juelson. 2003. Fetal alcohol syndrome in the Canadian corrections system. *Journal of FAS International* 1 (14): 1–10.

Burnett, A., and H.A. Omar. 2014. Firesetting and maltreatments: A review. *International Journal of Children and Adolescent Health* 7 (2): 99–101.

Burnside, L., and D. Fuchs. 2013. Bound by the clock: The experiences of youth with FASD transitioning to adulthood from child welfare care. *First Nations Child & Family Caring Society of Canada* 8: 40–61.

Chasnoff, I.J., A.M. Wells, and L. King. 2015. Misdiagnosis and missed diagnoses in foster and adopted children with prenatal alcohol exposure. *Pediatrics* 135 (2): 264–270.

Clarren, S.K., and J. Lutke. 2008. Building clinical capacity for fetal alcohol spectrum disorder diagnoses in Western and Northern Canada. *Canadian Journal of Clinical Pharmacology* 15 (2): 223–237.

Commonwealth v. Rompilla. 1995. 539 Pa. 499, 653 A.2d 626.

———. 1998. 554 Pa. 378, 721 A.2d 786.

Del Bove, G., G.V. Caprara, C. Pastorelli, and M. Paciello. 2008. Juvenile firesetting in Italy: Relationship to aggression, psychopathology, personality self-efficacy and school functioning. *European Child and Adolescent Psychiatry* 17: 234–244.

Doley, R., C. Ferguson, and R. Surrette. 2013. Copycat firesetting: Bridging two research areas. *Criminal Justice and Behavior* 40: 1472–1491.

Douglas, H. 2010. The sentencing response to defendants with foetal alcohol spectrum disorder. *Criminal Law Journal* 34: 221–239.

Edwards, W.J., and S. Greenspan. 2010. Adaptive behavior alcohol spectrum and fetal disorders. *The Journal of Psychiatry & Law* 38 (4): 419–447.

Fast, D., and J. Conry. 2004. The challenge of fetal alcohol syndrome in the criminal legal system. *Addiction Biology* 9 (2): 161–166.

Fast, D.K., and J. Conry. 2009. Fetal alcohol spectrum disorders and the criminal justice system. *Developmental Disabilities Research Reviews* 15 (3): 250–257.

Federal Emergency Management Agency. 2011. Fire death rate trends: An international perspective. *US Department of Homeland Security* 12(8). Retrieved from: http://www.nfpa.org/safety-information/for-consumers/arson-and-youth-fire-setting/young-firesetters.

Fernandes, Y., M. Rampersad, and R. Gerlai. 2015. Impairment of social behaviour persists two years after embryonic alcohol exposure in zebrafish: A model of fetal alcohol spectrum disorders. *Behavioural Brain Research* 292: 102–108.

Gelhorn, H.L., J.T. Sakai, R.K. Price, and T.J. Crowley. 2007. DSM-IV conduct disorder criteria as predictors of antisocial personality disorder. *Comprehensive Psychiatry* 48 (6): 529–538.

Gelhorn, H., C. Hartman, J. Sakai, S. Mikulich-Gilbertson, M. Stallings, S. Young, S. Rhee, R. Corley, J. Hewitt, C. Hopfer, and T. Crowley. 2009. An item response theory analysis of DSM-IV conduct disorder. *Journal of the American Academy of Child & Adolescent Psychiatry* 48 (1): 42–50.

Green, C.R., A.M. Mihic, S.M. Nikkel, B.C. Stade, C. Rasmussen, D.P. Munoz, and J.N. Reynolds. 2009. Executive function deficits in children with fetal alcohol spectrum disorders (FASD) measured using the Cambridge Neuropsychological Tests Automated Battery (CANTAB). *Journal of Child Psychology and Psychiatry* 50 (6): 688–697.

Hellman, D.S., and N. Blackman. 1966. Enuresis, firesetting and cruelty to animals: A triad predictive of adult crime. *American Journal of Psychiatry* 122 (12): 1431–1435.

Hopf, W.H., G.L. Huber, and R.H. Weiss. 2008. Media violence and youth violence: A 2-year longitudinal study. *Journal of Media Psychology* 20: 79–96.

Huff, M.B. 2014. Assessment and treatment of youth firesetting: A clinical perspective. *International Journal of Child and Adolescent Health* 7 (2): 117–123.

Jeffery, M. 2010. An Arctic judge's journey with FASD. *Journal of Psychiatry & Law* 38: 585–618.

Johnson, R., and P. Jones. 2014. Identification of parental endorsement patterns: An example of the importance of professional attunement to the clinical-forensic risk markers in juvenile firesetting and bomb making. *American Journal of Forensic Psychology* 32 (2): 1–18.

Kanehisa, M., K. Morinaga, H. Kohno, Y. Maruyama, T. Ninomiya, Y. Ishitobi, Y. Tanaka, J. Tsuru, H. Hanada, T. Yoshikawa, and J. Akiyoshi. 2012. An uncommon case of random fire-setting behavior associated with Todd paralysis: A case report. *BMC Psychiatry* 12: 132.

Kolko, D.J. 2002. *Handbook on firesetting in children and youth*. San Diego: Academic Press.

Kolko, D.J., and A.E. Kazdin. 1991. Motives of childhood firesetters: Firesetting characteristics and psychological correlates. *Journal of Child Psychology and Psychiatry* 32 (3): 535–550.

Krahe, B., I. Moller, L.R. Huessman, L. Kirwil, J. Felber, and A. Berger. 2011. Denensitization to media violence: Links with habitual media violence exposure, aggressive cognitions, and aggressive behavior. *Journal of Personality and Social Psychology* 100: 630–646.

Lambie, I., and I. Randell. 2011. Creating a firestorm: A review of children who deliberately light fires. *Clinical Psychology Review* 31: 307–327.

Lambie, I., F. Seymour, and T. Popaduk. 2012. Young people and caregivers' perception of an intervention program for children who deliberately light fires. *Evaluation and Program Planning* 35 (4): 445–452.

Lambie, I., I. Randell, and H. McDowell. 2014. Inflaming your neighbors: Copycat firesetting in adolescents. *International Journal of Offender Therapy and Comparative Criminology* 58 (9): 1020–1032.

MacDonald, J.M. 1966. *The threat to kill.* Available from: http://worldcat.org/z-wcorg/database.

MacKay, S., A. Paglia-Boak, J. Henderson, P. Marton, and E. Adlaf. 2009. Epidemiology of firesetting in adolescents: Mental health and substance use correlates. *Journal of Child Psychology and Psychiatry* 50 (10): 1282–1290.

Mattson, S.N., E.P. Riley, L. Gramling, D.C. Delis, and K.L. Jones. 1997. Heavy prenatal alcohol exposure with or without physical features of fetal alcohol syndrome leads to IQ deficits. *The Journal of Pediatrics* 131 (5): 718–721.

May, P.A., J.P. Gossage, W.O. Kalberg, L.K. Robinson, D. Buckley, M. Manning, and H.E. Hoyme. 2009. Prevalence and epidemiologic characteristics of FASD from various research methods with an emphasis on recent in-school studies. *Developmental Disabilities Research Reviews* 15 (3): 176–192.

McLachlan, K., R. Roesch, J.L. Viljoen, and K.S. Douglas. 2014. Evaluating the psycholegal abilities of young offenders with fetal alcohol spectrum disorder. *Law and Human Behavior* 38 (1): 10–22.

Morgan, N., D.A.G. Cook, C.E. Dorkins, and M.E. Doyle. 1995. An outbreak of copycat fire raising. *British Journal of Medical Psychology* 68 (4): 341–348.

Prentky, R.A., and D.L. Carter. 1984. The predictive value of the triad for sex offenders. *Behavioral Sciences & the Law* 2 (3): 341–354.

Rasmussen, C., and K. Wyper. 2007. Decision making, executive functioning and risky behaviors in adolescents with prenatal alcohol exposure. *International Journal on Disability and Human Development* 6 (4): 405–416.

Rompilla v. Beard, Secretary, Pennsylvania Department of Corrections, 545 U.S. 374 (Supreme Court of United States 2005).

Rompilla v. Horn, No. CIV.A.99-737 (ED Pa., July 11, 2000), App. 1307–1308.

———. 2004. 355 F.3d 233.

Ryan, K. 2009. *The Macdonald triad: Predictor of violence or urban myth?* Fresno: California State University.

Sakheim, G.A., and E. Osborn. 1986. A psychological profile of juvenile firesetters in residential treatment: A replication study. *Child Welfare: Journal of Policy, Practice, and Program* 65 (5): 495.

Singer, S.D., and C.H. Hensley. 2004. Applying social learning theory to childhood and adolescent firesetting: Can it lead to serial murder? *International Journal of Offender Therapy and Comparative Criminology* 48 (4): 461–476.

State of Washington v. Scholler. 2008. Snohomish County Superior Court, #08-8-00426-1 and #08-9-00443-1.

Stevens, S.A., J. Dudek, K. Nash, G. Koren, and J. Rovet. 2015. Social perspective taking and empathy in children with fetal alcohol spectrum disorders. *Journal of the International Neuropsychological Society* 21 (1): 74–84.

Stickle, T.R., and E.A. Blechman. 2002. Aggression and fire: Antisocial behavior in firesetting and nonfiresetting juvenile offenders. *Journal of Psychopathology and Behavioral Assessment* 24 (3): 177–193.

Streissguth, A.P., H.M. Barr, J. Kogan, and F.L. Bookstein. 1996. *Final Report: Understanding the Occurrence of Secondary Disabilities in Clients with Fetal Alcohol Syndrome (FAS) and Fetal Alcohol Effects (FAE).* Seattle: University of Washington Publication Services.

Surette, R. 2011. *Media, crime and criminal justice: Images and realities*. 4th ed. Belmomont: Wadsworth.

Tallichet, S.E., C. Hensley, and S.D. Singer. 2005. Unraveling the methods of childhood and adolescent cruelty to nonhuman animals. *Society & Animals* 13 (2): 91–108.

Texas v. Estrada, Bexar County, 2008 CR. 5920 (Texas Superior Court, 2010).

Thiel, K.S., N.J. Baladerian, K.R. Boyce, O.D. Cantos, L.A. Davis, K. Kelly, et al. 2011. Fetal alcohol spectrum disorders and victimization: Implications for families, educators, social services, law enforcement, and the judicial system. *The Journal of Psychiatry & Law* 39 (1): 121–157.

Wartnik, A.P., J. Brown, and S. Herrick. 2015. Evolution of the diagnosis of fetal alcohol spectrum disorder from DSM-IV-TR to DSM-5: The justice system in the United States – Time for a paradigm shift! In *Fetal alcohol spectrum disorders in adults: ethical and legal perspectives. An overview on FASD for professionals*, ed. M. Nelson and M. Trussler, 151–167. Cham: Springer.

Watkins, R.E., E.J. Elliott, A. Wilkins, J. Latimer, J. Halliday, J.P. Fitzpatrick, et al. 2014. Fetal alcohol spectrum disorder: Development of consensus referral criteria for specialist diagnostic assessment in Australia. *BMC Pediatrics* 14 (1): 178.

Watt, B.D., K. Geritz, T. Hasan, S. Harden, and R. Doley. 2015. Prevalence and correlates of firesetting behaviours among offending and non-offending youth. *Legal and Criminological Psychology* 20 (1): 19–36.

Wheeler, S.M., S.A. Stevens, E.D. Sheard, and J.F. Rovet. 2012. Facial memory deficits in children with fetal alcohol spectrum disorders. *Child Neuropsychology* 18 (4): 339–346.

Zipper, P., and D. Wilcox. 2005. Juvenile arson: The importance of early intervention. *FBI Law Enforcement Bulletin* 74 (4): 1–9.

Appendix A: Consensus Statement on Legal Issues of Fetal Alcohol Spectrum Disorder (FASD)

It is the jury's position that unnecessary and repetitive expenditures can be curbed if adequate services are provided at the point of first contact with child protection.

About the Consensus Statement

This consensus statement on Legal Issues of Fetal Alcohol Spectrum Disorder is the product of a unique IHE Consensus Development Conference held in September 2013. The event was a three-day juried hearing of evidence and scientific findings that allowed for the engagement and collaboration of citizens and decision makers in government and the justice system in addressing a specific set of key questions on legal issues related to FASD. (There were 28 experts who testified around the following 8 questions, to a jury composed of 14 people. The audience included about 400 participants).

Conference Questions

1. What are the implications of FASD for the legal system?
2. How can efforts to identify people with FASD in the legal system be improved?
3. How can the criminal justice system respond more effectively to people with FASD?
4. How can family courts and the family/child welfare legal system address the specific needs of people with FASD?
5. What are best practices for guardianship, trusteeship and social support in a legal context?
6. What legal measures are there in different jurisdictions to contribute to the prevention of FASD, and what are the ethical and economic implications of these measures?

Acknowledgements

The Honourable Ian Binnie CC, QC, Former Justice of the Supreme Court of Canada, led a panel of distinguished citizens and experts to develop

E. Jonsson et al. (eds.), *Ethical and Legal Perspectives in Fetal Alcohol Spectrum Disorders (FASD)*, International Library of Ethics, Law, and the New Medicine 75,
https://doi.org/10.1007/978-3-319-71755-5

recommendations and suggestions of policy improvements in addressing the unique position of people with FASD within the legal system.

The Honourable Marguerite Trussler QC, Retired Justice of the Court of Queen's Bench; Chairperson – Alberta Liquor and Gaming Commission, chaired the Steering Committee for Alberta Initiatives on FASD.

Disclosure Statement
All of the jury members who participated in this conference and contributed to the writing of this statement were identified as having no financial or scientific conflict of interest.

Consensus Statement Introduction

Fetal alcohol spectrum disorder (FASD) refers to a range of physical, neurodevelopmental, and behavioural impairments resulting from damage to the brain of the fetus caused by maternal alcohol use during pregnancy. These impairments may include growth retardation, malformations of the face, neurological disorders, and deficiencies such as problems with memory, learning, attention and social communication. The facial abnormalities associated with prenatal alcohol exposure are not always present, and, therefore, FASD is frequently invisible and undiagnosed. Nonetheless, the brain trauma that alcohol causes in the developing fetus is irreparable, lifelong, and devastating for the individual, the family and other caregivers. In Canada, at least one of every one hundred newborns is affected by FASD (an estimated 3800 newborns in 2010–11).

Although alcohol is the primary explanatory factor in the neurological profile of FASD individuals, we also recognize the impact of variables such as early childhood trauma, genetics, maternal nutrition, adverse environment and brain development. These factors tend both to confound and to mask the neurological deficits caused by the diffuse brain injury that exists in all cases of FASD regardless of where the person falls across the fetal alcohol spectrum.

FASD is present throughout Canadian society although accurate studies of prevalence in different segments of the population are not available. For reasons almost certainly related to their historical treatment in Canada, it is generally assumed, whether accurately or not, that Aboriginal people who are disproportionately represented in the criminal justice system are also likely overrepresented among the populations that have neurological impairments associated with FASD. We stress, however, that FASD also affects other populations in Canada.

The recommendations in the 2009 Consensus Statement on Fetal Alcohol Spectrum Disorder (FASD) – Across the Lifespan remain relevant today. While we have been asked to focus on FASD in the legal context, we recognize that FASD and its implications are issues of broader societal concern and that society has a corresponding responsibility to provide support to these affected individuals in all aspects of their lives.

This 2013 consensus statement explores the implications for the justice system when the needs of FASD-affected individuals go unmanaged in the broader community and ultimately surface in the legal context. Our recommendations should be read, however, in light of our strong support for a holistic community-based approach that gives primacy to the rights and voice of the child, while fostering a collaborative community response to the child's individual needs.

Our recommendations should also be read in the context of the recent amendments to the federal FASD Framework for Action, the August 2013 Canadian Bar Association call for legislative change to recognize the unique position of FASD individuals in the criminal justice system, and the upcoming review of the Canadian Diagnostic Guidelines definition of FASD.

We must also stress our recognition of the needs of the broader society. FASD is a possible explanation for behaviour. It does not provide absolution for misconduct. At the same time, people who have FASD suffer from neurodevelopmental disorders and, in some cases, serious functional deficiencies that in all fairness must be recognized and taken into account in the administration of justice.

During the course of this conference the jury has been presented with a great deal of evidence which demonstrates the immense problems and challenges that FASD presents to the justice system. This consensus statement attempts to respond to those problems and challenges and thus the focus of this statement tends to be on the problems associated with FASD. The jury wishes to acknowledge, however, that the evidence we heard also includes many stories of triumph and success. There are signs of hope. There is good reason to believe that, with determination and with properly allocated resources, the huge cost of FASD to both the individuals affected by it and to society at large, can be alleviated.

FASD is not a problem that will go away. The fact that its effects are believed to be concentrated so heavily in already disadvantaged Aboriginal communities adds to the urgency of finding solutions or at least alleviating the associated hardships.

The jury heard evidence that Albertans spend, on average, $721 per person each year on alcohol. There is also evidence of increasing alcohol consumption, including binge drinking among some young people. We also heard evidence that a woman's consumption of alcohol has a serious potential to adversely affect an embryo at the very early stages of development, even before a woman would know definitely that she was pregnant.

All of these factors suggest that while more resources should be devoted to the prevention of FASD, the problem is also one of better allocating existing resources. In this field, as elsewhere, an ounce of prevention is worth a pound of attempted remedies.

Question 1: What Are the Implications of FASD for the Legal System?

The FASD Challenge to the Legal System

The neurodevelopmental deficits associated with FASD present a fundamental challenge to the Canadian criminal justice system, which is premised on assumptions that people act in a voluntary manner that is determined by free will and that they can make informed and voluntary choices with respect to both the exercise of their rights and the decision to commit crimes. It is presumed that a person intends the natural consequences of his or her actions, and that, for example, an individual would never make a statement against his or her interest unless it was either true or coerced.

The evidence we have heard is compelling that those with FASD are likely to have a diminished capacity to foresee consequences, make reasoned choices or learn from mistakes. Therefore, their actions are likely to clash with assumptions about human behaviour at almost every stage of the justice system.

Throughout their lives, individuals with FASD are more likely to be involved in the legal system than individuals without FASD. Children with FASD are overrepresented in the foster care and group care systems, and their special needs and developmental issues have been identified by the courts in all aspects of the law from criminal prosecutions to guardianship, family violence and child protection applications.

Conflicting Consequences

The diagnosis of FASD may have multiple and conflicting consequences. Privacy issues are at stake. In the criminal context, courts in some (but certainly not all) cases recognize that FASD is a disability that reduces the moral culpability or voluntariness of a person's actions and may result in a lesser criminal sentence; but the same disability may result in a deemed inability to care for a child, leading to state intervention in the family or a change in custody, or deny a person's ability to rely on their insurer in a motor vehicle claim if they failed to disclose their FASD diagnosis.

The Elusive Nature of FASD

One fundamental problem is that FASD represents a broad spectrum of symptoms of greatly varied severity giving rise to a range of disorders/ disabilities and, consequently, varying degrees of diminished responsibility and capacity.

It would be relatively simple if individuals with FASD could be located on an index from 1 to 10 and the court could be told this suspect/applicant is a "3" or a "7" in terms of severity, but given the highly individualized symptoms and diagnoses such a simple one-dimensional categorization is impossible. While the elements of the neurological damage associated with FASD are well established, their expression and intensity vary from one individual to another.

In the absence of a simplified method of categorization, the legal system must adapt to individualized, context-specific diagnoses, and formulate manageable criteria or standards to deal with many different interactions with FASD sufferers.

Secondary Disabilities and Adverse Outcomes

As a result of permanent brain damage and other factors, a person with FASD is vulnerable to a number of secondary disabilities and adverse outcomes. These include leaving school, family and placement breakdown, homelessness, alcohol and drug abuse and related infectious diseases. Many youth with FASD have been taken into care and are being raised in foster families or group homes, often with several placements and possibly inadequately trained caregivers. These populations may overlap with the disproportionate apprehension of Aboriginal children in the child welfare system. Unemployment, mental illness, and involvement with the criminal justice system are common. We were told that a majority (about 60%) of individuals with FASD come into conflict with the law.

Underdiagnosis: The Invisible Population

Only a small portion of individuals with FASD show physical signs and the cognitive disabilities associated with FASD are often not apparent on standard intelligence tests. Without an awareness of other signs that may be symptomatic of FASD, the person affected by FASD can easily fall through the cracks.

Recommendations

Recommendations to tackle the implications of FASD in the legal system do not fit easily into a tidy framework. Recognizing that the context for some of the jury's recommendations will become more apparent later in this Statement, the jury begins with the following:

1. The ability of communities and families must be strengthened to deal – outside of the traditional criminal justice system – with "offending behaviour" of youths and adults.
2. Services must be provided within communities that would help create more stable homes and placements for those in care. The goal should be to help communities manage the problems associated with FASD so that those with FASD from that community can remain in the community as productive members of society.
3. FASD must be assessed using a multidisciplinary team approach; no one specialty is sufficient.
4. The development of biomarkers appears to be the most promising area of research to identify FASD affected individuals and should be pursued, although the use of them raises important legal and ethical issues.

5. Greater effort must be made to make the public aware of the cost of dealing with FASD in the legal system.[1]
6. Where at all possible those affected by FASD should be kept out of the criminal-justice system. In 2010/11 it cost an average of about $114,000 per year to keep a prisoner in federal prison, much more than it costs to provide services – criminal justice or otherwise – in the community. Studies suggest that between 10% and 25% of prisoners have FASD. It is estimated that each person with FASD costs governments $1.5–2.0 million over their lifetime including education, health and other services.[2] These costs, as well as the difficulties that people with FASD may experience in custodial institutions, include but are not limited to:
    - support for community-based housing (such as the At Home Chez-Soi/Housing First Program) and transition housing programs;
    - community education programs starting with children and youth; and
    - community support and intervention programs that are evidence-based in supporting individuals affected by FASD throughout their lifespan, particularly in key transition periods.
7. More resources should be focused on family and community supports that will allow those with FASD to live under supervision outside of the criminal justice system. The jury heard evidence about a cross-sectoral program in Alberta that supports people with FASD in the community for costs below $5000 per person served per year or $1.63 per capita, a figure that is far below correctional costs.

Training

8. Mandate training for all players in the legal system, including judges, crown, defence, corrections, police, probation officers, parole officers, and community frontline workers so that when they encounter a citizen, in a home or on the street, they have the background knowledge that will sensitize them to the cues that may suggest that the person they are dealing with has FASD.
9. Support innovative training programs that promote inter-sectoral dialogue and partnerships, and sustain longitudinal educational curriculums in order to ensure continuing education for all major stakeholders in Canada (such as corrections, health, social development, mental health, RCMP, provincial and federal court officials, education, and First Nations).

---

[1] The jury heard evidence that each person charged in the criminal justice system costs over $16,000 in policing, prosecutorial, court and correctional costs. In what is described as the revolving door phenomena, many people with FASD re-offend, often because they are unable to comply with various conditions placed upon them by bail orders, conditional sentences or parole.

[2] Governments benefit greatly through the taxation of alcohol, but spend only a tiny portion of these revenues on dealing with its adverse consequences. We heard evidence that Alberta collects $578 million in taxes on alcohol each year or $158 per capita but that the government spends only $3 per capita on the health effects of alcohol. There is a need for governments to devote more of those funds to education, research and services about the dangers of alcohol, including FASD.

10. Training needs to be carried out on an ongoing basis to ensure that people know not only the up-to-date best practices but also the services that are available in their communities to those who suffer from FASD.

Other Recommendations

11. Every child going into care of the state should receive a full medical examination and a full psychological examination that would include a screen for FASD to assist with the planning and implementation of appropriate services for the family. However, should this policy be implemented, the purpose of the assessment should be clearly stated to avoid the misuse of the FASD diagnosis against the mother. Similarly, admission procedures in correctional centres (either on remand or on sentence) should include screening for possible FASD to ensure that prisoners are dealt with appropriately by staff trained in the problems associated with FASD. Again, the FASD diagnosis should not be used against the prisoner, but should be used to help better accommodate and manage such persons within the correctional system.
12. Consideration should be given to the legal, ethical, and practical issues surrounding policies related to the sharing of a positive FASD diagnosis. For example, the suggestion that positive FASD diagnoses be kept on police files (e.g., CPIC) or child protection files to ensure that it is shared with others who may have contact with that individual in the future raises important issues of privacy. Nevertheless, if this information were known to police officers and child protection authorities – under certain specified conditions and with the appropriate training of those officials – it might help alleviate problems and promote just and fair outcomes.
13. Individuals with FASD often get into conflict with the law when they are not involved in a structured program. There is a need to build relationships between an individual with FASD or other neurological impairment and a circle of support that could include family members and social service workers to ensure that the individual has a therapeutic environment in which to live.
14. Housing stability and wraparound support are critical. Government should undertake to examine whether it might be more economical to develop small (e.g., 10-bed) housing units with 24/7 support from social service agencies to ensure that those people with FASD have established circles of support and therapeutic environments in which to live. The value and costs of such an approach need to be compared to the existing practice of revolving door processing by justice systems and incarceration.
15. FASD screening tools such as the Asante Centre's FASD Screening and Referral Tool for Youth Probation Officers should be examined in order to determine the best way in which they can be used to trigger a formal diagnosis in the court system or in other areas including but not limited to correction and child protection services.
16. There is a need for increased capacity for multidisciplinary diagnostic teams that can provide timely diagnosis at critical stages of the justice process (e.g., sentencing, child protection proceedings) and at other points in the individual's

life when decisions are made that might affect his/her welfare or that of his/her child. Care should be taken, however, not to divert diagnostic resources from the general population such that only those youths or adults who are caught up in the youth or adult criminal justice systems receive diagnostic services. In many locations, but perhaps especially in remote communities, mechanisms need to be developed to ensure that resources are both available and used most effectively to diagnose and create support plans for those with FASD.

Question 2: How Can Efforts to Identify People with FASD in the Legal System Be Improved?

The jury heard from many speakers about the importance of diagnosing people with FASD. At the same time, each diagnosis can cost in excess of $3000 and it is an intensive process with a potential to stigmatize those identified with FASD. The jury also heard that there are severe resource restraints on the availability of diagnosis in Canada, and in some parts of Canada, especially in remote areas including many First Nations, it is impossible to obtain a diagnosis.

While the jury has recommended increased screening and diagnosis, there is a corresponding need to ensure that those with FASD are supported in their efforts to live useful rather than disadvantaged lives in the community because they are so diagnosed.

Diagnostic Imaging

There is no imaging "signature" under current imaging methods that is specific to diagnosing FASD. However, advanced functional MRI, still in the research phase and not yet available for diagnostic purposes, does show significant reductions in brain volume, white and grey matter, and cortical abnormalities that, although not specific to FASD, are typical of those with neurological impairments associated with FASD.

Need for Early Identification and Intervention

There are promising models currently in place in Canada that could be used to effectively identify individuals who show signs of FASD and other neurodevelopmental disorders at an early stage. Integrated strategies can then be developed to manage these young children effectively before they come into conflict with the justice system. The Hub and COR (Centre of Responsibility) model that was started in Prince Albert, Saskatchewan, and has now spread to several other communities in the province, as well as communities across Canada, provides a promising model for approaching FASD in a multi-disciplinary and proactive manner. The Hub is a forum where individuals from corrections, health, social services, education and the police meet twice weekly to discuss cases in specific detail (within the limits of relevant information-sharing rules and regulations) in order to determine solutions for individuals assessed to be at acutely elevated risk.

Any member of the Hub may bring forward a case that has passed through their internal processes and has been deemed to be too complex or at too high a level of risk to be handled by the originating agency alone. The Hub provides immediate, coordinated and integrated responses through the mobilization of resources to address the situations facing individuals and/or families with acutely elevated FASD risk factors, as recognized across a range of service providers.

An individual suspected of having FASD or other neurological impairment may be identified by any participating agency, including the police service, prior to involvement with the justice system should he or she exhibit a level of acutely elevated risk. Once identified, the Hub mobilizes the necessary agencies or resources to address the risks facing the individual at that time, thereby potentially preventing the need to engage the legal system. The benefit of the Hub process is that it brings together individuals from multiple agencies to work collaboratively to resolve problems before they reach the justice system. This model is ideally suited to bring a quick response when someone suspects an individual may have signs of FASD or another neurodevelopmental impairment.

The Youth Criminal Defence Office program and the Youth Justice Advocacy program are also examples of effective intervention programs, launched in Alberta, to keep affected individuals out of the traditional legal system.

Identification of FASD in Court Proceedings

The reality of the court process (both civil and criminal) is that many decisions mwill have to be made without the provision of a full diagnosis. In some cases there may be indications but there will not be expert opinion evidence; the cases in which there are both are the exception. Those affected by FASD suffer disproportionately when decisions are taken on the basis of stereotypes, misinformation, or lack of relevant information. Decision-makers should have as much accurate information as is available and be aware of the practical limits on their knowledge.

Judicial Reluctance to Take "Judicial Notice" of the Symptoms and Attributes of FASD

"Judicial notice" is a doctrine that allows courts to find facts without expert or other evidence, provided the "facts" are notorious or capable of immediate and unarguable verification (for example that Christmas falls on December 25 every year).

If available, judicial notice is a shortcut to help solve the lack of courtroom resources, including the presence at trial of expert witnesses. However, appellate courts have stated that trial judges cannot simply take judicial notice of FASD.[3] Hence the individual with FASD is in a bind. No resources. No diagnosis. No evidence. No judicial notice. Therefore no fair and appropriate FASD-related accommodation is available within the usual rigours of the legal system.

Judicial Authority to Order Assessments

As one aspect of addressing the over-representation of Aboriginal people in the prison system, the Supreme Court of Canada has identified the importance of obtaining a report, providing background context, before imposing any sentence upon an Aboriginal offender.[4] Such contextual background information would be of equal importance to the court in the case of an accused person with FASD, not just in matters of sentencing. In youth matters, there is express authority in s. 34 of the Youth Criminal Justice Act for a court to order assessments where appropriate. There is no express parallel authority in the Criminal Code of Canada.

The jury is of the view, having particular regard to the restrictions on the scope of 'judicial notice', any ambiguity concerning the court's ability to order an FASD or other neuropsychological assessment as needed, should be resolved and if necessary, a provision similar to s. 34 of the YCJA should be incorporated into the Criminal Code.

Recommendations

17. The Supreme Court of Canada has recognized that the overrepresentation of Aboriginal persons among the inmate population constitutes a crisis in the criminal justice system. In the jury's view, the over-representation of people with FASD in correctional facilities and in care of child protection agencies is of overlapping and equal concern.
18. Federal, provincial and territorial governments should continue to support research that provides estimates of the prevalence of persons with FASD in correctional settings and in child protection care.
19. Federal, provincial and territorial governments, through the Heads of Corrections Committee, should explore effective case-management strategies for offenders with FASD who are serving their sentences in the community or in custody.

---

[3] *R. v. Harris*, 2002 BCCA 152 involved the sentencing of a 43-year-old with 62 convictions for breaking and entering and break of probation. A presentence report included information about possible FASD. The British Columbia Court of Appeal said the sentencing Judge erred by taking judicial notice of Mr. Harris' situation and making a diagnosis. Levine J.A. stated that "it is wrong in principle…for a sentence to be based on a conclusion about the mental capacity of an individual offender derived from assumptions and general knowledge." This conclusion was reached despite the Court of Appeal's recognition "that it is practically impossible for an adult to be assessed for FAS/FAE/ARND in this province" because of an unwillingness of the province to pay for such multidisciplinary and specialized assessments. See also *R v. Joamie*, 2013 NUCJ 19.

[4] *R v. Gladue*, [1999] 1 SCR 688.

20. Child protection authorities should explore effective case-management strategies for parents with FASD and children with FASD to ensure the functional needs of the parent or child are being provided for and adequate services are in place.

Question 3: How Can the Criminal Justice System Respond More Effectively to People with FASD?

The neurological impairments associated with FASD are likely to collide with the law, which generally assumes a level of intent, foresight and awareness. The evidence shows that, unless diagnosed, those with FASD are likely to be disadvantaged at the point of initial contact with police, in relation to the understanding of legal rights and options as well as the ability to respond to investigative processes (particularly interrogations), at the bail stage, the trial stage, the sentencing stage (where it is assumed by way of deterrence that the risk of adverse consequences will lead to an avoidance of those consequences), and the post-sentencing stage. At each of these stages, it is assumed that offenders are capable of making choices, understanding the consequences of their action, and learning from their mistakes. These assumptions do not accord with what is known about the functional disabilities associated with FASD.

A great risk created by the interaction of individuals with FASD and the legal system is a wrongful conviction. This danger is enhanced by the suggestibility of many people with FASD and the consequent risk of false confessions and guilty pleas of convenience.

The failure to have a full diagnosis of FASD should not be an excuse for ignoring relevant neurological impairments that may be associated with FASD. The imprisonment of an innocent man or woman, because of misunderstandings created by a condition over which an accused has no control, should shock the conscience of society.

FASD and the Pre-trial Process

Those with FASD facing criminal charges may often not fully appreciate the criminal nature and consequences of their actions, nor may they fully understand the legal proceedings and potential outcomes of their cases. Problems with memory, organizing, and contextualizing may make it difficult for them to remember or to relate important facts that would assist counsel in presenting a proper defence. It is characteristic of individuals with FASD to be suggestible and to have a desire to please others, and, therefore, to agree with leading questions. They may believe that a confession (true or false) is required and may therefore face an increased risk of giving false confessions and being wrongfully convicted.

Factors that make them more likely to give false confessions also make them less reliable as witnesses and complainants. When they are the victims of crime, those who have victimized them are therefore less likely to be convicted, an equally problematic outcome.

Taking Statements from Suspects or Witnesses with FASD

Alerting the authorities to an FASD issue

Section 10(b) of the Charter of Rights and Freedoms requires the police to inform people who are detained or arrested of their "right to retain and instruct counsel without delay." Some people with FASD, and no doubt others, may have trouble understanding this complex language.

Special rules of interrogation of suspects with known or suspected FASD

Although section 146 of the Youth Criminal Justice Act (YCJA) provides some special rules for the taking of statements from youths, the Criminal Code does not.

Videotaping statements would allow judges to better apply existing rules and safeguards that require valid waivers of Charter rights and allow only voluntary statements to be used as evidence. Videotaping would also help reduce the risk that a suggestible person with FASD might make a false confession that could possibly result in a serious miscarriage of justice.[5] In *R. v. Henry* it was held that statements taken from an individual with FASD who functions at the level of a seven-and-a-half-year-old should be excluded as involuntary.[6]

Recent judicial decisions that allow persistent or deceptive questioning of suspects by the police or that do not allow meaningful resort to counsel while an accused is being questioned by police may operate with great unfairness when applied to people with FASD.

Victims and witnesses in criminal trials may also have FASD. Videotaped police interviews with important witnesses who may have FASD would help determine whether misleading or otherwise problematic suggestions were made to the witness by the police.[7]

Waiver of Charter rights

In recognition of FASD disabilities, some courts have held that suspects with FASD lack the capacity to knowingly and voluntarily waive their Charter right to counsel.[8]

Recommendations

21. Parliament should give consideration to adding special rules to govern the questioning of suspects with known or suspected serious neurodevelopmental disabilities such as FASD.
22. Statements by a suspect should be videotaped.
23. The videotape requirement should extend to victims and witnesses as well as suspects with known or suspected serious neurodevelopmental disabilities such as FASD.

---

[5] This concern is not hypothetical. A false confession by Simon Marshall, a person with similar mental disabilities, led to a notorious miscarriage of justice in Quebec.

[6] *R. v. Henry*, 2002 YKTC 62 (CanLII).

[7] *R. v. C.M.S.*, 2004 YKSC 2.

[8] *R. v. Sawchuck*, (1997), 117 Man. R. (2d) 282, [1997] M.J., No. 186 (QL).

Exercise of Prosecutorial Discretion and Diversion

In many locations, a significant number of cases in court relate to "administration of justice" charges such as failure to appear, breach of probation, or failure to comply with a court order (typically bail conditions). Looking at all court cases for 2010/11, the proportion of all youth and all adult court cases involving an "administration of justice" charge as the most serious offence in the prosecution was as follows:

Jurisdiction	Youth	Adult
Canada	10.6%	21.0%
Manitoba	14.3%	30.5%
Saskatchewan	13.7%	28.8%
Alberta	11.8%	25.8%
Yukon	6.2%	28.6%
NWT	22.3%	34.4%
Nunavut	8.1%	26.8%

We heard evidence that a leading characteristic of people with FASD is an inability to organize their lives, meet deadlines, keep appointments, learn from experience and understand the consequences of failure to do any of these things. Accordingly, what are called "administration of justice" charges in effect criminalize those with FASD by setting the person up for further charges ("the revolving door"). These problems – e.g., the missing of court dates or other court-required appointments – can be addressed in three ways: (a) by the largely ineffective punishing of those with FASD for the violation, (b) by developing supports (e.g., reminders or by providing structures) so that the person does not violate conditions that are necessary, and (c) by ensuring that conditions required of all those involved in the youth/criminal justice system are necessary and useful for all those before the courts, especially those with FASD. Clearly the second two approaches are better both for the accused person and for society more generally.

Recommendations

24. Action should be taken – in legislative policy or in training – to reduce the number of "administration of justice" charges laid against FASD youths and adults. This might start immediately by ensuring that the nature and number of conditions (at pretrial release, on probation, etc.) placed on those apparently with FASD be realistic both in terms of the number and nature of the conditions.
25. Prosecutor's information sheets should be modified so that when a charge is laid against a person whom police suspect of having FASD or another neurodevelopmental disorder, the indications that the person may have FASD or some neurodevelopmental disorder can be noted.

Judicial Interim Release (Bail)

Persons with FASD will often have a history of non-appearance or of reoffending and are thus poor candidates for release based on past behaviour. This can lead to a likelihood of pretrial detention, guilty pleas based on convenience or, where release is granted, reliance upon numerous, stringent and unrealistic conditions.

Recommendations
In an application for judicial interim release where FASD is known or suspected:

26. Ready access by the court to rapid screening services should be routine. This is particularly important in bail matters as time will often be of the essence.
27. Bail conditions should be tailored to ensure the public safety and the attendance of the accused at trial, of course, but also with the recognition of the nature of FASD and tailored to the capacity and understanding of the person with FASD, who will likely not be able to perform conditions to the standard of the ordinary applicant.
28. Risk reduction strategies based on external supports rather than complex conditions should be considered. This may involve targeted use of sureties and/or the development of bail supervision programs appropriately tailored to the capabilities of accused with FASD.

Fitness to Stand Trial (Criminal Code S. 2)

The issue of fitness to stand trial can be raised by the judge or any party,[9] but as one judge has observed, the exceptions to criminal responsibility both with respect to fitness to stand trial and the mental disorder defence "were developed by judges several hundred years ago...when nothing was known about the complexity of the permanent brain damage that is Fetal Alcohol Spectrum Disorder."[10]

The standard for determining fitness to stand trial is very restrictive. A person is unfit to stand trial under s. 2 of the Criminal Code if he or she is "unable on account of mental disorder to conduct a defence at any stage of the proceedings before a verdict is rendered or to instruct counsel to do so, and, in particular, unable on account of mental disorder to (a) understand the nature or object of the proceedings, (b) understand the possible consequences of the proceedings, or (c) communicate with counsel." The courts have accepted that FASD is a mental disorder, but there are concerns that the other requirements of fitness to stand trial may be interpreted too restrictively in relation to an accused with permanent neurological disabilities.

[9] People with FASD who have been found unfit to stand trial have been subject to strict and long standing judicially imposed conditions, but s. 672.851 Criminal Code now provides that proceedings should be halted by a stay of proceedings if an unfit accused "does not pose a significant threat to the safety of the public" and if "a stay is in the best interests of the proper administration of justice." A person with FASD who satisfies such criteria would appropriately not be subject to a criminal trial or court-ordered conditions in the community.

[10] *R. v. Harper* 2009 YKTC 18 at para. 29.

Many speakers at the conference spoke about the difficulties in obtaining assessments of accused with possible FASD in the adult system and of the utility of s. 34 of the Youth Criminal Justice Act which enables judges to order the assessment of a young person by "a qualified person" at "any stage of proceedings." Such assessments can under s. 34(1)(b)(i) be ordered when the court has reasonable grounds to believe that the young person "may be suffering from a physical or mental illness or disorder, a psychological disorder, an emotional disturbance, a learning disability or a mental disability".

Recommendations

29. Judges in the adult system should have similar powers as are available under s. 34 of the Youth Criminal Justice Act to order assessments of accused, especially when there are reasonable grounds to believe that the accused suffers from FASD or any other intellectual impairment or neurodevelopmental disorder.

Guilty Pleas

The evidence raised a concern that there may be an enhanced need to ensure that where an accused with FASD pleads guilty, particular attention is paid to the voluntariness of the plea, the accused's understanding of the facts upon which the plea is based, his or her understanding of the consequences and the other options available.

FASD and the Trial

There is a need to ensure that appropriate information about the FASD condition is presented at trial so that proper legal safeguards are applied to protect an accused with FASD or facilitate the giving of accurate evidence by a victim or witness with FASD.[11] The issue is not only to prevent a wrongful conviction of an accused with FASD, but the wrongful acquittal in the case of a victim with FASD.

Consideration of Innovative Trial Courts

In some jurisdictions special courts have been established to deal with special subject matters (e.g., drugs) or people (family courts) or commercial matters (the commercial list in a trial court).

Recommendations

30. Consideration should be given to the establishment of special processes within the existing court structures to bring to bear the combined expertise and train-

[11] *R. v. P.D.T.*, 2012 ABCA 68 admitting statements in the face of an allegation but absence of evidence that accused has FASD.

ing of judges, prosecutors and defence counsel knowledgeable about FASD. This would serve the interest of fairness as well as efficiency.

Assessment of Credibility

A characteristic frequently associated with FASD is the inability to retrieve facts from memory in a coherent way, to remember the source of the information thus retrieved, to communicate what is remembered, and to respond to cross-examination in the stress of a courtroom. These characteristics may, unless understood in context by the trier of fact, unfairly affect an evaluation of the FASD individual's credibility.

Availability of *mens rea* Defences

FASD can be relevant to the assessment of whether the accused has the requisite fault or *mens rea* to be convicted of a criminal offence. With respect to offences that require subjective intent, the focus must be on the accused's own subjective awareness and purposes, and triers of fact should be alert to the relevance of evidence that the accused has FASD or other forms of intellectual impairments or neurodevelopmental disorders. These factors will, of course, likely be more relevant with respect to the higher forms of subject intent and knowledge. Even with respect to objective forms of fault, an incapacity to appreciate the relevant risk caused by FASD or other factors may be relevant.

Defences of Diminished Responsibility Such as *provocation*, *duress* and *self-defence*

These defences require that the accused act reasonably. The proper question is would a reasonable person with a form of FASD similar to that of the accused be considered to have acted reasonably? The assumption that people intend the ordinary and natural consequences of their actions may not apply to someone who, because of a neurological disability, is unable to anticipate what the effects will be, or control the impulse to react in a way not to be expected from an ordinary accused.

The Mental Disorder Defence (Criminal Code s. 16)

Accused who are found fit to stand trial may still raise the mental disorder defence. This defence has not been changed in any substantive way since the mid-1800s. Section 16 of the Criminal Code requires that an accused have a mental disorder that renders him or her incapable of appreciating the nature and quality of the act or knowing that it is wrong. Although courts have recognized FASD as a mental disorder, they have been reluctant to hold that it renders the FASD accused incapable of appreciating the nature and quality of the act or knowing that it is wrong.[12]

The availability of a better-tailored defence of diminished responsibility for those with mental disabilities could provide the legal system with more flexibility in dealing with the diverse circumstances of offenders with FASD.

Recommendations

31. A more refined approach to diminished responsibility might properly be considered by Parliament under its policies to assist people with disabilities, or by the courts under their powers under s. 8(3) of the Criminal Code to create new common law defences that are not inconsistent with statutes. In some cases a diminished responsibility defence could produce early release under tight controls, something that conditional sentences were intended to facilitate but which are now subject to increasing legislative restrictions from Parliament for reasons entirely unrelated to the particular disabilities of FASD individuals or others with neurological disorders.

Sentencing Offenders Who Have FASD

Section 718 of the Criminal Code instructs sentencing courts to consider certain objectives including denunciation, deterrence of the offender and others from committing offences, separating offenders from society, rehabilitation, reparations, and instilling a sense of responsibility in the offender.

Proportionality

Criminal justice is based on the principle that people who offend should be held accountable in proportion to what was done and the offender's responsibility for the offence. The principles are laid out more explicitly in the YCJA than they are in the Criminal Code. However, it is reasonable that this general principle holds for adults as well as youths.

Proportionality is required for sentencing both in the adult and the youth justice systems.[13]

---

[12] Kent Roach and Andrea Bailey "The Relevance of fetal alcohol spectrum disorder in Canadian Criminal Law from Investigation to Sentencing" (2009) 41 University of British Columbia Law Review 68; Mansfield Mela and Glen Luther "Fetal alcohol spectrum disorder: Can diminished responsibility diminish criminal behaviour?" (2013) 36 International Journal of Law and Psychiatry 46.

[13] The YCJA states that purposes such as rehabilitation are limited by the proportionality principle:

s. 38 (2)….

(c) the sentence must be proportionate to the seriousness of the offence and the degree of responsibility of the young person for that offence;

The Criminal Code provides that:

> **718.1** A sentence must be proportionate to the gravity of the offence *and the degree of responsibility of the offender*. (Emphasis added.)

Proportionality is not defined explicitly. It could, however, accommodate various forms of diminished responsibility related to impulsivity and suggestibility associated with FASD.[14] In particular, there is little judicial authority on how the "degree of responsibility of the offender" should be defined for those with disorders like FASD, but there is a developing judicial consensus that determining the offender's degree of responsibility requires more than a determination that the offender has committed a crime with the subjective or objective fault that is necessary for guilt and requires a judicial examination of relevant background factors that may be particular to the offender.[15]

Recommendations

32. Sentencing courts should take into account the challenges faced by those with an intellectual impairment or neurodevelopmental disorder such as FASD. This could be accomplished by deciding that for those with an intellectual impairment or neurodevelopmental disorder such as FASD, courts shall give primary consideration to the objective of rehabilitation and the imposition of a community sanction. Rehabilitation should be defined as including a reasonable prospect of managing the offender in the community.
33. For greater certainty, Parliament might enact a provision dealing with "diminished responsibility due to an intellectual impairment or neurodevelopmental disorder such as FASD." This functional approach would avoid senseless litigation about whether a particular case did or did not fall within a particular definition of a disorder (such as FASD). Instead it would focus on whether there was diminished responsibility and its immediate causes ("intellectual impairment or neurodevelopmental condition or disorder"). Although the meaning of the words "degree of responsibility of the offender" is not defined in the Criminal Code (or the YCJA), we recommend adoption of the following definition by judicial interpretation:

(d) all available sanctions other than custody that are reasonable in the circumstances should be considered for all young persons, with particular attention to the circumstances of aboriginal young persons;

(e) subject to paragraph (c), the sentence must

(i) be the least restrictive sentence that is capable of achieving the purpose set out in subsection (1),

(ii) be the one that is most likely to rehabilitate the young person and reintegrate him or her into society, and

(iii) Promote a sense of responsibility in the young person, and an acknowledgement of the harm done to victims and the community….

[14] *R. v. Ipeelee* [2012] 1 S.C.R. 433 at para 73, 96; *R. v. Arcand* 2010 ABCA 363 at para. 58.

[15] ibid.

> Degree of responsibility includes consideration of the offender's diminished capacity to comply with the law due to any intellectual impairment or neurodevelopmental disorder

34. For greater certainty, it is recommended that Parliament consider adopting the definition mentioned above as an amendment to s. 718.1 (b) of the Criminal Code and a parallel addition to s. 38(2) (c) of the YCJA and that Parliament make it clear that for such offenders primary consideration be given to rehabilitation.
35. While we believe there is ample scope under the existing legislation to achieve a fair and balanced result, consideration might also be given by Parliament to enact as follows:

> Evidence that an offender suffers from any intellectual impairment or neurodevelopmental disorder which impairs or diminishes the offender's ability to make judgments, foresee consequences, or perceive risks shall be deemed to be a relevant factor in determining whether alternative measures/extrajudicial measures should be made available to the accused.

36. When considering alternative measures under s. 717 (for adults) and under Part I of the YCJA, it be provided that

> If there is evidence that the offender suffers from any intellectual impairment or neurodevelopmental disorder, the police and crown attorney shall give primary consideration to the objective of rehabilitation of the offender and special efforts should be made to identify an appropriate set of alternative measures (or extrajudicial measures for youths) commensurate with the accused person's diminished responsibility for the offence. In crafting alternative measures/extrajudicial measures, the focus should be on those measures most likely to provide opportunities for the offender to be rehabilitated and reintegrated peacefully into society.

37. It should be made clear here and elsewhere – preferably in legislation – that the term "rehabilitation" in the Criminal Code and in the YCJA includes a "reasonable prospect of management in the community."
38. In line with the analysis previously outlined, in judicial interim release, consideration be given to the following amendment:

> For those who are charged with criminal offences, the police and/or the judge or justice at a judicial interim release hearing shall make special efforts to find structures that will ensure that the accused will appear in court and desist from committing offences. At the same time, for all accused, but in particular those with an intellectual impairment or neurodevelopmental disorder, police, judges and justices should ensure that conditions placed on the accused as part of a release order are ones that it is plausible to expect that the accused can comply with.

39. Parliament should consider adding balance to s. 718.2 by indicating mitigating as well as aggravating factors to be taken into account in the sentencing process. The Criminal Code currently lists a number of factors that are specifically to be considered aggravating. Although it indicates that judges should take into account mitigating factors (s. 718.2(a)) as well, no mitigating factors are listed. It is recommended, therefore, that the following words be added to this section to make it clear that the presence of FASD and similar intellectual impairments or neurodevelopmental disorders are mitigating factors in sentencing:

> Evidence that an offender suffers from an intellectual impairment or neurodevelopmental disorder which impairs or diminishes the offender's ability to make judgments, foresee consequences, or perceive risks shall be deemed to be a mitigating factor.

Release from Custody/Prison

The YCJA requires correctional staff to develop a release plan for all youths given "custody and supervision orders." In addition, the YCJA provides for a system of reviews (s. 94) of youth custody sentences whereby the youth can be brought back before the sentencing judge (or another judge) to determine if there should be a change in the sentence. Reviews for those with an intellectual impairment or neurodevelopmental condition or disorder can be especially important as a way of reintegrating the youth at the most opportune time when that youth – or circumstances in the community – has changed in such a manner that the youth can be best reintegrated into society by way of community supports rather than continuing to stay in custody.

Mandatory Minimum Sentences and Preservation of Judicial Discretion

Judges should have the fullest range of sentencing discretion in dealing with the diverse circumstances of offenders with FASD. The application of mandatory minimum sentences or offence-based restrictions on the availability of conditional sentences is intended to fetter discretion. The increasing use of such statutory restrictions will have a disproportionate and harmful impact on offenders with FASD. The courts cannot generally issue exemptions from mandatory sentences.[16]

Recommendations

40. Parliament should craft a statutory exemption that allows judges to justify departures from mandatory sentences where such exemptions are necessary to provide a fit sentence on an offender with a mental disability such as FASD. Such an amendment would allow the courts to develop an appropriate and case-sensitive sentencing jurisprudence for offenders with FASD.

Conditional Sentences

The Criminal Code permits a judge who would otherwise sentence an offender to a term of imprisonment to order a sentence to be served in the community (typically involving some form of "house arrest"), subject to strict conditions. In the last few years, Parliament has progressively restricted the availability of conditional sentences, resulting in imprisonment of FASD sufferers, which may aggravate rather

[16] *R. v. Ferguson*, [2008] 1 S.C.R. 96.

than alleviate their difficulties in eventually being able to live useful lives in the community. Unlike a breach of parole, a breach of conditional sentence will likely result in the offender serving the balance of the sentence in prison. Given the tendency of FASD sufferers to fail to perform conditions in a reliable and timely way, the conditions should not be "designed to fail," but be appropriate to the circumstances to the offence and the offender. Necessary conditions must be imposed, but none that are not necessary.

Recommendations

41. Parliament should consider greater availability of conditional sentences for persons with an intellectual impairment or neurological disorder such as FASD by allowing exceptions, with reasons, from the statutory exclusions that presently exist. Conditions should be crafted in such a way that they take into account the special challenges faced by those with FASD.

Special attention should be paid to the use of the various forms of temporary or conditional release reviews for youths as well as temporary absence, day parole, parole, etc. for adults, designed to reintegrate the offender safely into society. We understand that short-term risk management might suggest to some judges and releasing authorities that inmates who suffer from an intellectual impairment or neurodevelopmental disorder such as FASD be left in custody. But the reality is that these offenders are, eventually, going to be back in the community and it is in the public interest to use special efforts to develop and implement release strategies for these offenders that will be most effective in the long run.

A Final Word on Sentencing Objectives

The neurodevelopmental deficits associated with FASD challenge the basic principles of sentencing, which assume that offenders are capable of making choices, understanding the consequences of their actions, and learning from their mistakes so as not to repeat them. General deterrence, meaning that the punishment given to one person for breaking the law will operate to deter other persons, presupposes the ability of an FASD sufferer to process and translate information as well as to remember it.

Similarly, rehabilitation, as it is conventionally understood, is largely a neurodevelopmental process premised on the ability to understand, to learn, to remember, and to make choices. As none of these assumptions fits well with what is known about FASD, failure to take FASD into account during sentencing constitutes an injustice to offenders and to society at large. The offenders fail because they are held to a standard that they cannot possibly attain, given their disabilities.

Traditionally calculated sentences, calibrated for a non-disabled individual, may have a substantially more severe effect on someone with FASD. As one judge put it,

"One cannot but question what social policy is served by the use of the hard penal machinery of the criminal justice system to deal with the most chronic mentally disabled youth of our society."[17]

Problems in the Correctional System

Offenders with intellectual impairments or neurodevelopmental disorders such as FASD who are serving their sentences in custody are particularly vulnerable to exploitation and manipulation by other inmates. If corrections officials know that an inmate has FASD there are measures that can be taken to house the inmate on a secure range. In addition, knowing that an offender has FASD could help correctional officers understand the inmate's behaviour in prison and could result in fewer disciplinary charges for the inmates.

Knowledge of an offender's FASD status is also critically important in developing an effective correctional plan. This is true for offenders who are serving their sentences in custody as well as offenders who are serving their sentence in the community. It makes little sense to have a correctional plan that involves a treatment modality that relies heavily on neurodevelopmental reasoning for an offender who has reduced executive functioning. Even more important, however, is developing an evidenced-based approach to effective correctional programming for offenders with FASD.

The jury heard about a recent study that found that 9–10% of 91 participants/inmates at Stony Mountain Penitentiary were identified with FASD, while another 16–18% were possibly affected by FASD. These data suggest that not enough is done to diagnose and provide treatment for FASD in prisons. As one judge noted, if more residential facilities were available for people with FASD:

> *Fewer of these offenders would be incarcerated in jail; those who were incarcerated would not be incarcerated for as long, and, in the end, there is a very real likelihood that the revolving door of offending, often with increasing severity, would slow or be closed altogether for the individual FASD offender. In the end, society would be better protected and would also benefit from the knowledge that its youngest victims were now being assisted to find a meaningful life, despite the crime visited upon them in the womb.*

Recommendations

42. There should be broader access to multidisciplinary diagnostic services for individuals suspected of FASD in the federal correctional system. Present standardized intake screening tools used in the federal corrections context do not explicitly address FASD.
43. Diagnostic clinics in all correctional facilities in the provinces and territories should ensure timely and accurate diagnosis.
44. Mandated specialized training for correctional staff should be implemented to ensure that staff appreciate the response styles of inmates with FASD to ensure

---

[17] *R. v. D.* (W.), 2001 CanLII 380 at para 35 (SK PC).

that unnecessary confrontations are eliminated by staff being adequately equipped to respond without further escalation of the situation.

The recommendations related to sentencing and corrections (Recommendations 32–44) could have the effect of reducing, somewhat, levels of imprisonment. This should not raise concerns about public safety since various jurisdictions have found that levels of imprisonment can be strategically reduced without any reduction in public safety.[18]

Question 4: How Can Family Courts and the Family/Child Welfare Legal System Address the Specific Needs of People with FASD?

Given that the first point of contact for many individuals with FASD is within the family law system, special considerations to the unique challenges posed to parenting with FASD, or parenting children with FASD, are necessary to ensure that parents are not disproportionately disadvantaged in the child protection and family law context, based on their own neurological impairments associated with FASD or those of their child.

As individuals with FASD are likely to have diminished capacity to foresee consequences, make reasoned choices, or learn from their mistakes, their neurodevelopmental limitations associated with FASD present a fundamental challenge in the family law context.

Aside from the neurodevelopmental deficits associated with FASD, the jury heard evidence of the increased vulnerability of individuals with FASD to secondary disabilities such as leaving school, family and placement breakdowns, homelessness, alcohol and substance abuse, unemployment, and mental health problems. As child protection concerns generally mimic the secondary disabilities of FASD, it is not uncommon for parents with FASD to come to the attention of child protection authorities.

Although FASD presents challenges to parenting, the jury heard success stories which confirm that many parents with FASD, who might otherwise not be able to parent, could manage with appropriate supports.

Parents with FASD

The family is the basic unit of society and efforts should be made to maintain the familial bond. Resources should be provided to the family in a manner that supports the family unit and prevents the need to remove the child from the family.

Given the neurodevelopmental impairments often associated with FASD, many FASD parents may struggle with providing for the daily routine of their child. This is caused by difficulties with memory, difficulties in using consequences in an appropriate manner, problems in understanding the sensory cues of their child, and

[18] *R. v. D.* (W.), 2001 CanLII 380 at para 35 (SK PC).

challenges in learning from similar situations. It is therefore easy to be critical of the parenting skills of a parent with FASD. However, to overestimate a parent's abilities in light of their neurodevelopmental neurological impairment is to set them up to fail in their capacity to parent. Access to supports and resources can help with these struggles and should remain accessible to parents with FASD throughout their child's upbringing in order to adequately support their family unit.

Should intervention services be necessary, the manner in which they are carried out must be sensitive to the physical, behavioural and emotional consequences to the child that could result from apprehension. Research has shown that trauma surrounding stressful events may lead to structural changes in the child's brain. Where a child is apprehended, resources must be provided to ensure continued parent-child relationship in circumstances where the child is apprehended. This is the responsibility of the state.

When a parent with FASD becomes involved with the child protection authority, there are a number of stages when a parent may be disproportionately disadvantaged should the parent's neurological impairment associated with FASD be unrecognized.

There is a real possibility for parents with FASD to be unfairly disadvantaged at the initial contact with child protection authorities based on their inability to genuinely appreciate their legal rights and options.

The jury heard evidence that individuals with FASD are susceptible to suggestion and have a desire to please others. In light of these characteristics, the parent with FASD may inadvertently agree to insurmountable, unrealistic and unnecessary tasks in order to avoid confrontation with the person in authority and in an effort to expedite the return of their child(ren) to their care. This may be done without the parent with FASD ever speaking to a lawyer or being advised of his or her right to challenge the alleged child protection concerns. As a result, special measures must be taken to ensure that a parent with FASD provides an informed consent.

Given the evidence presented surrounding the memory impairments of individuals with FASD and their difficulties with organization and contextualization, when the parent with FASD agrees to an unrealistic list of tasks and appointments, they may be setting themselves up for failure. Their impaired reasoning and social judgment, impulsivity, suggestibility and low empathy may lead to responses that are perceived as contrary to a desire to comply with the child protection authority to have their children returned to their care. It is these very contrary response styles coupled with their failure to follow through that may result in further involvement with the system. The difficulty is that the parent with FASD may lack the capacity to understand or appreciate the specific direction or order.

Mandated training for frontline child protection workers is necessary to appreciate response styles of the parent with FASD, and to de-escalate unnecessary confrontations or limit the potential disadvantages associated with the parent's neurological impairment.

The terms with which the parent with FASD must comply in order for their child to be returned to parental care should therefore be specific to the child protection concerns, expressed in plain language, and unique to the parent's particular pattern of strengths and weaknesses.

Given that individuals with FASD have different learning difficulties and challenges, their unique learning styles must be taken into account when establishing their capacity to parent. Hands-on and experiential learning should be implemented as alternatives to traditional programming.

Finally, at the trial stage, problems with memory and in particular an inability to retrieve facts from memory in a coherent way, to link the information thus retrieved with its source, to communicate what is remembered, and to respond to cross-examination in the stress of a courtroom may impede their ability to properly instruct counsel and provide an alternative version of events, contrary to the position presented by the child protection agency, that would be accepted by the courts as valid given their apparent credibility. Steps must be taken to ensure that the trier of fact understands the unique limitations of this particular parent with FASD to avoid an unfair evaluation of the parent with FASD's credibility.

Where the family unit has been reunited, sufficient resources should be provided for long-term support. These should not be time-limited. Resources should include access to respite services for all caregivers, including parents with FASD.

The jury heard evidence of the direct impact of secondary disabilities on parents with FASD and how many decisions made on behalf of the family are incomplete, fragmented, and coming from multiple sources. It was suggested that timely and collaborative decision-making that is trauma-informed as well as training that anticipates the needs of individuals with FASD would assist the process. In addition, wraparound services should be established or expanded to help parents with FASD to navigate their way through the legal system. The jury supports the implementation of these suggestions and recommends that extra resources should be directed, or present resources reallocated, to provide for these suggestions.

The Family Law Office, a project of Legal Aid Alberta, is an example of an exemplary wraparound service. It offers a unique quality of service by offering a legal team comprised of a social worker and lawyer. The social worker attends with, and advocates for, the parent in the meetings with the child protection authorities, connects them to resources, and supports them to address all secondary disabilities, such as housing, addictions, employment, programming, mental health. The social worker then relays the information to the lawyer to ensure that what is expected of the parent is not misconstrued or forgotten. This team approach ensures that the legal process is understood by the parent and the parent is not unnecessarily disadvantaged based on the parent's neurological limitations.

CATCH (Collaborative Assessment and Treatment for Children's Health) is another innovative option of wraparound services presented. It consists of a comprehensive multidisciplinary case management team that is assembled to create relational informed decisions with respect of child protection matters. It involves cross-agency collaboration with mental health, developmental services, child protection, and community partners.

However, these services are limited, for various reasons, to certain parents. For example, they may be limited according to the parent's place of residence, ability to qualify for Legal Aid, and association with a specific child protection office. Inequities in access to these types of services should be overcome through expansion of these and similar services. Alternatively, additional resources should be allocated to programs that link parents with FASD to an advocate who can help them navigate through the legal process while addressing the secondary concerns of FASD.

Although a complete diagnosis is helpful to establish the strengths and needs of a parent with FASD as well as to inform service delivery, the absence of a complete diagnosis should not be an excuse for child protection authorities, lawyers, and judges to ignore the relevant neurological impairments that may be associated with FASD. Nor should a diagnosis of FASD be the basis for an apprehension of the children of a parent with FASD or a change in their custody.

If an apprehension is necessary and an accurate FASD diagnosis has not been made, an immediate diagnosis of the parent should be facilitated. A delay in the diagnosis could be detrimental to the family unit. The purpose of the diagnosis should be to inform service delivery, to structure appropriate assistance and programming for the parent, and to provide the child protection worker with alternative approaches to helping the parent with FASD to parent.

Access to FASD assessments should not be denied based on budgetary constraints or available resources. Parents should be entitled to an assessment in a timely fashion. Consequently, if the child protection agency denies the request for services or is unable to provide adequate services in a timely fashion, then the court should order that such services be provided from private contractors.

We heard that litigation delay may be problematic, but at the same time we recognize that sufficient time and opportunity must be provided to the FASD parent to access supports and acquire the skills necessary to continue to parent independent of child protection involvement. We recommend that sufficient resources be redirected to this purpose.

Should Adequate Services Not Be Put into Place to Provide Meaningful Opportunities to the FASD Parent, the Cycle of Multiple FASD Births Within a Family as Well as in Successive Generations Will Continue

If an apprehension is necessary, each child going into the care of the government should receive a full medical and psychological assessment that would include a screen for FASD. This screen should occur independent of the mother's admission of any consumption of alcohol during pregnancy. Should a diagnosis of FASD be confirmed, its sole use should be for planning and implementing appropriate services and not used against the mother as another child protection concern.

Children with FASD need to be given adequate care and services based on their functional need.

Foster parents and group home staff as well as prospective adoptive parents need to be properly trained and should be willing to work collaboratively with the parents and the child welfare system to the benefit of the child.

Parents of a child with FASD should receive training equivalent to that given to foster parents and group home staff specialized in caring for children with FASD. If a child is in the care of the government, such training should be provided to the parent by the child protection agency.

In circumstances where the child has FASD, all efforts should be made to prevent the development of secondary disabilities related to continued trauma. If a placement is necessary, it should be stable and with trained caregivers. It should maximize a healthy environment for an already vulnerable brain; avoid trauma, support attachment and development.

Access to resources and services for a child with FASD should not be timelimited or conditional and should be available when the youth transitions into adulthood. The need for resources for a child with FASD remains strong, particularly as the child transitions into adulthood, so that the child is not denied needed assistance.

Training

FASD-specific training of parents, caregivers, and foster parents, as well as child protection workers, lawyers and judges is critical at all stages of the child protection process.

Given the complex nature of child protection cases, ongoing training on the behavioural, neurological, and health implications of FASD should be mandatory for everyone involved with the parent or child with FASD. Child protection workers need to be able to identify the FASD parent and/or child in order to appreciate the limitations and provide adequate services in light of the neurological impairments. Lawyers need appropriate and ongoing training on FASD, in order to provide adequate representation of their client and to draft terms of an order that will assist their client, not set them up for failure. Judges need the required training to ensure that the trial process as a whole is not unnecessarily disadvantaging the parent with FASD and that all evidence is assessed in light of the parent's neurological impairment.

The bottom line, from the perspective of the jury, is that the primacy of the child's rights should never be pitted against the rights of the parent in light of the needs of the community. All participants in the family law context are entitled to equal consideration and adequate resources to provide them with a meaningful opportunity to preserve the basic family unit.

Recommendations

45. FASD-specific training should be made available for parents, caregivers, and foster parents at all stages of the protection process.
46. Fund accurate and timely diagnosis through provincial and territorial governments.
47. Provide transition planning for FASD-affected youth moving into adult services, with consideration of an extension of the original care agreement.
48. Provide stable placements for FASD-affected youth.
49. Direct or re-direct funding to proactive intervention strategies that maintain the family unit.
50. Minimize the negative impact or implications of the diagnosis.

51. Ensure that timelines contained in child protection laws accommodate the parent with FASD and provide meaningful opportunities to parent with their disability.
52. Develop policies to enhance the lives of parents with FASD and to break the cycle as well as the overrepresentation of FASD children and adults in the child protection system.
53. Allocate additional resources to prevent the inequities inherent to the disability when interacting with the legal system.
54. Target existing resources to address the unique and specific needs of the parent with FASD.
55. Provide meaningful ongoing training for judges, lawyers, and child protection workers to adequately be supported in their roles.
56. Government funding should be allocated or redirected to expand the wraparound and comprehensive services or provide for additional resources that pair parents with FASD with an advocate who can help them navigate through the legal process while addressing the secondary concerns of FASD.

Question 5: What Are Best Practices for Guardianship, Trusteeship, and Social Support in a Legal Context?

Children with FASD who reach the age of majority often lose the support of social agencies, ending up on the street with no mechanisms of assistance. Youth and adults with FASD exhibit very poor social judgment, as reflected in their tendency to go along with potentially disastrous courses of action, and their failure to understand such choices. A guardianship arrangement could potentially alleviate the severity of such consequences by giving the guardian, or if necessary the court, the power to prevent a catastrophic course of action.

The social and neurodevelopmental deficits, as well as the capacities of individuals with FASD, should be considered in order to broaden the framework to grant guardianship protection and provide the social supports that are generally unavailable to them beyond the age of majority.

A capacity assessment may be used to appoint a guardian and trustee for specific areas such as health care, housing, education/training, employment, and legal decision-making depending on the gaps in the respective domains. It is important that the legal guardian and trustee take an active casemanagement role in assisting the FASD individual with personal decisionmaking. A trusteeship order addresses other minimal assets, as well as income support programs and employment income. Guardians and trustees can act as navigators through the complexities of the legal system.

Should no guardian be involved, then upon application, the court should appoint a guardian ad litem to ensure that the person with FASD is adequately represented in the present legal matter.

Recommendations

57. Guardianship and trusteeship programs should be considered for adults with FASD who are found to have diminished capacity and therefore require assistance to manage their affairs.
58. Given the characteristics of an individual with FASD, such as impulsivity, ongoing guardianship and trusteeship is particularly important for those individuals with FASD who have received social support during their adolescence as they transition into adulthood.

Question 6: What Legal Measures Are There in Different Jurisdictions to Contribute to the Prevention of FASD, and What Are the Ethical and Economic Implications of These Measures?

When thousands of babies are born every year with serious brain injuries with a known and preventable cause, there must be effective measures for prevention. Equally important are the development and implementation of appropriate social supports as well as legal processes for the majority of individuals with FASD who come into conflict with the law. In that regard, it becomes important not to confine ourselves too tightly to "legal measures" but to expand our attention to other types of measures (the most obvious being education and training) to help prevent FASD. When doing so, however, care should be taken to ensure that communities of different sizes (e.g., smaller reserve communities) also have access to these preventative programs.

A number of measures have been studied with regard to alcohol awareness and harm reduction in the general population and, in particular, in women of childbearing age. These include alcohol warning labels, attempts to limit alcohol consumption, measures to ban the sale and service of alcohol to pregnant women, designation of 'dry' communities, criminalization of alcohol and drug use by pregnant women, interventions targeted at pregnant women with addictions, and subsidization of contraception.

Alcohol and pregnancy warning labels have been found to be effective but lose their impact over time. More intensive interventions are needed to reduce in-pregnancy drinking over the longer term. The language of messages should be considered carefully so as to not create unintended consequences and stress among women who consume low levels of alcohol in the time around conception and only later become aware that they are pregnant. In addition, the jury heard that there are data to suggest that these measures are least effective with binge or heavy drinkers.

Measures to ban selling or serving alcohol to pregnant women have been perceived as discriminatory based on gender. A less coercive approach is to support alcohol servers in promoting the offer of non-alcoholic beverages along with information brochures on FASD.

Criminalization of Alcohol and Drug Use by Pregnant Women

There have been attempts in the United States of America to use or expand existing legal measures to target women's substance use during pregnancy. Pregnant women have been charged with offences ranging from delivering drugs to a minor, to child neglect and chemical endangerment, which have resulted in arrest and incarceration in some states. Apart from any constitutional issues, medical and public health groups are concerned that these measures deter women from seeking prenatal care, accessing addiction treatment, or speaking openly about their substance use with health care providers out of fear of losing their child.

Interventions Targeted at Pregnant Women with Addictions, Including Forced/Involuntary Addiction Treatment for Pregnant Women and Requirements by Health Professionals to Report Prenatal Drug and Alcohol Use to Child Protection Services

These approaches, along with compulsory screening at birth, raise concerns that they may lead to or encourage under-reporting and may disproportionately impact marginalized women.

There are ethical issues surrounding some of the screening tools that have been suggested, such as meconium testing. It is this jury's opinion that ongoing research should address concerns with respect to informed consent, privacy, and appropriate follow-up once the results are obtained.

Issues surrounding prevention were considered at the IHE's First International Conference on Prevention of FASD in September 2013.

Recommendations

59. Develop a comprehensive FASD prevention strategy for Canada.
60. Develop gender-specific programs and create opportunities for women and men to discuss with their health care provider relationship issues, child care, and alcohol consumption.
61. Prevention programs should focus on those areas in which positive effects have been demonstrated. In particular, it may be worthwhile to examine interventions involving the mother-child unit. Such approaches might help reduce the likelihood of subsequent children with FASD after a child is found to suffer from an intellectual impairment or neurological disorder such as FASD.
62. Develop evidence-based mandatory training programs for front-line workers on how to talk to women in a secure, non-threatening fashion about the underlying causes of alcohol consumption.

A Final Word

It is clear that many complex legal issues associated with FASD remain to be resolved in order to ensure that FASD-affected individuals receive fair and equitable treatment in the justice system. Although there is higher awareness of the challenges faced by those with FASD than in the recent past, there is a danger that justice system personnel who do not receive ongoing training about FASD may interpret its symptoms as "defiance of court orders," "absence of remorse," and "apparent incorrigibility."[19] They may also fail to appreciate how people with FASD can, with appropriate supports, live happy and productive lives and contribute to society. It is in the interests of both individuals with FASD and society in general, to better understand FASD and to ensure that justice system personnel and others have the necessary training, tools and resources to support those living, often successfully, with FASD.

The goal of all of those working with people with FASD is to provide supports and guidance in the community so that they can live peaceful, productive and happy lives in the community. Our recommendations are made in the spirit of providing some additional mechanisms in the legal system to respond appropriately to those who suffer from FASD, thereby simultaneously improving their lives and improving the quality of our communities.

As Myles Himmelreich pointed out at the conference:

> *It is important for individuals such as myself with FASD to..... understand it so that we can better understand ourselves...... We need to know what it's like for ourselves and we can tell you what works and what doesn't work...... I'm an individual living with FASD, but please remember I'm not a diagnosis, I am a human being.*

There is no excuse for inaction on the basis of an uninformed view that nothing can be done. With appropriate improvements to family and community support for those with FASD, and in some areas guidance and more flexibility in the manner in which the legal system responds to the challenges of FASD, the quality of the lives of those living with FASD as well as our communities can be improved.

It has been our privilege as jurors to hear outstanding lectures from experts in a wide variety of relevant fields over a period of 2 days. It is our hope that this consensus statement, which builds on their expertise, contributes to a better understanding of FASD in the legal community, and, more importantly, that this understanding will lead to action.

---

[19] Justice Melvyn Green "A Judicial Perspective" Paper presented at the Fetal Alcohol Syndrome Disorders Symposium for Justice Professionals 1 March, 2006. We are happy to have heard that awareness of FASD among judges and others in the justice system has significantly improved since 2006.

Jury Members[20]

Chair – The Honourable Ian Binnie, C.C., Q.C.
Former Justice of the Supreme Court of Canada
Lenczner Slaght
The Honourable Judge Larry G. Anderson[21]
Provincial Court of Alberta
Ms. Danielle Collins
Lawyer
Family Law Office
Legal Aid Alberta.
Dr. Dennis Cooley
Assistant Deputy Minister
Ministry of Justice
Government of Saskatchewan.
Dr. Anthony N. Doob
Professor Emeritus of Criminology
Centre for Criminology & Sociolegal Studies
University of Toronto
Mr. Don Langford
Executive Director
Metis Child & Family Services Society Edmonton.
Dr. Valerie Massey
Registered Psychologist
D-V Massey & Associates
Adjunct Professor at the University of Alberta
Dr. Nicole LeBlanc
Pediatrician
Dr. Georges L. Dumont University Hospital Centre
Associate Clinical Professor from the Université de Sherbrooke and Université de Moncton
Justice Mary T. Moreau[22]
Court of Queen's Bench of Alberta
The Honourable Landon Pearson O.C.
Landon Pearson Resource Centre for the Study of Childhood and Children's Rights
Carleton University
Professor Kent Roach
Prichard Wilson Chair in Law and Public Policy

[20] Please note that the analyses and recommendations for the consensus statement do not necessarily reflect those of the organizations that the jury members are affiliated with.

[21] By reason of his judicial role, Judge Anderson did not participate in the formulation of recommendations relating to legislative changes.

[22] By reason of her judicial role, Justice Moreau did not participate in the formulation of recommendations relating to legislative changes.

University of Toronto
Mr. Bill Robinson
President and Chief Executive Officer
Alberta Gaming and Liquor Commission
Ms. Wilma Shim
Lawyer
Alberta Justice and Solicitor General
Ms. Lee Ann (Weaver) Tyrrell
Nurse, Lawyer, Policy Consultant for Government, Legal Guardian

Conference Speakers and Topics

What Are the Implications of FASD for the Legal System?

- **Overview of FASD**
  Sterling Clarren, CEO and Scientific Director, Canada Northwest FASD Research Network; Clinical Professor of Pediatrics; Faculty of Medicine, University of British Columbia; Clinical Professor of Pediatrics, School of Medicine, University of Washington
- **Prenatal alcohol exposure and abnormal brain development: Insights from animal studies**
  Kathy Sulik, Professor of Cell Biology and Physiology; Member of the Bowles Center for Alcohol Studies, University of North Carolina, Chapel Hill, NC, USA
- **Can FASD be imaged?**
  Sarah Treit, Centre for Neuroscience, University of Alberta
- **Characteristics of FASD**
  Carmen Rasmussen, Assistant Professor, Department of Pediatrics, University of Alberta; Research Affiliate, Glenrose Rehabilitation Hospital, Edmonton
- **Prevalence of FASD in the legal system**
  Patricia MacPherson, Senior Research Manager, Correctional Service of Canada
- **Socio-Economic implications of FASD**
  Philip Jacobs, Professor of Health Economics, Faculty of Medicine, University of Alberta; Director of Research Collaborations, IHE
- **Legal perspectives of FASD**
  Fia Jampolsky, Chair, Yukon Human Rights Commission; Lawyer, Cabott and Cabott, Whitehorse

How Can Efforts to Identify People with FASD in the Legal System Be Improved?

- **Potential impact, benefits and burdens of an FASD screening program in the corrections system**

Larry Burd, Professor, Department of Pediatrics, University of North Dakota School of Medicine; Director of the North Dakota Fetal Alcohol Syndrome Center and FAS Clinic

- **Review of current models for assessment and screening of FASD in the youth justice system**
  Albert Chudley, Professor, Department of Pediatrics, University of Manitoba; Medical Director, Winnipeg Regional Health Authority Program in Genetics and Metabolism

- **Building effective connections between courts and diagnostic clinics**

  Julianne Conry, Asante Centre, Maple Ridge, BC; previously, Department of Educational and Counselling Psychology and Special Education, University of British Columbia

How can the Criminal Justice System Respond more Effectively to People with FASD?

- At what points in the criminal justice process is an individual with FASD most vulnerable?
  Patricia Yuzwenko, Defence Lawyer, Youth Criminal Defence Office

- **How could an understanding of needs in FASD shape sentencing responses within the criminal justice system?**
  Jacqueline Pei, Assistant Professor, Department of Educational Psychology; Assistant Clinical Professor, Department of Pediatrics, University of Alberta

- **The effect of FASD on the reliability of confessions and the giving of testimony**
  Kaitlyn McLachlan, Clinical psychology, forensic specialization, Postdoctoral fellow, Department of Pediatrics, University of Alberta

- Policy and legal recommendations to the understanding of FASD, its challenges and potential solutions
  William Edwards, Deputy Public Defender, Los Angeles County Public Defender's Office

- **FASD and the modern sentencing theory debate; a path to criminal code reforms**
  Allan Manson, Professor in the Faculty of Law, Queen's University, Kingston, Ontario

- **Considerations in making effective sentences for persons with FASD**
  The Honourable Judge Sheila Whelan, Provincial Court of Saskatchewan

- Legislative impediments to judicial consideration of moral blameworthiness in sentencing offenders with FASD
  Jonathan Rudin, Program Director, Aboriginal Legal Services of Toronto; Chair, FASD Justice Committee

- How can a youth criminal defence advocacy model assist young people with FASD navigate the justice system?
  Cathy Lane *Goodfellow, Acting Senior Counsel, Youth Criminal Defence Office*

How can Family Courts and the Family/Child Welfare Legal System Address the Specific Needs of People with FASD?

- Working with parents with FASD in family and child welfare matters
  Lydia Bubel, Lawyer, Family Law Office, Alberta Legal Aid

- What specific characteristics of FASD need to be taken into account in family court and in the child welfare system?

  – Donna Debolt, Social Work Consultant, Edmonton, Alberta
  – Gail Andrew, Board Member, Canada FASD Research Network; Medical Site Lead, Pediatrics; Medical Director, FASD Clinical Services; Pediatric Consultant, Glenrose Rehabilitation Hospital

- How can children with FASD be best supported in foster care or other placements?
  Corey La Berge, Deputy Children's Advocate, Manitoba Legislative Assembly

What Are Best Practices for Guardianship, Trusteeship and Social Support in a Legal Context?

- **Broadening guardianship and lowering barriers to service eligibility; protective arrangements for people with FASD**
  Stephen Greenspan, Emeritus Professor of Educational Psychology, University of Connecticut; Clinical Professor of Psychiatry, University of Colorado

- **Clinical and ethical issues within capacity assessment of people with FASD**
  Arlin Pachet, Clinical Neuropsychologist, Adjunct Assistant Professor, Department of Psychology, University of Calgary

- **Views from a Public Guardian's perspective**
  Barb Martini, Director, Office of the Public Guardian

What Legal Measures Are There in Different Jurisdictions to Contribute to the Prevention of FASD, and What Are the Ethical and Economic Implications of These Measures?

- **Legal measures to contribute to prevention of FASD, effectiveness and ethical issues**
  Nancy Poole, Director, Research and Knowledge Transition, British Columbia Centre of Excellence for Women's Health; Research Consultant, Women and Substance Use Issues, British Columbia Women's Hospital

- **Legal and ethical aspects of meconium testing to identify alcohol use during pregnancy**
  Gideon Koren, Director, The Motherisk Program, The Hospital for Sick Children; Professor of Pediatrics, Pharmacology, Pharmacy and Medical Genetics,

University of Toronto; Professor of Medicine, Pediatrics and Physiology/Pharmacology; Ivey Chair in Molecular Toxicology, University of Western Ontario; Scientific Chair, CFFAR

- **A Personal Perspective**
  Myles Himmelreich, FASD Consultant, Edmonton, Alberta, Canada

Jury Recommendation Summary

Question 1

1. The ability of communities and families must be strengthened to deal – outside of the traditional criminal justice system – with "offending behaviour" of youths and adults.
2. Services must be provided within communities that would help create more stable homes and placements for those in care. The goal should be to help communities manage the problems associated with FASD so that those with FASD from that community can remain in the community as productive members of society.
3. FASD must be assessed using a multidisciplinary team approach; no one specialty is sufficient.
4. The development of biomarkers appears to be the most promising area of research to identify FASD affected individuals and should be pursued, although the use of them raises important legal and ethical issues.
5. Greater effort must be made to make the public aware of the cost of dealing with FASD in the legal system.
6. Where at all possible those affected by FASD should be kept out of the criminal justice system. In 2010/11 it cost an average of about $114,000 per year to keep a prisoner in federal prison, much more than it costs to provide services – criminal justice or otherwise – in the community. Studies suggest that between 10% and 25% of prisoners have FASD. It is estimated that each person with FASD costs governments $1.5–2.0 million over their lifetime including education, health and other services. These costs, as well as the difficulties that people with FASD may experience in custodial institutions, include but are not limited to:
   - support for community-based housing (such as the At Home Chez-Soi/Housing First Program); and transition housing programs
   - community education programs starting with children and youth; and
   - community support and intervention programs that are evidence-based in supporting individuals affected by FASD throughout their lifespan, particularly in key transition periods.
7. More resources should be focused on family and community supports that will allow those with FASD to live under supervision outside of the criminal justice system. The jury heard evidence about a cross-sectoral program in Alberta that

supports people with FASD in the community for costs below $5000 per person served per year or $1.63 per capita, a figure that is far below correctional costs.

8. Mandate training for all players in the legal system, including judges, crown, defence, corrections, police, probation officers, parole officers, and community frontline workers so that when they encounter a citizen, in a home or on the street, they have the background knowledge that will sensitize them to the cues that may suggest that the person they are dealing with has FASD.
9. Support innovative training programs that promote inter-sectoral dialogue and partnerships, and sustain longitudinal educational curriculums in order to ensure continuing education for all major stakeholders in Canada (such as corrections, health, social development, mental health, RCMP, provincial and federal court officials, education, and First Nations).
10. Training needs to be carried out on an ongoing basis to ensure that people know not only the up-to-date best practices but also the services that are available in their communities to those who suffer from FASD.
11. Every child going into care of the state should receive a full medical examination and a full psychological examination that would include a screen for FASD to assist with the planning and implementation of appropriate services for the family. However, should this policy be implemented, the purpose of the assessment should be clearly stated to avoid the misuse of the FASD diagnosis against the mother. Similarly, admission procedures in correctional centres (either on remand or on sentence) should include screening for possible FASD to ensure that prisoners are dealt with appropriately by staff trained in the problems associated with FASD. Again, the FASD diagnosis should not be used against the prisoner, but should be used to help better accommodate and manage such persons within the correctional system.
12. Consideration should be given to the legal, ethical, and practical issues surrounding policies related to the sharing of a positive FASD diagnosis. For example, the suggestion that positive FASD diagnoses be kept on police files (e.g., CPIC) or child protection files to ensure that it is shared with others who may have contact with that individual in the future raises important issues of privacy. Nevertheless, if this information were known to police officers and child protection authorities – under certain specified conditions and with the appropriate training of those officials – it might help alleviate problems and promote just and fair outcomes.
13. Individuals with FASD often get into conflict with the law when they are not involved in a structured program. There is a need to build relationships between an individual with FASD or other neurological impairment and a circle of support that could include family members and social service workers to ensure that the individual has a therapeutic environment in which to live.
14. Housing stability and wraparound support are critical. Government should undertake to examine whether it might be more economical to develop small (e.g., 10-bed) housing units with 24/7 support from social service agencies to ensure that those people with FASD have established circles of support and therapeutic environments in which to live. The value and costs of such an

approach need to be compared to the existing practice of revolving door processing by justice systems and incarceration.

15. FASD screening tools such as the Asante Centre's FASD Screening and Referral Tool for Youth Probation Officers should be examined in order to determine the best way in which they can be used to trigger a formal diagnosis in the court system or in other areas including but not limited to correction and child protection services.
16. There is a need for increased capacity for multi-disciplinary diagnostic teams that can provide timely diagnosis at critical stages of the justice process (e.g., sentencing, child protection proceedings) and at other points in the individual's life when decisions are made that might affect his/her welfare or that of his/her child. Care should be taken, however, not to divert diagnostic resources from the general population such that only those youths or adults who are caught up in the youth or adult criminal justice systems receive diagnostic services. In many locations, but perhaps especially in remote communities, mechanisms need to be developed to ensure that resources are both available and used most effectively to diagnose and create support plans for those with FASD.

Question 2

17. The Supreme Court of Canada has recognized that the overrepresentation of Aboriginal persons among the inmate population constitutes a crisis in the criminal justice system. In the jury's view, the overrepresentation of people with FASD in correctional facilities and in care of child protection agencies is of overlapping and equal concern.
18. Federal, provincial and territorial governments should continue to support research that provides estimates of the prevalence of persons with FASD in correctional settings and in child protection care.
19. Federal, provincial and territorial governments, through the Heads of Corrections Committee, should explore effective case-management strategies for offenders with FASD who are serving their sentences in the community or in custody.
20. Child protection authorities should explore effective case-management strategies for parents with FASD and children with FASD to ensure the functional needs of the parent or child are being provided for and adequate services are in place.

Question 3

21. Parliament should give consideration to adding special rules to govern the questioning of suspects with known or suspected serious neurodevelopmental disabilities such as FASD.
22. Statements by a suspect should be videotaped.

23. The videotape requirement should extend to victims and witnesses as well as suspects with known or suspected serious neurodevelopmental disabilities such as FASD.
24. Action should be taken – in legislative policy or in training – to reduce the number of "administration of justice" charges laid against FASD youths and adults. This might start immediately by ensuring that the nature and number of conditions (at pretrial release, on probation, etc.) placed on those apparently with FASD be realistic both in terms of the number and nature of the conditions.
25. Prosecutor's information sheets should be modified so that when a charge is laid against a person whom police suspect of having FASD or another neurodevelopmental disorder, the indications that the person may have FASD or some neurodevelopmental disorder can be noted.
26. Ready access by the court to rapid screening services should be routine. This is particularly important in bail matters as time will often be of the essence.
27. Bail conditions should be tailored to ensure the public safety and the attendance of the accused at trial, of course, but also with the recognition of the nature of FASD and tailored to the capacity and understanding of the person with FASD, who will likely not be able to perform conditions to the standard of the ordinary applicant.
28. Risk reduction strategies based on external supports rather than complex conditions should be considered. This may involve targeted use of sureties and/or the development of bail supervision programs appropriately tailored to the capabilities of accused with FASD.
29. Judges in the adult system should have similar powers as are available under s. 34 of the Youth Criminal Justice Act to order assessments of accused especially when there are reasonable grounds to believe that the accused suffers from FASD or any other intellectual impairment or neurodevelopmental disorder.
30. Consideration should be given to the establishment of special processes within the existing court structures to bring to bear the combined expertise and training of judges, prosecutors and defence counsel knowledgeable about FASD. This would serve the interest of fairness as well as efficiency.
31. A more refined approach to diminished responsibility might properly be considered by Parliament under its policies to assist people with disabilities, or by the courts under their powers under s. 8(3) of the Criminal Code to create new common law defences that are not inconsistent with statutes.
32. Sentencing courts should take into account the challenges faced by those with an intellectual impairment or neurodevelopmental disorder such as FASD. This could be accomplished by deciding that for those with an intellectual impairment or neurodevelopmental disorder such as FASD, courts shall give primary consideration to the objective of rehabilitation and the imposition of a community sanction. Rehabilitation should be defined as including a reasonable prospect of managing the offender in the community.
33. For greater certainty, Parliament might enact a provision dealing with "diminished responsibility due to an intellectual impairment or neurodevelopmental disorder such as FASD." This functional approach would avoid senseless litigation about whether a particular case did or did not fall within a particular defini-

tion of a disorder (such as FASD). Instead it would focus on whether there was diminished responsibility and its immediate causes ("intellectual impairment or neurodevelopmental condition or disorder"). Although the meaning of the words "degree of responsibility of the offender" is not defined in the Criminal Code (or the YCJA), we recommend adoption of the following definition by judicial interpretation:

Degree of responsibility includes consideration of the offender's diminished capacity to comply with the law due to any intellectual impairment or neurodevelopmental disorder.

34. For greater certainty, it is recommended that Parliament consider adopting the definition mentioned above as an amendment to s. 718.1 (b) of the Criminal Code and a parallel addition to s. 38(2)(c) of the YCJA and that Parliament make it clear that for such offenders primary consideration be given to rehabilitation.
35. While we believe there is ample scope under the existing legislation to achieve a fair and balanced result, consideration might also be given by Parliament to enact as follows:

    Evidence that an offender suffers from any intellectual impairment or neurodevelopmental disorder which impairs or diminishes the offender's ability to make judgments, foresee consequences, or perceive risks shall be deemed to be relevant factors in determining whether alternative measures/ extrajudicial measures should be made available to the accused.
36. When considering alternative measures under s. 717 (for adults) and under Part I of the YCJA, it be provided that

    If there is evidence that the offender suffers from any intellectual impairment or neurodevelopmental disorder, the police and crown attorney shall give primary consideration to the objective of rehabilitation of the offender and special efforts should be made to identify an appropriate set of alternative measures (or extrajudicial measures for youths) commensurate with the accused person's diminished responsibility for the offence. In crafting alternative measures/extrajudicial measures, the focus should be on those measures most likely to provide opportunities for the offender to be rehabilitated and reintegrated peacefully into society.
37. It should be made clear here and elsewhere – preferably in legislation – that the term "rehabilitation" in the Criminal Code and in the YCJA includes a "reasonable prospect of management in the community."
38. In line with the analysis previously outlined, in judicial interim release, consideration be given to the following amendment:

    For those who are charged with criminal offences, the police and/or the judge or justice at a judicial interim release hearing shall make special efforts to find structures that will ensure that the accused will appear in court and desist from committing offences. At the same time, for all accused, but in particular those with an intellectual impairment or neurodevelopmental disorder, police, judges and justices should ensure that conditions placed on the accused as part of a release order are ones that it is plausible to expect that the accused can comply with.

39. Parliament should consider adding balance to s. 718.2 by indicating mitigating as well as aggravating factors to be taken into account in the sentencing process. The Criminal Code currently lists a number of factors that are specifically to be considered aggravating. Although it indicates that judges should take into account mitigating factors (s. 718.2(a)) as well, no mitigating factors are listed. It is recommended, therefore, that the following words be added to this section to make it clear that the presence of FASD and similar intellectual impairments or neurodevelopmental disorders are mitigating factors in sentencing:

    Evidence that an offender suffers from an intellectual impairment or neurodevelopmental disorder which impairs or diminishes the offender's ability to make judgments, foresee consequences, or perceive risks shall be deemed to be a mitigating factor.
40. Parliament should craft a statutory exemption that allows judges to justify departures from mandatory sentences where such exemptions are necessary to provide a fit sentence on an offender with a mental disability such as FASD. Such an amendment would allow the courts to develop an appropriate and case-sensitive sentencing jurisprudence for offenders with FASD.
41. Parliament should consider greater availability of conditional sentences for persons with an intellectual impairment or neurological disorder such as FASD by allowing exceptions, with reasons, from the statutory exclusions that presently exist. Conditions should be crafted in such a way that they take into account the special challenges faced by those with FASD.
42. There should be broader access to multidisciplinary diagnostic services for individuals suspected of FASD in the federal correctional system. Present standardized intake screening tools used in the federal corrections context do not explicitly address FASD.
43. Diagnostic clinics in all correctional facilities in the provinces and territories should ensure timely and accurate diagnosis.
44. Mandated specialized training for correctional staff should be implemented to ensure that staff appreciate the response styles of inmates with FASD to ensure that unnecessary confrontations are eliminated by staff being adequately equipped to respond without further escalation of the situation.

Question 4

45. FASD-specific training should be made available for parents, caregivers, and foster parents at all stages of the protection process.
46. Fund accurate and timely diagnosis through provincial and territorial governments.
47. Provide transition planning for FASD-affected youth moving into adult services, with consideration of an extension of the original care agreement.
48. Provide stable placements for FASD-affected youth.
49. Direct or re-direct funding to proactive intervention strategies that maintain the family unit.

50. Minimize the negative impact or implications of the diagnosis.
51. Ensure that timelines contained in child protection laws accommodate the parent with FASD and provide meaningful opportunities to parent with their disability.
52. Develop policies to enhance the lives of parents with FASD and to break the cycle as well as the overrepresentation of FASD children and adults in the child protection system.
53. Allocate additional resources to prevent the inequities inherent to the disability when interacting with the legal system.
54. Target existing resources to address the unique and specific needs of the parent with FASD.
55. Provide meaningful ongoing training for judges, lawyers, and child protection workers to adequately be supported in their roles.
56. Government funding should be allocated or redirected to expand the wrap-around and comprehensive services or provide for additional resources that pair parents with FASD with an advocate who can help them navigate through the legal process while addressing the secondary concerns of FASD.

Question 5

57. Guardianship and trusteeship programs should be considered for adults with FASD who are found to have diminished capacity and therefore require assistance to manage their affairs.
58. Given the characteristics of an individual with FASD, such as impulsivity, ongoing guardianship and trusteeship is particularly important for those individuals with FASD who have received social support during their adolescence as they transition into adulthood.

Question 6

59. Develop a comprehensive FASD prevention strategy for Canada.
60. Develop gender-specific programs and create opportunities for women and men to discuss with their health care provider relationship issues, child care, and alcohol consumption.
61. Prevention programs should focus on those areas in which positive effects have been demonstrated. In particular, it may be worthwhile to examine interventions involving the mother-child unit. Such approaches might help reduce the likelihood of subsequent children with FASD after a child is found to suffer from an intellectual impairment or neurological disorder such as FASD.
62. Develop evidence-based mandatory training programs for front-line workers on how to talk to women in a secure, non-threatening fashion about the underlying causes of alcohol consumption.

MIX
Papier aus verantwortungsvollen Quellen
Paper from responsible sources
FSC® C105338

If you have any concerns about our products,
you can contact us on
ProductSafety@springernature.com

In case Publisher is established outside the EU,
the EU authorized representative is:
Springer Nature Customer Service Center GmbH
Europaplatz 3, 69115 Heidelberg, Germany

Printed by Libri Plureos GmbH
in Hamburg, Germany